Frock Coats and Epaulets

The Men Who Led the Confederacy

Alf J. Mapp, Jr.

MADISON BOOKS

Lanham • New York • London

To My Son

Published by Madison Books
4720 Boston Way
Lanham, Maryland 20706

3 Henrietta Street
London WC2E 8LU, England

Library of Congress Cataloging-in-Publication Data

Mapp, Alf J. (Alf Johnson), 1925–
Frock coats and epaulets : the men who led the Confederacy / Alf
J. Mapp, Jr.
p. cm.
Originally published: New York : T. Yoseloff, 1963.
Includes bibliographical references and index.
1. Confederate States of America—Biography. 2. Confederate
States of America—History. 3. United States—History—Civil War,
1861–1865—Biography. I. Title.
E467.M37 1996 973.7'42—dc20 96-2691 CIP

ISBN 1-56833-060-X (paper : alk. paper)

Distributed by National Book Network

⊗ ™ The paper used in this publication meets the minimum requirements
of American National Standard for Information Sciences—Permanence of
Paper for Printed Library Materials, ANSI Z39.48–1984.
Manufactured in the United States of America.

CONTENTS

FOREWORD

I am grateful to the public for its loyalty to this book. Readers in the United States, Canada, and Great Britain kept it alive for nearly two decades through repeated printings, including an Encore Edition as "a work published in English that has become a classic in the lifetime of its author." When new printings ceased, readers exhausted the supply of secondhand copies. Continued public demand brought forth new editions in 1982 and 1987 and additional printings. Now demand has brought this new and expanded edition with evaluations of recent Civil War research and important additions to the critical biographies. If you are one of the old friends whose insistence kept this work alive, I greet you again with deep appreciation. If the work is new to you, I welcome the opportunity to share with you my fascination with some of the most intriguing characters in American history.

ALF J. MAPP, JR.
Willow Oaks
Portsmouth, Virginia

MY PURPOSE

THE CONFEDERATE STATES of America lived only four years as a national entity. But, in history and literature, the ill-starred republic seems sure to live as long as the nation from which it sprang and to which it returned. This is true partly because the story of the Confederacy is now an integral part of the national heritage and partly because its fate is invested with the glamour of all lost causes valiantly fought for. It is true, too, because the Confederacy is part of the great traumatic experience of 1861–1865 that left its marks for good and ill on the personality of America.

But the story of the Confederacy fascinates for still another reason—it crowded the confused action of a huge stage with as many remarkable characters as have ever simultaneously answered history's cue. Some were remarkable for fiery genius, some for amazing courage. Some would have been great if their actions had never been illumined by the fires of war; others cast long shadows only because they stood in the spotlight of history. In their number, Malory could have found another white-bearded Arthur; Shakespeare another Prince Hal and a Falstaff; Milton an avenging angel flashing the sword of Jehovah; and Dickens a host of utterly delightful eccentrics.

It is my purpose, in the pages that follow, to present some of these intriguing personalities. In each chapter, one will hold center stage. The man who is a mere spear carrier in one chapter, or perhaps is only a disembodied voice from the wings, may be the chief protagonist in the next.

Some of these men were perfectly cast for their historic roles. Others were miscast because they chose the wrong parts or were pressed into them. Some who wore frock coats longed for epaulets. Some who wore epaulets had a propensity for orotund eloquence and a talent for political maneuver that fitted them better for the forum than for the field. How they played their roles helped to determine the fate of their nation and hence of the American people.

In telling briefly the story of each man's life, I have tried to let him reveal by his own words and actions the motivations of his conduct in time of national crisis. For this purpose, no one has improved on the anecdotal method used more than eighteen centuries ago by Plutarch. My primary concern here is not with military or political strategy, but with individual character. Strategy is here discussed only to the limited extent necessary for narration of the main course of events and an explanation of the way in which they were influenced by the personalities concerned.

My practice has been to accumulate enough facts about each of these leaders to fill several volumes and then to select from this mass those facts which, compressed within a single chapter, will help to give us some understanding of the character concerned. In some instances, illuminating details reveal the monolithic simplicity of a character that seemed complex. In other cases, the searching light reveals and accentuates unprobed recesses, giving us a chiaroscuro portrait of bold light and dark shadow—intensifying the drama but deepening the mystery. *For my purpose,* what Lee said to a wounded Union soldier after Pickett's charge is more important than the number of the enemy on Little Round Top that day; why Stuart desperately wanted General Pope's coat is more significant than the number of men he commanded at the close of 1862; what Davis did not know about his grandfather counts as heavily as what he said about constitutional law; the circumstances of Mrs. Benjamin's hasty departure from Washington assume greater dimensions than her husband's estimate of the senior senator from Alabama; and the thing that kept

Davis and Benjamin from shooting each other in hot blood explains a great deal more about Confederate history than a transcript of the diplomatic correspondence which the two conducted with Lord Russell.

My subject is Confederate leaders, civil and military. But it is also human nature.

The particular subject of human nature as exhibited in Confederate leadership has for me an irresistible appeal, because I am an American concerned with my country's exciting story and because that story has a special meaning for me as a son of the South. I had two great-grandfathers in the Army of Northern Virginia. One was a lieutenant under "Stonewall" Jackson. After the war was over, he entertained with great delight the Yale classmates who had been his opponents in the Army of the Potomac. The other was a teenaged private who rode around McClellan's army with "Jeb" Stuart. In a way, he had the more remarkable record of the two. "Grandfather talk" with friends from Virginia to Alabama has revealed to me the probability that he was the only private in the Confederate armies.

ALF J. MAPP, JR.

ACKNOWLEDGMENTS

THE NATURE of this book imposes obligations that the author can never acknowledge in detail. Though original research in old letters, diaries, and newspapers is the basis of many statements, the great bulk of my research has been among secondary sources. These sources are now so numerous that the writer on any comprehensive topic related to the war of 1861–65 will exhaust himself long before he exhausts the sources. The bibliographies at the end of separate sections of the book list only the handful of works found most helpful in the preparation of *Frock Coats and Epaulets*. Each section is the distillation of facts numerous enough to fill many shelves. Even so, the book that began to emerge was so long that, in the interest of brevity, I reluctantly abandoned the idea of separate portraits of such important and intriguing characters as Alexander H. Stephens, Nathan Bedford Forrest, Stephen Mallory, Raphael Semmes, and P. G. T. Beauregard. And I had to resist the temptation to include petticoats as well as frock coats and epaulets. To the many historians whose patient research or experience with actual events produced the records on which I have drawn, I owe a great debt.

To one of these I acknowledge a pre-eminent obligation. The late Douglas Southall Freeman, twice winner of the Pulitzer Prize for biography and widely regarded as the greatest of American biographers, has made more important contributions to Confederate scholarship than any other man. My personal indebtedness to him extends even further than that of most writers on the Confederacy, for Dr. Freeman encouraged me to write my first book, *The Virginia Experi-*

ment. In *Frock Coats and Epaulets,* honesty has compelled me to depart from Dr. Freeman's concept of Lee as a "simple man." But it has in no way lessened my recognition of his vastly superior knowledge of Lee and the whole field of Confederate operations, and in no instance have I been truer to my mentor's example than in obeying the dictates of my own integrity.

Among those whose helpfulness has made this book possible are the staffs of the Virginia State Library, Richmond; the Virginia Historical Society, especially Mr. John Melville Jennings; the Confederate Museum (Richmond), especially Miss India Thomas; the library of the College of William and Mary in Williamsburg, especially Mr. Herbert L. Ganter, archivist; the Sargeant Room of the Norfolk (Va.) Public Library, especially the late Miss Mary Churchill Brown; and the Library of Congress, Washington, D.C.

ALF J. MAPP, JR.

Introduction

SOME PLAIN TALK
ON REBELS AND YANKEES

Since 1963, when *Frock Coats and Epaulets* was first published, the years have been unkind to Confederate leaders. Recent decades have seen a hostility reminiscent of the 1930s toward many venerated heroes, from Columbus to Washington, from Jefferson to Winston Churchill. The vilification of the hero has become such a passionate pastime that any of the departed great retaining a shred of earthly vanity must dread the recurrence of anniversaries providing excuses for renewed attacks. Our times have been especially hard on the Confederates because many persons who are politically correct, but not factually so, have insisted on picturing them as risking, and sometimes sacrificing their lives, for the hateful institution of slavery. In this view, they may, like Darth Vader, have fought with skill and courage, but like him they were servants of an evil empire.

Much of the condemnation springs from glib assumptions about the motivations of participants in the Civil War. Recently many people—educators, politicians, journalists, and concerned citizens of every sort—have lamented that large numbers of United States high school seniors are unable to explain the causes of the Civil War. Far be it for me to encourage anyone to believe that American high school students have an adequate knowledge of their country's his-

11

tory. But a question about the causes of the Civil War is no proper touchstone for testing student proficiency. On closing a popular school text, or turning off a televised docudrama, one may bask in a comforting feeling of having mastered the causes of the nation's defining conflict, but the complacency is not justified.

Professional historians who have devoted decades of study to the subject have failed to reach agreement not only on the origins of the war but on its supposed inevitability. Some have echoed William Seward's prophetic description of it as an "irrepressible conflict" while others have seen it as the result of preventable blunders. Some accord the North a majority of stupidity while others grant the palm to the South, and some see the "honors" equally divided. Some say that the war would not have come if a large black population had not been concentrated in the South, and then leap to the conclusion that the war from the beginning was fought to free the slaves. They see it as a noble crusade by Northerners to free blacks held by Southerners who fought tenaciously to keep them in bondage.

The war *might* not have come if the South had not had a source of cheap labor conducive to agricultural development that proceeded apace in contrast to the industrialization of the North and thus helped to produce two regionally defined societies in fierce conflict over tariffs, commercial legislation, and a host of constitutional issues that each came to regard as intimately involved with its survival. Seen in this light, the black labor force was one of a variety of factors contributing to regional economic differences leading to damaging competition and eventually to the arbitrament of arms.

Avery Craven said it succinctly. An Iowan trained at Harvard and the University of Chicago, teaching later in Middle Western universities as well as ones in Australia, England, and Germany, he brought to the analysis of Civil War origins no special sympathy for the South but a catholicity far above parochialism. He said: "By 1860, slavery had become the symbol and carrier of *all* sectional differences and conflicts. . . . It produced those fighting terms, 'The Abolition Crusade' and 'The Slave Power.' It colored every issue and often hid the more basic issue behind the words 'right' and 'rights.' "[1] Others carrying no special brief for the South were far more emphatic. Arthur C. Cole said that slavery "was scarcely the crux of the sectional issue." Charles A. Beard, a leader of the "liberal" school of American historians and political scientists, stressed the crucial role of economic conflicts about tariffs and centralized banking and said that slavery "hardly deserved a footnote in the history of the Civil War."

Despite the number and complexity of causes contributing to the outbreak of hostilities, many persons have persisted in seeing the Federal soldiers as crusaders for freedom and their Confederate opponents as ipso facto defenders of evil. That this view should be attractive to many who regard themselves as either the genetic or cultural heirs of the victors is understandable. Robert Penn Warren, who was a shrewdly analytical biographer and historian as well as one of the world's great novelists and poets, wrote in 1961 that according to the "doctrine of the Treasury of Virtue" the Civil War was "a consciously undertaken crusade so full of righteousness that there is enough overplus stored in Heaven, like the deeds of the saints, to take care of all small failings and oversights of the descendants of the crusaders, certainly into the present generation."[2]

Certainly the opponents of such crusaders appear to be villains of the deepest dye. Many decent people find it impossible to empathize with such vile embodiments of depravity. Yet a look at the historical record reveals that most leaders on both sides were decent but fallible people without sufficient saintliness or Satanism to separate them from their fellow humans.

Robert E. Lee and Abraham Lincoln, each canonized in popular hagiography, were indeed noble characters, but both compromised on the foremost moral issue of their times. Lee was dedicated to a

[1]Avery Craven, *An Historian and the Civil War* (Chicago, 1964), 163.
[2]Robert Penn Warren, *The Legacy of the Civil War: Meditations on the Centennial,* Quoted in *A Robert Penn Warren Reader* (New York, 1987), 293.

demanding code of ethics and was remarkably compassionate in dealing with individuals of every background. But although he repeatedly decried the institution of slavery and eschewed for himself the role of slaveholder, he found it almost impossible in the social and legal context of his society to free the slaves inherited by his wife. Abraham Lincoln, although the favorite symbol of compassion in the history of the American Presidency and from his early days a hater of slavery, nevertheless at first refused to free the blacks because he gave a higher priority to preserving the Union. When Union General John C. Fremont, four and one half months into the Civil War, attempted to free the slaves within his Missouri command, Lincoln rebuked him, saying that so far the war had had "nothing to do with slavery" and he wished to keep it that way.

When Lincoln finally issued an Emancipation Proclamation in September 1862, he specifically exempted from its provisions the states of Illinois, Pennsylvania, New Jersey, Delaware, and Maryland, as well as some Federally held areas behind the Confederate lines, for fear of offending Unionists in those places. Even so, his most effective general, Ulysses Grant, himself a slaveholder, declared "If I thought this war was to abolish slavery, I would resign my commission, and offer my sword to the other side." William Tecumseh Sherman had already written that, as a general, it was "neither his duty nor pleasure to disturb the relation of master and slave.[3] . . . As to freeing the negroes, I don't think the time is come yet. When negroes are liberated either they or [their] masters must perish. They cannot exist together except in their present relation, and to expect negroes to change from slaves to masters without one of those horrible convulsions which at times startle the world is absurd."[4]

Grant was a paragon of perseverance throughout the war and a

[3]James M. Merrill, *William Tecumseh Sherman* (Chicago, New York, and San Francisco, 1971), 209.
[4]William Tecumseh Sherman, *Home Letters of General Sherman*, M. A. DeWolfe Howe, ed. (New York, 1909), 229.

model of magnanimity at Appomattox. Sherman was an inventor of the modern concept of total war, with perhaps a nod of acknowledgment to the Roman conquerors of Carthage in the Punic Wars and to some less sophisticated people before and since. Both had qualities worthy of emulation, but we should not seek, in their ideologies, relevance to our own times. And the same is true of their Confederate counterparts. In neither case should ideological irrelevance blind us to the entertainment and instruction inherent in their lives.

I

JEFFERSON DAVIS : Aristocrat by Design

(Cook Collection of the Valentine Museum, Richmond)

I

JEFFERSON DAVIS : Aristocrat by Design

The Missing Grandfather

THE MAN WHO symbolized the planter aristocracy of the South in the War between the States was uncertain of his own grandfather's origin.

Richmond, sitting proudly on her seven hills, appraised with a practiced dowager's eye the strangers who entered her gates when Virginia's capital became the capital of the Confederacy. She should have been a good judge of aristocracy. She had certainly seen enough aristocrats. But most of them had been aristocrats of the Virginian stamp—urbane without being urban, their manners informal but reserved—polished men, indeed, but with a luster rather than a shine. Richmond had few criteria by which to recognize aristocracy as it burgeoned in younger and more ebullient societies, some a single generation removed from the frontier and more Western than Southern in spirit. So the dowager by the James was sometimes doubtful as to who belonged and who didn't among the influx of strangers. She reserved judgment about Kentucky's John C. Breckinridge, who could be courtly and eloquent but who sometimes carried the delivery of the stump into the drawing room, until the keepers of her *Almanach de Gotha* recalled his impeccable Virginia heritage. And she was perplexed for a time by that Georgia aristocrat, Robert Toombs,

17

who wore his tobacco-stained vest as proudly as if it had been an armorial vestment.

But, of one of the newcomers, Richmond could be sure. Jefferson Davis was a patrician. The elegance of his carriage as he strode down the street, his easy grace as he sat a horse, the imperial slimness of his figure, the fine-chiseled features of his long face, the air of disciplined sensitivity, all bespoke the thoroughbred. He was the embodiment of the qualities deemed aristocratic by an ancient society, a candlelight civilization.

And yet Jefferson Davis did not know who his great-grandfather was. He himself had been born June 3, 1808 in the frontier country of Kentucky in a log cabin not many leagues from the one in which Abraham Lincoln was born about eight months later.

In the East, the Davis cabin would have been regarded as a very humble home, but frontier neighbors saw it through other eyes. Not only did it have four snug rooms, but it boasted the unexampled luxury of glass windows. This effete importation from Georgia drew the curious from miles around. Of course, if any family in the area should pamper themselves with such comforts, it would likely be the Davises. The head of the family, Samuel Emory Davis, had had enough education to be a county clerk in Georgia after serving as a captain in the Revolutionary forces.

When young Jefferson Davis was born, his parents decided his middle name should be Finis. The choice is understandable. He was the fifth son and tenth child. When he was born, his oldest brother, Joseph, was a 23-year-old law student.

Jefferson was only two years old when his father sold his Kentucky property, which he had greatly improved by hard labor and intelligent management, and moved to the Deep South. After a few months' residence in Louisiana, he bought land in Wilkinson County, Mississippi.

In Kentucky, Samuel Davis had raised blooded horses, and the sale of his stock brought him a small fortune in terms of frontier economy. He was now able to build a substantial frame house with plastered walls. The double doors of the cypress-paneled hall opened onto a wide veranda extending across the entire front of the house. From this shady refuge, the family could look out on the live oak trees with their festoons of Spanish moss that cast lengthening shadows with the approach of twilight, transforming them into gnarled and bearded old men. There was a brooding fierceness to the land as it baked in the noonday sun, but it had a weird beauty in the intimacy of a cicada-haunted, moonlit night. The boy who had been born in a log cabin would have a plantation childhood.

Little Jefferson would have looked perfectly at home in the greatest plantation mansion on the James or most elegant town house in Charleston. The refined features of this small, golden-haired boy with big brown eyes made him look more patrician than many a child unquestionably to the manor born.

His father was determined that he should have such educational advantages that his manners and conversation should be equally appropriate in a manorial setting. Working in the hot fields side by side with his slaves, Samuel Davis saved money to send little Jefferson to a good private school in Kentucky. The strength of his desire to give his son every advantage is attested by the fact that Samuel, though he was a Baptist, sent the boy at the age of seven to a Catholic school conducted by Dominican Friars.

In the two years that Jeff had attended a log cabin school in the woods, he had had little opportunity to learn much. On the woodland trail to the school, however, the little fellow demonstrated one day that he had learned an important lesson at home. The necessity for courage had been instilled in him by both parents. When, with his sister Pollie, he saw a large, great-antlered buck, he said, "We will not run." And he stood his ground while the animal walked up to him, sniffed until stared down, and then ran off.

Such incidents would pale before excitements that awaited the boy on his 700-mile journey to Springfield, Kentucky. He would ride with Major Hines, one of brother Joseph's friends, and the major's wife, seven-year-old son, sister-in-law, and niece accompanied by two Negro servants of the Hines'.

During the journey of several weeks, Jeff had his first glimpse of the kind of life characteristic of his frontier origins. For days there were no farms, no stores, no white habitations. But deer and turkeys were abundant. At night, Jeff and the rest of the party slept under the trees while a blazing campfire discouraged prowling panthers. Somewhere, in the darkness beyond the circle of firelight, silent-footed Indians flitted among the trees.

At Nashville, there was a special treat. Major Hines had stirred Jeff's imagination with stories of his service at the Battle of New Orleans under Andrew Jackson. Now Jeff would have a chance to meet "Old Hickory." The general was at his plantation, The Hermitage. The white-columned mansion of his dreams had not yet been erected and Jackson lived in a large, solid log house. But the thin-faced, lofty-browed, old warrior had an imposing natural dignity, an unaffected grand manner, that made an indelible impression on the boy. The child remained at The Hermitage two weeks. The awe and admiration inspired in him by the general never left him, even when he became a national figure and was the intimate friend of Presidents. It is possible that Jeff's military aspirations were inspired in part by the visit with Jackson.

At St. Thomas Catholic School, seven-year-old Jeff was set apart by the fact that he was the youngest pupil and the only Protestant. He had a bed in the room of one of the priests, Father Angier, who acted as his unofficial guardian. At the school, he acquired a taste for disciplined scholarship. The British diction of the friars probably had a tempering influence on Jeff's Deep Southern speech, and may account for the fact that his enunciation in later years was not far different from that to which Richmonders were accustomed.

During this period of his schooling, Jeff evidenced quick-witted resourcefulness when he was ordered to be whipped as a result of a school prank. A number of boys were responsible for a veritable barrage of cabbages, squashes, and potatoes that caused an uproar one night among the sleeping monks. The cover of darkness had been gained by extinguishing the light burning before an icon. Little Jeff bargained for freedom from punishment if he would reveal the name of the boy who had put out the flame. Having gained this concession, he admitted that he was the offender.

The influence of the boy's school environment caused him to ask to become a Catholic. Evidently, his family had exacted a promise that he not be converted to that faith, because the head of the school discouraged this interest.

When Jeff was nine years old, his mother could no longer bear separation from him and he returned home, traveling on the Ohio and the Mississippi by the new and exciting means of steamboat.

Thinking that he had become such a man in his absence that his own mother would not recognize him, the little boy ran under the old live oaks up to the familiar hospitality of the broad veranda where she sat and, pretending to be a stranger, asked if she had seen any stray horses. Bounding toward him and enfolding him in her arms, she exclaimed, "I see a stray boy."

Next he was placed in a boarding school at Washington, Mississippi. Here he was not far from Natchez, where brother Joseph was rapidly solidifying his position as member of a virile, half-aristocratic, half-plutocratic oligarchy.

The next year, a new academy opened near Jeff's home. He enrolled and was able to live with his family while attending school. The principal, John A. Shaw, awakened the boy's interest in many fields of knowledge, and Jeff testified in later life that this transplanted New England pedagogue was his most influential teacher. Nevertheless, Jeff quit school while at this academy. His wise father voiced no objections but put him to work picking cotton. After two days of work in the blazing sun, the boy developed a great thirst for knowledge. He completed his studies at the school about the time of his thirteenth birthday and entered Transylvania University at Lexington, Kentucky.

Easterners of that day were prone to regard anything west of

Virginia as provincial, but Transylvania was a cosmopolitan institution of learning with an able faculty recruited from Europe as well as from many parts of the United States. Jefferson soon excelled in history, Bible studies, Latin, and Greek. The college library seemed to become the center of his life. He spent so much time in reading that he largely abandoned participation in sports. But he always had time for making friends and earned great popularity with fellow students, faculty and townspeople. He soon won the reputation of being the best scholar in the school. He became popular in polished society, a frequent visitor at the nearby home of Henry Clay, and a great favorite with motherly women who remarked on his handsomeness and refinement.

"Shine in Society"

Such attainments must have brought great satisfaction to Jeff's father. On June 25, 1823, when Samuel Davis was struggling hard to make ends meet, he wrote Jeff with an eloquence of heart that triumphed over faulty grammar, confiding to the boy the high hopes that he reposed in him. He concluded : "Use every possible means to acquire useful knowledge as knowledge is power, the want of which has brought mischief and misery on your father in old age—That you may be happy and shine in society when your father is beyond the reach of harm is the most ardent wish of his heart."

Samuel Davis, whose educational advantages had placed him above his neighbors on the Kentucky frontier, had never had the economic or cultural resources to keep pace with leaders of the plantation society in Mississippi. Among former Virginians and South Carolinians who exemplified the graces of an old civilization, he frequently felt inadequate. Among those who could speak of their own long pedigrees in a deprecating way that was a sure sign of unshakable social security, a man's self-confidence sometimes suffered if he did not know who his grandfather was. The ironic fact is that there is some reason to believe that Davis was descended from Evan Davis, a great planter and one of the earliest settlers in a principal citadel of Southern aristocracy, the Northern Neck of Virginia. It is not surprising that Samuel knew little of his family background, since he was only nine years old when his father died. Nor is it surprising that, having enjoyed few educational advantages, and having made his way in a rough frontier society, he lacked some of the graces that may have been second nature to his forebears. Young Jeff would never know who his great-grandfather was, but he had a father of whom he could justly be proud.

Ignorance about his ancestors in a society sometimes accused of Shinto enthusiasms seems not to have worried Jeff as much as it did Samuel. Nevertheless, the father's anxiety in this matter seems to have had an effect in shaping the son's ideals and manners. This influence is reflected in the contempt which Jefferson Davis later felt for genealogical studies. It also explains his extreme sensitivity regarding his prerogatives as a gentleman and his almost excessively punctilious conformity to the code of the Southern aristocrat. Just as some planters of eighteenth-century Virginia became more representative of the English ideal of aristocracy than many of the nobles whom they sought to emulate, so Jefferson Davis became a more convincing embodiment of Southern aristocracy than many bluebloods who occasionally displayed a lordly disdain for some of the more exquisite refinements.

A little over a year after Samuel Davis wrote the letter, he was dead. In the meantime, Jeff's sister Mary had also died. The double blow almost overwhelmed the sensitive youth. He wrote to his sister-in-law, "If all the dear friends of my childhood are to be torn from me, I care not how soon I follow." It was with a sad heart that three days later he prepared to enter upon a new life by accepting an appointment to the United States Military Academy. Despite his military enthusiasms, Jeff had hoped to finish his course at Transylvania and then study law at the University of Virginia.

He had been junior class orator at the Kentucky college and looked forward to the enjoyment of senior honors earned by popularity and intellectual excellence. Brother Joseph promised the boy that, if he still wanted to go to the University of Virginia after a year at West Point, he would send him.

When he arrived at West Point late in the summer of 1824, Jeff found that the term had already begun. A faculty member who was Joseph Davis's friend begged that the boy be permitted to enter if he could pass a special examination. The mathematics professor and the teacher of foreign languages were his inquisitors. Jeff had not studied arithmetic at Transylvania and he crammed for the examination in desperation. He happened to know the answer to the first big question asked by the mathematics teacher and gave it so promptly and explicitly that the examiner saw little need for further questions. The language teacher was considerably impressed with the lad's proficiency in Greek. Jeff had passed.

The strict regimentation of life at the Point was uncongenial to him. Not only was he held to a rigorous schedule, but the numerous prohibitions were so severe that even novels and plays were on the proscribed list.

One of his principal compensations was his friendship with Albert Sidney Johnston, which had begun at Transylvania and was now resumed at the Academy. Five years Jeff's senior, Johnston was already a leader at the Point. His high scholastic standing, manly character, and appealing personality qualified him as the teen-aged boy's personal hero. Through Johnston, Jeff came to know other outstanding cadets, such as Leonidas Polk.

Jeff's career at West Point was a notable one, but not for scholarship. Despite the brilliant promise of his years at Transylvania and his genuine intellectual interests, he stood just above the median in his class at the end of the first year. In both his second and third years, he was in the lower half. In 1828, he was graduated 23d in a class of 33. Perhaps his lack of interest in mathematics partly explains his poor showing. But his extracurricular activities—the things that really made his school career notable—may have left him little time for study. The nature of these activities is suggested by the fact that he acquired 120 demerits in his first year, 70 in his second, and 137 in the third. In his senior year, in conduct, he stood 163rd in a class of 207.

Through the four years his reputation for honor remained un-smirched. But he effectively demonstrated the capacity of an honor-able but imaginative and high-spirited youth for getting into trouble of bewildering variety and complexity.

In August 1825, he was ordered to appear before a military court to answer charges that he had been at Benny Havens', a tavern off-limits to the cadets, and there had drunk "spiritous" liquors. Jeff admitted visiting the place but pleaded not guilty of the more serious charge on the technicality that malt liquors, cider, and porter were not "spiritous." The court found him guilty on September 3, 1825 and sentenced him to dismissal. But his honesty had earned him the tribunal's respect and it recommended the remission of the sentence. Pardoned by the Secretary of War, Jeff was permitted to continue his education.

Later, the irrepressible boy returned to Benny Havens' on another lark. Warned that an instructor was coming, he fled so precipitately that he tumbled down a 60-foot bluff and came near death.

In the South, Christmas was a joyful occasion celebrated with fire-works, eggnog parties, and other delights frowned on in many parts of the North. At Christmas time in 1826, Jeff and some of his colleagues from below the Potomac decided to enliven the austere confines of West Point with an old-fashioned Southern Christmas. They did not have the fireworks, but they did obtain the ingredients for eggnog. Before light on Christmas morning, Jeff was eagerly dash-ing about inviting fellow cadets to a big eggnog party at No. 5 North Barracks. Somebody told him that Captain Ethan Hitchcock, the same officer who had caught him at Benny Havens', was alert to the fact that something was going on. The 18-year-old cadet ran to the room, flung open the door and yelled, "Put away the grog, boys, Old Hitch is coming." The silent, horrified stare of the other boys told him that something was wrong even before he turned around and saw that Captain Hitchcock had entered behind him.

"Old Hitch" sent Jeff to his quarters under arrest. Despite the embarrassment of his position, the young man had no trouble in getting to sleep. In fact, he slept through one of the most violent disturbances in the history of the Academy. Nineteen of the cadets at the party drove off Captain Hitchcock and his fellow officers with stovewood clubs. One of the faculty members had to take refuge in his quarters from a cadet who pursued him with drawn sword. Hitchcock himself barely missed being shot by Jeff's roommate. An hour and a half later, the riot was quelled, but broken windows and ripped-out stair rails were mute evidence of its violence.

The chief offenders were court-martialed and dismissed. Jeff refused to divulge any information about his roommate's activities, and for that reason was confined to quarters for weeks. This martyrdom brought him great popularity, which he hugely enjoyed.

Some of his instructors viewed him in a far more baleful light. One seemed to feel an almost chemical repulsion for Jeff. The Mississippian's proud bearing exacerbated the antipathy. The teacher indulged in an unimaginative brand of pedagogic sarcasm whenever he addressed the boy, and Jeff, in turn, tried to stare him down, just as he had the stag in faraway days in Kentucky.

One day, the teacher cut deep when, with a significant look at Jeff, he referred to those "who, in an emergency, would be confused and unstrung, not from cowardice, but from the mediocre nature of their minds." Not long afterwards, the boy got his revenge. During a lesson in the use of explosives, the fuse of a grenade was accidentally lighted. Jeff was the first to notice it. As though he were asking a routine question, he said to the instructor: "What shall we do, sir? This fire-ball is ignited."

The astonished professor shouted, "Run for your lives!" and dashed for the door.

Calmly, Jeff picked up the grenade and threw it out the window.

There could be no doubt of Jeff's courage and daring. In matters of discipline, his record was not good, and it would be difficult to predict the career of the tall, handsome Mississippian who at the age of 20 was graduated from the United States Military Academy and commissioned a brevet second lietenant.

On Hawkeye's Trail

Jeff divided his three months' furlough following graduation between his old home, where his mother still lived, and the Natchez plantation of brother Joseph. The 43-year-old Joseph was not so taken up with his rapidly growing wealth or his 18-year-old bride that he did not have plenty of time for his younger brother. Indeed, the relationship had grown less fraternal and more like that of father and son. Jeff also renewed the association with James Pemberton, the Negro who had been his personal servant before West Point days. The two were united by a bond of friendship stronger than the tie of master and slave. When Davis boarded the Mississippi River boat for St. Louis and duty at nearby Jefferson Barracks, he took James Pemberton with him.

Soon he was transferred to Fort Crawford, a wilderness trading post on the Wisconsin River. The young lieutenant would have been better prepared for life at this post if the family had never left the log cabin in Kentucky. He was soon given an assignment that might have been drawn from the pages of James Fenimore Cooper. The fort stood amid almost treeless prairies. Timber was necessary for badly needed repairs. Davis took a small party of men up river in an open boat in search of cedar and pine. Two French-Canadian trappers were his guides.

One day they were pursued by whooping Indians in swift canoes. Despite the best exertions of Davis and his men, the Indians gained on them rapidly. With the gap between pursuers and pursued closing inexorably, the lieutenant got a sudden inspiration. He and his men, in desperate haste, converted a blanket into a sail. The boat almost turned over, but it picked up speed immediately. Eventually the Indians turned back, abandoning all hope of using their scalping knives that day.

Davis established his lumber camp at a point about 175 miles from his home fort. Except for a few intrepid trappers and bands of Indians, the rule of the black bear and the elk were unchallenged in the great forest. Once Davis and his party hardly had time to take cover before an Indian war party landed. The braves searched, but not in the thoroughgoing tradition of Cooper's Indians. Davis held his breath while one came within 12 feet of him and then returned to his canoe.

A little later, Davis was ordered to Ft. Winnebago, on the portage between the Wisconsin and Fox Rivers. Here he came to know friendly as well as hostile Indians. Many white men were contemptuous of the aborigines, but Davis conceived a great respect for them. He did not think that a formal education such as he had received at West Point was the only kind that counted. He confessed that, as he grew to know the Indians better, he was impressed with "the variety of things they could do and he could not."

Davis was acquiring a liberal education on one of America's wildest frontiers, and he gloried in the experience. Physical diversions could not lure him completely from his beloved books, but he could not resist the delights of the square dance when the fiddles began to scrape. He found fewer people to share another of his favorite pastimes, riding "crazy horses," unbroken broncos that could kill a man. Several times he nearly met death, but he always mastered his mount.

His frontier skills were put to a fresh test when he was sent on reconnaissance into the territory between the Ft. Winnebago portage and an obscure Illinois village called Chicago. To the best of his knowledge, he and his companions were the first white men to enter upon this savage scene. They lived off the land as they went, eating fish, waterfowl, and wild rice. On one scouting trip, their path was blocked by a party of unfriendly Indians. Davis spurred his horse forward and grabbed the scalp lock of the brave directly in front of him, dragging the astonished warrior with him and then dropping him to the ground. While the other Indians looked on in amazement, Davis and his party made their escape.

When Davis was 23, he had a happier experience with Indians. On orders from Fort Crawford, he set up a sawmill on the Yellow River. Association with the Indians was frequent, and Davis strove to keep relations friendly. He had the height, the erect carriage, the dignity, and the courage that Indians so much admired. The chief adopted him as his own son, and Davis was henceforward known to the tribesmen as "Little Chief."

Working in the heavy snow and the cold rains, Davis was laid flat on his back by an illness that became pneumonia. He had to be his own physician, and James Pemberton was his nurse. In the hours when his mind returned from its fever-ridden wanderings, he explained his plans to the faithful servant, who in turn transmitted them to the workers. Some days, it seemed that the young officer was losing his battle for life. Then the fever broke and there came a time when James Pemberton could take up his emaciated master in his arms and carry him to the window to look out on the glittering expanse of snow. Eventually, Davis was up and about his duties, but he never fully recovered from his illness. Ever afterward, he was particularly susceptible to respiratory ailments, which were sometimes accompanied by excruciating facial neuralgia and partial loss of vision.

His next duty was back at Fort Crawford where he supervised the construction of a large addition to the post. A burly soldier engaged in the work declared publicly that he would thrash "that baby-faced lieutenant" if he tried to order him around. He deliberately disobeyed one of Davis's orders and, when corrected, persisted in his disobedience before the entire working crew. The man reached for a plank, which he may or may not have considered using as a weapon. No one ever knew because, before the defiant soldier had a chance to do anything, Davis grabbed a heavy stick and struck him down. He then proceeded to whip him as though the giant were a child. He stopped only when the big man begged for mercy. Then, in the most dignified manner, Davis said, "This has been a fight between man and man and I shall not notice it officially."

Many of the men, accustomed to rough-and-ready ways, conceived a new admiration for the lieutenant. This sentiment may not have been universal, but nobody else defied his orders.

In the course of this project, Davis was sent on a special assignment which gave him a chance to prove that he was good at gentle persuasion as well as forceful conversion. He was ordered to remove squatters who had built cabins in the area of Dubuque, Iowa. The Federal government was negotiating with the Indians for control of the territory, but the land still belonged to the aborigines and the presence of the squatters was imperiling the tentative peace. Therefore, Davis was instructed to use the bayonet if necessary.

Davis recoiled from the application of naked force, especially since women and children were involved. Yet harsh tactics might be inevitable. A force commanded by another lieutenant had failed utterly in its efforts to move the people from their cabins. Now Davis and his 50 soldiers had to face about 400 armed squatters.

He addressed the most hostile audience he was ever to face. As he turned from side to side, he looked into cold gun barrels and cold eyes. The crowd shouted insults at him, but a barrage of words was better than one of bullets. So he talked on until they began listening. He showed that he fully appreciated their feelings and realized the hardship that execution of his orders would impose. But he explained the government's problem, and told them that they could move back into their cabins as soon as Federal agents completed negotiations with the Indians for transfer of the land. He received no ovation, but he could count the speech a success since he had not been shot. After the crowd dispersed, he went from cabin to cabin, making a plea to common sense and offering wagons to facilitate their moving. Then he went away for a few days to give passions time to cool.

When Davis returned to the community of squatters, he was warned not to go into the Log Saloon. Men were waiting there to kill him. Being the sort of young man he was, one who liked to "ride crazy horses," the lieutenant strode into the saloon with a smile on his face. The room was crowded with scowling men. "My friends," said Davis, beaming with good will, "I am sure you have thought over my proposition and are going to drink to my success. I treat you all." Nobody refused the invitation, and as the night wore on, some of the miners seemed to get positively fond of the young lieutenant.

The next day the squatters left their cabins peaceably. There was no show of force. None was needed.

In 1832, Davis was made aide to Brevet Colonel Zachary Taylor, who had been made temporary commander at Fort Crawford. A native of Virginia, "Old Rough and Ready" was descended from some of the Old Dominion's leading families. Though more limited in formal education than many Virginia aristocrats, he was in other ways typical of the Commonwealth's country gentry. He cared little about dress. Some West Point men would be astonished when he began wearing a straw hat with his uniform. Davis was infinitely attentive to all the details requisite to a gentlemanly appearance, but the two men were kindred spirits in their courage and in their love of fair dealing. They became good friends.

About this time, the Governor of Illinois called for volunteers for what promised to be a full-scale Indian war. When mutiny broke out in the force raised in Joe Davies County, Davis was sent to the trouble spot. Arriving on a Saturday, he operated so diplomatically and at the same time firmly that by Monday he was able to convert a mass of mutinous men into an obedient regiment.

Davis loved action and was ambitious, but he deplored the threat of war with the Indians. He believed that justice was on the side of Black Hawk. He was incensed that men of his own race should have burned the Indians' homes and beaten their squaws. He could sympathize with Black Hawk's anguish over the destruction of his ancestral burying ground.

In these troubled days, Davis sometimes found congenial company at John Dixon's log house, a combination inn and store, at Dixon's Ferry, Illinois. Another young man, less than a year younger than Jefferson Davis, a fellow native of Kentucky who like him had no enthusiasm for war with Black Hawk, also found interesting conversation at Dixon's house. It would be interesting to know whether these two met, because their names—-Davis and Lincoln—would be linked in history.

Davis was in Mississippi on leave when sharp fighting broke out in

May of 1832. By the time he returned to duty, the Black Hawk War was nearly over. He reluctantly but obediently played a part in the old chief's final defeat. Black Hawk and his son had escaped death or capture. Davis was given the unwelcome assignment of hunting him down. On the way to Prairie du Chien, Davis and his party were intercepted by some Winnebago Indians who, in the hope of concessions from the Federal government, handed over the Old Chief, bound and helpless.

Davis rode back with the lean old warrior who sat his horse as proudly in his white deerskin suit as a Southern planter in his white linen. Then it became Davis's duty to escort Black Hawk and a number of other prisoners down river to Jefferson Barracks.

Even before Davis had met Black Hawk, the old chief had his sympathy. Now, by his dignity in defeat, he commanded his respect. In a lengthy statement that the chief dictated in October 1833, he was critical of the treatment accorded him at the barracks. But he described Davis as "a young war chief who treated us all with much kindness." He further testified, "He is a good and brave young chief with whose conduct I was very much pleased." He cited particularly an incident at Galena, where a crowd collected to see the famous captive. Davis, he said, "would not permit them to enter the apartment where we were—knowing from what his feelings would have been if he had been placed in a similar situation, that we did not wish a gaping crowd around us."

In subsequent years, Davis took no pride in his part in the Black Hawk War. "The real heroes," he declared, "were Black Hawk and his savages."

Courtship and Court-Martial

The lieutenant was loath to return to what promised to be a dull round of duties at Fort Crawford. During his recent leave, he had toyed with the idea of leaving the army to enter the railroad business, but had been discouraged by brother Joseph.

But an important addition had come to Fort Crawford. When Davis called on Colonel Taylor, he found a slender, 18-year-old girl, whose large, bright gray eyes had a quality more compelling than most of more decided hue. From her wavy hair to her softly rounded chin, she was beautiful, and her figure was charming. To the young man's excited imagination, she appeared a gleaming angel, but the tilt of her nose lent a touch of piquant, down-to-earth humanity. She was Sarah Knox Taylor, the colonel's daughter.

In conversation, Davis learned that she was well educated for a girl of her time, though at that stage he doubtless would have imputed hidden wisdom to the most inane remark that she could have made. He later learned that she was also an expert dancer. And before many days, he knew, in addition, that he wanted her to be his wife.

The world was a glorious place until the time came to confide his intentions to the colonel. Taylor's oldest daughter had married an army officer. He told Davis he had vowed that the other two should not. Disappointed but not discouraged, Davis continued to press his suit.

At length, the colonel forbade his daughter to see Davis. The two young people met surreptitiously. Evidently suspicious of what was going on, Taylor tried to get the lieutenant transferred to another post. The next spring, Davis was assigned to recruiting duty with a new regiment of dragoons. He would have to leave for Lexington, Kentucky, but he carried with him the consoling thought that before long he would return to Fort Crawford. Besides, he had been promoted to first lieutenant.

When Davis returned to the fort, he again asked the colonel for his daughter's hand. And again he was refused.

But, at the end of the summer when the lieutenant embarked with his regiment for the wilds of Arkansas, he carried with him a flower from Sarah Knox Taylor in token of their secret engagement.

Shortly after arriving in Arkansas, Davis was made adjutant. For half a month, he and his men lived on a daily diet of buffalo meat for breakfast, buffalo meat for lunch, buffalo meat for supper, with no bread or vegetables to vary the monotony. Once, on a long march, they were reduced to eating cold flour.

But Davis's heart suffered more than his stomach. On December 16, 1834, with no prospect of seeing Sarah Knox Taylor before the end of the year, the lonely lieutenant wrote her :

"Dreams, my dear Sarah, we will agree, are our weakest thoughts, and yet by my dreams I have been lately almost crazed, for they were of you, and the sleeping imagination painted you not as I felt you, not such as I could live and see you, for you seemed a sacrifice to your parents' desire, the bride of a wretch that your pride and sense equally compel you to despise." Then, he said, he had had another dream, a pleasant one in which he and his fiancée had been together.

At last had come a letter from Sarah in which she expressed herself reassuringly, almost in the same words she had used in the second dream. "Kind, dear letter," the young man wrote, "I have kissed it often and it has driven away mad notions from my brain." The ardent lover closed his own letter, "Adieu, ma chere, très chere amie."

Davis had a new worry not many days later. The day before Christmas dawned gray and wet. He had been troubled with respiratory difficulties ever since his severe illness from pneumonia, so he remained in his tent at reveille. When the major sent for him to account for his absence, he cited the regulation requiring that rolls be called in quarters when it was raining. The major shouted at him in anger, whereupon Davis walked off. The major then placed him under arrest, confining him to quarters.

In March, he was arraigned before a general court-martial in Memphis, Tennessee on charges of "conduct subversive of good order and military discipline."

Davis, perhaps partly through his diligent conformity to an ideal of aristocracy, had already developed an air of poised assurance that nearly all women and a good many men admired, but which irritated some people beyond measure. The major was evidently one of the uncharmed. He was astonished and probably apoplectic when Davis, given a chance to speak for himself, turned upon his accuser with the calm self-confidence of a prosecutor with a full arsenal. The lieutenant gave a dispassionate summary of the facts of the case, pointing out that he had been within his rights according to military law when he failed to attend reveille. Then, standing proudly erect with a look of injured dignity that seemed to put his commanding officer and the whole United States Army on trial instead of himself, Davis declared, "On the day when I learn that the caprice of a commander can increase or decrease the obligations of my commission, can magnify or diminish the quantum of military offense contained in military acts, I shall cease to consider myself a freeman and no longer feel proud of my sword."

Pointing out his commanding officer's conduct as a horrible example of a situation that the army should move to correct, he said, "If an officer shown to be harsh and disregardful of the feelings of others, irritable and forgetful . . ., if such an officer can with the jaundiced eye of passion see in simple questions and facings about, contemptuous and disrespectful conduct, there can be little security for his subordinates in his official intercourse."

Then, assuming a more modest tone, he said, "The humble and narrow reputation which a subaltern can acquire by years of the most rigid performance of his duty is [of] little worth in the wide world of fame, but yet is something to himself."

Then, abruptly shedding his humility, he addressed the court with the firmness of a man demanding his due, not pleading for mercy. "If I have complied with the first part of the eleventh paragraph of the second article, General Army Regulations, and my commander has shown a disregard to the last part of the same paragraph," he said, "then have I by my arrest and charges been injured, and I look to the court for redress."

The court acquitted him and he strapped on his sword.

Davis obtained a furlough and went back to Mississippi. The recent experience of the court-martial, although the decision was in his favor, may have contributed to the dissatisfaction he felt with his army career. But also in his mind was the fact that his occupation seemed to stand in the way of his marriage to Sarah. Not only had her father expressed opposition on the grounds of Davis's vocation, but he himself saw little prospect of being able to support a family adequately on army pay. He visited brother Joseph at Hurricane, his plantation home on the Mississippi below Vicksburg. The plantation life with its graces and amenities was a welcome change from the barracks. Learning the direction of his younger brother's thinking, Joseph offered him the use of 1,800 acres of uncleared land sliced from his own 6,900-acre plantation if Jeff wished to leave the army and become a planter.

The lieutenant resigned from the army effective June 30, 1835. His furlough would extend until then, so there was no need to report again at his Western post.

He had already written Sarah Knox about his decision and eagerly awaited her father's approval now that the old obstruction had been removed. But, when her reply came, Davis learned that Colonel Taylor still withheld his blessing. Nevertheless, the determined girl had told her father that, with or without his consent, she would marry Davis. The girl went to the home of her widowed aunt, Elizabeth Taylor, near Louisville. Jefferson met her there and they agreed to be married on June 17.

Colonel Taylor sent her trousseau money enclosed with an affectionate letter. But both he and her mother found it inconvenient to attend the ceremony. On the morning of her wedding day, Sarah Knox wrote her mother : "I am very much gratified that Sister Anne is here. At this time, if one member of the family is present, I shall not feel so entirely destitute of friends. But you, my dearest mother, I know, will still retain some feelings of affection for a child who has been so unfortunate as to form a connection without the sanction of her parents, but who will always feel the deepest affection for them, whatever may be their feelings toward her."

But she was not so "destitute of friends" as she supposed. Two of her uncles, Hancock and Joseph Taylor, arrived for the wedding as did one of her father's sisters, a Mrs. Gray. A Taylor first cousin showed up and was pressed into service as best man.

Under the circumstances, Davis felt more than the usual bridegroom's anxiety as, dressed in black broadcloth, he stepped into his buggy and headed out of Louisville for the three-mile ride to the home of Sarah's aunt. Before he got out of town, he was accosted by an excited man, the county clerk. Davis reined to a stop and the man asked to see the marriage license, which he himself had issued earlier. Davis handed it down to him. "I am informed," the clerk said, "that the young lady is not of age and that her father is intensely antagonistic to the marriage." He then methodically tore up the license and walked away.

Calling on all his self-discipline to resist striking the man, Davis put the whip to his horse and hurried on to the plantation. The wedding guests had already gathered when he reined in with a sweating horse, and anxiety mounted as he entered into a soft-voiced but agitated conversation with Sarah's Aunt Elizabeth and Uncle Hancock. The threat of scandal hung over the family. Hancock Taylor rode back to Louisville with Davis. There the uncle swore before the clerk that Sarah was of age, which indeed she was, and a new license was issued.

When Davis arrived back at the plantation, Sarah's gentle gray eyes were brimming with tears. But a little later he, tall and slim in his black broadcloth, and she, wearing a bonnet and traveling dress, stood in the parlor before an Episcopal minister who joined them in matrimony. The family dissension caused by the event and the extreme anxiety occasioned by the argument over the license had put everyone's nerves on edge. Hancock Taylor's 11-year-old daughter looked around the room, watching the tears course down the faces of the witnesses. Then she noticed that the groom was not crying, too, and "took a dislike to him, deciding he must be heartless."

Sweet Song of Death

Most gloomy apprehensions were left behind when Davis and his bride stepped aboard a Mississippi River steamboat—surely there was never a more romantic honeymoon conveyance than these floating palaces of white and gold and red plush—that was to carry them down river to Vicksburg. At first they set up housekeeping in Joseph's house, now a showplace of the Natchez area boasting running water and what was probably the largest private library in Mississippi.

Sarah Knox soon proved that she could bring to housekeeping the same seemingly effortless precision that characterized her dancing and could handle a kitchen spoon as effectively as she could a delicate fan. She exemplified the type of Southern aristocrat who was accustomed to house servants, but, having no fears of losing caste, took pride in domestic tasks.

Davis was up at dawn every day to get an early start in the cool hours with the work of clearing his wooded acres. Later in the day brother Joseph joined him, and the two would direct the black laborers.

Felling the trees and burning out the briars and canebrakes was hot work in that August of 1835. The serpentine mists that coiled upward from the swamps were like the heat itself made palpable.

One day Davis came down with fever. The doctor said that it was malaria, a diagnosis that brought a chill dread to Sarah Knox's heart, because the same disease had claimed the lives of two of her sisters. The next day she herself began burning with fever. As the days passed, both failed to benefit from the prescribed treatments.

At last they resorted to a change of scene. They went by boat to Bayou Sara to stay with Davis's sister Anna. In this very area, Sarah Knox's sisters had died.

After arrival, both husband and wife suffered turns for the worse. Davis's life was thought to be in danger, and the fact that Sarah Knox seemed to be in almost as serious a condition was kept from him. One day a sound hauntingly familiar penetrated his fevered brain. It was the voice of Sarah Knox singing "Fairy Bells," the song of their courtship. The mists from the swamps seemed to be swirling about him, dissolving his powers of thought, but he staggered out of the room and toward the sound. There before him on her bed was Sarah Knox. There was no recognition in the gray eyes that had always looked on him so tenderly. In her delirium, she must have been with him in a happier time and place, for exultantly she sang their song of love. In trembling arms, Davis held her to him as, quite literally, she poured out her life in song.

On Davis's insistence, funeral services were conducted in his room. Services for Davis himself, it seemed, would have to be held within a few days. Then the crisis passed, but more than a month went by before he was able to return to brother Joseph's home.

His physical recovery was slow. His emotional recovery was far slower, and probably was never complete. Sarah Knox had died on September 15, a bride of less than three months. Davis was tortured by the thought that his bringing her to the Delta country had caused her death. The fact that he had married her and taken her away despite the strong resistance of her family deepened his feeling of responsibility.

Toward the end of October he set out on a tour, but he took only his sorrow with him from Mississippi to Havana to New York City, to Washington and back again to Mississippi. Finding no comfort in travel, he became a recluse. For seven years, he seldom left the area around Hurricane.

One great comfort was the company of brother Joseph. Not only was he like a devoted father, but he was an able mentor as well. Though he himself eschewed public office, his counsel was sought by the ablest politicians in Mississippi. Fellow planters respected him for the model management of his plantation, one of the best run in the state. Mississippi lawyers acknowledged that he was one of the state's half-dozen top leaders in the profession. And businessmen had unbounded admiration for a man who, by his own exertions, was either a millionaire or close to it.

During these years of retreat, Jefferson Davis grew intellectually through association with his brother. His knowledge of constitutional law was deepened by study of the volumes in Joseph's celebrated library. His interests were broadened by reading newspapers and periodicals from all over the United States and from Britain to which Joseph subscribed.

From Joseph, Jefferson also learned lessons in plantation management. Slavery, as Jefferson saw it at Hurricane, seemed a beneficent institution. Overseers were not authorized to punish the Negroes. When the slaves gave offense, they were tried by a jury of their peers —their fellow slaves. Joseph retained the right to pardon the convicted or reduce the sentence if he believed a jury was too harsh. The slaves were encouraged to keep laying hens, and Joseph bought eggs from them at prevailing market prices. Academic learning was encouraged among the few who showed interest and aptitude.

Of course, such idyllic conditions did not prevail on most plantations. On the average such establishment, life was as far removed from the Hurricane ideal as from *Uncle Tom's Cabin*. When the fashion centers decreed hoop skirts for milady, an amused observer of Joseph's and Jefferson's management methods drew a laugh by declaring, "Now the Davis brothers will have to widen their cotton rows to make room for the lady pickers' hoops."

In 1838, Davis began to apply more independently some of the lessons he had learned from Joseph. Acting as his own architect and construction superintendent, he built an airy, one-story house surrounded by a continuous gallery. He had cleared a field of briars to provide a building site amid noble oaks and he called the place Brierfield. He found escape now in Shakespeare, Byron, Burns, and Sir Walter Scott as well as in the factual works which he had previously devoured. Increasingly, he turned to the Scriptures for spiritual sustenance.

Davis took a personal interest in his slaves that seemed to be dictated even more by humanitarian than by economic motives. Among the innovations that he introduced was a day nursery to take care of the small children while their parents worked.

Life Intrudes

In 1843 Davis was drawn out of his tight little plantation world. Just one week short of election day, the Democrats of Warren County withdrew their candidate for the state legislature. The Whigs so dominated the district that it was hard to get a Democrat to accept his party's nomination and consent to being trotted out as a sacrificial lamb. Besides the overwhelming strength of the Whigs and Davis's eleventh-hour entry into the contest, he had another disadvantage. This one was acknowledged by one of his backers, the *Vicksburg Sentinel,* which said : "There may be some in the country to whom Mr. Davis from the secluded privacy in which he lived is unknown; to these we repeat : 'Mr. Davis is what we have stated—every inch a man.' "

The election results were a foregone conclusion. But Davis might well have paraphrased one of his favorite authors, and said : "From this nettle defeat, we pluck the flower victory." In an all-day debate in the course of the campaign, he was pitted against the greatest orator in Mississippi, Sergeant Smith Prentiss. Though Davis lost the election, his incisive logic etched his name and image on the brains of Mississippi voters. In Illinois a few years later, another little-known candidate, debating with the celebrated Stephen A. Douglas, would similarly lose an election and gain a reputation.

Joseph Davis had long dreamed of a high destiny for his younger brother. He now urged upon him a political career. The pressure on Jeff Davis to continue in politics was strong in his part of Mississippi. His own interest had been aroused by the excitement of the campaign.

Because of his seven years of seclusion, with so much time given to the study of history and constitutional law, he could bring to politics a mind vastly superior in learning and philosophical cast to that of most practitioners of the art. But the combination of studies and protracted seclusion had confirmed whatever tendency he had toward dogmatism.

In December, when Davis rode to Vicksburg to attend a political caucus, he stopped by his niece's plantation to leave a message. The recipient of the message was the 17-year-old daughter of Mr. and Mrs. William Burr Howell of Natchez, friends of Joseph's. He was to tell her that Joseph was expecting her the next day for a Christmas house party.

The girl proved to be tall, slender, and animated, with a face more arresting than beautiful except for the large, luminous brown eyes.

That night Varina Anne Howell wrote her mother a lengthy description of the 35-year-old messenger, whom she had seen for only a few minutes. With a strange mixture of girlish naïveté and acute perception, she wrote :

I do not know whether this Mr. Jefferson Davis is young or old. He looks both at times; but I believe he is old, for from what I hear he is only two years younger than you are. He impresses me as a remarkable kind of man, but of uncertain temper, and has a way of taking for granted that everybody agrees with him when he expresses an opinion, which offends me; yet he is most agreeable and has a peculiarly sweet voice and a winning manner of asserting himself. The fact is, he is the kind of person I should expect to rescue one from a mad dog at any risk, but to insist upon a stoical indifference to the fright afterward. I do not think I shall ever like him as I do his brother Joe. Would you believe it, he is refined and cultivated, and yet he is a Democrat !

When Davis returned from Vicksburg, Varina was still at the plantation. In the mornings, he and the girl would ride over the fields. Varina thought that he was a knightly figure on his magnificent white Arabian steed. And he thought that the dark-eyed girl in the blue riding habit, sitting a bay horse in lithe and slim-waisted grace, was a noteworthy addition to the beauty of the landscape. At first, Davis seems to have thought of her as little more than a child, albeit a highly attractive one. But evenings before a cheerfully snapping log fire in the music room melted the barrier of years. She could discuss both ancient and modern classics. She brought to arguments on politics the same good-humored high-spirits that she showed as a horsewoman. Both brother Joseph and James Pemberton thought highly of her, and their approval was important to Jefferson. Almost before he realized what was happening, Jefferson was enthralled with the girl and she had given her heart unreservedly to him. Not until February did Varina leave Hurricane for her home. By that time, they were engaged.

In the ensuing days, Jefferson and Varina suffered so from the pangs of love that, whenever a letter from one was delayed, the other was tortured with thoughts that the loved one might be ill.

Davis visited the Howells, a proudly aristocratic family, and won their approval. But courtship was interrupted by the demands of politics. He was named elector-at-large for the Democratic party in the presidential contest and stumped for James K. Polk all over the state of Mississippi. Varina, who at first had found it so hard to believe that a man could be both a refined gentleman and a Democrat, now found her friends equally incredulous on the same point. Her sensibilities were kept so raw by abrasive criticisms of Davis that she finally went to bed in a bad nervous state. By the time the contest was over, even inveterate Whigs were saying that Mr. Davis was an exception to the general run of Democrats. Varina recovered her usual poise and the wedding was set for February 26, 1845.

When Davis stepped aboard the steamer to take him to Natchez for his wedding, he must have felt that the act symbolized a break with the old life and the beginning of a new. But, much to his surprise, a fellow passenger was Zachary Taylor, now a general. Then and there, at a moment tragically late for both, and more so for one no longer with them, father-in-law and son-in-law were reconciled.

After the wedding, the couple boarded a river boat and steamed down the Mississippi. They debarked at Bayou Sara, drove to Jeff's sister's place, and there together placed flowers on the grave of Sarah Knox.

Beginning life at Brierfield after a festive month in New Orleans, Varina proved a competent plantation mistress. There could be no question of her devotion to her husband, but family relations were sometimes made tense by a tug of war between her and brother Joseph, each of whom coveted the position of chief influence in Jefferson's life.

Virtually every politician who runs for Congress "consents" to do so at the "urging of friends" but the traditional announcement was quite literally true in Davis's case. Without opposition, he became the Democratic nominee for the United States House of Representatives.

The man of action who galloped all over the district making speeches wherever a crowd could be gathered together seemed a far cry from the recluse of a few years before. He arranged to arrive in Woodville a day ahead of his scheduled appearance so that he could spend some time with his mother. When he entered the house, she was dressed in her best finery—but for burial. There would be no welcoming arms this time for the "stray boy."

After the funeral, Davis rode more than 40 miles to Natchez to tell Varina of his mother's death and an hour later, mounting another horse, rode the more than 40 miles back to Woodville to keep his speaking engagement.

Davis won the election. Before he left for Washington he had the privilege of introducing one of his heroes, John C. Calhoun, to a Vicksburg audience. As accustomed as Davis was by now to the stump, he asked his 19-year-old wife not to look at him while he spoke and she obediently kept her eyes riveted on her lap. Because nothing must go wrong on this important occasion, Davis had memorized his speech, contrary to his usual practice. Haltingly, he began to recite it and then suddenly branched out extemporaneously with a spontaneous vigor that captivated his audience and caused Calhoun to regard him as a man worth watching.

On December 8, 1845 Davis became a member of Congress. He brought to the office not only a greater knowledge of constitutional law than most veteran congressmen, but also a greater firsthand knowledge of the country. He had lived and worked in North, East, and West as well as in the South.

But he had much to learn about the practical politics of Washington and John C. Calhoun became his mentor.

The new congressman's teen-aged bride became his indispensable secretary, enthusiastically working for hours on end, taking his dictation and helping with research. Not much inclined to early rising, despite his farm background, Davis worked far into the night, his creative energies waking to their full power at an hour when many of his colleagues were in bed.

Davis quickly earned in Washington a reputation as a "thinker and scholar," which made him seem peculiar to some of his fellow politicians and admirable to others. His studies in the library at Hurricane had acquainted him with British theories of the legislator's role. In that country, where a man need not be a resident of the constituency which elects him to Parliament, a legislator is regarded as representing the nation as a whole rather than a particular district. Though the exigencies of American politics were quite different, Davis conscientiously sought to fulfill the English ideal. When a fellow congressman, with log-rolling in mind, asked if he would support a river and harbor bill because it would benefit Mississippi, he replied: "I feel, sir, that I am incapable of sectional distinction upon such objects. I abhor and reject all interested combinations."

His philosophical breadth of view was a little too much for some in the chamber when on December 19, 1845 he spoke against a policy of using the nationalization laws to protect "native Americanism." It was among savage nations, he said, that "a stranger was counted an enemy, and the same word designated both; but, as civilization . . . advanced and prevailed, the gates of admission were gradually thrown open. Like another celebrated system which prevails in this country, namely a protective tariff, this barbarian doctrine of exclusion has been called 'the American system.' Such a doctrine was never heard among the patriots of the Revolution." Looking around the chamber, he asked, "Do you gentlemen forget that, among the signers of the Declaration of Independence, were eight actual foreigners and nine who were the immediate descendants of foreign parents?" He declared, "To live for one's country, in its broadest, truest sense is . . . to live for mankind."

When politicians raised the cry of "54-40 or fight" and the United States seemed about to go to war with Britain over Oregon, Davis called for strengthened defenses but cautioned that war was "a dread alternative" and should be "the last resort." When debate on the Oregon issue degenerated into sectional controversy, Davis defended his own Southland, but in words that reminded his hearers of the superior claims of national interest. Tall, slim, and graceful, he was a commanding figure as he declared : "It is as the representative of a high-spirited and patriotic people that I am called on to resist this war clamor." His modulated voice conveyed an impression of controlled power as he said : "From sire to son has descended our federated creed, opposed to the idea of sectional conflict for private advantage and favoring the wider expansion of our union. If envy and jealousy and sectional strife are eating like rust into the bonds which our fathers expected to bind us, they came from causes which our Southern atmosphere has never furnished."

As Davis sat down, a short, bullet-headed old fellow with a cannonball body rose from his desk and, rolling as he walked, moved toward a cluster of his friends. "That young man, gentlemen," he pronounced with the finality of a musket shot, "is no ordinary man. Mind me, he will make his mark yet. He will go far." The opinion was listened to with respect, for this old Yankee, whose verbal ammunition had found many a target in that chamber, was the most distinguished man on the floor—the only man to serve in Congress after being President of the United States, John Quincy Adams.

The possibility of war with Britain was soon shoved into the background. On May 11, 1846, President Polk told Congress : "Mexico has passed the boundary of the United States and shed American blood upon American soil. War exists, and exists by the act of Mexico."

At once, Davis's military ardor erupted through the crust of cool reserve that had distinguished him during the Oregon crisis. The treaty of peace ending the struggle now begun, he said, should "be made at the city of Mexico, and by an ambassador who cannot be refused a hearing, but will speak with that which levels walls and opens gates—American cannon." He dashed off a letter to the Vicksburg *Sentinel* announcing his desire to command a regiment from his own county.

He declared : "My education and former practice would, I think, enable me to be of service to Mississippians who take the field. If they wish it, I will join them as soon as possible, wherever they may be."

A few days later, Davis spoke in the House in support of a Resolution expressing "appreciation to General Taylor for his conduct on the Mexican Frontier." No one hearing the speech could bring a charge of narrow sectionalism against Davis, but he was open to a charge of extravagant national chauvinism, magnifying in his enthusiasm the "triumph of our arms." He described himself as "an American whose heart responds to all which illustrates our national character, and adds new color to our name."

The world knew that the estrangement between Jefferson Davis and his former father-in-law was ended when it heard the Mississippi Congressman say of General Taylor : "The world held not a soldier better qualified for the service he was engaged in. Seldom in the annals of military history has there been [a victory] in which desperate daring and military skill were more happily combined."

Then, as a loyal alumnus of the United States Military Academy, Davis seized the opportunity to reply to recent criticisms of West Point graduates. Many politicians, mindful of Revolutionary traditions, still believed that the citizen soldier was more than a match for the professional military man. Davis cited the "professional skill" exercised by General Taylor in the border battle, and asked whether anyone would maintain that "a blacksmith or tailor could have secured the same results."

Up jumped Representative Andrew Johnson of Tennessee, his bulldog face contorted with rage. A former tailor whose wife had taught him to read and write, he was one of the most class-conscious men who ever sat in Congress. He immediately assumed that Davis's rhetorical reference to "a tailor" was intended as a slur on him. He snarled out a denunciation of the group to which he claimed Davis belonged : the "illegitimate, swaggering, bastard, scrub aristocracy."

Davis, who had not even been thinking of Johnson when he made the statement, at first was astonished and confused by the little

Tennesseean's tirade. However, he said at once that he had intended no personal disparagement.

Two days later, Davis, whose code demanded even greater regard for the sensitivity of a man who was not a gentleman than for one who was, made a more extended explanation of his reference to the hypothetical tailor. "Among those to whom I have been long known, no explanation could be necessary," he said, "but here, having been misunderstood, it seems to be called for. Once for all, then, I would say, that if I know myself, I am incapable of wantonly wounding the feelings, or of making invidious reflections upon the origin or occupation, of any man." He explained that he had picked the occupations at random to illustrate the fact that "a military education does not qualify for civil pursuits, nor does preparation for any of the civil pursuits, in itself, qualify for the duties of a soldier."

Johnson did not forget, and could not forgive. The imagined insult continued to fester under his thin skin.

While Davis awaited a call to military duty, he was asked to prepare a report investigating charges of misconduct by Daniel Webster while serving as Secretary of State under President Tyler. As a result of the investigation, Webster was completely exonerated. Some people later questioned why Davis, as a Southerner, had taken so much pride and pleasure in the vindication of a New England statesman. The Mississippian replied: "No man who knew Daniel Webster would have expected less of him, had our positions been reversed. None could have believed that he would, with a view to judgment, ask whether a charge was made against a Massachusetts man or a Mississippian."

In this same period, Davis, though he was afire with military ardor, spoke against a proposal to confer upon the President the power to appoint general officers of the army. He spoke as a strict constitutionalist.

About the same time, another freshman congressman, Abraham Lincoln of Illinois, made his maiden speech in Congress. Even taller that Davis, but ruggedly lean whereas the Mississippian was imperially slim, Lincoln provided a striking contrast to the Mississippi congressman, who also had been born in a log cabin on the Kentucky frontier. Both were eloquent, but each in his own way. Davis's speeches were of the school of Burke, distinguished by polished but complicated syntax and delivered in melodious tones, with graceful gestures. Lincoln's speech was simple and trenchant, exemplifying the art that conceals art, but was delivered in a discordant voice, accompanied by gestures that, though awkward, had a rude force. Their speeches differed as much in content as in style. Davis pleaded for the cause of Union and reverence for the constitution. Abraham Lincoln spoke only in defense of the right of revolution which he called a preserver to "the liberty of the world."

To the Halls of Montezuma

When the Mississippi Rifles, a volunteer regiment, asked Davis to be its colonel, he accepted and remained in Washington only long enough to support the Walker Tariff Bill, a free trade measure in which he strongly believed.

Before leaving Washington, Davis extracted a promise that his regiment would be equipped with percussion rifles. Winfield Scott, General in Chief of the Army, objected to the percussion rifle as an untried weapon, and thought that flintlock muskets were more dependable. Events proved Davis right, but he had irritated Scott. Though pompous, Scott was an astute man and was favorably impressed when Robert E. Lee disagreed with him on good grounds. But when Davis stood his ground he was such a rigid embodiment of gentlemanly propriety that even a Virginia aristocrat such as Scott could take offense.

While en route with his regiment from New Orleans to the mouth of the Rio Grande, Davis received a letter from General Taylor. There was no question about how the colonel now stood with the man who had once been his father-in-law. In the letter, signed "Truly and sincerely your friend," Taylor declared, "I can assure you I am more than anxious to take you by the hand and to have you and your command with or near me."

Arriving at the Rio Grande on August 12, Davis found no transports awaiting him. After fourteen days with none in sight, Davis indignantly wrote Secretary of the Treasury Walker: "We have met delay and detention at every point. The quartermasters at New Orleans have behaved either most incompetently or maliciously, and I am now but two days in possession of the rifles ordered forward before I left Washington."

Transport came at last, and Davis's volunteer regiment—though the last to arrive—was in time for the advance on Monterey. Davis's Mississippi Rifles and Campbell's Tennessee Rifles were in the hardest part of the fighting.

These two regiments were assigned the task of capturing a tannery which, with its stone walls under the protection of an artillery redoubt, made a good fort for the defending Mexican infantry. The regiments marched forward despite a savage cross fire of artillery until Davis's men stood directly in front of the building with the Tennesseans on their left. A moment's reflection was enough to make a coolly reasoning man turn back. Davis had no instructions, had no idea of the importance of his assignment to the general plan and now seemed to have no sustaining troops except the one regiment of Tennesseeans. Frowning down on him was a stone fortress bristling with guns. In that moment, he shouted : "Now is the time ! Great God ! If I had 30 men with knives, I could take the fort."

The lieutenant colonel of the Mississippi Rifles yelled, "Follow me," ran forward, mounted the wall and was shot down a moment later. Davis was hardly a step behind the lieutenant colonel, with his riflemen mounting the parapet and dropping down behind him. The Mexicans dashed for the exit on the other side and ran about 75 yards to another fort. They were closing the gates of their refuge when Davis and his men reached the spot and forced an entrance. The Mexicans threw up their hands in surrender.

At that moment, a lieutenant arrived with orders from General

Quitman for the Mississippi Rifles to retire. It was infuriatingly frustrating to have to withdraw when on the verge of triumph. But Davis had learned lessons of military discipline at West Point. So he ordered his men back. But, as he went, he cursed with a skill and vehemence that amazed some who had thought of him as the model of propriety.

The Mississippi Rifles saw little action on the second day at Monterey, but the third day brought real excitement. Davis, with four companies—two of Mississippi Rifles and two of Tennessee infantry—entered the town on the heels of a retreating enemy. With the support of other companies and a Texas regiment, he occupied the fort which he had been on the verge of capturing two days before. It had been denuded of artillery and abandoned by the Mexicans. Learning that the enemy was concentrated in the main plaza, the Americans advanced upon the square, seizing a two-story house and holding it for several hours until the converging fire of the enemy forced abandonment of the structure. Davis spotted a tall stone house from which he would be able to direct a plunging fire upon the Mexicans in the plaza. To reach it, the Americans would have to cross a street swept by the fire of small arms and artillery. Quickly, Davis directed the men in setting up a street barricade to protect their passage. He exulted that they would spend the night in a stone fortress commanding the heart of Monterey.

While they labored with the speed of enthusiasm, a messenger came up to Davis. All the troops in Davis's rear had retired and he was ordered to withdraw. He knew that such an order would not have been given if the circumstances of action in the Plaza had been known. He also knew that leading his men back under the enemy's guns would involve greater risk than pressing on to his objective. But orders were orders. Back he marched, stepping forward ahead of his men to test the enemy's fire. There is no record of his cursing as he dodged bullets on the way back. Perhaps he was speechless.

The next day, September 24, Mexican General Ampudia requested a parley on terms of surrender. Davis was one of three commissioners appointed by General Taylor to arrange the terms.

The city, with its supplies, would be surrendered. The Mexican troops would be permitted to retire peacefully.

The next morning was appointed for receipt of the signed terms by the Americans. Many of the United States officers feared that the Mexicans planned to seize the American negotiators as hostages or kill them. Davis had already decided to ride alone into the Mexican camp to "call for" the signed papers. As he rode past Taylor's headquarters on his way, the general called out, "Hello, Davis! Where are you going?"

Davis explained his intentions. The general objected, "Not by yourself."

"One man is as good as twenty," Davis said. "If they mean foul play, they would destroy twenty as well as one, and if there is danger, nothing but an army will do."

At length, though, he consented to the company of his old friend, Col. Albert Sidney Johnston. The articles of surrender were delivered without incident. But all the effort and anxiety were of little avail. Washington disapproved the terms of capitulation and fierce fighting resumed.

In the meantime, Davis had obtained a sixty-day leave to be with his wife, who had grown sick with anxiety for his safety. He returned to Mexico and resumed command of the Mississippi Rifles in January 1847.

Toward the last of February, the plight of Taylor's army was critical. He had fewer than 5,000 effective troops. Moving down on him, confident of the kill, was Santa Anna with a force estimated to number 20,000. Almost every high-placed observer except Taylor himself regarded American defeat as virtually inevitable. The general fell back to Buena Vista, but only to prepare for battle.

In the early morning of February 23, when Davis's men moved forward on the double quick, the American and Mexican armies were already engaged. The rising sun revealed acres upon acres of glitter—the massed effect of the burnished guns and sparkling equipage of the Mexicans giving their army, as an observant young sergeant noted, "the appearance of a forest of icicles reflecting the rays of a bright summer's sun."

With bands blaring and banners waving, the shimmering mass flowed over the barren plain toward the American forces. "Forward!" shouted Davis, as he plunged ahead on his great bay horse. When the Americans and Mexicans were about a hundred paces apart, both sides opened fire. Davis's men were forced back and formed in the rear of protecting batteries. Again the Mexican bands struck up, the blare of their brass snatched up and flung down by the wind like boastful taunts. If Santa Anna had his way, Buena Vista would be fought in grand opera style.

American artillery soon provided some percussion effect that silenced the bands. A quickened rate of fire spread dismay among large numbers of the enemy.

In the charge, a musket ball had entered Davis's foot, embedding in the flesh a portion of his spur. But he still sat his horse and commanded his regiment in a firm voice.

By this time, a considerable portion of the Mexican cavalry had been massed in front and to the left of the Mississippi Rifles and a small detachment of Indiana troops standing with them. Other American units were engaged elsewhere with the enemy, and could not come to Davis's aid. His men must withstand a charge by a force at least nine times their number. In a moment of desperation, Davis devised his now-famous "V formation."

The name has led many people to picture the formation as a sort of wedge-shaped prow upon which the wave of the enemy was shattered. Such was not the case. The V was an obtuse angle, a very spraddled V, and its apex was not pointed at the enemy. Quite the reverse. The wide-open jaws of the V awaited the onslaught. The men were "deployed as skirmishers at very short intervals, the front rank to fire, the rear rank to reserve fire, then step forward and fire while the other rank was reloading."

Davis told his men to hold their fire until ordered to shoot. The Mexican cavalry thundered forward like an avalanche, darts of light gleaming from their lances, tricolored pennants streaming like comet tails. A portly officer, his flashing sword raised, trotted in the lead.

Suddenly, as the cavalry swept forward in the faces of one wing of the V and thus parallel with the other wing, the Mexicans realized that they were encountering something different from the traditional hollow square of infantry prepared to receive attack. They were visibly shaken. But the little bugler just behind the commander sounded the charge. The Mexicans broke into a gallop that carried them into a shattering volley.

For two hundred yards, the ground was carpeted with dead cavalrymen. Wildly neighing horses wheeled to right and left among the dead as if in response to phantom riders.

Davis's men fell back to the protection of their batteries. Showers of grape and cannister demoralized the already confused Mexicans. Stumbling over each other and their fallen comrades, they fled.

When Davis's wound was being dressed, General Taylor burst in upon him excitedly. "My poor boy!" he exclaimed. The general had been told that Davis was killed, and had sent out messenger after messenger to ascertain the truth without waiting for any of them to return. To every rumor of Davis's death, the white-haired old general had stubbornly replied, "I'll never believe it."

For the rest of his life, Davis would recall with pride the success of his V formation. Acclaim for his inventiveness and courage poured in from all parts of the United States. In England, the great Duke of Wellington was fascinated by the Mississippian's innovation. General Taylor, in his official report, declared that Davis's "distinguished coolness and gallantry" entitled him to "the particular notice of the government." But it is doubtful if Davis was ever prouder than at the moment when the grizzled old warrior who had once been estranged from him clasped his hand and said, "My daughter was a better judge of men than I."

The burst of glory at Buena Vista ended Davis's active service in the Mexican War. Three months later, the enlistment of his regiment having expired and the war in Northern Mexico having ended, he sailed for home with his men, some of them hobbling on crutches like himself and many of them resting in pine coffins.

Cheering throngs and pretty girls tossing flowers awaited them at New Orleans. Sergeant Smith Prentiss praised Davis in orotund phrases that drew even greater applause than his hostile sallies in the famous all-day debate of 1843.

More praise came in a letter from President Polk, who informed him that he was promoting him to brigadier general of volunteers. Ever the strict constitutionalist, and determined not to depart from the stand he had taken in Congress, Davis thanked the President but informed him that the Chief Executive had no authority to appoint militia officers, since that power belonged to the states alone.

Figure Skating in the Senate

Before Davis was ready to discard his crutches, he was appointed by the Governor to fill temporarily the United States Senate seat vacated by the death of Jesse Speight. The Governor acknowledged that the interim appointment was in response to popular demand. It was not the first time that a political career had been advanced faster by spectacular success in the field than by sober competence in the forum—and it would not be the last. Davis was distinguished from many of his contemporaries being pushed forward politically on the basis of Mexican War records by the fact that he had prepared for public service in the study and on the stump as well as in camp.

Almost from the day he entered the Senate, he was recognized as a man of rare gifts, even in a chamber dominated by those two giants of eloquence with eyes of burning anthracite : the crag-browed Webster and the lion-maned Calhoun. His first speech was in support of a bill to increase the army, and the crutches on which he leaned— symbols of his own military sacrifice—were props not only to his body, but also to his argument.

Davis's growing reputation owed little to circulation in society. Varina often urged him to attend more receptions as a matter of political expediency, but the two usually spent the evening over a pile of papers beneath his study lamp as the clock ticked tediously on while elsewhere chandeliers blazed and toes were tapping.

The Mississippian was not only serious, but troubled. He stated in the press that he was alarmed over "the spirit of hostility to the South, that thirst for political dominion over us, which, within two years past, has displayed such increased power and systematic purpose."

In tariff matters, and in other concerns, the interests of the industrial North had clashed constantly with those of the agricultural South. An agrarian society often democratic in practice but unyieldingly aristocratic in concept was in constant conflict with an urban-dominated society often aristocratic in practice but vehemently democratic in theory. In the nineteenth century, two Americas clashed : that of the eighteenth century and that of the twentieth. In the first, the one personified by the South, Washington and Jefferson would have been at home. In the second, personified by the North, virtually all the great founding fathers except Franklin would have been aliens. In the West, allegiance was for a long time divided between the world of the South that based its claims on the title deeds of the past and the world of the North that relied on "natural law" to justify the demands of an onrushing machine age. Debate stormed about the black and his role in society, but the larger question was the kind of society in which both the black and the white would live. Few men could perceive that the final answer was inevitable. Some hotheads both North and South were so unaware of this central fact that already they were eager to provide an answer by the arbitrament of arms. And, all the while, the question was being answered as the huffing, snorting, screaming steam engine—fit symbol of the new age of mass production and mass communication—roared across the brooding fields and quiet prairies of the pastoral past.

The plantation home, so often the white-columned reproduction of an Attic shrine, was the true temple of Southern society. To Davis, it was not the house of his fathers, to be taken for granted. In its many-chambered spaciousness, it was something that in his individual case had grown with him and to him. It was a dwelling place that was bone of his bone. To be separated from it would be to be left defenseless to the world, to be parted from the only kind of life meaningful to him. When he perceived that it was threatened with destruction by forces from without, he abandoned by rapid degrees the objectivity with which he had viewed issues on a national plane. Every part of his cultural habitation became precious to him, and he fought for it with vehemence.

He had long regarded slavery as an institution that could be benevolent and which, if suddenly removed from the South, might leave a vacuum creating a vortex of passion and destruction. He now began to argue that slavery, to be most benevolent, must not be restricted to a few states: that in its dispersion, with only a few slaves to any one master, a paternal relationship could best be preserved. As Northern attacks against the "peculiar institution" mounted, and as they degenerated into vehement denunciations of Southern society as a whole, Davis began to suspect—and eventually to believe passionately—that slavery was a necessary step in the preparation of blacks for "civil liberty and social enjoyment."

Beneath Davis's fine-spun web of sophistry was a substantial framework of legal argument. He pointed out that the Constitution recognized the status of slaves as property, a fact admitted by many Northern lawyers, including Abraham Lincoln. He reminded the Senate that the United States was the creature of the States, rather than the States being the creatures of the Federal government. His logic was impeccable. After all, the States had existed before the national government. Indeed, Virginia had ratified the Constitution with the proviso that she did not by ratification forfeit the right of secession. By acquiescing in Virginia's reservations, the other States had conceded that all enjoyed the right of secession.

Using logic with the cold precision of a steel blade, Davis smoothly cut intricate figures on the thin ice of American political precedents. His graceful performances won the admiration of dispassionate lawyers and other connoisseurs of debate. They were admired by most of his constituents, even though some would have preferred a more heated exercise of his talents. But the time was past when converts could be won by neat arguments presented with restraint. His elaborate skating on thin ice, though expertly done, was irrelevant in view of the great thaw coming to unfreeze a *status quo* that had existed since the earliest days of the federated republic. Soon the roiled flood waters would be inundating the traditional metes and bounds of American life, and a President of the United States would declare, "The dogmas of the quiet past are inadequate to the stormy present."

Davis's arguments about the rights of the States, including the right of secession, were valid, solidly rooted in constitutional law. Unlike him, his opponents could not justify their arguments by the compact of the States—the Constitution, with its majestic phrases limned in faultless copperplate and attested by reverenced names. So they appealed to what they called a "higher law." To be conscientious and legally right was not enough. In the ship money case, Charles I, as conscientious a monarch as ever sat upon the English throne, was right by laws that reached back through Elizabeth to Alfred and the nation's birth. Yet the Parliamentary leaders invoked a "higher law" and, before the strife was ended, Charles had paid for his correctness with his head. With Davis as with Charles, the law was with him but history was against him.

Davis's political sentiments quickened his partisan ardor. Speaking for the Democratic Party in the Presidential campaign of 1848, he declared :

Separating myself as far as possible from the prejudices I may very naturally feel for the creed of my entire political life, it seems to me evident and demonstrable that the South should fraternize with the Democracy. This is the party of strict construction, of checks and balances, and constitutional restraints. We of the South are the minority, and such we must remain. Our property, our security in the Union, depend upon the power of the constitutional curb with which we check the otherwise unbridled will of the majority.

Nevertheless, the campaign was an embarrassing one for Davis. Zachary Taylor was the candidate of the Whig party. Davis had rejoiced in the nomination, but he could not forsake his own party to work for the general's election. Taylor made the situation as easy for the younger man as he could. He wrote thanking him for "many acts of kindness . . . the smallest portion of which I greatly fear I will never have it in my power to repay." He concluded with fatherly advice :

I have your own advancement more at heart than my own. You are now entering on the stage of action, while I must soon retire from it; you must therefore pursue that course which your good judgment will point out, as far as your honour and the good of the country are concerned, without regard to my advancement. It is sufficient to me to know that I possess your friendship, which is all I ask or wish.

In electioneering, Davis stressed the fact that both Taylor and the Democratic candidate, Lewis Cass, were good and able men. He maintained that the important—and overriding—factor in the contest was the difference in parties. When Taylor was elected, Davis was named to the joint committee of notification.

In fairness to Davis, it must be said that although with Calhoun's physical decline he became the Senate's chief apologist for slavery, he foresaw without regret the day of its abandonment. "Leave natural causes to their full effect," he argued, "and when the time shall arrive at which emancipation is proper, those most interested will be most anxious to effect it. . . . Leave the country to the south and west open, and speculation may see in the distant future slavery pressed by a cheaper labor to tropical regions where, less exertion being required to secure support, their previous preparation will allow them to live in independent communities."

Nor was Davis a monomaniac on the subject of slavery. To him, as to many slavery opponents in the North, the issue of slavery itself was subordinate to the economic and political struggle between the two sections. Each slave state added to the Union was a recruit for the Southern side, each nonslave state a recruit for the Northern. It was logical that the South, being now in the minority, should be the stout defender of state sovereignty while the North, enjoying a majority, should seek to enforce its will by strengthening the central government. "It is the characteristic of all legislation for special interests," Davis argued, "that the benefits inure to the strong; thence it has ensued that appropriations for internal improvements have mainly been made at the North and East. . . . Henceforth we must become relatively weaker in the national legislature, and therefore rather expect an increase than cessation of the unjust discrimination heretofore made against us."

With this sense of being part of a threatened minority, Davis, on June 23, 1848, while the bill to admit Oregon was pending, proposed an amendment that "nothing contained in this act shall be so construed as to authorize the prohibition of domestic slavery in said territory. . . ." On August 10, the Senate approved the resolution of Stephen A. Douglas to extend the 36° 30′ line of the Missouri Compromise to the Pacific, thus confining slavery to the area south of that line. Davis voted for it as the best bargain obtainable. But the House, reflecting more accurately than the Senate the numerical preponderance of the North, rejected the measure by a vote of 121 to 82. The engulfment of the South and its way of life was thus plainly forecast. "Who does not see . . . ?" Davis asked.

The same truth was recognized by Henry Clay who, seeking to preserve the Union by compromise, pleaded in 1850 that California be admitted "without any restriction or condition on the subject of slavery." Clay was a feeble figure as he rose in the Senate. Death had already laid its hand upon him and personal ambition had loosed its hold. Without the physical strength of former years, he now commanded a moral force that transcended in effectiveness all the arsenal of stratagems which he had employed in other times. Turning to Northern senators who were pressing their advantage over the South, he demanded: "What do you want who reside in the free states? . . . You have got nature itself on your side."

Webster, Calhoun, and Davis were conspicuous in the days of

debate that followed. But William H. Seward of New York struck the keynote of the North in the sectional clash when he answered Davis's and Calhoun's carefully reasoned legal arguments with the statement, "There is a higher law than the Constitution."

The Southern keynote was sounded by Senator James Mason of Virginia, reading the words of Calhoun, who, too weak to speak, sat, wraithlike, swathed in flannels, fixing the chamber with luminous eyes. The giants were fading, but they were still giants. Calhoun pleaded for a compromise that would permit both Northern and Southern vetoes of congressional legislation. "If you of the North will not do this," he said, "then let our Southern states separate and depart in peace."

And Senator Shields of Illinois forecast what the result of secession would be when he asked, "Does any man suppose that the great Northwest . . . will ever peaceably submit to see the Mississippi River in the possession of a foreign government?"

History contrives few set pieces like this great drama almost on the eve of war. Webster, Clay, and Calhoun, the three giants of the Senate, confronted each other in the same chamber when the age of giants was almost at an end. Coming from North, West, and South, they represented not only an age that was passing but also a nation threatened with extinction. And, peering with haunted eyes into the boiling cauldron of national strife, they read in fire and smoke, and voiced like Shakespeare's spirits of the heath, the prophecies of a people's doom.

A leading actor in the scene to unfold spoke his own prophetic line. Said Davis:

If I have a superstition which governs my mind and holds it captive, it is a superstitious reverence for the Union. . . . God forbid that the day should ever come when to be true to my constituents is to be hostile to the Union. . . . [But] if there is a dominant party in this Union which can deny to us equality . . . this would be a central government raised on the destruction of all the principles of the Constitution : and the first, the highest obligation of every man who has sworn to support that Constitution would be resistance to such usurpation. . . .

He threw back his patrician head as though he were once again preparing to repel the charge at Buena Vista. "If, when thus fully warranted, they want a standard-bearer, in default of a better, I am at their command."

In 1851, Senator Mason of Virginia introduced a new fugitive-slave bill designed to strengthen the hands of the Southern States in securing the return of slaves who had fled to free states. Enough Northern support for the bill was mustered to give the South a majority and the measure was signed into law by Millard Fillmore, who had succeeded to the Presidency upon Taylor's death. Influential in passage of the measure was Daniel Webster.

Davis early foresaw that Northern states, appealing to a "higher law," would refuse to obey the statute on fugitive slaves just as they had ignored constitutional provisions on the status of the slave. In a speech to the Senate, he declared, "I deny the power of Massachusetts to nullify the law and remain in the Union, but I concede to her the right . . . to retire from the Union—to take the 'extreme medicine,' secession." About four months later, on June 28, 1851, in a speech at Capon Springs, Virginia, Massachusetts' own senator conceded the right of the Southern states to secede over the same issue. In organ tones undiminished by age, Webster declared, "If the Northern states refuse, wilfully and deliberately, to carry into effect that part of the Constitution which respects the restoration of fugitive slaves, and Congress provide no remedy, the South would no longer be bound to observe the compact. A bargain cannot be broken on one side and still bind the other."

The vilification to which Webster was subjected in his home state insured that the Southern states would be hard-pressed to find Northern allies in the future.

In March 1851, Davis had entered upon a new six-year term in the Senate. In September, he was persuaded by Mississippi Democrats to accept the nomination for Governor. As when he first ran for office, he was called upon because of an emergency caused by withdrawal of the original nominee. This time, he was his party's standard bearer at real sacrifice. Most of his senatorial term remained before him and he already had gained a national reputation through Senate service.

Many Southerners, though sorry that he did not endorse Calhoun's doctrine of nullification, regarded him as political heir apparent to the great South Carolinian.

Opposing Davis in the general election was Henry S. Foote, with whom he had served in the Senate. They had been colleagues only by parliamentary technicality. Neither would have found the other's company at dinner an aid to digestion.

Foote, although a Whig, was running as the Unionist candidate. Some of Davis's supporters said that the Foote of one party had become the head of another. The crowds laughed, but voted for Foote. At that, despite the handicap of his eleventh-hour candidacy and a return of facial neuralgia that restricted his campaign, Davis had lost by only a narrow margin.

To the normal harshness of defeat were added the exacerbating factors of sacrifice of his Senate seat and the fact that he had been beaten by a despised rival.

Back he went to Brierfield, finding consolation in plantation life and domestic pleasures. Was he again to become a recluse? Many Mississippians thought so. They were prepared for a cool, academic lecture when he emerged from contemplation in his retreat to address the Mississippi Democratic Convention in 1852.

But they saw a different Davis. This was not the man who sometimes seemed to covet the role of schoolmaster to the nation. This was the rider of "crazy" horses, the leader of daring charges. Reason was not abandoned, but emotion was in the saddle. As Davis warmed to his subject, he was not content to refer to his defeat in terms of gentlemanly self-deprecation. He shouted, in a voice vibrant with passion, "Fraud and falsehood and Free Soil and Foote and Fillmore have triumphed in Mississippi, but success thus acquired must be as temporary as its means were corrupt."

He launched into an attack on the Fillmore administration that brought cheers from the convention. This intemperate speech accomplished overnight what Davis's well-reasoned campaign addresses had failed in. It restored the popular enthusiasm that had greeted him on his return from Mexico. Politically prominent Mississippians began to work for his nomination to the Vice Presidency.

That place on the Democratic ticket went instead to William R. King of Alabama. The Presidential nomination was thrust upon a genuinely reluctant dark horse, the handsome, sensitive, and conscientious Franklin Pierce of New Hampshire. The Whig nominee for President was General Winfield Scott. Davis, whose early irritation with Scott had ripened into dislike during the Scott-Taylor feud, took personal pleasure in the Whig defeat.

He also had a personal reason for delight in Pierce's resounding victory. The Mississippian and the New Hampshireman, despite sectional differences, had been close friends in Washington. But Davis had campaigned hard for Pierce for another reason. He believed that, with a Democratic administration in office and headed by a man of Pierce's moderation and integrity, there was hope for preservation of the Union.

No North, No South

On December 7, 1852, the President-elect wrote to Davis, requesting his counsel in person as a friend. When the two talked, Pierce offered Davis a post in the cabinet. By this time, the Mississippian was once again reluctant to leave his broad acres and his books. Pierce urged Davis in the strongest terms to accept the appointment, pleading the need for his old friend's help with the heavy burdens of an unsought office and telling him that together they could work to heal sectional splits. In this period of indecision, Varina became ill. She was pulled on the rack—drawn on one side by strong ambition and on the other by a realization that her husband's health and nerves would suffer from a return to public life. At length, Davis accepted the post of Secretary of War.

To his task he brought not only the virtues of military training and war experience, but also a much rarer quality : imagination. As an administrator he was far less conservative than as a political philosopher. He soon revised the regulations of the service, introduced variations in standard tactics (he still remembered his "V" formation with pride), and organized a permanent medical corps. He saw that the troops were provided with rifles of modern design (Just let Scott try to block him this time !) and added the minie ball to American arsenals.

In his first annual report as Secretary of War, he broached the most imaginative proposal of all. "Napoleon when in Egypt," he said, "used with marked success the dromedary . . . in subduing the Arabs whose habits and country were very similar to those of the mounted Indians of our Western plains. . . . For like military purposes, for expresses and for reconnaissance, it is believed, the dromedary would supply a want now seriously felt in our service."

Camels in the American desert ! Hardheaded men hooted at the idea. But to incredulity, sneers, and laughter Davis replied with a seemingly inexhaustible fund of facts drawn from both history and contemporary experience. Opposition only strengthened him in his resolve. At last on May 14, 1856, 34 camels stalked with awkward, ruminative dignity down a gangplank and onto Texas soil. This experiment in ecology was still in progress in 1861 when the Federal Government's attention was diverted from the Western deserts by an "experiment in rebellion."

Davis's importance in the administration transcended the fact that he was a great Secretary of War. In British terms, he was clearly first minister in Pierce's cabinet. Just before his inauguration, Pierce had seen his small son mangled in a railroad accident. For a long time afterward, he carried a heavy burden of grief. The tragedy had brought on a nervous illness in Mrs. Pierce. Under these circumstances, the President often felt the need to confer with a trusted

friend of proved discretion. Davis became his confidant and coun-
selor. Often Pierce quit the gloomy chambers of the White House to
spend an evening with the Davises. Varina was a charming hostess.
Her quick wit, which sometimes offended the slow-minded, was
enjoyed by Pierce. And many decisions of state were born in conversations with Davis. The Mississippian, an avowed expansionist, soon
had at least as much to do with American foreign policy as Secretary
of State Marcy. His voice certainly counted for more than Marcy's in
the choice of ambassadors for several sensitive posts. Some Northerners complained that the South, through Davis, was running the administration. Pierce was sensitive to this criticism, but he did not stop
visiting Davis. He simply slipped out of the White House under cover
of darkness and walked without escort to his friend's home.

Faced with the responsibility of serving a whole nation, Davis no
longer spoke in terms of narrow sectionalism. Increasingly, he was a
spokesman for the Administration in many parts of the nation and
nearly always he pleaded for the Union. On one four-day tour, he
spoke in Wilmington, Delaware; Trenton; Princeton; Philadelphia;
and New York. Praising Pierce in Wilmington, he declared : "He is a
glorious patriot. He knows no North, no South, no East, no West."
With prolonged cheering, a Philadelphia crowd expressed its enthusiasm for Davis's dream of a transcontinental railway, not only for
national defense but also for national unity. In New York City, at
the world scientific convention in the Crystal Palace, he spoke in
terms of broad internationalism. "Throw open the ports of all the
world," he said. "Let the civilized nations represented here declare
we are one brotherhood and that whatever can be produced more
cheaply in another country shall be brought thence. Thus we will
have a bond of peace that will not be in the power of unwise rulers
ever to break."

But, all the while, he was true to the principles of States' rights to
which he had declared allegiance as Mississippi's representative. He
warned a Trenton audience of "the danger of consolidation, centrali-

zation, and the re-establishment of despotism upon the liberties of the people."

During his service as Secretary of War, Davis became one of the commanding figures on the national scene. Despite the strength of sectional prejudice, metropolitan audiences in the North saluted his eloquence. Postmaster General James Campbell declared that his cabinet colleague's knowledge was "encyclopaedic" and many years later pronounced him "the best educated man whom I ever came in contact with." Carl Schurz described him as a "grand personage" of the "well-known strong American type."

There were some who did not find Davis so attractive. They were repelled by a quality that Schurz admired: a "kind of dignity which does not invite familiar approach." And, though most Army men were enthusiastic about the Secretary of War, the General in Chief reserved for him some of his choicest epithets. Winfield Scott had become almost an embodiment of American military tradition and he was accustomed to having his own way, with little regard to the passing parade of War Secretaries. Davis, even more than most men, was insistent upon the prerogatives of his official rank and his status as a gentleman. He shared with Scott a necessity for justifying himself— for replying in writing to every written accusation. Both men expended in vitriolic correspondence more time and energy than two intelligent men in positions of high responsibility could afford to waste. By May 21, 1856 the quarrel between the two had descended to so low a level of acrimony that Davis wrote the old soldier:

"Having early in this correspondence stamped you with falsehood, and whenever you presented a tangible point, convicted you by conclusive proof, I have ceased to regard your abuse, and as you present nothing in this letter which requires remark, I am gratified to be relieved from the necessity of further exposing your malignity and depravity."

One instance in which Davis enforced his will over Scott's objections was in the selection of three American officers to observe the Crimean War and bring back lessons from which the United States might profit. "Old Fuss and Feathers" thought that a young captain selected by the Secretary was much too green for such an assignment. But Davis, arguing that the appointment was justified by the young man's unusual promise, sent him anyway. The captain in question was George B. McClellan.

Through his close relationship with the President, Davis played a major role in two of the principal events of the Pierce administration : the Gadsden Purchase and passage of the Kansas-Nebraska Bill.

In the first of these, his intervention was decisive. When Mexico threatened war over 45,000 square miles of disputed territory south of the Gila River in New Mexico and Arizona, Davis counseled purchase of the land and suggested that the President appoint James Gadsden as minister to Mexico to conduct the negotiations. The profitable bargain that averted war bears Gadsden's name, and credit should be given the distinguished South Carolinian for the finesse with which he carried out his assignment. But the inspiration for the move and much of the guidance from Washington during the transaction came from Davis.

His role in passage of the Kansas-Nebraska Bill was far less prominent but perhaps, as some historians argue, no less decisive. On Sunday, January 22, 1854, Senator Stephen A. Douglas of Illinois called on Davis and appealed to him for entrée to the White House. In appearance, the "Little Giant" was as much a bulldog as Andrew Johnson, but a less snappish, better bred bulldog. Nevertheless, he had all the bulldog tenacity of the Tennessee senator in addition to much greater subtlety. He seldom showed his teeth, but when he sank them into an issue that he could exploit he seldom let go. Douglas was prepared to introduce a bill that might help to put him in the White House, but if it was to have any hope of success it must have the endorsement of the present occupant of the Executive Mansion. Douglas was not on such terms with Pierce that he could approach him directly with any confidence. He, therefore, sought Davis's intervention. To reinforce his plea, Douglas brought with him several prominent Southern senators.

The Kansas-Nebraska Bill would be a substitute for the earlier Nebraska Bill, which would have organized the area in question as a single territory to be known as Nebraska. Under the new bill, the area would be divided along the 40th parallel into two territories, Nebraska in the North and Kansas in the South. In deciding whether slavery would be permitted in the two new territories, the principle of "popular sovereignty" should prevail. Douglas held out to the North the hope that Nebraska would vote to prohibit slavery, to the South the hope that Kansas would vote to legalize it. Douglas would like to introduce this measure the next day with the imprimatur of the White House.

With some misgivings, Davis eventually consented to approach Pierce. The President granted one of his rare Sunday audiences. The coolness with which he received Douglas would have discouraged most men, but the Illinoisan persevered. When the senator left the White House, his bill had the President's endorsement.

Davis feared that introduction of the bill would provide fresh fuel for the fires of sectional conflict. He was quickly proved right. The bill was passed, but only after three months of rough debate in which the rudest verbal blows reopened old wounds. In its final version, it repealed the Missouri Compromise which, since 1850, had helped to hold in check some of the most ardent partisans in both North and South. Before the year was out, controversy over the Kansas-Nebraska Act had caused a realignment of political forces in the North and West. Discontented Whigs, Free Soilers, and anti-slavery Democrats united to form the Republican party.

It is virtually certain that Douglas's bill could not have been passed without Presidential support. Knowing that fact, he would not have introduced it without assurance of White House endorsement. Thus he would not have provoked the bitter three months' debate. Some students of Pierce's life believe that the President would never have granted Douglas an interview if Davis had not intervened. The Mississippian had much cause to regret his part in the interview.

Ensuing months proved that, in opening the door to the White House, he had also opened the door on a whole new era of conflict.

Until then, there had been some hope for conciliation. Moderation in the interest of national unity had been urged not only by some of the passing giants, but also by some of the coming generation of leaders. Even now, in lashing out against the Kansas-Nebraska Act, an Illinois representative expressed some views strikingly similar to those of Davis. Abraham Lincoln, speaking October 16 at Peoria, advocated gradual emancipation but said he did not know how it could be accomplished. "I have no prejudice against the Southern people . . .," he asserted. "I surely will not blame them for not doing what I should not know how to do myself." Though personally hostile to slavery, he insisted that property rights guaranteed by the Constitution should be protected and urged a practical Fugitive Slave Law.

But in this same year William Lloyd Garrison, who had been jailed in 1829 for his tirades against New England slave traders, had his revenge as, to the applause of representative men, he publicly burned a copy of the Constitution, branding it "a covenant with death and an agreement with Hell."

One of the greatest comforts to Davis in days of worry was the smile with which his small son Samuel greeted him on each day's return from work and the romp on the floor which had become a joyous ritual. One day, the little boy was too sick to play with his father. The disease was never diagnosed, but within three weeks he was dead. Even Varina heard Davis say little about the loss, but after the child's death "he walked half the night and worked fiercely all day."

On February 25, 1855 a daughter was born. Christened Margaret Howell, she was doubly precious because of the earlier loss.

In 1856, fighting over slavery was so bloody in Kansas that both Pierce and Douglas, because of their connection with the Kansas-Nebraska Act, had no chance to win the Democratic nomination for

President. Both that and the election of 1856 were won by James Buchanan.

Davis consented to the efforts of friends who wished to back him for the United States Senate, and was elected. On March 4, when the Pierce administration came to an end, the President told Davis: "I can scarcely bear the parting from you. You have been strength and solace to me for four anxious years and never failed me."

Davis could look back on years of remarkable accomplishment. He had shown a tendency to waste energy and effort in justifying himself to disgruntled individuals, and sometimes in a vain effort to get a high-ranking subordinate to confess to being in the wrong. He had also spent considerable time and energy in a more amiable if equally consuming fashion. He had given liberally of his crowded hours to disgruntled privates, worried wives of soldiers, and even to a mentally deficient man who visited him repeatedly before eventual confinement in an institution. But, despite the habit of devoting an enormous proportion of his time to details, Davis probably had accomplished more in four years than any of his predecessors as Secretary of War.

Caught in the Vortex

He took his seat in the Senate on March 5. Two days later, the Supreme Court handed down one of its most historic pronouncements: the Dred Scott decision. The court held that a Negro slave was not a citizen of the United States, that a slave's removal to a free state could not make him a freeman, and that the Missouri Compromise was unconstitutional because the Fifth Amendment prohibited Congress from depriving persons of their property without due process of law.

The decision could not have been more in accord with Davis's thinking if he had written it himself.

Many elements in the North were enraged. Before the decision there had been threats of secession in the South. Now it seemed that some of the Northern states might secede first. As early as 1815, at the Hartford Convention, representatives of the New England states had proclaimed the doctrine of interposition : the right of a state government to interpose its sovereignty between its citizens and the Federal government. The doctrine was revived, and some felt that a bolder step might be necessary. In open convention in Worcester, Massachusetts in January 1857, two of the Bay State's most influential citizens, Wendell Phillips and Thomas H. Higginson, proposed secession.

Davis's service as Secretary of War had intensified his appreciation of the Union. The threat of its dissolution, whether by Northern or Southern action, filled him with dread. He refrained from speaking on the slavery issue. And, when he returned to his constituents at the end of the congressional session, he pleaded with them to do all that they could to promote national unity.

But his words were caught up in the whirlwind and soon he himself would be snatched into the vortex. When Buchanan was attacked in the Senate for applying the Dred Scott decision to Kansas, Davis replied : "Sir, we are arraigned day after day as the aggressive power. What Southern senator, during the whole session, has attacked any portion or any interest, of the North. . . . You have made it a political war. We are on the defensive. How far are you to push us ?"

Davis became the most respected spokesman for the South. Horace Greeley wrote : "Mr. Davis is unquestionably the foremost man of the South today. Every Northern senator will admit that from the Southern side of the floor the most formidable to meet in debate is the thin, polished, intellectual-looking Mississippian with the unimpassioned demeanor, the habitual courtesy, and the occasional unintentional arrogance, which reveals his consciousness of the great commanding power."

Greeley saw Davis as an embodiment of the spirit of an earlier generation of Southern aristocracy. It was a role for which he had been molded by Samuel Davis and Brother Joseph, as well as by his own efforts. But, perfectly trained for the part, he had stepped upon the national stage at a time when a large proportion of the audience had begun to regard his chosen character as archaic.

One characteristic of the traditional Southern aristocrat was the easy acceptance of responsibility as a birthright. This trait Davis did not have. Responsibility always rested heavily upon him. The burden of Southern leadership in the Senate, which he felt to be his at this critical juncture in national history, was a crushing one. His "fine steel courage" carried him through the bitter fights of February 1858. Then the frail body collapsed. Serious laryngitis and painful neuralgia disabled him. One side of his face was paralyzed. His left eye, red and swollen, bulged from its socket. For four weeks, he was speechless and blind.

A distinguished Philadelphia specialist who examined the eye said that he could not understand why it had not burst. Davis felt for his writing slate and scrawled, "My wife saved it." Many years later, Varina, who had indeed been a faithful nurse, wrote, "All the triumphs of my life were and are concentrated in and excelled by this blessed memory." No word of complaint escaped Davis through the painful examination, although he nearly fainted from the agony. The physician was astonished. "Such patience," he said, "surpasses that of man; it is godlike."

As Davis's slow recovery began, visitors flocked to his bedside. An Anglophobe legislator might there encounter Lord Napier, the British ambassador, and a hot-tempered Southern secessionist might on entering pass a departing abolitionist. A daily visitor was Senator Seward, who, by publicly describing the approach of sectional conflict as "irrepressible," helped to make it so. When told, at an early stage of Davis's illness, that the Southerner might lose the affected eye, Seward, with tears welling, said, "I could not bear to see him maimed —he is such a splendid embodiment of manhood." Though one of the chief leaders of the Northern forces in the Senate, the New Yorker would give Davis regular reports on the course of the intersectional debates, often cheerfully telling him, "Your man out-talked ours."

Seward remained an enigma to Davis. Once, when the Northerner said that he made some of his speeches indicting the South because they were "potent to affect the rank and file in the North," Davis asked, "But, Mr. Seward, do you never speak from conviction alone?"

"Nev-er," was the emphatic reply.

Davis raised his blindfolded head from the pillow and, with his voice charged with emotion even though reduced to a whisper, declared, "As God is my judge, I never speak from any other motive."

Seward put his arm about Davis and gently lowered the patient's head. "I know you do not," he said. "I am always sure of it."

This visit depressed Davis. He finally consoled himself with the thought that Seward had only imparted a "feigned confession" in an effort to be amusing.

Seward saw no reason to apologize for what he was, but he sincerely admired Davis and found the Mississippian's example a comfort rather than a reproach. Seward apparently liked the assurance that somebody was maintaining the standards that he believed he personally could not afford.

There came a day when, despite the remonstrances of both Seward and Varina, Davis insisted on riding to the Senate to speak on an appropriation for the coast survey. "It is for the good of the country and for my boyhood's friend, Dallas Bache, and I must go if it kills me." It did not kill him but he came near fainting—after carrying his point.

Gradually, he increased the length of his daily attendance as his strength increased. Some days, the iron will tyrannized over the suffering body and whipped on the raw nerves beyond endurance. On one such day, when Davis was addressing the Senate on an Army appropriation bill, Judah P. Benjamin, a bland and round-faced senator from Louisiana, interrupted to criticize a small point in Davis's discourse. Davis, his temper flaring, charged that Benjamin was trying to misrepresent a clear statement. In the heated exchange that followed, Davis, as usual in such cases, appeared haughty. The appearance of arrogance deeply stung Benjamin who, as a Jew, had sometimes been made to feel an alien.

That day, Davis received a note from Benjamin challenging him to a duel. Even when ill, Davis, with his military experience, probably would have been more than a match for the portly Benjamin who had never used any weapon but his eloquence. He tore up the note, vowing : "I will make this right at once. I have been wholly wrong."

He did make it right, by a generous apology in the Senate. Benjamin replied in the same vein. Oddly enough, the incident was the start of a long friendship between the two men. At first, Davis may have been motivated by a desire to be especially kind to one whom he had wronged. Benjamin, though a practical politician adjusting to the shifting tides of reality, admired Davis's idealism. Davis had a capacity for commanding the respect of big-hearted cynics such as Seward and Benjamin. Perhaps he appealed to a suppressed strain of idealism.

Soon, to facilitate his recuperation, he vacationed in Maine. Here, his nerves quickly healed. He found the people hospitable and they found him charming. In Portland, he was honored with a serenade and responded with a speech in which he asserted, "The bickerings of little politicians, the jealousies of sections must give way to dignity of purpose and zeal for the common good."

In a speech at the Maine State Fair, he declared, "The whole Confederacy [which, in that day, meant the Union] is my country, and to the innermost fibers of my heart I love it all, and every part." But he left his audience in no doubt about his views on States' rights. "My first allegiance," he said, "is to the State of which I am a citizen."

Davis inspired real affection in Maine. Before he left, he was asked to review troops in Portland and was awarded an honorary degree by Bowdoin College.

In Massachusetts, his personal triumph was repeated. He was asked to speak in Faneuil Hall, the shrine of Yankeedom. Caleb Cushing introduced him as a man of "surpassing wisdom" who might "aspire to the highest places in the executive government of the Union." A standing ovation greeted Davis when he rose to speak.

With well-chosen words, a mellifluous delivery, and graceful gestures, he charmed his audience. Then he defended the South in vigorous terms. Before closing with an eloquent plea for preservation of the ties of Yorktown, he went so far as to condemn the "pharisaical pretension" of New England abolitionists. Hearty applause followed.

Speaking in New York to a cheering audience before returning to Mississippi, Davis gave what was probably his most effective statement of his views on the crisis threatening the Union. He defined it as "a contest upon the one side to enlarge the majority it now possesses and a contest upon the other side to recover the power it has lost." He solemnly warned : "If one section should gain such predominance as would enable it, by modifying the Constitution and usurping new power, to legislate for the other, the exercise of that power would throw us back into the condition of the colonies. And if in the veins of the sons flows the blood of their sires, they would not fail to redeem themselves from tyranny, even should they be driven to resort to revolution."

Back home in Mississippi as 1859 drew to a close, Davis worked for the preservation of the Union. He faced unflinchingly the possibility of war, but, strongly influenced by the friendship shown him in New England, told his constituents that, if a "Northern army should be assembled to march for the subjugation of the South, they would have a battle to fight at home before they passed the limits of their own State."

He told his people, though, that if an abolitionist were elected President, "you will have presented to you the question of whether you will permit the government to pass into the hands of your avowed and implacable enemies. In that event . . ., I should deem it your duty to provide for your safety outside of the Union of those who have already shown the will, and would have acquired the power, to deprive you of your birthright and reduce you to worse than the colonial dependence of your fathers."

Before the New Year, gaunt old John Brown had been hanged by order of the United States government for the insurrection at Harper's Ferry. The South was alarmed and driven to talk of violence by the threat of Abolitionist invasion. In the North, despite Brown's earlier criminal record, he was regarded by many as a saintly martyr to the tyrranical slavocracy. His swinging body, black against the sun, was a grim pendulum marking the running out of time : time for concilia-tion, time to save the Union.

When the 1860 Democratic National Convention met in Charles-ton, South Carolina, the division between Northerners and Southern-ers was so bitter that the Deep South delegates walked out. Senator Douglas was the leading candidate, but failed to win the two-thirds majority necessary for nomination. For 57 ballots, Massachusetts voted solidly for Jefferson Davis. Ironically, one of the Mississippian's most enthusiastic supporters was Benjamin F. Butler. If the Deep South delegates had remained in their seats, Davis, who was not even an active candidate, might have won the nomination.

The convention adjourned without a nominee.

In the resulting mitosis, the Democratic Party in convention assembled became two cells : a Northern one and a Southern one. Douglas won the nomination of the Northern Democrats, Vice Presi-dent John C. Breckinridge that of the Southerners.

The Constitutional Union Party, the tired old Whig war horse in new trappings, carried John Bell to inevitable defeat.

In the Republican convention, Seward was swept aside by the rough-and-tumble onrush of Lincoln supporters. The galleries were packed with his shouting followers. Not only the South, but some of the citadels of the East, trembled when the prairie lawyer won the nomination amid the wildest demonstrations. A Lincoln enthusiast declared, "A thousand steam whistles, ten acres of hotel gongs, a tribe of Comanches, might have mingled in the scene unnoticed." But the South heard the "fire bell in the night" which Thomas Jefferson had prophesied.

Davis's ears had been straining for the sound, but he was still not prepared for the shock. Desperately, he sought promises from Bell, Breckinridge, and Douglas that they would withdraw in favor of a candidate who might unite the forces opposing the Republican party. The first two agreed, but Douglas would not.

By a minority of the popular vote, but a majority in the electoral college, Lincoln was elected. His supporters had committed him before his party and the nation to policies for which he had no relish. Essentially a man of moderation and broad humanity, he was presented to the public as an instrument of vengeance. Wendell Phillips spoke for many of Lincoln's followers when he exulted, "The Republican Party is a party of the North pledged against the South."

In December, Davis was among the senators and representatives of nine Southern states who signed a declaration addressed "To Our Constituents" and saying : "The argument is exhausted. . . . We are satisfied the honor, safety, and independence of the Southern people require the organization of a Southern Confederacy—a result to be obtained by separate state secession."

Davis signed in much greater travail of spirit than some of his colleagues who optimistically assumed that the Southern states would be permitted to depart in peace. He foresaw war. Once again his nerves were taut, and the old neuralgic pains returned.

There still were men in all parts of the nation who felt the same deep concern. A Senate committee of thirteen, which soon took the name of its chairman, John H. Crittenden of Kentucky, was created to search for means of reconciliation. It consisted of five Republicans, five non-Republicans from Northern and border states, and three representatives of the Deep South.

Davis was asked to be a member. After being assured that there would be no inconsistency in his serving and signing the Southern declaration "To Our Constituents," he consented, saying, "If, in the opinion of others, it is possible for me to do anything for the public good, the last moment while I stand here is at the command of the Senate."

At the Crittenden Committee's first meeting, Davis suggested that no recommendations be made to the Senate that were not concurred in by a majority of the committee's Republicans. Crittenden proposed a compromise that would involve abandonment of the South's position, supported by the Dred Scott decision of the Supreme Court, that the Constitution protected the right to introduce slavery in all the territories. At the same time, it would provide remuneration for escaped slaves by communities which obstructed application of the federal fugitive slave laws. Slavery would be prohibited in all territories north of the 36° 30′ line and protected in all south of it. The Southerners were generally disposed to accept the compromise. The Republicans refused to commit themselves without instructions from the President-elect, Mr. Lincoln.

That very afternoon, the thunderbolt fell. Washington learned that South Carolina had seceded. Ardent secessionists in most of the Southern states urged their governments to follow. Despite his painful affliction, made worse by the course of events, Davis met daily with the Crittenden Committee. The only hope for averting national tragedy was that the Republican members of the committee would agree to compromise. Even that help might now be too late. But wishes fed hopes as Davis and his colleagues from the Southern and border states awaited Lincoln's counsel to the Republican members. The word came: "Stand firm. The tug has to come, and better now than any time hereafter."

So the tug came. And now—in the administration of a septuagenarian President who had tiptoed carefully around the sleeping dogs of war. Not hereafter—in the administration of a somewhat dismayed Illinois politician who had been carried into office on the shoulders of a howling mob.

Davis urged Buchanan to withdraw federal troops from Fort Sumter, thus ending the explosive situation in South Carolina. Secession, he reminded him, was the constitutional right of every state. But Buchanan, at first irresolute, eventually refused to alter the fort's military status. On January 9, the ship *Star of the West,* attempting to provision and reinforce the federal garrison at Sumter, received the blunt warning of a cannon ball across the bow. She kept on until two shots crashing into her hull persuaded her to turn back. The next day Mississippi seceded.

In a speech to the Senate the day after Mississippi's action, Davis protested the assertion that "the cause of the separation was the election of Mr. Lincoln." He insisted that Lincoln as an individual was not a bugaboo to the South, that the South feared instead the forces of which Lincoln was the instrument. "The man," he declared, "was nothing save as he was the representative of opinions, of a policy, of purposes, of power, to inflict upon us those wrongs to which freemen never tamely submit."

He then made a direct appeal to Congress to intervene for peace. Once again he rose above sectionalism as he said :

Today it is in the power of two bad men, at the opposite ends of the telegraphic line between Washington and Charleston, to precipitate the State of South Carolina and the United States into a conflict of arms . . . .

And still will you hesitate? Still will you do nothing? Will you sit with sublime indifference and allow events to shape themselves?

No longer can you say the responsibility is upon the Executive. He has told you the responsibility now rests with Congress; and I close as I began, by invoking you to meet that responsibility. . . . If you will, the angel of peace may spread her wings, though it be over divided States; and the sons of the sires of the Revolution may still go on in friendly intercourse with each other. . . . Thus may it be; and thus it is in your power to make it.

The applause in the galleries was so loud and long that the presiding officer had to call on the sergeant at arms to restore order. The out-burst of enthusiasm was followed by a "deep hush." The Senate chamber was as void of initiative as it was empty of sound.

Shortly after this speech Davis was confined to his bed, suffering intensely from neuralgic pain and nearly blind. But, on January 21, he rose from his bed to give the Senate official notification of Mississippi's secession. When he stood up at his desk, his emaciated form clothed in black broadcloth, his neck swathed in black silk, his remaining vitality seemingly concentrated in the eyes that stared with almost preternatural brightness from their deep hollows, he might have been saying farewell not only to his Senate colleagues, but to life itself.

He stood like a silent specter while suspense mounted. When he opened his mouth, his opening words of formal notification were barely audible. Then his voice swelled to its old strength. "Secession," he said, "is to be justified upon the basis that the States are sovereign. There was a time when none denied it." He went on, expounding the Constitutional law, more an abstraction than a man.

And then the inner warmth of the man radiated through the exterior restraint. His glance swept the chamber, lingering here and there with affection.

I see now around me some with whom I have served long. There have been points of collision. But whatever of offense there has been to me, I leave here. I carry with me no hostile remembrance. . . . I have, senators, in this hour of parting, to offer you my apology for any pain which, in the heat of discussion, I have inflicted. I go hence unencumbered by the remembrance of any injury received, and having discharged the duty of making the only reparation in my power for any injury offered.

As he sat down, the sound of weeping came from the galleries.

A week later, the Davises were aboard a train carrying them back to Mississippi—out of the United States. At station after station along the way, the pain-wracked, nerve-tortured man responded to demands for a speech. He got weaker and weaker as he voiced his solemn warnings of grave days ahead. The observant conductor, alarmed for the health of his distinguished passenger, finally started yanking the cord as soon as Davis said, "My friends and fellow citizens," signaling the engineer to separate the speaker from his demanding audience by a huffing and puffing exit down the rails.

At Jackson, Mississippi, the Governor came aboard to present Davis a commission as major general, and notify him that he had been named commander of the armed forces of Mississippi.

Davis was glad that his role seemed destined to be a military one. He remembered fondly the days of the Mexican War when his young brother-in-law, serving under him, had written: "There is not a man in his regiment who would not sacrifice his life to obey him. . . . I verily believe that if he should tell his men to jump into a cannon's mouth, they would think it right and would all say, 'Colonel Jeff knows best, so hurrah, boys, let's go ahead.' " Such loyalty was seldom found in politics. In war loyalties were absolute. On the battlefield, problems were clear cut, the precision of black and white only occasionally marred by a smudge of gray. Friends and enemies wore identifying uniforms. For a man of Davis's temperament, strong in courage but tortured by the disparity between logic and human behavior, the battlefield was easier on the nerves than political strife.

Back at Brierfield, awaiting developments in the crisis, he was thankful that he had no part in the assembly of delegates from the seceded states—now six in number—which had convened at Montgomery, Alabama.

Tapped for Martyrdom

On the afternoon of February 10, while assisting his wife with some rose cuttings, Davis was startled by the arrival of an excited messenger on horseback. As he glanced at the telegram handed him, such a look of grief came to his face that Varina "feared some evil had befallen our family." For a long interval he said nothing, and she was too apprehensive to question him. Then, "as a man might speak of a sentence of death," he told her that he had been elected President of the provisional government of the Confederate States of America.

Three days and 25 speeches later, Davis arrived in Montgomery at 10 P.M. Artillery salutes were fired as his train came into the station. Davis feared that more practical uses for the guns would soon be found. But his great frustration at this moment was that so many influential men complacently assumed there would be no war. One of Mississippi's strongest political leaders refused to believe that Davis had said war might result from the peaceful withdrawal of a sovereign state.

A little later, William Lowndes Yancey, chairman of the reception committee, escorted Davis onto the balcony of the Exchange Hotel, beneath which waited an eager crowd of men and women. "The man and the hour have met," he said. The crowd roared.

Davis told them that he hoped for peace, but declared, "If war should come . . . we shall show . . . that Southern valor still shines as brightly as in the days of '76." And he added, "If, in the progress of events . . . necessity shall require that I shall enter the ranks as a soldier, I hope you will welcome me." This man, it could safely be predicted, would take seriously his official status as commander-in-chief of the Confederate forces.

Two days later, on February 17, Davis rode in a carriage with wizened little Alexander Stephens, vice president of the Confederacy, to the State Capitol, where Congress was assembled. As they rode past cheering throngs, a sprightliness was imparted to the parade by the music of the band. Somebody said it was a minstrel tune that had been orchestrated for the first time. They called it "Dixie."

After a formal reception by Congress, Davis stepped out onto the portico to take the oath of office. Once again, here was one of history's set pieces. The classic white columns were traditional symbols of the South's plantation society. And the dignity and lean, long-limbed grace of the man taking the oath were perfectly expressive of the idea of Southern aristocracy.

As the President began his inaugural address, he seemed to become more than the perfect representative of his people. Doubtless, he had in mind Washington and London and Paris as much as Montgomery. He struck a universal note. His words and his manner made his listeners aware that, amid the confused alarums of their time, they stood on the windswept stage of history.

Our present political position has been achieved in a manner unprecedented in the history of nations. It illustrates the American idea that governments rest on the consent of the governed, and that it is the right of all those to whom we would sell, and from whom we would buy, that there be the freest practicable restrictions upon the interchange of these commodities. . . .

There can be, however, but little rivalry between ours and any manufacturing and navigating community, such as the Northeastern States of the American Union. It must follow, therefore, that mutual interests will invite to goodwill and kind offices on both parts. . . .

If, however, passion or lust of dominion should cloud the judgment or inflame the ambition of those States, we must prepare to meet the emergency and maintain, by the final arbitrament of the sword, the position which we have assumed among the nations of the earth.

Then he spoke of what the people might expect from him. "You will see many errors to forgive, many deficiencies to tolerate; but you shall not find in me either want of zeal or fidelity to the cause. . . ."

His listeners in Montgomery were inspired. So were those throughout the South who read his words. In the North, some newspapers said that, if war should come, the South would have the advantage of being led by the superior President.

Davis wrote Varina : "We are without machinery, without means, and threatened by a powerful opposition; but I do not despond, and will not shrink from the task imposed upon me. . . ."

Had he despaired, he would have been excusable. Not only was a nation of 5,500,000 free citizens (assuming that Virginia, Tennessee, Arkansas, and North Carolina would join the Confederacy) in danger of attack from a nation of 22,000,000. Not only was the balanced economy of the North with its superior industry, transportation, and financial resources pitted against the agricultural economy of the South. But, if war came, the South, in opposing an established and cohesive republic, would have to act through an instrument of government constitutionally pledged to recognition of "the sovereign and independent character" of each state.

Davis took hope from several external factors. He believed that there might be in the North enough opposition to war against the South to prevent a massive effort by the federal government. This hope was not as fantastic as it may now seem. There is much evidence to support Carl Sandburg's assertion in his biography of Lincoln that about one fourth of the population of the Northern states believed in the justice of the Southern cause. Davis was sustained, too, by the

hope that Britain and France, because of dependence on cotton and
other considerations of national interest, would intervene to halt a
war between the United States and the Confederacy.

Nevertheless, Davis might without exaggeration have told his
Montgomery audience what President-elect Lincoln had told his
Springfield neighbors a week earlier, that he had before him a task
"greater than that which rested upon Washington."

Davis promptly dispatched an agent to Europe to purchase arms
and ships. He charged an appointee with the responsibility of estab-
lishing a powder plant. He also sent an agent into the United States
to purchase armaments. To some of the Northern manufacturers,
silver dollars still had a solid ring that could be heard above the strains
of "Yankee Doodle."

The need for ships of war was really desperate. United States Naval
officers who resigned their commissions to serve the Confederacy first
sailed their ships into Northern ports and surrendered them. Davis
would not have had them do otherwise. He believed in "the splendid
folly of honor." Nevertheless, their action meant that the Confederacy,
with its vast shoreline and penetrating bays and rivers, had not a
single warship.

On February 25, Davis named three "discreet" commissioners, two
of whom had opposed secession, to negotiate with the government of
the United States and settle all disagreements "around a conference
table with honor and dignity to both sides." But the failure of this
effort was forecast by the course of a Peace Convention of twelve
Northern and eight Southern states called in Washington on Virginia's initiative. The convention suggested a compromise plan to
the Senate. While its fate teetered in the balance, many men pressed
Lincoln to condemn or endorse the proposal. He conceived that he
should remain aloof. The compromise was defeated by one vote.

Anxiously, Davis awaited Lincoln's inaugural address for a clue
to the course of the new administration. Some Southerners hoped that
Lincoln would be influenced by a much circulated editorial that the

famous James Gordon Bennett had published in the influential *New York Herald*. In the issue of February 19, Bennett had said :

> For the future, the Northern President should profit by the example of his Southern rival, who does not attempt to tell the Southern people that the crisis is nothing, that nobody is hurt (on the contrary he acknowledges that the revolution hurts both North and South), but declares that the South is ready to meet any hardship rather than to abandon its principles. Mr. Lincoln must look this state of things in the face. It cannot be turned off with a joke; and when next he opens his mouth we trust he will not put his foot in it. If Mr. Lincoln aspires to be the second Washington of this great Confederacy, let him come out emphatically in his inauguration in favor of the Crittenden resolutions as amendments to the Constitution; let him call an extra session of the new Congress and in his first message boldly reiterate this plan and its submission at once to the people through the States; let him appoint his cabinet but not dispose of another office in his gift till this great and overwhelming question is settled.

The North, as much as the South, misgauged Lincoln. He was not, as he was so often called, a clown or a buffoon. He was not a malignant man, but one of keen sympathies. He was certainly not, as some of the North's most brilliant men asserted, lacking in intellect. He was an authentic genius, and genius sometimes appears in eccentric disguise. He was a man of tremendous ambition, as his closest associates have testified. He grew to manhood in a frontier society where the law and politics provided the only road to commanding achievement. But he was more a man of contemplation than of action. For all his hearty telling of funny stories, he was an introvert. Had he been born into a more sophisticated society, he might, with his remarkable gift for expression, have followed the route of letters to enduring fame. As it was, his ambition, in combination with his environment, caused him to essay the role of man of action. For that role, he was as temperamentally unfitted as Hamlet.

There would shortly come a time when the United States needed as President not so much a man of vigorous action as one of enduring patience, not so much an efficient executive as a voice for its highest aspirations. For this role, Lincoln was superbly fitted.

On March 4, he was inaugurated. He declared, "I have no purpose directly or indirectly to interfere with the institution of slavery in the States where it exists." But he also said, "No State, upon its own mere action, can lawfully get out of the Union." More significant than either statement was his omission of any plan for compromise.

On April 1, Seward, now Lincoln's Secretary of State, proposed that Fort Sumter be evacuated. Lincoln made Seward realize that his advice on this point was not wanted. But, as the crisis grew, the President continued to debate with himself on alternative courses of action. On April 6, he notified South Carolina that he had dispatched an expedition to provision the garrison. On April 11, South Carolina formally requested Major Anderson, Sumter's commander, to surrender the fort. He said that he would when his supplies were exhausted. Since, by Lincoln's own statement, supplies were on the way, South Carolina rejected Anderson's offer.

At 4:30 A.M. the next day, shore batteries opened fire on Sumter. On April 13, after 34 hours of bombardment which demolished much of the fort without killing a single federal soldier, the garrison surrendered. The war was on.

Lincoln declared that "insurrection" existed and called on all the States for troops to suppress it. In quick succession, Virginia, Arkansas, Tennessee, and North Carolina withdrew from the Union and cast their lot with the Confederacy.

On May 21, Richmond was chosen as the permanent capital of the Confederate States of America. Thus it was that, in early June, Davis and his cabinet and a whole army of government clerks moved in on a Richmond somewhat apprehensive of this invasion from the South.

Like most Presidents of the United States, Davis had not been free to choose his cabinet simply on the basis of getting the best man for each job. Geographical considerations loomed even larger in making appointments in a struggling new-born Confederacy than in an established republic. So did the necessity of finding high places for disappointed aspirants to the Presidency.

The Secretary of State was Robert Toombs of Georgia. Vigorous and vehement, he sometimes lunged upon the scene breathing out threatenings and slaughter and at other times was ready to regale the world with boisterous good humor. Some people thought that he should have been elected President, and he agreed with them.

Secretary of the Treasury C. G. Memminger, a South Carolina moderate in a nest of fire eaters, lacked both the imagination and the graces of some of his Charleston associates, but had a sturdy competence.

The Secretary of War, Leroy Pope Walker, was a volatile Alabama lawyer, loyal and courageous, but impatient of detail and lacking in administrative experience.

The Navy portfolio was held by Stephen Mallory, an antisecession Floridian who had risen from poverty and obscurity with a pertinacity that spoke well for his initiative but which had irritated many people in his home state.

Smooth and smiling Judah P. Benjamin, keenest-minded of the cabinet officers, was attorney general. Some people objected to the fact that the Louisianian was a Jew. Davis, according to some of his close associates, was insistent that Benjamin have a high place in the government. The President's admiration for Benjamin was said to date from the time of their near duel.

The Postmaster General was John Reagan of Texas, who cared little for social finesse, and whose quiet competence was seldom suspected by those who met him casually.

With these officials and their subordinates together with a horde of preferment seekers descending on Richmond, the capital, according to its social columnist, T. C. De Leon, "felt much as the Roman patricians might have felt at the advent of the leading families of the Goths." Richmond would later revise this estimate. In the meantime, Davis was excluded from all hasty criticism of the newcomers. The *Richmond Daily Enquirer* seemed to regret only that he was not a

Virginian. "The mantle of Washington falls gracefully upon his shoulders," the newspaper said. "Never were a people more enraptured with their Chief Magistrate than ours are with President Davis."

The old Brokenbrough house, a neo-classic mansion, was offered to Davis as a gift from the citizens of Richmond. He refused the property as a present, but accepted the use of it as a residence after its purchase by the Confederate government. It became known as the White House of the Confederacy.

Davis kept Robert E. Lee near him in an anomalous position as a military adviser with undefined duties. The President probably had more respect for Lee than for any other soldier in the South except his boyhood hero, Albert Sidney Johnston. It soon became apparent that Davis was determined to be his own Secretary of War. The most minute correspondence of the War Department was submitted to him, and he insisted on tending to a great deal of the paper work even when a return of his neuralgic pains sent him to bed. He supervised the disposition of the untrained volunteer forces in Virginia, as well as the 6,000 trained troops under Beauregard and those under Joseph E. Johnston, both assigned to defense of Virginia's northern frontier.

Imposition of a federal blockade of Southern ports; federal occupation of Alexandria, Virginia; seizure of the area around Fortress Monroe; the raising of the regular army of the United States to 42,000; the massing of forces on the Potomac under Union General Irvin McDowell: all these things led inescapably to the conclusion that a Northern invasion force would soon be rolling forward to the battle cry "On to Richmond!"

By the middle of June, it seemed likely that Manassas, an important rail junction in Northern Virginia, would be the first objective of the invaders. This point was held by Beauregard, who was greatly outnumbered by McDowell. Davis ordered Johnston, who had abandoned Harper's Ferry as untenable, to join forces with Beauregard. Plans for the defense of Manassas were formulated in a council of war in Davis's bedroom. Despite his illness, the President hoped to be on the battlefield several days before the fight began.

When the Union and Confederate armies clashed at Manassas on July 21, Davis could not bear to remain away from the scene. As he neared the battlefield, riding his bay horse, he was alarmed at the sight of many wounded men being carted or carried from the field. He paused to speak words of sympathy to these. Soon a great many stragglers appeared. He exhorted them to return to the fray, but his urging was mostly in vain. He was half-prepared for news of a Confederate defeat when he reached General Johnston. The trim little commander, relishing the moment, told Davis: "Mr. President, I am happy to inform you that the enemy is at this moment in full retreat."

Davis called for vigorous pursuit of the foe, but already darkness was closing in, the federal troops were nearing the defenses of Washington, and the raw Confederate soldiers were "demoralized by victory." Reluctantly, and by degrees, the idea of organized pursuit was abandoned.

Davis sent Lee a telegram which touched off celebrations in Richmond: "We have won a glorious though dearly-bought victory. Night closed on the enemy in full flight and closely pursued."

Exuberant crowds greeted Davis on his return to Richmond two days later. A speech was called for and the Virginians cheered Davis lustily when he said, "The grand old mother of Washington still nourishes a band of heroes."

The quick victory at Manassas multiplied Davis's problems. Swaggering overconfidence and utter complacency hampered his attempts to build up the new nation's defenses.

There were other problems, too. While Davis liked being his own Secretary of War, he would have liked the nominal secretary to be at least a dependable undersecretary in charge of administration. Walker maintained that office work was not the proper business for a gentleman. It certainly was not the proper business for the gentleman from Alabama. As details crowded upon him, he grew increasingly nervous and frequently took to his bed. These circumstances, combined with Davis's own predilection for the military, caused the hard-working President to spend so much time with the

War Department that he could give only cursory attention to other aspects of his administration.

Within the War Department, there were serious problems apart from the shortage of men and matériel. Beauregard was revealing a sensitive ego, well nourished by popular adulation. He always expected more than was done for him. Joseph E. Johnston gave promise of being a greater thorn than Beauregard. When Joe Johnston learned that, in appointing full generals, Davis had placed him fourth, he was outraged. How could he be outranked by Adjutant General Cooper, Albert Sidney Johnston, and R. E. Lee "for the benefit of persons neither of whom has struck a blow for the Confederacy"?

Johnston addressed to Davis nine pages of protest. The legal arguments used by the general and the President to justify their contentions regarding the Chief Executive's right to make such appointments under existing law might still present a fine point for judicial decision. The essential fact is that neither Johnston nor Davis was judicial. Johnston, proud and highly sensitive, sincerely believed that his dignity had been injured. As he so often did in such circumstances, he bolstered his injured ego by proud references to his adherence to the code of a soldier and a gentleman and to the family tradition that he had sought to maintain.

These references infuriated Davis, who was just as proud as Johnston and particularly sensitive to overweening references to family tradition. As was customary with him in such cases, Davis replied with a cold superiority calculated to prove that he was perhaps an even loftier gentleman that his verbal antagonist.

Because of the varying backgrounds and similar temperaments of Davis and Johnston, a disagreement was growing into a feud. The struggling Confederacy could ill afford such conflict between the commander-in-chief of its armies and one of its four top generals.

Though the War Department was Davis's primary interest, minute details in all departments awaited his approval. Highly efficient personally, he had never learned to delegate authority. The tragedy was that, even more than most executives, he needed to delegate because his physical and nervous constitution always caused him great suffering when he was overworked.

As his problems grew more vexing, he was frequently abrupt with ambitious politicians and importuning officers. Sometimes, after he had been curt to an old friend, he would sit morosely at the dinner table and scarcely touch his meal. He had never learned to "suffer fools gladly," and he offended many a congressman whose oral capacity was not encroached on by cranial development.

In his handling of Confederate finances (relying on the withholding of cotton to force European intervention rather than applying the purchasing power of the commodity), as well as in his exaggerated faith in the ability of West Point to transform even mediocre material into good generals, he thought in abstractions. When the abstractions did not square with empirical evidence, he turned more and more to endless paper work. On paper, most problems could be reduced to abstractions.

The principal flaw in his great record as United States Secretary of War had been his tendency to waste time and energy in attempts to get his opponents to admit that they were in the wrong. The correspondence between Davis and Johnston never sank to the level of that between Davis and Scott. But both instances revealed the same need for justification on Davis's part, though admittedly his provocation was great in both.

With all his faults, however, Davis brought considerable gifts to the office of President. He had been a great Secretary of War, and the experience gained in that office was valuable to him now. Admittedly, this advantage was counterbalanced by the fact that the War Department of the United States, had been brought to a high peak of efficiency by Davis himself. Davis's West Point training gave him a far better understanding of military problems than most civilian Presidents would have had. Again, there was a corresponding disadvantage. If he had not been a graduate of West Point, he might not so often have been tempted to play soldier and might not so often have underrated the capacity of officers who lacked West Point training.

If Davis's mind was rigid and sometimes overly theoretical, it was nevertheless brilliant, capacious, retentive, and disciplined. Furthermore, he was an articulate and sometimes moving spokesman for the aspirations of the South. He might often be too self-conscious in adherence to the Southern gentleman's code, but he was in truth a high-minded gentleman of courage. And, through his own efforts and those of his older brother and father, he had been molded into an image of leadership acceptable to his people. Even underprivileged Southerners preferred, at this stage of their history, to give their homage to a man with the aura of aristocracy. And the same inflexible will that sometimes made him incredibly stubborn also enabled him to surmount pain and discouragement. He would know a great deal of both.

The Fice Dogs of Fate

Disappointed candidates for President of the provisional government and politicians offended during Davis's short tenure were murmuring in discontent when the general elections for the permanent government were held throughout the South. But the people were still rejoicing over the victory at Manassas and Davis was swept into office without formal opposition. Under the Confederate Constitution, he and Alexander Stephens were elected to six-year terms.

The powers of the office to which Davis had been elected were not so clearly defined. The constitutional language awaited the amplification of experience. Where possible in matters of disputed authority, Davis preferred to work through Congress, but he was ready to put the full weight of his office behind necessary measures. In November, in the final session of the Provisional Congress, Davis had cited the vital need of a rail link between Danville, Virginia and Greensboro, North Carolina. The proposed 40 miles of track would connect Richmond with Atlanta by a route shorter and less vulnerable than those already available. North Carolina authorities, raising the cry of "States' rights" with even greater fervor than before the war, said that they would not consent to the construction. Davis called upon Congress to go ahead with the work under the war powers of the Confederate government. The work was done.

Congress was not always so cooperative in matters of defense. With the vastly outnumbered Confederacy in a struggle for its life, both houses of Congress passed two measures that, by increasing furloughs and exemptions, would have weakened the Southern armies—perhaps by 30,000 men almost immediately. Davis was infuriated. He not only vetoed both bills, but reminded Congress that the administration of the armies was not a legislative function. Like a pedagogue admonishing misbehaving charges, he told the Congressmen that they ought to stay within the limits of law and common sense.

On February 22, 1862, Davis was inaugurated as President of the Confederate States of America. The occasion was not a happy one for him. In some ways, the "permanent" government seemed more impermanent than the provisional one. States had already challenged the authority of the Confederacy. North Carolina was furnishing more soldiers to the Confederacy than most states and Georgia was supplying the leadership of Longstreet and John B. Gordon, but the governors of those two states were so jealous of their sovereignty that the Confederacy was threatened with sabotage.

Prices of food and clothing had risen alarmingly, in some cases more than 100 per cent within less than a year. The Confederacy was buying arms and provisions with paper convertible not into coins, but into more paper : Confederate bonds bearing 8 per cent interest, with the interest payable in paper.

Federal seizure of the Confederate commissioners James M. Mason and John Slidell, en route to Europe on the British mail steamer *Trent,* had briefly raised Southern hopes. Great Britain, incensed over the insult to her sovereignty, had demanded that the prisoners be released. Unofficially, Lincoln had vowed, "I would rather die than give them up." War between the United States and Britain had seemed imminent. But the cool-headed Seward had persuaded

Lincoln to accede to Britain's demands. One more Confederate hope
had been frustrated.

Davis had sent Lee into Western Virginia, about to become West
Virginia by a secession of its own, to save the area from federal dom-
ination. But, for a variety of reasons, including inefficient and
quarreling subordinate officers, Lee had failed. Many people were
saying that the Virginian was only a "dress parade general." But
Davis had decided that Lee had qualities of greatness and he stead-
fastly refused to shelve him.

Kentucky had been lost to the Federals. Tennessee was in grave
danger. The rail artery through the Southwest was in direst peril.
And, while these misfortunes occurred or threatened on the perimeter
of the Confederacy, the efficient George B. McClellan was organizing
with superb skill a grand army poised for a drive on Richmond itself.

Mindful of all these dangers, Davis rode in his black carriage, under
dark skies and through steady rain, to his inauguration in Capitol
Square. Mrs. Davis followed in another carriage. She was surprised
to notice that the slow-moving vehicle was flanked by solemn-faced
blacks in white gloves. She asked the coachman why they were there.
He turned around. "This, ma'am, is the way we always does in Richmond for funerals and sichlike."

The inaugural ceremony took place under a rain-pelted awning
by the bronze equestrian statue of George Washington. As Davis, very
thin and pale, walked to his seat, cheers burst from the crowd huddled
beneath black umbrellas. His face was tight-drawn as he rose to speak.
From the platform, the audience below must have looked like a field of
sable mushrooms sprouting from the mud.

With the rain drumming on their umbrellas, most of the crowd
heard little of the President's carefully reasoned address in which he
explained the legal rightness of the Southern cause. It being Washington's birthday, the President made appropriate references to that
earlier secession in which Northerners and Southerners had been
joined. In conclusion, looking upward with hands upraised, he
pledged, "With humble gratitude and adoration, acknowledging the

Providence which has so visibly protected the Confederacy during its brief, but eventful career, to Thee, O God, I trustingly commit myself, and prayerfully invoke Thy blessing on my country and its cause."

To Varina, her husband, "as he stood pale and emaciated, dedicating himself to the service of the Confederacy, evidently forgetful of everything but his sacred oath, . . . seemed . . . a willing victim going to his funeral pyre." She had so strong a sense of foreboding that, "making some excuse," she regained her carriage and went home.

For a moment the fragile figure stood on the platform, the tension of inner conflicts evident in the taut posture and the bow-string tightness of the jaw muscles. Above him was the figure of Washington, majestically composed, the serenity of the countenance reflecting perfect assurance that all problems would yield to common sense, the uplifted hand pointing out unequivocally the direction that he knew to be right.

Amid the problems that made Davis's life a nightmare, he had two props aside from his spiritual convictions and his intense devotion to a way of life under attack. One was his wife, who believed he was one of the greatest men on the planet. The other was Judah P. Benjamin, who a few years before had been ready to shoot him.

In the course of his Confederate career, Benjamin held three different cabinet posts. But, whatever his official title at any given time, he was always the chief confidant of the President in the daily business of the government. Davis valued Benjamin for his brilliance and industry, but even more for his cheerfulness and agreeableness. Davis thought Benjamin was an adviser, but almost always the smiling cabinet officer gave the President the advice he wished to hear. Benjamin's chief influence was not in suggesting new policies or procedures but in confirming Davis in views to which the President was already predisposed. It is not surprising that Davis, with his sensitive ego, his overwhelming determination to be right, and his almost unbearable need to be appreciated, grew to regard Benjamin as indispensable.

When, right after the inauguration, Richmond heard confirmation of the report that Roanoke Island in North Carolina had fallen, Congress demanded Benjamin's scalp. After service as Attorney General, the Louisianan had succeeded Walker in the War Department. Acting on bad advice, he had refused to reinforce the Confederates on the island. Davis had to let Benjamin go if he was to save the effectiveness of his administration. But, while he dropped him from the War Department, he made him Secretary of State and hailed the move as a promotion.

Other factors had contributed to Benjamin's removal. One was the zealousness with which he had carried on the President's feud with Johnston. Johnston had powerful friends in Congress. When Benjamin, largely through ignorance of military etiquette, had precipitated a threat of resignation by "Stonewall" Jackson, Benjamin's enemies had an emotional weapon with which to pressure the Administration.

Davis's theoretical cast of mind carried with it a certain logic of realism. He saw that conscription was necessary, and called for a draft law embracing men between the ages of 18 and 35. Immediately, he was bitterly attacked from many sides. Vice President Stephens protested the move as an act of despotism. Senator Barnwell Rhett, of South Carolina, one of the most ardent secession leaders, now said that forcing men into the army would violate the very freedom for which the Southern states were fighting. Governor Joseph E. Brown of Georgia was loud in opposition. He was determined that, if the law was enacted, he would defy it wherever possible and circumvent it where defiance was not feasible. The law was passed, but from that time onward Davis faced a strong, united opposition.

The President aroused genuine fears among some when he declared first Norfolk and then Richmond to be under military law. Equally stern measures had already been adopted by the Federal government, but a people who had taken "States' Rights" for their battle cry found such moves hard to accept. The inadequacy of local police to deal with enemies within Norfolk and Richmond justified President Davis's action. Unfortunately, his choice for chief of the Richmond military district was Major Winder, who sometimes forgot civilians were not privates under his command.

The problems that had been slowly closing in on Davis now rushed at him from all directions. On April 2, McClellan's powerful army reached Yorktown in its steady movement up the Peninsula toward Richmond. On April 6 and 7, the two great battles of Shiloh were fought. Albert Sidney Johnston, the general in whom Davis had the greatest confidence, was killed and the Confederacy suffered a major defeat in the West. Island No. 10, a vital Confederate fortification in the Mississippi River, fell to the enemy about the same time. On April 20, Farragut forced his way up river to New Orleans, opening the lower Mississippi to Yankee gunboats and transports. On May 1, Norfolk and Portsmouth (with its important shipyard) were occupied by the Federals.

And all the while, McClellan moved inexorably toward Richmond with Joseph E. Johnston retreating before him.

Johnston had advocated a concentration of the forces of many States to strike a disastrous blow at the enemy in the vicinity of Richmond. He contended that territory should be sacrificed to gain a mass of maneuver, that destruction of the enemy's striking power outweighed loss of ground.

The holding of territory was more important to Davis than to Johnston. He feared that, once the Federals had occupied a section, freeing all the slaves and offering them special inducements to serve the Federal government, that area (even if regained) would never again be a well-integrated part of the Confederacy.

Nevertheless, Davis's views were not, as is sometimes supposed, completely contrary to Johnston's. While he placed a high value upon territory, he would have liked to risk reductions of the defensive forces in some parts of the South in order to concentrate forces at other points where the enemy was more vulnerable. But he headed a Confederacy rather than a cohesive federal republic. Governor Brown of Georgia had suspended conscription in his state until the Georgia legislature had passed it and he then had appealed to the courts to invalidate the action of the assembly. Governor Zebulon Vance of North Carolina attacked conscription in such strong terms that many observers thought he was inviting drafted soldiers from his state to desert. If Davis had attempted to denude the defenses of Georgia and North Carolina to concentrate forces for a decisive attack on McClellan in Virginia, what would have happened? He probably would have had to contend with rebellion or secession.

Davis wrote Brown a 2,500-word letter of closely reasoned arguments for conscription. With unanswerable logic, he demonstrated the constitutionality of the draft. But Brown would not acknowledge that Davis was right. He simply reiterated his emotion-charged statements of opposition, counting on them to stir voters who had no time to digest disquisitions on the Constitution.

Not appreciating Davis's problems, Johnston thought that the President was completely lacking in imagination. Baffled by the complexity of Johnston's character, Davis thought that the general was determined to avoid a fight. Influenced partly by his wife, Johnston came to believe that the administration was plotting against him. There was ill feeling between Mrs. Johnston and Mrs. Davis, who had once been affectionate friends, and these women now did nothing to reconcile their husbands.

When Davis, once again absorbed in the theoretical, reproved Johnston for not brigading his harassed army according to States, the exasperated general made little more effort to communicate with Richmond than if it had been a foreign capital.

During this period, Davis, who had long been concerned with spiritual matters but had never joined a church, was privately received into the Episcopal communion. Religion was too personal a thing to be flaunted in public. He was no demagogue who would use profession of faith to win favor with his highly religious constituents.

That same day, a big dance was in progress at the White House. Davis, weary and nervous, hated these noisy affairs. Though he greeted the guests with the politeness that his code demanded, he withdrew within himself as a refuge. Many of the guests thought he was arrogant.

During this party, the President received a message. Without altering his expression, he drew his wife aside. As casually as if he were asking about the supply of refreshments, he quietly told her:

"The enemy's gunboats are nearing Richmond. You and the children must leave town tomorrow."

The party went on. Davis was still the self-contained host. His wife was as animated as ever. Surely, the discord of war was far from these music-filled rooms. These polished floors could never know the tread of bloody boots. The guests felt a sense of security. They lingered late.

The next day, at Davis's command but against her own wishes, Varina left for Raleigh, North Carolina with the children.

The Federal gunboats were turned back by improvised shore batteries. To some, this fact simply seemed to mean that Richmond would be taken by land rather than by water. Already, McClellan's tents were visible from the rooftops of the city.

Davis was laboring from early in the morning until late at night, attempting to prepare for any eventuality. Benjamin's smile was virtually the only one he saw these days. He was harassed by petty criticism on all sides. An anxious public sought a scapegoat. It seemed unpatriotic to blame anybody in uniform. A civilian politician who always looked as though he were superior to fate as well as to most mortals was a far more suitable target. Davis, in moments of reflection, realized that he was spending too much time and energy in answering the carpers. But he could not change ingrained habit that was a psychological necessity. He wrote his wife, "I wish I could learn to let people alone who snap at me, in forbearance and charity to turn from the cats as the snakes. . . ."

When Davis finally received word from Johnston that the general had crossed the Chickahominy about 25 miles from Richmond and would defend the crossing, he was greatly relieved. He rode out on horseback, expecting to visit with Johnston at the Chickahominy encampment. A short distance outside the city, he sighted an aggregation of tents. He asked who was there, and was told they were Hood's Texas brigade. Knowing that this brigade was with Johnston, he exclaimed : "No ! Hood's Brigade is down on the Chickahominy." Told that Johnston's headquarters were in a brick house to his right, he protested : "No. He's down on the Chickahominy." When he learned Johnston had changed his plans, Davis was shocked. He went at once to Johnston. The general explained that he had found the marshy ground near the Chickahominy unsuitable for defense. Davis asked if Johnston intended to fight where he was, on the outskirts of Richmond. Johnston's answer was equivocal and he seemed to regard Davis as a meddler.

The President was a proud man, but he swallowed his pride rather than quarrel with Johnston when the fate of the capital was uncertain.

Johnston did fight on the outskirts of Richmond, at Seven Pines, on May 31. He was severely wounded. Davis, always drawn by the sound of guns, was there when the general was taken from the battlefield. He bent over him with all the solicitude of a brother.

Though Davis's sorrow over Johnston was genuine, he was thankful that he now had the opportunity to appoint Lee as the general's successor.

With Jackson keeping Federal reinforcements occupied in the Valley of Virginia, Lee and the Army of Northern Virginia rolled McClellan back down the Peninsula.

Davis was entitled to some feeling of personal satisfaction. When newspaper editors and politicians had demanded that Lee be shelved, the President had never lost faith in him. Protests were loud when he named Lee to succeed Johnston, passing over General Gustavus Smith. Davis's stubbornness had served the cause well. It had saved Robert E. Lee for top command.

In the months that followed, Lee continued to justify Davis's faith.

With Jackson as his brilliant chief lieutenant, Lee defeated an invading army under Union General John Pope, thrashing him at Cedar Mountain and Second Manassas and driving him from Virginia soil. The boastful Pope had unwittingly helped the Confederacy before his departure. His cruel treatment of civilians, so strongly in contrast with McClellan's chivalry, had prompted a new wave of enlistments. Men eager to strike a blow were rushing to the Confederate colors.

Lee persuaded Davis that the time was at hand for invasion of the North. Both the general and the President counted heavily on the aid of Maryland's Southern sympathizers as the Army of Northern Virginia forded the Potomac River September 14. A successful campaign north of the Potomac might bring England and France to the aid of the Confederacy. The *London Times* and other British newspapers were loud in praise of Confederate generals and statesmen. Prominent lawyers in Britain and on the Continent argued as stoutly as Davis himself that the Southern States had every legal right to secede. Gladstone was known to favor recognition of the Confederacy, even though he had not yet made the celebrated speech in which he told Parliament, "Jefferson Davis has created a nation." Davis found it possible to share some of Benjamin's optimism. Events seemed to be justifying the President's faith in Lee and in the "opinions of mankind."

Not so well-placed was the President's faith in another general, Braxton Bragg. This fact was not at first apparent, even to Davis's enemies. While Lee was taking boldly aggressive action against the Union forces in Virginia and Maryland, Bragg was on the offensive in Kentucky. Aided by two dashing cavalrymen, Nathan Bedford Forrest and John Hunt Morgan, he rallied pro-Southerners in Kentucky and put the Federals on the defensive in the West. The whole situation in that theater brightened when, as the Confederates enjoyed successes on land, Farragut's fleet suffered reverses on the Mississippi.

On September 17, 1862, at the Maryland village of Sharpsburg near the Antietam, hopes fed by the chancellories and parliaments of the Old World were abruptly shattered. Lee's invasion of the North was halted. Politicians overseas had never viewed the Confederate cause with starry eyes. But there had been the gleam of acquisitiveness, and now that was replaced by a jaundiced glaze. The end of Lee's campaign in Maryland was a major diplomatic defeat for the Confederacy.

Lincoln was determined to make it a diplomatic victory for the Union. He had been holding for some time an Emancipation Proclamation, which he had wished to issue earlier. But Seward had pointed out that issuance of such a document when Union armies were hard pressed would be regarded abroad as a measure of desperation. Now, after Sharpsburg, Lincoln could play from strength. By way of explanation, he had written Horace Greeley: "If I could save the Union without freeing any slaves, I would do it. . . . What I do about slavery and the colored race, I do because I believe it helps to save the Union. . . ."

Lincoln's own statement of his purpose explains the anomaly that the Emancipation Proclamation declared the slaves to be free only in areas in which the federal government was powerless to free them. Slaves were declared free only in States controlled by the Confederate government. In Virginia, cities and counties occupied by federal forces were specifically exempted from its provisions. And freedom was not proclaimed for the slaves in Illinois, Pennsylvania, New Jersey, Delaware, and Maryland, all Union states. Lord John Russell, the British Foreign Minister, declared, "If it were a measure of Emancipation it should be extended to all the States of the Union . . . [It] is not granted to the claims of humanity but inflicted as a punishment."

In some parts of the United States, the reaction to the proclamation was violent. Issued September 23, 1862, it was to become officially effective January 1, 1863. When, two months after that date, the first military conscription act went into effect, riots raged in New York City. By mid-July, mobs were roaming the Northern metropolis and lynching blacks. After issuance of the proclamation, General

Ulysses Grant had declared, "If I thought this war was to abolish slavery, I would resign my commission, and offer my sword to the other side."

But these dissents counted for little in the larger context of public sentiment at home and abroad. Some Northerners, despite all Lincoln's public declarations that the war was not being fought to free the slaves, had fought all along for that purpose. For innumerable others, Lincoln's proclamation released a well-spring of genuine idealism that for the first time provided an acceptable justification for all the bloodletting. And in England, his lordship, the Foreign Minister, evaluating the contents of his dispatch boxes with a dispassionate eye, might conclude that the Emancipation Proclamation was shallow propaganda; but the recently enfranchised British working class— the Cockney laborers, the Midlands mill workers, the Yorkshire miners—saw a new Magna Carta emblazoned with shining rubrics of sacrificial blood. Emerson said truly that a force had been unleashed that would work while men were sleeping. As Lincoln said, the response was "all that a vain man could wish."

Davis painstakingly pointed out that the document was legally ineffective because it applied only to Confederate territory. To him, it was transparent propaganda, and he could not understand how men could fail to realize that fact if it was pointed out to them. Davis's Secretary of State, Benjamin, wasted no energy in indignation. He only regretted that the Confederacy had not had an opportunity to effect a similar master stroke. Later, he urged Davis to emancipate the slaves in the Confederacy. But Davis objected, among other things, that such an act would be illegal. Once again he was baffled by the non-Euclidean public mind.

Though men did not yet know it, the twentieth century had at last defeated the eighteenth century on the battleground of the nineteenth.

In that same September of 1862, when Lee's invasion of the North ended at Sharpsburg and Lincoln issued his Preliminary Emancipation Proclamation, Varina returned to Richmond. Her white silk-clad presence made the White House once again a haven amid the horrors of war.

Davis needed her more as the months passed. There were some bright spots: "Jeb" Stuart's spectacular cavalry raid into Pennsylvania in October and Lee's defeat of Burnside at Fredericksburg in December. But the news from the West came in the accents of doom. General Bragg, advancing on Louisville from Chattanooga, had been halted at Perryville by General Buell's Army of the Ohio. The mercurial Bragg was plunged into despair. He now surrendered the initiative that he had so boldly exercised. Though his casualties had been about the same as Buell's and the battle had been a draw, he withdrew from the field and holed up in Murfreesboro, Tennessee.

The Southern people, who had been elated over Bragg's offensive, now were infuriated by his sudden switch to defense. In the press and in Congress, he was pilloried. To demands that he be removed or chastised, Davis was adamant. He did not subject Bragg to the barrage of questions that he would have fired at Johnston under similar conditions. Davis was impressed with the fact that Bragg always kept his army efficiently organized in accordance with the best West Point standards and that he had due regard for protocol in addressing the President as commander-in-chief.

Nevertheless, Davis could not blink the fact that some change was needed. On November 24, he named Joe Johnston to over-all command of the Department of the West, with headquarters in Chattanooga. Given the ill-defined scope of Johnston's authority, and the perpetual misunderstanding between him and the President, disaster was predictable.

On December 10, Davis, desiring to see the Western situation for himself, visited Johnston at Chattanooga. There was polite conversation over the teacups, but no meeting of minds. Davis wanted decisive action in the West. Johnston wanted clarification of his duties, particularly his relationship with Bragg, technically his subordinate. But the President and the general each talked to a man with closed ears.

Union General Rosecrans attacked Bragg on December 31. The

Battle of Murfreesboro (December 31, 1862—January 3, 1863), a flaming bridge between the old year and the new, reduced to ashes Confederate hopes for an offensive in the West. Brought to indecision by anxiety, Bragg hesitated until his opportunity to defeat Rosecrans was lost. Then he abandoned the field and his base, retreating toward Chattanooga. Not until Bragg's chief lieutenants gave the general a vote of no-confidence did Davis grudgingly admit that this favorite should be replaced.

The active command of the Army of Tennessee then officially passed to Joseph E. Johnston. Predictable disaster became almost certain.

But tragedy struck first in the East. Early in May, Lee and Jackson, in one of the most brilliant victories in modern history, defeated a Union force more than twice the size of theirs, sending Hooker's army reeling back across the Rappahannock. But this victory was more costly to the South than most of its defeats, for Stonewall Jackson was fatally wounded. The combination of Lee and Jackson—one of the greatest fighting teams in the annals of war— was no longer at the service of the Confederacy.

Richmond gave Jackson the biggest funeral in the city's history— not a planned pageant of death, but the spontaneous outpouring from homes and offices and warehouses of those who had followed his fortunes in life and now chose to follow his coffin. After the funeral, Davis returned to his own quarters like a man in a trance. A visitor entered the room and greeted him. The President stared back without comprehension. Then his training as a gentleman reasserted itself even though other reflexes refused to work. "You must excuse me," he said. "I am still staggering from a dreadful blow. I cannot think."

Having struck in Virginia, disaster now skipped to the West like a capricious tornado. By five victories between the first and the seventeenth of May, Grant separated Johnston from General John C. Pemberton, defender of Vicksburg. After siege, the city fell on July 4.

At the same time, Lee was stopped at Gettysburg. Lee had presented this second invasion of the North as a great gamble, and Davis had endorsed it with full knowledge of the facts. But there is reason to believe that he had secretly shared the belief of many Southerners that Lee's army was invincible.

Lee submitted his resignation. Davis refused it in a letter of generous praise. It no longer required courage to retain Lee, as it had in the early days of the war. Now virtually all Southerners believed that he was indispensable. Since the death of Jackson, Lee was easily the foremost hero of the South. Davis never evidenced the slightest jealousy over Lee's primacy in the pantheon of popular estimation. The Virginian was the nearly perfect embodiment of the code which was part and parcel of the President's faith.

For Johnston, Davis had no kind words. He held him responsible for the loss of Vicksburg and told him so in a detailed letter, the tone of which was set by the phrase "my orders as your superior officer."

After Vicksburg and Gettysburg, some Southerners lost the will to fight and others who had never had it were emboldened to demand peace negotiations. A secret society seeking peace was formed in western Georgia and the northern parts of Alabama and Mississippi. A similar organization arose in mountainous areas of Tennessee, Virginia, and North Carolina. In western North Carolina, peace sentiment was sufficiently strong for Unionists to declare their convictions without ostracism by their neighbors or retribution by the State government.

Vice President Stephens, acting like a one-man independent government, headed for Washington, purportedly to discuss prisoner exchange but actually to sound out Lincoln on peace negotiations. At Fortress Monroe, he was stopped by a message from the now confident Federal government: "The customary agents and channels are adequate for all needful . . . conferences between the United States forces and the insurgents."

Desertions in Confederate ranks mounted until they equaled proportionately the heavy desertions from the Union forces. As quick as he was to pass judgment on men in terms of the most adamant abstract principles, Davis could not bear to know that a deserter was condemned to death, once a wife or parent had made him aware that an individual personality was concerned. He pardoned so many deserters that even the humane Robert E. Lee begged him to desist in the interest of morale. But the general's plea was of no avail.

Morale in the armies of the Confederacy was not helped by the lack of food and clothing. This deficiency was due partly to the South's inadequate facilities and resources, a problem made worse by the ravages of the invader. But it was also due in part to inefficiency of distribution under the Commissary General, Lucius Northrop. That officer had been a West Point classmate of the President's. Nothing in his previous experience fitted him for the role, but no amount of criticism had thus far changed Davis's convictions about his qualifications for the job. Northrop's concern with protocol and established procedure may have appealed to the President. Historians of the Confederacy have written much about "constriction of the thin gray lines." The story of retreat should be told, too, in terms of strangulation by thin lines of red tape.

Already, the shortage of food and sky-high inflation had caused a civilian riot in Richmond in the terrible year of 1863. A crowd of women and a few boys had collected outside the government offices and finally, numbering more than a thousand, had spilled like a boiling flood downhill to Main Street and into produce stores on Cary. Led by an Amazon with fire in her eyes, the screaming mob of muscular women bore down on hapless merchants cowering behind locked doors. Swinging axes and clubs they smashed the windows like Parisian harridans of the French Revolution.

Despite their athletic prowess, they were still women. And their femininity asserted itself when they broke into a milliner's stock, appropriating hats as one of the necessities of life along with the bread which they had originally sought.

The riot was rapidly becoming an orgy of destruction, a release for all the pentup passions and frustrations of life in a beleaguered city. Davis hurried from his office to the very heart of the violence. By that time, the city battalion was threatening to fire on the enraged women.

Davis climbed up on a cart and called out. He probably could not be heard above the din. The erect, emaciated figure in their midst must have caught the women's attention. He wore a goatee now, and the grayness showed in both hair and beard. The mob began to quiet down out of curiosity. Davis must have thought of the angry squatters that he had faced in Dubuque when he was a "baby-faced lieutenant."

The crowd of milling women, now hushed to hear their President, comprised a more privileged audience than the one that had heard him deliver his inaugural address a few blocks away in the shadow of Washington's statue. They saw and heard a man, not an abstraction. Davis was visibly moved by the suffering that had provoked them to violence. They soon realized that they were listening to a human being concerned with their problems. He told them that their tactics would only keep all food out of the city. He said that the bayonets now threatening them should be freed for use against the enemy, so that all might once again eat their bread in peace. Slowly, the mob dissolved.

Small wonder that, with such domestic problems afflicting the Confederacy while failures in the field forecast disaster, Davis had a return of the old neuralgic pain and that this time even the sight of his good eye was threatened.

And the news read by those tortured eyes only tightened the tension of his nerves. The proportions of the diplomatic defeats at Vicksburg and Gettysburg became apparent in September when Britain, in obedience to United States demands, informed Richmond that iron-clad rams being constructed for the Confederacy would never be permitted to leave Liverpool.

In the same month, events reached a climax in the West. Rosecrans successfully maneuvered Bragg out of Chattanooga, "Gateway to the East," without having to fire a shot. Davis rushed Longstreet with 11,000 troops to Bragg's aid. At Chickamauga, near Chattanooga, the Confederates defeated Rosecrans so badly that only the magnificent self-command and personal force of Union General George H. Thomas prevented a rout. Rosecrans retired into Chattanooga, and Bragg, instead of pursuing, merely invested the city. The Confederate general failed to realize the scope of his own accomplishment and threw away the opportunity to win undisputed success. In November, Bragg was defeated at Lookout Mountain and was routed from Missionary Ridge.

With his untutored, straight-to-the-mark eloquence, Confederate General Nathan Bedford Forrest asked, "Why does the man fight battles?" In more roundabout ways, virtually all of Bragg's officers asked the same question. The commander's dyspeptic personality did not help ameliorate the general dissatisfaction. By October, the officers were almost in revolt and Davis again hurried to the West to study the situation for himself. In Bragg's presence, he asked each of the subordinate generals what he thought of the commander. To a man, they agreed that he "could be of better service elsewhere."

At last, Bragg—retreating into North Georgia—resigned. With grave misgivings and hurt pride, Davis reappointed Johnston to active command of the Army of Tennessee. But, still loyal to Bragg and to his own judgment of men, Davis brought his friend to Richmond as military adviser to the President. How could an ignorant man like Forrest take the measure of a West Pointer like Bragg? Natural military genius did not catch Davis's eye unless it was clad in polished armor.

The people of the Confederacy were desperate, and they turned on Davis the hatred born of desperation. His tender regard for Bragg placed the seal on his growing unpopularity.

In March, Lincoln commissioned Grant a lieutenant general and made him the commander of Union armies in the field. Grant began the costly but persistent destruction of the only two remaining Confederate armies of real consequence—Lee's Army of Northern Virginia and Johnston's Army of Tennessee.

Numbers and time were on Grant's side. The Confederate forces, pitifully smaller than their adversaries and now daily diminished by desertions, were made up in large part of beardless boys and white-bearded men.

In these circumstances, Davis was urged repeatedly to offer slaves their freedom in exchange for military service. But, ever the strict constitutionalist, he had convictions unaltered by exigency. The central government of the Confederacy, he maintained, had no more right to free slaves than the central government of the old Union.

On April 30, Davis must have anticipated the poet's thought that "April is the cruelest month." Outside the windows of his office, the trees were poignantly alive with the bright, new green of April in Virginia. Their shadows were lengthening on the brick pavements. The warm air, redolent of the tobacco warehouses, carried to a sensitive nose a delicate foretaste of the floral fragrance that was the heavy distillation of spring nights in the South. Joe, the little son who sometimes seemed a reincarnation of his small brother who had died in Washington, would be playing now on the lawn of the Executive Mansion or around the classic portico and its rails which challenged his acrobatic skill.

How long would he play there? The children and Varina might soon have to flee Richmond. With spring would come Grant's great offensive against the city. Every blossom of burgeoning life was like a funeral flower for the capital.

Suddenly Varina was at the door, her dark eyes soft with sympathy, a tray in her hand. She pushed aside the papers in front of him and placed the tray on his desk, uncovering the dishes with which she hoped to tempt his appetite.

A servant burst into the room. "Little Joe's done fallen off the porch rail onto the walk and we're scared he's dying."

Davis and Varina dashed down the steps and along the sidewalks to the White House. They ran through the silent rooms to the little boy's bed chamber. There he lay, apparently asleep with the gentle look that he so often wore when he let the smiling mask of mischief drop. But only a few times did the little chest rise and fall, and then there was the stillness of death.

Downstairs, later, Davis was tautly controlled. A courier arrived with an urgent message for the President. He looked at the note. Then, turning to Varina with a trancelike expression, he asked, "Did you tell me what was in it?"

He tried to write an answer, but could not. "I must have this day with my little child," he said. And, staring fixedly ahead, he slowly mounted the stairs.

After dark, friends began to arrive. The windows of the mansion were still open. The odors of the spring night, heavy as incense, entered on the breezes that blew in the curtains and flickered the gaslights.

In some chamber, a woman of the household staff was weeping. Little Jeff, still confused by what had happened to his brother, was protesting, "I have said all the prayers I know, but God will not wake Joe." All else was silence except for a sound from above the high-ceilinged living room—the regular fall of footsteps, the sound of a man pacing back and forth, alone.

Four days later, Grant crossed the Rapidan and entered the Wilderness. The next day Lee attacked his right flank, and in a three-day battle the Virginian completely outmaneuvered his opponent.

Then came the bloody battles of Spotsylvania Court House and Cold Harbor. In the month ending June 12, Grant's losses equaled Lee's total strength. But the Union had men to spare.

Grant then decided to approach Richmond by way of Petersburg and laid siege to the smaller city.

On July 17, while Petersburg neared the end of its first month of siege, Sherman's army crossed the Chattahoochee River and encamped only eight miles from Atlanta. Johnston had fought skillful defense actions and had conducted an efficient retreat. But Davis wanted an offensive and he believed that one was practicable. Bragg backed him up in the conviction that Johnston should launch an offensive. But Johnston himself still talked in defensive terms when he consented to talk at all.

Was Johnston going to give up Atlanta without a fight? Should he be removed from command? For a gentleman of Davis's code, the decision was embarassingly difficult because of the bad blood between him and the general. For a long time, he paced alone. When at last he went upstairs to bed, he exclaimed to Varina, "If I could take one wing and Lee the other, I think between us we could wrest a victory from these people."

The next morning the President wired Bragg, who was now with Johnston's army, for advice. Bragg advised removal of Johnston. With the cabinet's approval, Davis relieved Johnston of command and appointed John Hood in his place.

Hood launched an offensive, and on September 1 had to evacuate Atlanta.

In that same month, Davis was forced to face a bitter fact: "Two thirds of our men are absent . . . most of them absent without leave."

In January, February, and March, Sherman moved north through South Carolina and into North Carolina, leaving a trail of ashes. By now, Davis—in response, for once, to public clamor—had named Lee commander-in-chief of all Confederate forces. Lee had restored Johnston to command of the Army of Tennessee, which was still making its enforced tour of the South with an unwelcome cavalry escort provided by Sherman.

Political negotiations for peace without duress were now manifestly impossible. Davis had appointed Confederate commissioners to confer with Lincoln and Seward aboard the Union transport *River Queen*. But Davis's insistence on Southern independence and Lincoln's adamant stand for union had doomed the conference from the start.

Toward the end of March, Lee, outnumbered more than two to one, made a desperate effort to break through Grant's lines and failed.

Flight

When Davis came home from the office, Varina knew from his pale face and compressed lips that something terrible had happened.

Taking her into trembling arms, he told her that she and the children must leave Richmond.

She realized argument was useless. Even in this moment of domestic grief, her husband's mind was fixed upon the abstractions by which he lived and for which he was prepared to die. He told her, "I do not expect to survive the end of constitutional liberty."

He gave her a pistol, telling her, "You can at least force your assailant to kill you."

He went to the train station with Varina and the children, and boarded their car. Then, in the awkward moment of parting when anything to be said seemed so unimportant beside what must be left unsaid, his little daughter grasped him and clung to him in a trembling paroxysm of grief. Davis put her down, took one look at the white faces of his little family against the rusty red plush of the worn upholstery, and then strode briskly from the car.

On Sunday, the first Sunday of April 1865, Davis was in his pew at St. Paul's Episcopal Church when a man walked up the aisle and handed him a telegram. It was from General Lee, and read: "I advise that all preparation be made for leaving Richmond tonight. I will advise you later, according to circumstances."

Quietly, Davis rose from his seat and walked out of the church. That night a crowd was gathered at the station when Davis and several of his cabinet boarded a train for the South. Immaculate in Confederate gray waistcoat and breeches and a Prince Albert, a broad-brimmed hat on his patrician head, his carefully trimmed goatee gray in the depot lights, he was the living ideal of the Southern planter, the embodiment of a legend that could outlive reality. Some who saw him then thought that he was not merely resigned to his role, but actually content with it.

Richmonders saw two Presidents within the space of a day. A few hours after Davis left the city, Lincoln entered it. He walked to the White House of the Confederacy and sat in the very chair that Davis had sat in. The fortunes of war, political and military, had brought these two sons of the Kentucky frontier to occupy the same seat. The lean, rawboned Lincoln with the look of rugged patience contrasted sharply with the fine-drawn, thin-skinned, patrician-looking man who had sat there a short while before. Later, Lincoln stood in Capitol Square beneath the equestrian statue of Washington in whose shadow Davis had stood at his inauguration. The face of Washington was obviously not that of a man who cracked jokes on momentous occasions. Washington had been cast in bronze before he was ever a statue. But Lincoln was of a different mold. He stared at Washington's outstretched arm, which pointed southward. "Washington is looking at me," said Lincoln, "and pointing to Jeff Davis."

Already, Lincoln's soldiers were making plans for capture of the Confederate President. Privately, Lincoln confided that he hoped Davis would escape.

The Confederate President had not gone far. And, though he had parted with many impediments to flight, the prerogatives of his office were not among them. He had halted in Danville, where he was tendered the use of a comfortable home. Citizens of this small, Southside Virginia tobacco town preened themselves on its being the new capital of the Confederacy.

Davis was buoyed by these proofs of enthusiasm for the cause. An artist once remarked that Davis had the face of a poet. Certainly there was something in him that responded to the poetry and the drama of events. Almost unquestionably, he felt himself a man of destiny. He loved English literature, and the figure of the leader at bay rallying his forces has been a dear one to the Saxon imagination since the days of Alfred. Certainly, Davis—his nerves worn raw by his Richmond trials, then pulled taut by the necessity for flight—was now quivering with exhilaration. Partly he was stimulated by fresh adulation, partly by escape from the immediate physical scene of old problems, and undoubtedly in large measure by his consciousness of an heroic role.

He issued a proclamation, not to prepare the people of the South for defeat but to encourage them to fresh exertions. He declared that tremendous benefits would accrue from the freeing of the "finest army of the Confederacy" from the duty of defending Richmond.

"We have now entered a new phase of the struggle," he declared. "Relieved from the necessity of guarding particular points, our army will be free . . . to strike the enemy in detail far from his base. . . . Animated by that confidence in your spirit and fortitude which has never yet failed me, I announce to you, fellow countrymen, that it is my purpose to maintain your cause with my whole heart and soul."

Impatiently, Davis awaited word from Lee's army. He was confident that Lee, having abandoned Richmond, was on his way to Danville. Here the "finest army of the Confederacy" could defend its new seat of government.

But, as Saturday night arrived without any word from Lee, Davis became anxious and summoned his cabinet to a meeting around the dining room table in the house which he occupied. The tight-faced President, his smooth-browed and relaxed secretary of state, and the other government officers, wearing expressions ranging between these two extremes, were speculating on Lee's whereabouts when a teenaged lieutenant entered the room with a message from the general himself. The young man was John S. Wise, son of fiery General Henry A. Wise. He handed to one of the men credentials showing that he was authorized to deliver his message orally.

Then, standing at the opposite end of the table from the President, he told him that Lee had retreated west beyond the railroad to Danville and could not turn south to the city.

The news was a shock, but Davis addressed Wise with a quiet courtesy which the lieutenant found surprising under the circumstances. "Do you think General Lee will be able to reach a point of safety with his army?" the President asked.

Without hesitation, the lieutenant replied: "I regret to say, no. From what I saw and heard, I am satisfied that General Lee must surrender. It may be that he has done so today."

Then young Wise proved as outspoken as his father. "In my opinion, Mr. President, it is only a question of a few days at furthest, and if I may be permitted to add a word, I think the sooner the better; for, after seeing what I have seen of the two armies, I believe the result is inevitable, and postponing the day means only the useless effusion of noble, gallant blood."

Young Wise saw shock on nearly every face before him. He realized then that "none of them had heard such a plain statement of this unwelcome truth before."

On Monday, Davis learned that Lee had surrendered the day before. In the rain and the dark, with too many cars attached to a wheezing engine, a train pulled out of Danville bearing southward Davis, his cabinet, and all the refugees who could squeeze inside the cars. Davis had withdrawn within himself and even the members of his cabinet dared not intrude upon his mood. No such inhibitions afflicted a young woman refugee who, overjoyed at finding herself seated very near the President, seized the opportunity to talk to him incessantly. Her chatter was as monotonous as the click-click of the rails—and much faster.

Stoneman's Union cavalry was rapidly closing in on the Presidential train. Someone set fire to one railroad trestle as soon as the last car passed over it. The timbers were ablaze before the two rear lanterns merged into a fading penumbra and vanished in the mist.

The train stopped in Greensboro. Here Davis would have established another capital, but the people were willing to forego the honor. They expected to see blue uniforms in the street almost hourly and had already held a pro-Union rally. Davis had to remain on the train a long time before a grudging landlord found a room for him.

The second night in Greensboro, the cabinet members gathered in the President's room to hear reports from Generals Johnston and Beauregard. Seats were too few. Davis began with pleasantries as though he were in Richmond with the strong gray wall of the Army of Northern Virginia at its peak between him and his enemies. But only Benjamin was inclined to smile. Johnston's face was like hard, polished marble except for the vertical frown marks above his nose, like warning exclamation points. Beauregard's face was equally rigid, like pock-marked stone except for the sad, accusing "bloodhound eyes."

Davis saw that he had misgauged his audience. He immediately became as solemn as they. "I think we can whip the enemy yet," he said, "if our people will turn out."

Silence followed. Then Davis asked for the generals' views.

They spared him nothing. They stated, and buttressed with cruel facts, their conviction that the South was beaten.

Finally, with tight-lipped self-control maintained with incalculable effort, Davis authorized Johnston to seek terms from Sherman. When the generals and the cabinet members filed out of the room, Davis was a model of dignified composure. A few hours later, he left town— recumbent in an ambulance.

Arriving in Charlotte on April 19, Davis received a warm welcome reminiscent of Danville. But he also received a telegram announcing the assassination of Abraham Lincoln. Andrew Johnson, the grim little bulldog who had buried his hatred of Davis in a shallow grave as a dog buries a bone against the exigencies of another day, was President of the United States. "I certainly have no special regard for Mr. Lincoln," said Davis, "but there are a great many men of whose end I would much rather have heard than his."

In Charlotte, individual members of the official party began to tell the President goodbye as they prepared to flee for their freedom. When Davis left Charlotte for Yorkville, South Carolina, still hoping to find a new capital, only Benjamin, Reagan and Mallory remained of the cabinet. The President was well enough to ride horseback.

On May 3, the diminished caravan reached Abbeville, South Carolina. There was a letter from Varina, who was now in Washington, Georgia : "Oh, my dearest, precious husband, the one absorbing love of my whole life, may God keep you from harm."

Just before Davis himself reached the Georgia town, Benjamin and Mallory parted from him. Breckinridge, who had rejoined Davis after participating in Johnston's negotiations with Sherman, said goodbye to the President in the town.

At this point, Davis might have saved himself by fleeing either to the coast or to the West, where there were still unsurrendered Confederate forces. But, instead, accompanied by a few loyal soldiers, he headed for Florida. He must find his wife and children. He dared not think of her fate if she fell into the hands of vengeful Yankees. And he was forced to admit that not all the disillusioned Confederates stumbling home, some more than half drunk, were impeccable gentlemen. Rumor was abroad that large sums of money were secreted on Varina's person.

Near one midnight, Davis and his companions were riding southward over a sandy road. Suddenly the sharp cry of "Halt!" came out of the darkness. Instantly, they drew rein. "Who comes there?" was the next demand.

"Friends," Davis replied in a firm voice.

Recognizing a familiar voice, the sentry stepped nearer. It was Davis's secretary, Burton Harrison.

A few minutes later, Davis held Varina in his arms. She and the children had fared well under Harrison's protection.

The next day, Davis rode on with his family. But the morning after, reassured by the fact that Harrison would still be with them, he told the little party goodbye with the hope of reaching some point in the West from which the fight could be carried on.

The separation was short. Lost in a fog, Davis and his companions soon came unexpectedly upon his wife's party. Once again, the two groups traveled together. This time they made camp near Irwinsville, in South Georgia. Harrison urged the President to push on. He was afraid that the Federal cavalry might be nearer than the fifty miles supposed to lie between them and Irwinsville. But Davis "seemed entirely unable to apprehend the danger of capture."

Davis thought it unnecessary to move on. But, in case marauders should come, he lay down in his wife's tent with all his clothes on, even his gray frock coat, thinking to keep watch over his family. But, through utter weariness, he sank into a deep sleep.

He would not have slept so easily if he had known the orders issued to a Federal colonel in the area:

"You will have every port and ferry on the Ocmulgee and

Altamaha rivers . . . well guarded, and make every effort to capture or kill Jefferson Davis, the rebel ex-President, who is supposed to be endeavoring to cross."

Davis was roused at daylight by a black servant, who told him there was firing across the creek. Stepping out of the tent, he saw men on horseback deploying along the road. He knew at once that they were not mere marauders, but Federal cavalry.

Davis's horse stood by the road, saddled, and the President's pistols were in saddle holsters. The Yankee horsemen were almost at the tent, but Davis made a dash for the horse, throwing a cloak around him as he ran. Varina threw a shawl about his shoulders.

Before he could reach his horse, a horseman yelled, "Halt!" Turning toward him, Davis looked into a carbine. Again the man yelled "Halt!" Davis lunged forward and the man took careful aim. At that moment Varina flung her arms about her husband.

By this time, the little camp was full of Union soldiers. Davis detached himself from his wife's embrace and walked back toward the tent with her. Now Davis's companions were all prisoners, too. Turning to one of them, Colonel F. R. Lubbock, he said, "I would have heaved the scoundrel off his horse as he came up, but she stopped me."

"It would have been useless," the colonel said. Davis did not argue the point. He sat down by a small fire which had been built behind the tent.

A moment later Colonel Pritchard, commander of the Union cavalry, dismounted and walked toward the President. The officer was savoring this moment. "Well, old Jeff, we've got you at last."

Davis flung his head back. "The worst of all," he shouted, "is that I should be captured by a gang of thieves and scoundrels."

Already, grinning, blue-coated cavalrymen were emerging from Mrs. Davis's tent with their plunder. But Pritchard assumed an attitude of injured dignity and said, "You're a prisoner and can afford to talk that way."

A few minutes later, Pritchard told the President that he must get up and move along. The cry was eagerly taken up by saber-wielding young men, who yelled, "Move along, old Jeff!"

Herded into an ambulance, Davis and his family rode to Macon under heavy guard. When they reached the city several days later, Davis was escorted to the headquarters of Brevet Major-General Wilson. The Union officer handed the Confederate President a Presidential proclamation from Washington. With a scornful eye, Davis scanned the phrases:

Whereas, it appears from evidence in the Bureau of Military Justice, that the atrocious murder of the late President, Abraham Lincoln, and the attempted assassination of the Honorable William H. Seward, Secretary of State, were incited, concerted and procured by and between Jefferson Davis . . . and other rebels and traitors against the government of the United States . . . , Now, therefore, to the end that justice may be done, I, Andrew Johnson, President of the United States, do offer and promise . . . one hundred thousand dollars for the arrest of Jefferson Davis.

"There is one man at least," said Davis, "who knows the charge to be false."

"Who is that?" asked Wilson.

"The man who signed the proclamation, for he well knew that I greatly preferred Lincoln to himself."

Through Suffering, Apotheosis

On May 22, at 2 P.M., Davis, his face flushed but arrogant in its composure, descended the gangplank of the steamer *Clyde*. His right arm was tightly grasped by Union Brevet Major-General Miles, elegant in his blue and gold uniform. The general had dressed carefully for the historic moment.

Thus Davis returned to Fortress Monroe, where, a little over a decade before, when he had been laboring as Secretary of War to preserve the Union, he had been accorded a military escort under quite different circumstances. Then his name had blazed in the sky in a shower of fireworks, and the crowd had cheered him lustily.

Davis's cell was the inner room of a casemate. Here he was parted from Reagan, the faithful postmaster general, who had chosen to share the last moment possible with his chief.

Reagan, now that the moment was here, could think of nothing to say that seemed adequate. Davis asked him to read the sixteenth psalm aloud. "It gives me comfort."

In his honest Texas drawl, Reagan read : "Preserve me, O God : for in thee do I put my trust. . . ."

The two men shook hands. Reagan turned his sad face away and walked out. The Texan, though a gentleman in the highest sense of the word, put little store in the hallmarks of gentility that Davis had been taught to prize so highly. This intensely practical postmaster general, who despite incredible difficulties had kept his department going throughout the war and at a profit, was little bemused by some of the abstractions which Davis found absorbing. But Reagan knew the high-hearted man within the shell. Of Davis, Reagan later wrote, "I loved him as I never loved any other man."

The circumstances of Davis's confinement were effectively described by the *New York Herald,* which exulted : "He is literally in a living tomb. . . . It may, in fact, be said, that neither the great Napoleon at Elba or St. Helena, the lesser Napoleon at the Fortress of Ham, nor any other state prisoner of the centuries, was subjected to greater surveillance. . . ."

The masonry walls, the barred windows and doors, the lamp always burning in the cell, night and day, the guard's eye always upon him, the four-score armed men outside—all these made escape indeed impossible. But they were not deemed sufficient.

Davis was sitting on the end of his cot toward evening of the second day, reading from his *Book of Common Prayer.* The door clanged open and he looked up to see, standing before him, a captain in the Union army.

"Mr. Davis," said the man, "I have an unpleasant duty to execute."

Behind the officer was a man wearing a blacksmith's apron and carrying the tools of the trade.

Davis looked into the officer's eyes. "You do not intend to put fetters on me?"

"Those are my orders," said the soldier.

"Those are orders for a slave," Davis protested, "and no man with a soul in him would obey such orders."

"Those are my orders," the officer repeated.

"I shall never submit to such an indignity!" Davis cried out. "Did General Miles give that order?"

"He did."

"I would like to see General Miles."

"The general has just left the fort."

Davis then asked that execution of the order be postponed until the general's return. He also asked that a telegram be sent in his name to the President.

"Mr. Davis," the officer replied, "you are an old soldier and know what orders are. It is needless to say that an officer is bound to execute an order given him."

"There can be no necessity for such an order to make my imprisonment secure."

"My duty," said the soldier, "is to execute this order and it is folly for you to resist."

Davis was on his feet. Despite the way his suit bagged on his scarecrow limbs, despite all the visible evidence of nerve torture, he was an imperial figure. Fixing the officer with a look of scorn he pointed to a sentinel, and said, "I *am* a soldier and I know how to die. Let your men shoot me at once."

There was a moment of silence. Davis put his foot on a stool and stood quietly.

The officer turned to the blacksmith. "Smith, do your work."

The blacksmith stooped to fasten the clasp of the shackle around the President's ankle. Davis's fist shot out in a blow that floored the man.

Struggling to his feet, the smith raised his hammer to strike Davis. The officer grabbed the upraised arm.

Next, the sentinel and Davis were struggling for possession of the guard's musket. The sentinel succeeded in breaking Davis's grip on the weapon.

The officer sent for four of the strongest guardsmen. In unison, they closed in on Davis. He struck the first one, but they overpowered him and threw him down on the cot. Still, it was all that the four of them could do to hold him down while the blacksmith riveted one clasp around one ankle and fastened the other with a freight-car lock.

The officer ordered the men back to their quarters. Davis lay motionless except for his heavy breathing. Then, when the officer himself was almost outside the door, Davis raised himself up and threw his feet to the floor. The heavy chains clanged on the stone. Not a murmur came from the compressed lips, but—in defiance of the iron will—tears rolled down the tight-drawn cheeks.

The next day, Dr. John H. Craven, surgeon of the fort, visited the prisoner. He later reported :

"Stretched upon his pallet, and very much emaciated, Mr. Davis appeared a mere fascine of raw and tremulous nerves—his eyes restless and fevered, his head continually shifting from side to side for a cool spot on the pillow, and his case clearly one in which intense cerebral excitement was the first thing needing attention."

Newspaper stories of the shackling of President Davis soon brought bitter criticism not only from the foreign press, but also from influential Northern newspapers. In obedience to public opinion, the fetters were removed.

Dr. Craven, who had been strongly prejudiced against Davis before meeting him, was moved first to pity, then to sympathy and admiration, in the course of daily visits. Repeatedly, he informed General Miles and others that the patient might not survive if the conditions of his imprisonment were not eased.

Dr. Craven was removed. But his successor soon began to take a sympathetic interest in Davis's plight and concurred in Craven's recommendations.

At last, after General Miles's transfer to another post, Davis was granted a little more freedom. Still, though, his family were not permitted to visit him.

He no longer suffered the tortures which he had described to Dr. Craven : "The consciousness that the Omniscient eye rests upon us in every situation is the most consoling and beautiful belief of religion, but to have a human eye riveted on you in every moment of waking or sleeping, sitting, walking or lying down, is a refinement of torture on anything the Comanches or Spanish Inquisition ever dreamed. . . . The lamp burning in my room all night, shooting its rays . . . into my throbbing eyeballs, one of them already sightless from neuralgia, is torture of most intense agony."

But, now that these tortures were past, his life was still miserable. The opportunity to hear a little from the outside world brought its own quota of pain. Davis learned that his public image was that of coward and villain. When he was captured, he wore his wife's cloak, which he had grabbed by mistake in the dark tent, and she had thrown a shawl about his shoulders. Rumor and malice had quickly distorted the story until even in the South it was quite generally believed that he had donned petticoats and skirts in the hope of eluding detection. Davis found this distortion of his public image as painful as the very real ravages wrought upon his physical self by painful confinement. He learned that many Northerners sincerely believed that he had plotted the murder of Lincoln. He was confident that he could clear his public record if only he could be tried in court. But his constitutional right of trial was denied him. Month after month passed while, without benefit of trial, he suffered the punishment of imprisonment.

But the traditional American sense of justice, at first all but smothered by hate and hysteria, began to assert itself. Prominent New Yorkers, most of them stout foes of secession, began to insist that Davis be given a hearing. These citizens obtained the services of

Charles O'Conor, one of America's greatest lawyers. He wrote to Davis, offering to confer with him at any time. Davis replied with deep gratitude. But military censors did not permit his letter to be sent. Suspecting the censorship, O'Conor then sought permission to talk with Davis. This right of the prisoner to confer with an attorney was denied by both the Attorney General and the Secretary of War.

Reasons for the denial of civil rights to Davis are made clearer by a statement by Chief Justice Chase to officers of the Johnson Administration. "If you bring [Davis and his colleagues] to trial," he said, "it will condemn the North, for by the Constitution secession is not rebellion. Trials for treason in the civil courts are not remedies adapted to the close of a great civil war. Honor forbids a resort to them after combatants in open war have recognized each other as soldiers and gentlemen engaged in legitimate conflict. . . . It would be shockingly indecorous for the ultimate victor in such a conflict to send his vanquished opponent before the civil magistrate to be tried as if he were a mere thief or rioter."

Meanwhile, indignation about Davis's illegal confinement mounted in influential circles. Seeking an easy way out, friends of the Administration intimated to Davis that he could be freed without trial if he would only apply for pardon.

Davis, contending that a request to be pardoned for treason would be an admission of guilt, flatly refused.

President Johnson sought Chase's advice. The Chief Justice told him, "We cannot convict him of treason."

At last, with famous Northerners including Horace Greeley offering to sign Davis's bond, the federal government presented its case against Davis to a grand jury in Norfolk, Virginia. That body found that he had committed treason while "moved and seduced by the instigation of the devil."

Subsequently, the federal judiciary declared that the indictment had been "lost from the records of the court."

On June 5, 1866, after Davis had been in prison for 13 months, Attorney William B. Reed appeared before the federal court in

Richmond to plead for "a speedy trial on any charge that may be brought against Mr. Davis, here or in any other civil tribunal in the land. We may be now here representing, may it please the Court, a dying man."

On May 4, 1867, after nearly two years of imprisonment, Davis was conducted to Richmond to appear before the federal court, Judge Underwood presiding. Excitement in Richmond ran so high that Davis was guarded by a company of infantry when he was driven by carriage the next morning to the old Custom House, where the court sat. Ironically, the building which Davis now entered was the old Confederate office building. Beneath its roof he had wrestled with the problems of command, had conducted his voluminous correspondence with irate governors and recalcitrant generals. And here he and Varina, on another spring day not unlike this one, had received the news of little Joe's fall.

When Davis entered the packed courtroom, the excited crowd saw a thin old man with gray hair, gray goatee, and furrowed cheeks. But it was not hard to see in this emaciated frame the figure of the proud young officer who many years before, at a court martial, had placed his accuser on trial. One who was present in the Richmond courtroom wrote :

"Mr. Davis, though looking better than I expected, is only the shadow of his former self, but with all his dignity and high, unquenchable manhood. As he entered the densely crowded courtroom, with his proud step and lofty look, every head reverently bowed to him and a stranger would have sworn that he was the judge and Underwood the culprit."

The courtroom drama lasted only a few minutes. The attorney general of the United States rose to declare that it was not the government's "intention to prosecute the trial of the prisoner at the present term of the court." Davis was then released on $100,000 bond, subscribed by prominent Northerners, to have "liberty of free locomotion," until the government was prepared to try him.

The crowd understood that the Administration had taken an easy way out. Davis would never be tried, but he was a free man. When he stepped into the street, escorted by his two lawyers, the infantry guard had vanished. A laughing, weeping crowd pressed in upon him. Suddenly a wild cry went up and was chorused by the throng. It was the rebel yell.

As he stepped into the carriage, and as he rode to his hotel, that same fierce cry of jubilation followed him. Then, as he left his carriage and walked toward the hotel door, someone shouted, "Hats off, Virginians!" In an instant, silence prevailed and virtually every head was bared in reverence.

The scapegoat of the Confederacy had become its martyr. Through suffering, Jefferson Davis had gained apotheosis.

In the first years of his freedom, he traveled, receiving hearty welcomes in Canada, Cuba, Britain, and the European continent. Though Paris staged parades in his honor, he declined an invitation from the Emperor. He could not forget the monarch's policy of encouraging the Confederacy while withholding recognition.

Davis became president of a Tennessee insurance firm that failed, carrying with it most of his savings. Brother Joseph died, and so did another son.

But at last he found peace. He made his home at Beauvoir, a plantation on Mississippi's Gulf Coast. He sat in his rocker on the verandah and looked across the short space of lawn, green with the tropical lushness of the Gulf country, to where the blue waves lapped gently against the glistening white barrier of the shell bank. And he looked beyond, to where the blue of the Gulf mingled with the blue of the sky. Behind the house stretched a thousand acres of pine and cypress. The scene was different from that of the plantation where Jefferson Davis had been reared. It was painted in the truer-than-life postcard hues of the tropics. But in spirit the scene was not different. The sense of warm earth brooding under a brassy sun was there. The white-columned verandah was very nearly the same. But the Jeff Davis who sat upon it was quite different from the golden-haired, small boy of those earlier days. He was a silver-haired, goateed Southern gentleman in white linen. Looking at him, it was hard to believe that the war was over and lost, and with it a way of life.

In these days, he wrote a two-volume apologia for that way, the *Rise and Fall of the Confederate Government*. Characteristically, he asserted in it that the war had proved secession impracticable but had not proved it illegal.

In 1886, he toured the South, receiving in the capitals of Mississippi, Alabama, and Georgia such adulation as would have been denied him during most of his Presidency.

On December 6, 1889, when he was in his 81st year, he died in New Orleans en route home from a visit to Brierfield, where he had walked with his memories in a cold rain. Varina was with him.

The New York *World* declared, "A great soul has passed away."

Four years later, he returned to Richmond, in a coffin instead of a carriage. Richmond had begged for the honor. The old dowager by the James was surer than ever of what she had maintained long ago : that Jefferson Davis was a gentleman. In Hollywood Cemetery, where lie so many of Virginia's immortals, "close where the James goes rolling by," he was laid to rest.

In 1907, William E. Dodd, a Virginian who had won international distinction as a diplomat and as an interpreter of Southern history, said of the Richmond cemetery, "There the visitor to the capital of the 'lost cause' may now stand by the grave of its most perfect representative." The "perfect representative" of the Old South—Jefferson Davis would have liked that description. So would Brother Joseph. And so would Samuel.

Davis was content to leave his utterances and his career to the verdict of history. What does history say about him? Historians say many different things. His supporters and detractors are campaigning almost as vigorously as in his lifetime. But history has not made a pronouncement. The ballots are not yet in.

In the opinion of at least one elector who is trying hard to be objective, it must be conceded that Davis was not successful as President of the Confederacy. His saving of Lee's services for the infant government was almost counterbalanced by his incessant quarreling with other generals and stubborn support of incompetent officers. He brought to the Confederacy not only the asset of a stiff backbone but also the liability of a stiff neck.

But a great question remains : who could have done a better job? Certainly not the other Southern politicians who believed that they should have been President. Few had his intellectual stature. None excelled him in moral conviction. None equaled him in loyalty to the Confederacy as a region and an abstraction. No better prepared leader could have been found outside the ranks of politicians. Robert E. Lee had the moral stature and the intellectual force to head the government, but he had no experience in statecraft. Lincoln, for all his genius, was less suited than Davis to be the leader of a revolutionary government. Addiction to action-arresting contemplation is often admirable in a philosopher and occasionally tolerable in the head of a firmly established republic. But it is impossible in the leader of a revolutionary movement.

What American statesman might have been equal to the task that confronted Davis? What man could successfully have united the Confederacy's factions, patched up its constitutional weaknesses, organized its government and armed and disciplined its citizens while withstanding invasion both by land and along an unprotected seacoast? We must move backward through the whole roster of American Presidents before we find a name that makes us pause and say, "Maybe." If any American statesman could successfully have filled the role that Davis was called upon to play, that man was George Washington. The great Virginian had played a similar part in his day, though he did not simultaneously direct the armies of a rebel republic and head its civil government. And he did find the European allies that Davis sought in vain.

The characters of men are as different as their fingerprints. But one President of the United States was strikingly like Davis in gifts and personality. Woodrow Wilson is one of the few American chief executives who have equaled Jefferson Davis in intellectual stature. Both men had, in seclusion, grown in knowledge but acquired the encrustation of dogmatism. Both were emotional men who imposed an iron discipline upon their own rebellious nerves. Both were self-conscious adherents of a high code. Both were intensely loyal to their ideals and to men who, in their judgment, embodied them. Both were intolerant of opposition. With both, self-justification was an obsession. Each needed the reassurance of an "adviser" who could read his mind. Wilson had Colonel House. Davis had his Benjamin.

Each was narrowly legalistic in his approach to public problems and each was baffled by the public's small regard for logic. Each impressed casual acquaintances as cold, but aroused strong emotions in intimate friends and, when deeply moved, could stir multitudes by oratory.

Just as Wilson, in an era of rampant nationalism, thought in terms of a League of Nations, so Davis, in a time when states' rights enthusiasts thought of their states as their countries, gave his intellectual allegiance to the South as an entity.

Each was a wartime President, but Davis had to struggle with traditions whereas Wilson could summon them to his aid. Each man was reviled in his time, but each became a martyr to the cause he served.

Davis was not a Washington in a time and place that demanded a Washington. With no more inaccuracy than is involved in most generalizations, we can say that he was a Woodrow Wilson. To be a Wilson was not enough, but it was to be head and shoulders above most occupants of the White House. As for history's verdict, that is another matter. Clio is not an unbiased judge of men. She records what is behind but looks ahead. She doubtless will be influenced by the fact that Wilson voiced the aspirations of the future, while Davis spoke for the dreams of the past.

JEFFERSON DAVIS
Bibliography

Davis, Varina Howell. *Jefferson Davis, Ex-President of the Confederate States of America, a Memoir by His Wife,* Vols. I and II. New York, 1890. Making due allowances for the bias of a devoted widow, these volumes are still the best source books on Davis. They contain, besides reminiscences of Mrs. Davis, who was an intelligent and articulate woman, Davis's own account of his early life as well as the recollections of many who knew him.

Eaton, Clement. *Jefferson Davis.* New York and London, 1977. This is the best objective, full-length biography of Davis. Particularly valuable are the insights into his domestic life.

Strode, Hudson. *Jefferson Davis.* 1st ed. 3 vols. New York, 1955–64. Strongly pro-Davis, but informative and appealingly written.

Rowland, Dunbar. *Jefferson Davis, Constitutionalist,* Vols. I–X. Jackson, Miss., 1923. A collection of Davis's letters, papers and speeches preserved in the Mississippi Department of Archives and History.

Dodd, William E. *Jefferson Davis.* Philadelphia, 1907. An interesting interpretive study by a man who was both an historian and himself an active participant in government.

Taylor, Richard. *Destruction and Reconstruction.* New York, 1955. The memoirs of the brilliant Confederate lieutenant general who was both Davis's devoted brother-in-law and a staunch friend to Johnston. Particularly valuable are passages describing the conflict between Davis and Johnston, pp. 22–25, 42–45; Davis's habit of "listening to narrators who were more disposed to tell what was

132

agreeable than what was true," pp. 250–252; the years of his imprisonment and subsequent freedom, pp. 302–304. Taylor's account of the Massachusetts delegation's enthusiastic support of Davis at the Democratic National Convention in 1860 derives special validity from the fact that Taylor was a Louisiana delegate to the same convention.

Patrick, Rembert W. *Jefferson Davis and His Cabinet*. Baton Rouge, 1944. A scholarly study as valuable for its sketches of Davis's associates as for its portrayal of the President himself.

Eckenrode, H. J. *Jefferson Davis, President of the South*. New York, 1923. A provocative study whose usefulness is somewhat impaired by the author's tendency to cut the cloth of history with his eyes firmly fixed on his favorite anthropological theories.

Davis, Jefferson. *The Rise and Fall of the Confederate Government*, Vols. I and II. New York, 1881.

Craven, Avery O. *The Coming of the Civil War*. New York, 1942. Excellent analysis of the causes of conflict.

Coulter, E. Merton. *The Confederate States of America, 1861–1865*. Baton Rouge, 1950. The best book on the problems of the Davis Administration.

Eaton, Clement. *A History of the Southern Confederacy*. New York, 1954. Affords insight into problems faced by Davis, especially pp. 46–60.

McElroy, Robert. *Jefferson Davis, the Unreal and the Real*.

Bradford, Gamaliel, Jr., *Lee the American*. Boston and New York, 1912. Especially Chapter III, "Lee and Davis," pp. 48–73.

Dowdey, Clifford. *Experiment in Rebellion*. Garden City, 1950. Good picture of wartime Richmond.

Hendrick, Burton J. *Statesmen of the Lost Cause: Jefferson Davis and His Cabinet*. Boston, 1939.

Johnson, R. U. and Buell, C. C. (eds.). *Battles and Leaders of the Civil War*. New York, 1887–1888. Especially Vol. II, pp. 439–449, Mrs. Burton Harrison's description of Davis and the impression he made on Richmond society, together with her evocation of the Richmond atmosphere in 1862.

Meade, Robert Douthat. *Judah P. Benjamin: Confederate Statesman*. New York, 1943.

Govan, Gilbert E. and Livingood, James W. *A Different Valor, the Story of General Joseph E. Johnston, C. S. A.* Indianapolis, 1956. Hypercritical but valuable references to Davis.

Southern Historical Society Papers, Vol. V, Richmond, 1878, pp. 97–126; Vol. XXVI, Richmond, 1898, pp. 96–101. Informative on the retreat of the cabinet from Richmond and on Davis's flight and capture.

Kean, Garlick Hill. *Inside the Confederate Government: The Diary of Robert Garlick Hill Kean,* ed. Edward Younger. New York, 1957. Comments by the head of the Bureau of War, generally caustic in tone but enlightening regarding Davis's conflicts with subordinates.

Jones, J. B. *A Rebel War Clerk's Diary at the Confederate States Capital,* Vols. I and II. New York, 1935.

Haskell, M. Monroe, Jr. and McIntosh, James T., eds. *The Papers of Jefferson Davis.* Vol. I. Baton Rouge, 1971.

Woodworth, Steven E. *Jefferson Davis and His Generals: The Failure of Confederate Command in the West.* Lawrence, Kan., 1990.

Williams, T. Harry. *Lincoln and His Generals.* New York, 1952. Affords basis of comparison between Lincoln and Davis in handling of generals.

Richmond Dispatch, Richmond Enquirer, and *Richmond Examiner* for appropriate dates of Davis administration (microfilms in Virginia State Library). Particularly informative concerning the opinions and tactics of the President's critics is the *Richmond Examiner.*

NOTE: The works listed above and following subsequent chapters are simply those that have been most useful in the preparation of *Frock Coats and Epaulets,* and appear in the order of their usefulness.

II

ROBERT E. LEE : Man of Disciplined Fire

II

ROBERT E. LEE : Man of Disciplined Fire

Two Boys

A BOY WAS BORN in Westmoreland County, Virginia on January 19, 1807. By the time he was six years old, his father had been in jail twice and had fled the country. Poverty haunted the child's early years.

On the same date and in the same county a son was born to a couple who had united in their marriage two of the most aristocratic names in America. The father had been a great general of the Revolutionary War, had been three times Governor of Virginia, and had been mentioned prominently as a presidential possibility. The boy was born in a mansion that rivaled the great manor houses of England.

These two boys were one and the same : Robert Edward Lee. His father was General Henry (Light Horse Harry) Lee, who had won great distinction in fighting under Washington and later had memorably epitomized his chief as "first in war, first in peace, and first in the hearts of his countrymen." The boy's mother was the former Ann Carter, great-granddaughter of Robert (King) Carter of Corotoman, greatest of Tidewater river barons and ancestor of more famous Americans than any other prominent man of his generation. But unwise investments and exceedingly generous loans to friends had rendered Henry Lee unable to satisfy his creditors and he had gone twice to debtors' prison. The people of Westmoreland had elected him a magistrate after his emergence from prison in order to demonstrate the confidence and esteem in which they still held him. But his financial difficulties increased and eventually he had to put a considerable part of the Atlantic Ocean between himself and his creditors. And so, too, when Robert was only three years old, the family had left the beloved old mansion of Stratford.

An amateur psychiatrist acquainted with the facts of Robert E. Lee's childhood might have predicted that he would grow into a maladjusted man. Reared in an atmosphere compounded of ancestral pride and acute embarrassment, of vestigial elegance and growing poverty, his personality might easily have been warped by conflicting pressures.

Much depended upon the mother, who was the sole parent of the child through most of his formative years. She exemplified the qualities of piety and common sense for which the Carters were distinguished. Through frequent visits to the Carter kin at Shirley on the James, and in fireside conversations at the house in Alexandria which became her home, she impressed young Robert with the traditions of courage and public service to which he was the heir. General Harry Lee's advice was much sounder than his practice, and his cogent letters to his son buttressed the mother's prudent counsels.

In his early teens, the boy completed a course of study at the Alexandria Academy, where he displayed considerable aptitude for Latin and mathematics.

At the age of seventeen, a handsome, brown-eyed, broad-shouldered lad, he applied in person to the Secretary of War for an appointment to West Point. He must have been glad that he bore with him a sheaf of endorsements from some of the most prominent men in Virginia, for that official was no less formidable a person than the renowned John C. Calhoun. His burning eyes and exploding shock of hair gave him a look of startling intensity before which even mature men quailed.

In 1825, young Lee entered the Military Academy. Partly because it provided him with a free education and partly because of filial sentiment for his father's field of glory, he had chosen the profession of arms. The habits of self-discipline inculcated by his mother stood him in good stead under the strict regimen of the Academy. His good conduct record became legendary. Upon graduation he stood first in his class in artillery and tactics and a close second in general scholastic performance. He had won the most coveted distinction in the gift of the Academy, the office of corps adjutant. While making this record, he had found time to serve as acting assistant professor of mathematics and to read such varied extracurricular fare as the *Federalist Papers*, books on seamanship, and Rousseau's *Confessions* in the original French. Independent of his assigned studies, he devoured works on Napoleon's strategy.

His instructors thought of him as a model youth and even fellow cadets remarked on his natural dignity. The bare outlines of his record might suggest an embryo stuffed shirt. But that impression is given the lie by the recollections of his youthful associates. Joseph E. Johnston, a fellow cadet, recalled in later years that young Lee "was full of sympathy and kindness, genial and fond of gay conversation, and even fun. . . . He was the only one of all the men I have known that could laugh at the faults and follies of his friends in such a manner as to make them ashamed without touching their affection for him. . . . " Strangely enough, the brilliance of Lee's achievements seems to have inspired little malicious envy. Johnston said that Robert had "a superiority that everyone acknowledged in his heart."

In Virginia circles, Robert's behavior, and that of his brother Smith, seemed quite conservative when compared with that of their older brother Carter. The two younger Lees were both teetotalers and Carter, the life of many a party, boasted that he drank for the three of them.

Of the three, Robert was closest to his mother. When he left for West Point, sped by her cheerful blessing, she had confessed to another, "How can I live without Robert? He is both son and daughter to me." Almost immediately after graduation, Robert became her constant companion. Long a semi-invalid, she had grown extremely ill and Robert became her nurse. The role was one familiar to him from many of his mother's past sicknesses. Some analysts of his character think that he first learned in her sick room the hard lesson of patience under adversity. On July 10, 1829, with Robert at her side, she died.

Next month, Brevet Second Lieutenant Robert E. Lee was ordered to report for duty to the Corps of Engineers at Cockspur Island in the Savannah River, Georgia. Directing construction work in the muck of a swamp and in water almost to his shoulders, Lee proved that his 5-foot 10-inch physique was as rugged as it looked.

In the summer of 1830, Lee returned on furlough to Virginia and most of his time was spent in the vicinity of Arlington. That famous Custis mansion, with its great Tuscan columns, was built like a Roman temple, and certainly Robert was votary to one who dwelt within. Mary Custis, more attractive in figure than in face, had a good-humored charm that Lee found irresistible. Her father was not particularly happy about Robert's visits. Lee's social background would more than satisfy Mr. Custis, whose chief pride in life was the fact that he was the stepgrandson of George Washington. But he did not want his daughter to become too attached to an impecunious young man dependent on a second lieutenant's pay for a living.

Nevertheless, when Lee returned to his duties on Cockspur Island, Mary was much in his thoughts, even though he solaced his loneliness with a mild flirtation or two in Savannah.

By Lee's next trip to Arlington, it was apparent that, however Mr. Custis might feel about him, Mrs. Custis was a charmed ally. One day when Mary bent over the sideboard to cut the young man a piece of cake, he leaned forward too. His black hair almost touched her blonde curls. In a soft voice, he asked her to be his wife.

On June 30, 1831, handsome in his blue full dress uniform, Robert E. Lee stood in the old mansion before a tall, lean parson. "The minister," Lee said, "had few words to say, though he dealt them as though he had been reading my death warrant, and there was a tremulousness in the hand I held that made me anxious for him to end."

Actually, in those days, Lee was a very happy man. His bantering good humor and delight in teasing his friends were even more evident than usual.

In August, Lee moved with his bride into quarters at Ft. Monroe, Virginia where he was assigned to work with the engineers. The Chesapeake breezes afforded pleasant relief from the heat of summer. Lee's immediate superior was Capt. Andrew Talcott, an able man with a beautiful wife. Both became fast friends of the Lees.

Legs and Footsteps

It is a remarkable tribute to Lee's personality that he was not considered odd by his fellow officers. The post was a high-living one with imported liquors and imported female companions. Lee didn't drink, didn't swear, and didn't gamble. But he could lend a strong supporting arm to a drunk companion and see him safely to his bed. When young officers imbibed too freely, he understood their desire to escape from hard routine, and said, "The poor devils . . . are drilled off their feet." When Mrs. Lee left the post for long visits, she was secure in the knowledge that Robert, unlike some of the other husbands, would not seize the opportunity for illicit romance.

Nevertheless, Robert was far from immune to feminine charms. His eyes always kindled at the sight of a beauty. Once, at a party, his sister introduced him to a group of young ladies. "Sweet, innocent things," he recalled with joy, "they concluded I was single, and I have not had such soft looks and tender pressure of the hand for many years." Once, when he was writing to a friend, he looked down toward the beach, and wrote : "As for the daughters of Eve in this country, they are formed in the very poetry of nature, and would make your lips water and fingers tingle. They are beginning to assemble to put their beautiful limbs into the salt water."

In the fall of 1832, Lee became the father of a boy. The child was named George Washington Custis Lee, in honor of the maternal grandfather, who was now one of Robert's most enthusiastic admirers. Lee's domestic happiness was complete. "I would not be unmarried for all you could offer me," he told a friend, and he declared, "Master Custis is the most darling boy in the world."

The circumstances of his work were not so happy. Opportunities to design buildings, wharves, and fortifications were pleasantly challenging, but deep-rooted controversies between the staff and line officers were disagreeable. Nevertheless, Lee did his work well and with remarkable economy.

Late in 1834, Lee was transferred to Washington to serve as an assistant in the office of General Gratiot, adjutant general. The Lees now made their home at Arlington. The office work was confining and the long rides from the capital to the plantation were disagreeable in bad weather. But Mary was happy to be home again and Lee delighted in the traditions of Arlington and the family's association with George Washington. Most young men adopt as an ideal some man of eminence in their chosen profession. If Washington was not already Lee's ideal, he became so in this period.

The next two years brought heavier domestic responsibilities. A girl was born to the Lees. Mrs. Lee's health, probably never robust, declined considerably and she was much in bed and frequently nervous. In 1836, just up after an extended illness, Mrs. Lee contracted the mumps at the same time that the two children were suffering from the whooping cough. Lee wrote his old friend Talcott that the little Lees were "whooping, coughing, teething, etc., and sometimes all three together." One of Lee's cousins said of him, "I never saw a man so changed and saddened."

Domestic cares were not altogether responsible for his state of mind. General Gratiot was a kindly gentleman. But the office routine was as wearying as it was confining and Lee could not see that it led to promotion. In February 1837, he wrote Talcott a note as bleak as the Washington weather:

You asked what are my prospects in the corps? Bad enough . . . as to what I intend doing, it is rather hard to answer. There is one thing certain, I must get away from here. . . . I should have made a desperate effort last spring, but Mary's health was so bad I could not have left her, and she could not have gone with me. I am waiting, looking and hoping for some good opportunity to bid an affectionate farewell to my dear Uncle Sam. . . .

By the end of June, the entire picture had changed. Mrs. Lee's health was much improved. A new, lusty-lunged little Lee, promptly named William Henry Fitzhugh, had entered the world, and, to cap it all, Lee was sent to St. Louis to apply his engineering skill to a fascinating problem of real magnitude : channel changes in the Mississippi that were threatening to destroy the waterborne commerce of St. Louis.

Lee had to battle the elements, human apathy, and a scarcity of supplies as well as the Father of Waters. But his persistence and ingenuity triumphed. By the building of dykes he directed the mighty river to the task of clearing and maintaining its own channel. The speeches of public officials and the columns of leading newspapers rang with praise of the young Virginian's achievements.

Lee's services on the Mississippi from 1837 to 1839 had not only earned him an enviable reputation in his corps and in the engineering profession, but had also taught him new lessons in accomplishing big things with small resources and in getting along with civilian authority. The mayor of St. Louis had been impressed with Lee's "rich gift of genius and scientific knowledge." But he noted that Lee's character matched his mind in breadth and nobility.

He wrote of him : "He had none of that coddling, and petty, puerile planning and scheming which men of little minds and small intellectual caliber use to make and take care of their fame."

Though Robert E. Lee enjoyed his work in Missouri, his heart was always in Virginia—partly because his family was there a great part of the time and partly because he was a true son of Light Horse Harry Lee, who always called Virginia "my country." During a visit home, he wrote one of his Carter cousins :

I think [the West] is a great country and will one day be a grand one;

all is life, animation and prosperity; but . . . it is far more pleasant for *me* to be here than there. I felt so elated when I again found myself within the confines of the Ancient Dominion that I nodded to all the old trees as I passed, chatted with the drivers and stable-boys, shook hands with the landlords, and in the fullness of my heart—don't tell Cousin Mary—wanted to kiss all the pretty girls I met.

On this trip, Lee greeted a new daughter, the fourth of the children whom he now began to call his "annuals."

In his letters, he had shown great anxiety about the instruction of his offspring. Now one of them taught him a lesson which he never forgot. The thirty-three-year-old father went walking in the snowy fields of Arlington with his eight-year-old son Custis. Looking back to see how the little fellow was making out, Lee saw that the boy, by prodigious efforts, was managing to plant his feet in the footsteps of his father. "When I saw this," Lee said, "I said to myself, 'It behooves me to walk very straight when this fellow is already following in my tracks.' "

Lee returned to further labor on the Mississippi and its tributaries, punctuated by brief visits home, and then reported back to Washington late in 1840 for a new assignment. Shortly afterward, his fifth child, another daughter, arrived. The struggling young lieutenant confessed that her appearance could have been "dispensed with for a year or two more." But he added, "However, as she was in such haste to greet her Pa, I am now very glad to see her."

From the winter of 1840 until the late summer of 1846, Lee was busy in a succession of routine tasks, mostly concerned with the inspection and repair of coastal defenses. These activities had some educational value, but Lee doubted that they would lead to promotion beyond his newly won rank of captain. At thirty-five, having been thrilled by the performance of an enchanting actress, he confided to an intimate friend his amazement that feminine beauty still excited him because he felt so old in every other way. When a few months short of the milestone of forty, he was weighed down with domestic responsibilities and the dull weight of occupational routine, and was almost resigned to a belief that he would not fulfill his youthful ambition for military distinction.

Then, on August 19, 1846, three months after the United States declared war on Mexico, Lee received orders to report to Brigadier General John E. Wool for services south of the border.

The School of War

In ensuing months, Lee became engineer and acting inspector general with Wool's forces. He won distinction by his skill and indefatigable labors in bridging streams and by his boldness in scouting. In January of 1847, he received orders that would enable him to see action in the most exciting part of the war. He was to join General Scott at Brazos. Lee, who had impressed Scott in earlier years as much by the independence with which he maintained his convictions as by his brilliance, was immediately made a member of the general's staff. Thus he was placed close to one of the most remarkable military leaders in American history on the eve of the great campaign of Vera Cruz. Scott's vast bulk, ponderous pomposity, and excitable temperament made it easy to caricature him as "Old Fuss and Feathers," but beneath the fuss and feathers was a wise old bird of singular toughness and sharp talons.

Vera Cruz was then the most powerful fortress in the Western hemisphere. To take it, General Scott conducted the first sizable amphibious operation in United States military history. In that effort and in ensuing campaigns, he proved himself the nation's greatest master of scientific warfare. Lee was privileged not only to take part in the action, but also to participate in the planning. Though only a captain, he was one of the four members of what Scott called his "Little Cabinet." Lee was an outstandingly privileged student in the school of war.

On March 24, the third day of the siege, Lee gained his first experience in combat. He did not find it exhilarating. His duty was to direct a battery trained on the town. He seems to have been almost careless of personal safety, but fearful for his brother Smith Lee who was bravely manning one of the guns. Something else upset Lee.

Afterwards, he wrote his nephew: "The shells thrown from our battery were constant and regular discharges, so beautiful in their flight and so destructive in their fall. It was awful! My heart bled for the inhabitants. The soldiers I did not care so much for, but it was terrible to think of the women and children."

Vera Cruz surrendered March 27, and the formal occupation was two days later.

More interested in finding and defeating the main army of the enemy than in capturing towns, Scott now led his army into the interior in pursuit of Santa Anna. On April 14, the Americans found themselves at the Rio del Plan. A high mountain fronted upon the plain and its pass was occupied by Santa Anna, who had placed formidable fortresses on the commanding ridges. At this crucial moment, Lee was assigned to reconnaissance. The fortified mountain of Cerro Gordo was an insurmountable obstacle. If the Americans were to go around it, a passage must be found through ravines which, on the basis of preliminary exploration, appeared impassable.

Lee proceeded to explore these ravines in search of a place where a road could be constructed. Soon he came upon a spring with a well-traveled path leading to it. He then realized that he must be in the rear of the Mexican lines.

Confirmation came all too quickly when Mexican soldiers suddenly came into view. They were approaching rapidly. There was no time to leave the spot. Quickly, Lee dropped to the ground behind a huge log. The Mexicans drank from the spring. Before they left, others came.

Lee realized that this could go on all day and that his only hope of remaining undetected was in lying still with perfect self-control for hours on end. He could not afford the luxury of moving a muscle when two of the Mexicans sat down on the very log behind which he was lying.

More Mexican soldiers gathered at the spot and began to move around the spring and the surrounding bushes. Then one of them stepped over the log, almost bringing his foot down on Lee. The captain held his breath. The Mexican never looked down, and passed on without knowing that he had stepped over a captain of the United States Army.

All through the afternoon the Mexican soldiers came and went. Then came twilight and at last, mercifully, the almost palpable blackness of a tropical night. Slowly moving his aching joints, the Virginian got to his feet and, by virtue of an uncanny sense of direction, made his way back to headquarters.

Two days later, Lee, carrying a heavier load of responsibility than many a general, led General David E. Twiggs's division through the ravines that Santa Anna had said would be impassable even to a mountain goat. Because of Lee's brilliance and judgment, the Americans were able to turn the enemy's left and won the historic victory of Cerro Gordo.

Twiggs poured out his gratitude with unmilitary prodigality. He began by saying that anything he might write would "add little to the good reputation of Captain Lee" and then filled a paragraph with praise of his "gallantry and good conduct" deserving "the highest praise" and frankly attested his reliance on Lee's knowledge and judgment. Colonel Bennett Riley, admitting that comment on Lee was "not appropriately within the range" of his report, nevertheless seized the opportunity to testify to the Virginian's "intrepid coolness and gallantry . . . when conducting the advance of our brigade under the heavy flank fire of the enemy."

General Scott said: "I am impelled to make special mention of the services of Captain R. E. Lee, Engineers. This officer, greatly distinguished at the siege of Vera Cruz, was again indefatigable during these operations, in reconnaissance as daring as laborious, and of the utmost value. Nor was he less conspicuous in planting batteries, and in conducting columns to their stations under the heavy fire of the enemy."

Lee garnered more praise than any other officer involved in the Cerro Gordo operation and he was later brevetted major "for gallant and meritorious conduct in the battle."

Of course, Lee was gratified by his success, but he was not drunk with vainglory. He wrote his young son Custis, "You have no idea what a horrible sight the field of battle is."

By the middle of May, Scott was in Puebla, about 200 miles from Mexico City. Three months later, though handicapped in supplies and transportation, and commanding a force numerically inferior to the enemy, he marched through the mountains into the Valley of Mexico with the capital as his goal.

In his reconnaissance reports, Lee revealed a .sound sense of strategy on which Scott became increasingly dependent. Raphael Semmes, a naval officer who would achieve international fame, wrote :

The services of Captain Lee were invaluable to his chief. Endowed with a mind which has no superior in his corps, and possessing great energy of character, he examined, counseled and advised with a judgment, tact and discretion worthy of all praise. His talent for topography was peculiar, and he seemed to receive impressions intuitively, which it cost other men much labor to acquire.

By August 17, the Americans were at the village of St. Agustin, only nine miles south of Mexico City. But the short route to Mexico City was guarded by two fortifications, at San Antonio and Churubusco. Under these circumstances, a direct advance would be foolish. A possible alternative was the crossing of the Pedregal, a huge lava flow. If successful, this move could place the Americans north of Santa Anna's forces at San Antonio. But could a path be found across the Pedregal?

Lee found a route. He guided others over it and became a sort of one-man communications force, carrying messages between units of the army. His mission was as weird as it was remarkable. He groped his way over the lava through a night whose enveloping blackness was pierced only irregularly by flashes of lightning that made the landscape seem as strange as the mountains of the moon. He was curtained off from many sounds by the roar of a torrential rain. It was almost as though he were feeling his way across the surface of the planet when it was new, and the lava had cooled, but darkness was still upon the face of the deep and the rains came.

Lee's activities made possible the success of three engagements, one in the Pedregal, one at Padierna, and one at Churubusco. And these victories caused the Mexicans to seek an armistice, which was signed August 24. Lee was in all three battles and was in the field continuously for 36 hours. Neither enemy bullets and shells nor weariness induced by his extraordinary labors wrenched from Lee any visible signs of fatigue or nervousness. Only once did any happening of the incredible 36 hours wring from him an overt emotional response. When he saw his old friend Joe Johnston shivering in an agony of grief over his nephew's death in battle, Lee held out his hand to his old schoolmate and burst into tears.

Gen. David E. Twiggs, Gen. Gideon Pillow, Gen. James Shields, and Gen. Franklin Pierce vied with each other in praising Lee in their official reports. Gen. P. F. Smith said : "His reconnaissances, though pushed far beyond the points of prudence, were conducted with so much skill that their fruits were of the utmost value— the soundness of his judgment and personal daring being equally conspicuous." And General Scott himself said that Lee was "as distinguished for felicitous execution as for science and daring." Lee was brevetted lieutenant colonel, and Scott amplified his original praise by saying that Lee's activities in the Pedregal constituted "the greatest feat of physical and moral courage performed by any individual, to my knowledge, during the campaign."

Negotiations between the United States and Mexico broke down and the armistice was terminated September 7. Scott took Chapultepec and on September 14 was able to raise the American flag above the National Palace in Mexico City. In the closing days of the war the dictates of duty did not carry Lee into dramatic exploits rivaling the adventures in the Pedregal, but he did serve for more than 50 hours without sleep and ceased his labors only when he fainted. Furthermore, he was frequently called into consultation by Scott and did not hesitate to express disagreement with his chief on several vital points. Lee was also notable for the fact that, far from indulging in the many controversies that divided the officers occupying the capital, he quietly essayed the role of peacemaker.

In the Mexican War, Lee had learned valuable lessons in strategy from a great master, Winfield Scott. Moreover, the pupil had captured the master's admiration to such an extent that, ten years after the war, Scott would pronounce him "the very best soldier that I ever saw in the field."

Lee had proved that, as his previous record would indicate, he was brilliant and resourceful. The fires of battle had illumined a side of his character heretofore hidden in the shadow of his reserve. He was daring to the point of audacity, and banked fires smoldered behind his marble dignity. He was a man of discipline, but also a man of fire.

Lee the Emancipator

Lee returned home still clean-shaven except for a mustache, but with new lines in his face and some white hairs in his head, which he fancied that his wife and children stared at constantly. Otherwise, his most notable souvenir was a bottle of whisky that a friend had made him promise to carry off to war nearly two years before. The seal was still unbroken, as was Lee's resolve not to drink alcoholic beverages.

For a while he was on office duty in Washington and for the next four years was assigned a variety of engineering tasks, including the study of coastal defenses, land surveys in Florida, and the construction of Fort Carroll at Baltimore.

His chief delight now was in his family. The "little people," as he called his children, idolized him. The "greatest treat" for the younger ones was to climb into his bed in the morning and lie close to him while he told fascinating stories. In the evenings, he told stories too, but on the basis of "no tickling, no story." He would take off his slippers and place his bare feet in his children's laps so that they could tickle the soles while he talked. Those same feet, remarkably small for a man of Lee's large hands and massive torso, were good at broadjumping, as he proved in many a contest with the older boys.

But Lee could be exacting as well as gentle. In after years, his youngest son said, "I always knew that it was impossible to disobey my father." Lee was ambitious for his children, too. He knew that Custis was highly intelligent and, while the boy was at West Point, he wrote him: "You must press forward in your studies. . . . You must be number 1. It is a fine number. Easily found and remembered. Simple and unique."

In the spring of 1852, much to his surprise, Lee was assigned to the superintendency of the United States Military Academy at West Point. He believed that he lacked sufficient academic experience for the job and begged to decline an honor beyond his abilities. His request was denied, and on September 1, 1852 he became superintendent.

Lee soon pleased the board by the shrewd economies that he was able to effect without in any way lowering the standards of the institution. He improved the living quarters of the instructors. He introduced greater order into the facilities and procedures of the Academy. He was generally strict in matters of discipline, but inclined to be lenient when a boy incriminated himself by telling the truth.

At West Point, Lee was a student as well as an educator. In his private chambers, he studied not only military science, but also geography, history, literature, and architecture.

One of the most significant events in Lee's personal life during his superintendency was his confirmation in the Episcopal Church. He may have been moved to considerations of faith and immortality by the death of his mother-in-law who, by his own testimony, "was to me all that a mother could be." Two months later, he wrote a friend: "The blow was so sudden and crushing, that I yet shudder at the shock, and feel that I have been arrested in the course of life and had no power to resume my onward march." Whatever his reasons, Lee's action in joining the church was an expression of the simple piety characteristic of him from boyhood. His life had long been so exemplary that his conversion made no observable difference in his behavior. It did not even break him of the habit of falling asleep in church.

In March 1855, Lee was commissioned lieutenant colonel and made second in command of the Second Cavalry, a new regiment commanded by Col. Albert Sydney Johnston and formed for service in the West. In Texas Lee gained experience in the art of maintaining soldiers' morale under conditions of tedium and extreme discomfort. Anticipated battles with the Indians did not materialize. In dealing with them, Lee put diplomacy to good use; though, when asked to disrobe as part of a ceremonial, he balked at anything beyond removing his tie. There was no real excitement, only variation in tedium. He was frequently called from camp for court-martial duty.

Lee was even more interested in the happenings of the outside world than in the events of his immediate sphere. He foresaw the election of President Buchanan and wrote to Mrs. Lee, "I hope he will be able to extinguish fanaticism North and South, cultivate love for the country and Union, and restore harmony between the different sections." But, after the inauguration, he wrote her of his fears that violence would result from "the systematic and progressive efforts of certain people of the North to interfere with and change the domestic institutions of the South. . . . They must . . . be aware that their object . . . can only be accomplished by them through the agency of a civil and servile war."

Lee, however, was no apologist for the "peculiar institution" of slavery. He had long believed in gradual emancipation of the slaves, and had made a life of freedom in Liberia possible for those of his own slaves who wanted it. He re-emphasized his position in a letter to his wife:

In this enlightened age, there are few I believe but what will acknowledge that slavery as an institution is a moral and political evil in any country. It is useless to expatiate on its disadvantages. I think it, however, a greater evil to the white than to the black race. . . . Their emancipation will sooner result from the mild and melting influence of

Christianity than the storms and tempests of fiery controversy. . . . If [the abolitionist] means well to the slave, he must not create angry feelings in the Master. . . . Is it not strange that the descendants of those Pilgrim fathers who crossed the Atlantic to preserve their own freedom of opinion have always proved themselves intolerant of the spiritual liberty of others?

Though Lee was assigned to frontier duty in Texas from 1856 to February 1861, he was actually with his regiment there only from March 1856 to October 1857 and for an additional year beginning February 1860. The death of Mr. Custis left labyrinthine problems of legal settlement, which young Custis Lee inherited with the estate of Arlington. Lee was repeatedly granted leave to attend to the many harassing details which fell his lot. The Lees joined the ranks of the land-poor gentry and for a time Lee necessarily assumed the roles of hard-working farmer and hard-pressed businessman. Custis Lee thought that, since his father bore all the burden of Arlington, he should also enjoy whatever fruits might eventually accrue from his efforts. He therefore sent the deed to the property to his father. Lee quickly returned it, replying, "Your dear grandfather distributed his property as he thought best, and it is proper that it should remain as he bestowed it."

During this period Mrs. Lee lapsed so far into painful invalidism that Lee feared she might never recover. His daughters were also sick a good deal of the time. Amid his cares at Arlington, Lee did not lose his warm smile but, in a letter to Custis, he confessed, "I have no enjoyment in life now but what I derive from my children."

John Brown's Raid

Lee was at Arlington the morning of October 17, 1859 when lush-bearded, young Lieutenant "Jeb" Stuart, a West Point cadet during Lee's superintendency, arrived with an order for Lee to report immediately to the Secretary of War. There was an insurrection at Harper's Ferry. It might be the start of a revolution, for the federal armory and arsenal were located in that place. Troops from Ft.

Monroe, Marines from the Washington Navy Yard, and Maryland militiamen were converging on the spot.

A few hours later, still wearing civilian clothes but bearing a presidential proclamation, Lee was with Stuart aboard a locomotive rumbling toward Harper's Ferry, where Lee was ordered to assume command of all forces.

Arriving after nightfall, Lee learned that insurgents under the leadership of one who later proved to be John Brown had holed up in an engine house with prominent civilian hostages, after killing both Negro and white citizens of the community.

Perceiving that the disturbance was on a smaller scale than the War Department had suspected, Lee telegraphed instructions to hold back the troops being sent from Fort Monroe and decided that it was not necessary to dignify the small-scale criminal effort by issuance of the presidential proclamation. He surrounded the engine house with Marines and militia and awaited daylight.

The next morning, Stuart, under flag of truce, presented Lee's demand for surrender. With a carbine in his hand, gaunt old John Brown stalled for time. He counted on the government's fear for the safety of the hostages. A shout rang out from the engine house, "Never mind us, fire!" Lee recognized the voice as that of a good friend, Lewis W. Washington, great-nephew of the general. With a thrill of pride, Lee exclaimed, "The old Revolutionary blood does tell!"

Five minutes later, bullets and bayonets had ended the insurrection. Brown was superficially wounded. Lee showed him every consideration, even promising that the prisoner would not have to submit to questioning at the time if he did not feel equal to it.

Lee quickly quashed rumors adding to public unrest and established order with a quiet assurance that ruled out the possibility of mob vengeance against the prisoners.

Lee, of course, did not share the views of Northern abolitionists who saw Brown as a crusading saint; neither did he share the fears of some Southerners who saw Brown as captain of the vanguard of widespread, organized rebellion. In his official report, prepared while Harper's Ferry still seethed with excitement, he said of Brown's effort, "The plan was an attempt of a fanatic or madman." Lee had acted with efficiency, perspective, and self-control.

John Brown's raid was but one in a quickening succession of events symptomatic of the growing rift between North and South.

Back on the Texas frontier, Lee read with mounting anxiety the reports of national division. A committee of Texans on December 3, 1860 called for a convention to decide whether the State should secede. Lee was one of the few men in the United States still standing on solid middle ground between the extremists of North and South. He wrote Custis:

Feeling the aggressions of the North, resenting their denial of the equal rights of our citizens to the common territory of the Commonwealth, etc., I am not pleased with the course of the "Cotton States," as they term themselves. In addition to their selfish, dictatorial bearing, the threats they throw out to the "Border States," as they call them, if they will not join them, augur little for the benefit. While I wish to do what is right, I am unwilling to do what is wrong, either at the bidding of the South or the North. One of their plans seems to be the renewal of the slave trade. That I am opposed to on every ground.

When Lee wrote again on January 29, he had learned of the secession of four States. His words revealed that he had decided where his duty lay in the national crisis. He said:

The South in my opinion has been aggrieved by the acts of the North as you say. I feel the aggression, & am willing to take every proper step for redress. It is the principle I contend for, not individual or private benefit. As an American citizen, I take great pride in my country, her prosperity & institutions, & would defend any State if her rights were invaded. But I can anticipate no greater calamity for the country than a dissolution of the Union. It would be an accumulation of all the evils we complain of, and I am willing to sacrifice everything but honor for its preservation. I hope, therefore, that all constitutional means will be exhausted before there is a resort to force. Secession is nothing but revolution. The framers of our Constitution never [would have] exhausted so much labor, wisdom and forbearance in its formation, and surrounded it with so many guards and securities if it was intended to be broken by every member of the Confederacy at will. . . . In 1808 when the New England States resisted Mr. Jefferson's Imbargo law & the Hartford Convention assembled secession was termed treason by Virginia statesmen. What can it be now? Still, a Union that can only be maintained by swords & bayonets, & in which strife & civil war are to take the place of brotherly love & kindness, has no charms for me. I shall mourn for my country & for the welfare & progress of mankind. If the Union is dissolved & the government disrupted, I shall return to my native State & share the miseries of my people, & save in defense will draw my sword on none.

Lee's calmly measured words masked great suffering. Shortly before, in a more emotional vein, he had written : "I wish for no other flag than the star spangled banner and no other air than 'Hail Columbia.' I still hope that the wisdom and patriotism of the nation will yet save it."

These were melancholy days for Lee. Threats to the State and the nation he loved were a dark backdrop for his personal troubles. His children received cheerful letters from him, and associates in Texas were impressed by an outward composure that bordered on impassiveness. But, six months before, in a letter to a beloved relative, he had confessed :

At this distance from those you love and care for, with the knowledge of the vicissitudes and necessities of life, one is rent by a thousand anxieties, and the mind as well as body is worn and racked to pieces. . . . Touching your kind wishes for my speedy return, you know the embarrassment that attends it. A divided heart I have too long had, and a divided life too long led. That may be one cause of the small progress I have made on either hand, my professional and civil career. Success is not always attained by a single undivided effort; it rarely follows a halting, vacillating course. My military duties require me here, whereas my affections and urgent domestic claims call me away. And thus I live and am unable to advance either. But while I live, I must toil and trust.

Lee's attitude was understandably human. Nurtured in traditions of family greatness and having so distinguished himself at West Point and in Mexico as to attract prophecies of greatness, he was now at the age of fifty-three a lieutenant colonel with at least 22 men standing between him and the rank of brigadier. Advancement from captain to lieutenant colonel had taken 22 years. After 31 years in the army, and with the responsibility for a large family including an invalid wife, he was drawing only $1,205 a year. Lee's sense of failure was increased when Joe Johnston, a classmate who had won distinction at West Point but had not equaled Lee's record either there or in Mexico, eclipsed him by becoming a brigadier general. Lee knew that, by his refusal to curry favor and his outspoken defense of unpopular officers whom he believed in the right, he had jeopardized his own chances for promotion. But his admiration for his old friend and his generosity of spirit were such that he soon wrote Johnson a letter of congratulations, beginning, "My dear general : I am delighted at accosting you by your present title, and I feel my heart exult within me at your high position."

As the national crisis deepened, his mood was increasingly that of a letter to Custis in which he said, "My little personal troubles sink into insignificance when I contemplate the condition of the country, and I feel as if I could easily lay down my life for its safety."

In February 1861, seven States (including Texas) had seceded. Lee received orders from the War Department relieving him of duty with his regiment and directing him to report in person to the General-in-Chief in Washington by April 1.

What did Scott have in mind? General Twiggs, commander of the Department of Texas and Lee's immediate superior, had recently exclaimed in irritation, "I know General Scott fully believes that God Almighty had to spit on his hands to make Bob Lee!"

Some admirers of both Scott and Lee thought that the old General cherished the hope that his young fellow Virginian would some day succeed him as General-in-Chief.

Once, when war with Britain seemed possible, Scott had said, "If war comes, it would be cheap for our country to insure Lee's life for $5,000,000 a year."

" . . . In Whose Behalf Alone"

Exactly what transpired during Lee's interview with Scott remains a mystery to this day. Speculation mounted in the outer office as the door to the General's inner sanctum remained closed for one hour, then two, and finally three hours, before Lee emerged from the room.

Scott's associates noticed that the general was solemn for the rest of the day, and Lee had no time for informal conversation with old friends at the War Department. It is generally assumed that Scott at least suggested to Lee that the younger man might command the Union forces in the field in the event of civil war. Some believe that the General held out to Lee the possibility of heading so formidable an army that war might be averted.

On April 18, Lee returned to see Scott. He revealed to the old General that Francis P. Blair, acting as the informal but authorized emissary of the Secretary of War, had offered him command of the Union Army. Then Lee told Scott his reply: "Though opposed to secession and deprecating war, I could take no part in an invasion of the Southern States."

The old General looked at Lee with the earnest sadness of a disappointed father. "Lee," he said, "You have made the greatest mistake of your life; but I feared it would be so."

Nine days later, the *Richmond Enquirer* quoted Scott as saying he would rather have received the resignation of every general in the United States Army than that of Colonel Lee. By that time, Virginia, hitherto strongly Unionist in sentiment, and alarmed by the defection of the Deep South, had herself seceded in response to Lincoln's call for troops from the Old Dominion to invade her sister States. And Virginia, impressed with Lee's record in the Mexican War and cherishing the name of Lee with its precious Revolutionary associations, was calling upon him to take command of the Common-wealth's defending forces.

When Lee, handsome in his high silk hat, boarded the train for Richmond in response to that call, he did so with a clear conscience. A textbook in use at the United States Military Academy shortly before his own student days had taught the right of secession. His own native State, in ratifying the Constitution, had stated that it reserved the right to secede. Even the great idol of New England, Daniel Webster, had once eloquently defended the right of secession. The fact that Lee had received a free education at the United States Military Academy gave him no compunctions about defending his native soil from the invading United States Army. He knew that Virginia had contributed her share to the maintenance of West Point.

But the sense of justification could not erase his sorrow. In an affectionate letter to General Scott, Lee had movingly expressed his pain at parting from his old chief and from the service to which he had devoted "all the best years of my life and all the ability I possessed." The sorrow of parting had eclipsed past disappointments so that, in retrospect, he could say, "I have experienced nothing but kindness from my superiors and a most cordial friendship from my comrades."

He was sad, too, because he was one of the minority of realists at a time when crowds in both North and South were celebrating in advance the quick victories that would surely be theirs. At Orange, villagers had assembled at the station and they called for Lee until he stepped to the rear of the train and bowed. At Gordonsville, where he changed trains, a jubilant throng demanded a speech. All this inane joy jarred against Lee's sensibilities in what was for him a moment of mourning. If the crowd wanted a speech, he would give them one. He spoke with his usual courtesy, but he urged them to stop lounging about stations and put "their affairs in order for a long, bloody war" whose support would "strain all their resources."

That night, Governor John Letcher offered Lee command of all

Virginia forces, with the rank of major general. The appointment was quickly and unanimously approved by the Convention. The next morning, Lee walked through Richmond streets from the Spotswood Hotel to his new, one-room office in the Post Office Building. The old capital was now strangely unfamiliar. Its ordered grace had been replaced by the atmosphere of an armed camp with fresh troops arriving almost hourly. Four members of the Convention called to escort him to Jefferson's columned capitol to appear before the Convention. Waiting in the rotunda before entering the hall, he looked long and hard at the statue of Washington. Despite the inhibiting influence of modesty, the obvious parallel must have been apparent to one with his sense of history.

But, lest anyone mistake it, John Janney, president of the Convention, drew the parallel and underlined it at length so that it would be inescapable to the most obtuse. Lee must have found it awkward to stand for so long a time while the orator addressed him in the most flattering terms, but he must have been touched by the complimentary reference to Light Horse Harry Lee and by the statement, "I bid you a cordial and heartfelt welcome to this hall, in which we almost yet hear the echo of the voices of the statesmen, the soldiers and sages of bygone days, who have borne your name, and whose blood now flows in your veins."

Lee replied in deep, measured tones:

Mr. President and gentlemen of the Convention, profoundly impressed with the solemnity of the occasion—for which I must say I was not prepared—I accept the position assigned me. . . . I would have much preferred had your choice fallen on an abler man. Trusting in Almighty God, an approving conscience, and the aid of my fellow citizens, I devote myself to the service of my native State, in whose behalf alone will I ever again draw my sword.

The delegates rushed forward to grasp his hand. It is remarkable that Alexander Stephens, who was far from enthusiastic about secession and was a far from credulous observer of men and politics, was strongly impressed with Lee's manner and was as convinced as his colleagues that Lee's words had the force of sincerity despite their resemblance to the perfunctory rhetoric of the hustings. Here was a man who apparently believed uncompromisingly in the maxims of the copy books. Stephens was more convinced than ever after a brief, private conversation with Lee. At this time, Stephens reminded the Virginian that Lee's rank of major general of Virginia forces might create special problems since the Confederacy had no higher rank than brigadier general. Without hesitation, Lee replied that "he did not wish anything connected with himself individually, or his official rank or personal position, to interfere in the slightest."

"Granny" Lee

Lee went amiably about his duties two days later when the Virginia Convention yielded temporary control of the Virginia forces to the Confederacy. Lee's responsibility for the defense of Virginia was an appalling one. As in the Revolution, the Old Dominion's extended coastline and large rivers provided many channels of attack for the enemy. There were only 60,000 small arms in the arsenals of the Commonwealth and all but 6,000 of these were antiquated flintlocks. Lee could take comfort in the fact that his old commander and great personal friend, Colonel Andrew Talcott, a competent engineer, was in charge of the posts guarding the river mouths.

Lee personally enjoined the commanders of these posts to be ready to repel instantly any attack, but not to provoke one until the State was in a proper posture of defense. Such orders were but common prudence at a time when many of the volunteers were being sent to their stations with no guns whatever. But some Southerners who were disposed to believe that a good Confederate could lick a Yankee soldier with his bare hands were highly critical of Lee. A personal observer for Confederate Secretary of War Walker informed authorities in Montgomery that Lee's caution suggested the possibility of treachery. Some Virginians, imputing less ignoble motives to the General but chafing at inaction, soon began to call the commander "Granny Lee."

Volunteer forces in Eastern Virginia grew faster than they could be armed, but Western Virginia, long hostile to the leadership of Tidewater and Piedmont, was not moved by any enthusiasm for the impending struggle.

Despite the many obstacles, Lee began to bring order out of chaos. He placed batteries on the Potomac, strengthened the defenses of both the York and the James, and with great prescience concentrated many of his best troops at the village of Manassas, a railroad junction in Northern Virginia.

By the middle of May, Lee learned that Federal forces were congregating on the Potomac near Washington, and at Fortress Monroe at the lower end of the Peninsula, the neck between the James and the York. Later in the month, Federal forces occupied Alexandria, Virginia. About the time that these threats materialized, President Davis and his chief lieutenants moved into Richmond, which now replaced Montgomery as capital of the Confederacy. To Lee's other vexations was added the necessity of adjusting to newly constituted civil authority.

Public adulation of Lee had turned to sharp criticism, but to his staff he was more the hero every day. Young Colonel Walter Herron Taylor noted that Lee seemed "to address himself to the accomplishment of every task that devolved upon him in a conscientious and deliberate way, as if he himself was directly accountable to some higher power for the manner in which he performed his duties." He could also tell that, although Lee did not complain, he hated office work and longed for the field. The general had a decided verbal aptitude but "nothing seemed to tax his amiability as much as the necessity for writing a lengthy communication." His chief recreations were horseback riding in the late afternoon with members of his staff and talking with children.

As in so many other periods of crisis in his life, Lee's apparent composure under frustration and criticism caused those near him to marvel. By July his central task of organization had been completed despite the fearful odds and, in a letter to his beloved Mary, he revealed that the toll on him had been greater than the world suspected. The iron control could be relaxed a little now. He wrote: "As usual, in getting through with a thing, I have broken down a little and had to take to my bed last evening, but am at my office this morning."

In this month, the Battle of Bull Run, or First Manassas, was fought. The Confederates, under Johnston and Beauregard, put the Yankees to inglorious flight. The outcome of the battle proved Lee's wisdom in concentrating forces at Manassas. But the quick Southern victory gave wings to an optimism that soared to ridiculous heights and greatly increased Lee's difficulties in pursuing a policy of preparation and prudence.

A Richmond observer had described Lee as "cold, quiet and grand." She did not suspect that Lee had sent Johnston a note overflowing with generous emotion: "I almost wept for joy at the glorious victory. . . . The feeling of my heart could hardly be repressed on learning the brilliant share you had in its achievement."

Soon Lee himself had a chance to see action. With Davis's permission, but with his official status equivocal, Lee was on his way to the western counties to see for himself just what was going on in the mountains.

Separated from Eastern Virginia by a barrier of sentiment no less formidable than the physically dividing mountain ridges, this part of the State posed hard problems. General George McClellan, before taking command in Eastern Virginia, had triumphed over Confederate forces there. Now a Federal force of undetermined size stood guard over the Cheat Mountain Pass, strategically vital to the defense or conquest of the area.

Confederates under General W. W. Loring were concentrated at nearby Huntersville. The general could scarcely have received Lee with less enthusiasm if the Virginian had been a Yankee. He resented the fact that Lee or someone in Richmond had deemed the presence of the staff chief to be necessary. Loring had much more military experience than Lee. Lee's position was embarrassing because of Loring's attitude, because of his own indefinite status, and because of the fact that he had never commanded more troops in the field than four squadrons of horse and those only on a 40-day scout in 1856. For these reasons, Lee did not order Loring to speed up his proposed march to Cheat Mountain, despite the fact that he foresaw the delay would cost the army a badly needed victory.

As in his Mexican War days, Lee found an alternate route through rugged country. But, because of flooding rains and seas of mud, together with the low morale of Loring's army, the projected battle ended in a few scattered shots, much confusion and a march back to camp. A colonel who had begged Lee for the privilege of leading the advance column had thoroughly botched the job.

Lee had undoubtedly been too trusting in granting the privilege of leadership to a man whose ability and character he did not know. But, under the vaguely defined circumstances of his mission, it is hardly fair to blame him for not being firmer with Loring. And certainly he was not responsible for the weather.

Lee's next mission was to the Kanawha Valley where the fiery Henry A. Wise and the stubborn John B. Floyd, both former governors of Virginia, had brought the squabbles of the forum into the field. These political generals, though intelligent and able men, were firing verbal shots at each other rather than shells at the enemy and seemed to be united only in hostility to Richmond. Through diplomacy and the happy conjunction of orders for Wise to report to Richmond, Lee was able to improve conditions. But he was unable overnight to prepare the forces of Wise and Floyd for a successful assault on the enemy.

Lee cannot be blamed for declaring, after a fresh indication of negligence on the part of one of the Confederate officers: "This is in keeping with everything else I find here—no order, no organization; nobody knows where anything is; no one understands his duty; officers and men are equally ignorant."

Before the end of October, the area which Lee had sought to

defend had seceded from Virginia to become West Virginia, a new state in the old Union.

When Lee reported to President Davis in Richmond early in November, the chief executive was startled by the patriarchal appearance of the officer whom he had sent into the West. The chin that had been clean shaven now wore a long white beard. The profile had a look of antique grandeur such as one might find in classic statuary or on some ancient coin stamped with the likeness of a mythological hero. No one could deny that Lee looked like a great leader, but some people in Richmond were saying that he was merely "a showy presence" with "an historic name."

Lee consented to tell Davis the sad story of inefficiency in the Western forces only after exacting a promise that the President would reveal this information to no one else. Lee's critics were as numerous, as stridulent, and as persistent as a chorus of cicadas on a summer night, but he would not resort to alibis. Davis marveled at Lee's self-discipline. "Through all this . . . ," the President later wrote, "he stood in silence without defending himself . . . for he was unwilling to offend anyone who was wearing a sword and striking blows for the Confederacy."

Three days later Davis sent Lee to South Carolina to assume command of shore defenses. A Federal fleet lay off Charleston. This time, mindful of his dealings with Loring, Lee obtained assurance that he would exercise complete powers of command with Richmond's backing. Even so, the President thought it necessary to write a letter to the Governor of South Carolina, praising Lee's ability and moral strength. Virginia and South Carolina were not far apart. Lee's name now provoked sneering remarks and head-shaking in Charleston parlors as well as Richmond drawing rooms.

When the general arrived in Charleston, he found the old city in a bustle of excitement foreign to its usually muted and mellow tone. The booming of cannon off the coast told of a furious fight. Lee rode to the shore but could not learn what was happening until darkness settled and the firing ceased. He then learned that the enemy fleet had put two small forts out of operation and now controlled the sound.

Lee quickly set up headquarters in a small abandoned house far from other habitations. He subjected himself and his staff to a Spartan regimen of work minus luxuries. The daily fare corresponded in plainness to the tinware off which it was eaten, but one of Lee's officers said that the General "always seasoned the meal with his good humor and . . . jests." There, and in trips through the low country of South Carolina and Georgia, he planned defenses for the much indented coastline from Charleston to Savannah. He blocked some river mouths with debris and used his engineering skills to strengthen greatly the forts of Charleston and Savannah.

The little that South Carolina people saw of General Lee impressed them more favorably in his behalf than Davis's generous letter of recommendation. The celebrated poet Paul Hamilton Hayne said Lee was "perhaps the most striking figure we had ever encountered," a man with "the quiet, dauntless step of one every inch the gentleman and soldier." Lee became a local hero when, in the great Charleston fire that engulfed his hotel along with many stores, churches, and dwellings, he rescued a baby and helped several women to escape.

"Hope the Enemy Will Be Polite"

When Lee left Savannah in the spring of 1862 on orders to report to Richmond, he had added to the defenses of the South Carolina and Georgia coasts systems of earthworks on so large a scale as almost to constitute an innovation in warfare. But he did not delude himself that all was secure. Earlier, he had written one daughter, "Another forlorn hope expedition. Worse than West Virginia." To another, he had written, "I hope the enemy will be polite enough to wait for us."

Lee resumed his role of military adviser to the President at a time when the Confederacy's life was seriously threatened. The loss of Forts Henry, Donelson, and Columbus placed the whole Mississippi basin in grave jeopardy. Roanoke Island, North Carolina had fallen to the Yankees. General Joseph Johnston's forces had retreated from Manassas to the Rappahannock. Unknown to the public, powder supplies were too low to permit a major battle. On March 24 a flotilla of Union troopships docked at Ft. Monroe, and it became apparent that the next major thrust of the enemy would be through Tidewater to Richmond. Lee correctly predicted that the blow would be on the Peninsula, between the York and James rivers. He began reinforcing "Prince John" Magruder, the elegant commander in that area.

Early in April, two major blows fell in the West. General Albert Sydney Johnston was killed at Shiloh, and the fall of one more fort gave the Yankees control of the Upper Mississippi. The next disaster might be in Tidewater. Lee directed Joseph E. Johnston to move his men to the Peninsula.

Pessimistic about the value of earthwork defenses in that location and an ardent believer in concentration of forces, Johnston soon urged on Davis and Lee the abandonment of the Peninsula, the port of Norfolk, and the Naval Shipyard in neighboring Portsmouth. The army, with all reinforcements that could be rushed to it, would be concentrated just outside Richmond. The persuasive Gustavus W. Smith, who had resigned his job as street commissioner of New York City to become a Confederate general, supported Johnston's contentions.

In a long day of argument, Lee, backed by Secretary of War Randolph, maintained that Johnston's strategy would threaten the very life of the Confederacy. About an hour past midnight, the President overruled Johnston and ordered a spirited defense of the Peninsula.

Lee was frustrated in his desire for field service but he scored a notable achievement when, largely as a result of his own persistent urging, a Conscription Act, backed by the President, was passed by the Confederate Congress. The act, though not all that Lee sought, had been pushed through over strong opposition, particularly from North Carolina and Georgia.

Lee's quiet influence was being felt in the Valley of Virginia, too, where his strategy was being translated into triumph by the lightning tactics of "Stonewall" Jackson.

Nearer Richmond, no successes brightened the gloom. On May 4, Johnston retreated up the Peninsula without notifying the government. A bloody defeat was sustained at Williamsburg. When Johnston complained of interference with his command and asked to be relieved, Lee used sincere friendship and skillful diplomacy to assuage his old comrade's hurt feelings.

But, when Norfolk fell, Lee stepped in to strengthen the artillery at Drewry's Bluff on the James and to block the channel. By the middle of the month, an enemy ironclad had been forced to withdraw after going up the river as far as the fortified point.

By May 24 the enemy was in Mechanicsville, five miles from the capital. Lee offered his services in the field in any capacity that Johnston might deem of most assistance. On the last day of the month, when clouds dark with menace lowered over Richmond like a funeral pall, Lee rode out to Johnston's headquarters on Nine Mile Road. Counting on the waters of the Chickahominy—at their highest flood in two decades—to block reinforcement of the Federals, Johnston planned on that day to seize the village of Seven Pines. The battle began at 3 P.M. and, drawn irresistibly by the sound of fire, Davis soon appeared at Johnston's headquarters. Through the failure of subordinates, Johnston's plans misfired. The general himself was felled by a shell fragment and was borne off the field on a litter.

General Smith, ranking officer, normally would become Johnston's successor. Lee had no intimation that Davis had other plans until, as he and the President rode back to Richmond through lines of ambulances and wagons trailing the blood of their occupants, the chief executive turned his tense, drawn face to the Virginian and said: "General Lee, I shall assign you to the command of this army. Make your preparations as soon as you reach your quarters. I shall send you the order when we get to Richmond."

The Army of Northern Virginia

The next day Lee was in command of a beaten army that had suffered frightful losses. Relations with his chief lieutenants constituted a special problem. General Smith could hardly be expected to be enthusiastic about Lee's promotion. General James Longstreet promptly complained, "The entire [enemy] army seems to be opposed to me. . . . If I can't get help, I must fall back."

In his first order to the troops, announcing his own accession as commander, Lee gave the army a new name: Army of Northern Virginia. The word "Northern" implied that Lee intended to fight most of Richmond's battles near the Potomac frontier between the Union and the Confederacy.

Lee used psychology in other ways. He called a conference of all his general officers, about forty in number, and gave each a chance to give advice. At that meeting, most of the hostility toward Lee vanished among the high-ranking officers.

The men in the ranks had been insulted when Lee set them to digging trenches. Some maintained that such was not soldier's work, not even white man's work. Lee asked, "Why should we leave to [McClellan] the whole advantage of labor?" A hostile Richmond press poked fun at Lee's reliance on shovels and dubbed him "the King of Spades." But the very men required to dig the trenches soon began to look forward with great eagerness to Lee's daily appearances astride his great gray horse Traveller and his cheerful words of encouragement. On his first ride, he wore a white suit instead of his uniform, and he was so jolly that some of the boys mistook him for a prosperous distiller dispensing whisky to lift the general morale.

Major E. P. Alexander, an observant young artilleryman, was convinced of Lee's diplomatic prowess and found him likable and kindly. But he still had serious doubts about him as a commander. One day he voiced his doubts to Colonel Joseph Ives, who had served on Lee's staff in South Carolina.

"Tell me this . . . ," he said. "Has General Lee the audacity that is going to be required for our inferior force to meet the enemy, . . . to take the aggressive, and to run risks and stand chances?"

Ives reined his horse to a full stop and turned toward his questioner: "Alexander, if there is one man in either army . . . head and shoulders above every other in audacity, it is General Lee! His name might be Audacity. He will take more desperate chances and take them quicker than any other general in this country, North or South; and you will live to see it, too."

Lee soon proved his audacity by sending Jeb Stuart and his cavalry on the historic scouting expedition that carried him completely around McClellan's vast army and became celebrated as the "Chickahominy Canter." This expedition brought back news that McClellan's right wing was exposed, and the report moved Lee to fresh audacity. He summoned to join him in the defense of Richmond Stonewall Jackson and his valiant Army of the Valley. This daring juncture of forces provoked much solemn head-shaking and refurbishing of the old adage about putting all one's eggs in one basket.

With the two forces combined, Lee would have about 85,000 men. Union troops numbered about 105,000. But Lee would withdraw most of his men from the Richmond trenches and concentrate his strength in an attack on the force of 25,000 comprising McClellan's right.

On the afternoon of June 23, Lee explained his plans to Jackson, a most unmilitary looking figure in his dusty, shapeless uniform, and to the stolid-faced Longstreet. Jackson's troops were to strike at the flank, while other units attacked elsewhere. Jackson said that he could march his troops to a junction with the Army of Northern Virginia by the morning of the 26th.

By eight o'clock on the appointed day, most of Lee's army was in position. From the heights above Mechanicsville, Lee watched and waited for the sound of Jackson's guns, which would signal a general forward movement. Shortly after 3 P.M., Lee saw the smoke of artillery in the distance and assumed that Jackson had opened fire. But Jackson, delayed by unfamiliar roads, oppressive heat, and utter weariness, had not even appeared. A. P. Hill, fearing that further delay would make execution of Lee's plan impossible, had attacked the enemy prematurely. In the midst of the confused scene were President Davis and a number of politicians who had ridden out from Richmond to watch the battle. An observer said that Lee, "facing the cavalcade and looking like a god of war, . . . exchanged with the President a salute with the most frigid reserve." He then demanded, in deep Jovian tones, "Who are all this army of people and what are they doing here?"

In the silence that followed, Davis twisted in his saddle under the expectant gaze of the rest of the party. "It isn't my army, General," said Davis.

"It certainly isn't my army, Mr. President," said Lee, "and this is no place for it."

"Well, General, if I withdraw, perhaps they will follow," Davis replied. Raising his hat, he rode away, followed by his chastened retinue. Lee was not always pleasant, after all.

The next day, Jackson was again delayed and as a result the day closed with little or nothing gained and the opportunity to destroy McClellan perhaps irrevocably lost. Lee's official report was worded with typical restraint : "Could the other commands have cooperated in this action, the result would have proved most disastrous to the enemy." But the next day, when Jubal Early expressed fear that the enemy would escape, Lee's neck reddened and jerked with irritation and he exploded, "Yes, he will get away because I cannot have my orders carried out!" Again, on this day, the errors of subordinates cost Lee a decisive victory.

Nevertheless, severely hampered in execution though it was, Lee's strategy succeeded in driving McClellan from base to base until, at Malvern Hill on the first of July, he halted under the protection of Union gunboats in the James.

For the time, Richmond was safe. The city rejoiced and some of Lee's former critics praised him lavishly, but he himself was disappointed. His achievement was considerable, but it could have been so much greater. Perhaps Lee, more familiar with the theory than the practice of grand strategy, failed to realize that his subordinates were his inferiors in intellect and efficiency. Lee refrained from direct criticism of Jackson, perhaps because he was convinced that the hero of the Valley Campaign was a far abler man than his performance on the Peninsula would indicate. Jackson, not given to blind faith in other generals, had no reservations about Lee. He declared, "I would follow him blindfolded."

However he might have judged or misjudged his own officers, Lee had accurately taken the measure of his opponent. He had predicted before the campaign: "McClellan will make this a battle of posts. He will take position from position under cover of his heavy guns. . . . " As the war wore on, Lee would demonstrate again and again that he was as skillful in reading the minds and temperaments of his opponents as in surveying strange terrain.

In the disillusionment following McClellan's retreat down the Peninsula in the Seven Days' Battles, Major General Halleck was appointed General-in-Chief of the United States Army. He consolidated the Federal Armies of Virginia under General John Pope, a loud-mouthed officer who boasted to his troops: "I have come to you from the West, where we have always seen the backs of our enemies: from an army whose business it has been to seek the adversary and to beat him when found." If his rhetoric was intended to intimidate the Confederates as well as boost the morale of his own troops, he failed in half of his purpose. Pope was widely quoted as saying, "My headquarters are in the saddle." The quotation inspired a Confederate joke that the Union general didn't know his headquarters from his hindquarters.

Nominally, those headquarters were in Northern Virginia and to this area he ordered both McClellan and General Ambrose Burnside, who was at Fortress Monroe. Pope envisioned a triumphal march from the neighborhood of Alexandria to Richmond.

Quickly divining Pope's intentions, Lee rapidly moved his own army westward toward the Valley. In the second Battle of Bull Run, also known as Second Manassas, the two wings of Lee's army united to put the Union forces to flight. The boastful commander was lured into the fight in the belief that he was attacking an isolated force commanded by Jackson.

Pope's defeat made McClellan look good again. Pope was ousted to make way for "Little Mac."

Lee's strategy, ably served by Jackson and Longstreet, had sent the invading Federal Forces across the Potomac to the Washington defenses. The sweeping victory was doubly precious because of heavy Confederate losses in the West.

Lee himself had been injured in the campaign. He had often exposed himself to the hail of enemy bullets despite the pleadings of fellow officers and had never once been wounded. Instead, he was injured when he fell from the faithful Traveller, who shied at a startling shout from Lee's own men. Some of the men near Lee marveled at the fact that not so much as one small "damn" escaped his lips, even though the bones of one hand were broken and the other hand was sprained.

With his hands in splints, Lee could not ride out on his usual tours of inspection. But his mind was ranging afar, across the Potomac and into Maryland. He planned an invasion of that State.

The prospect was inviting for several reasons. Invasion of the North might increase the substantial sentiment for peace already existing in the Union. If successful, the campaign would be more one of liberation than of conquest since there was so much "pro-Southern" feeling in Maryland. Such a triumph for the Confederacy might bring aid sought from Britain and France. But there were many factors that would have discouraged a George McClellan or a Joseph E. Johnston from attempting an invasion of Maryland. These factors were nowhere better summarized than by Lee himself in a letter to Davis:

"The Army is not properly equipped for an invasion. . . . It lacks much of the material of war, is feeble in transportation, the animals being much reduced, and the men are poorly provided with clothes and in thousands of instances are destitute of shoes. . . . What concerns me most is the fear of giving out of ammunition."

Nevertheless, Lee resolved to invade Maryland. As Colonel Ives had said, "His name might be Audacity."

Invading the North

For four days, brigades of Lee's army forded the upper Potomac while bands played "Dixie" and "Maryland, My Maryland." Some were gay cavaliers whose arms and accouterments glittered in the distilled gold of a September sun and others were lean, ragged, and dirty men who marched with a swagger or rode with the dash of circus riders.

In a public statement written by a Marylander on his staff, but expressing Lee's own nobility of purpose, the General declared:

Marylanders shall once more enjoy their ancient freedom of thought and speech. We know no enemies among you, and will protect all, of every opinion. It is for you to decide your destiny freely and without constraint. This army will respect your choice, whatever it may be; and while the Southern People will rejoice to welcome you to your natural position among them, they will only welcome you when you come of your own free will.

Lee had anticipated that the Federal garrisons at Harper's Ferry and Martinsburg, in his rear, would be abandoned when McClellan learned that the Confederates were north of the Potomac. He was disappointed in this expectation. So long as both posts remained in Federal hands, his whole Maryland campaign was imperiled. Therefore, against Longstreet's urgent warnings, he boldly divided his force, even though it was numerically inferior to the enemy, sending Jackson with his three divisions back across the Potomac to take Harper's Ferry.

Lee explained to one of his generals that he was making what appeared to be a hazardous move because of his estimate of McClellan as "an able general, but a very cautious one." Lee explained: "His army is in a very demoralized and chaotic condition and will not be ready for offensive operation—or he will not think it so— for three or four weeks. Before that time I hope to be on the Susquehanna."

Jackson recrossed the Potomac September 11. On the night of the 13th, Lee was surprised to learn that Federal infantry was being massed below South Mountain, a position occupied by a Confederate division under D. H. Hill. Lee did not know why McClellan had thrown off his usual cautious restraint and was moving with such rapidity. He could not know that one of Hill's officers had used a copy of Special Order 191, detailing Lee's plan of campaign, to wrap a packet of cigars and that this copy had been found by a Union private and passed upward through the chain of command to McClellan.

On the 14th, successive enemy charges all but overpowered the Confederates on South Mountain. Some regiments ran out of ammunition but held their ground by throwing stones. The Texas brigade, spying Lee on Traveller, yelled "Give us Hood! Give us Hood!" A gallant but impetuous officer, Hood had been under technical arrest since Second Manassas for breach of discipline.

Lee lifted his hat and promised: "Gentlemen, you shall have him." Lee then told Hood, "If you will merely say that you regret this occurrence, I will release you and restore you to the command of your division." Hood refused and Lee compromised. "I will suspend your arrest, until the impending battle is decided." Hood rode out to his men, and their boisterous cheering quickly evidenced the inspiriting effect of his presence.

Long after nightfall, firing ceased. The Confederates still held South Mountain, but they would have to abandon it. Lee frankly said: "The day has gone against us and this army will go by Sharpsburg and cross the river."

Lee's army was now in the gravest peril. If Jackson did not succeed in taking Harper's Ferry, Lee would have to retreat into Virginia or be destroyed. Late that night Lee received from Jackson the comforting news that the Federal garrison should fall to his forces the next day.

By the light of the moon and through heavy dust clouds like rolling fog, Lee's men marched westward, crossing Antietam Creek about dawn. The Confederate forces assembled in the area of Sharpsburg, a village in the midst of a triangle of cornfields, orchards, and woods, at the junction of Antietam Creek and the Potomac. Approaching Lee's force of 18,000 was a Federal army estimated at 90,000 and certainly numbering at least 70,000. In these circumstances, Lee was relieved to learn that Jackson had taken Harper's Ferry and could march to Lee before the end of that day.

By 2 P.M., McClellan's forces appeared in a cloud of dust on the other side of the Antietam. Union and Confederate artillery began exchanging shots at a desultory rate attuned to the slow dragging of a hot afternoon. Behind the Union artillery, the blue coats were massing.

The next morning, Jackson rejoined Lee. The Federals attacked only briefly during the day, and at dark a gentle rain replaced the falling shells. The quiet was deceptive. Before dawn, the rattle of muskets and thunder of big guns woke the Confederates.

Daylight brought tragedy. The blue tide engulfed the line guarded by Jackson and D. H. Hill. Three Confederate divisions were mangled. Almost phenomenally calm amid the general confusion, Lee quickly redisposed his forces. Moving swiftly but with clear purposefulness, the commander seemed to be almost everywhere at once, infusing his men with fresh resolve. Again, regiments were forced to fight on after ammunition was exhausted. With only bayonets as weapons, the men stood firm.

Suddenly a fresh cloud of dust appeared. They must be other Union troops. It was hardly credible that A. P. Hill could have marched the 17 miles from Harper's Ferry in seven hours with the remainder of Jackson's men left behind to take care of prisoners.

"What troops are those?" Lee asked a lieutenant.

"They are flying the Virginia and Confederate flags," was the reply.

As calmly as if he were merely a spectator at a dress parade, Lee said, "It is A. P. Hill, from Harper's Ferry."

Just as calmly, he ordered a battery of the 10th North Carolina to fire on approaching Federals, though warned that this action would draw enemy fire to the spot where he stood.

"Never mind me," he said in the same even tones, and proceeded to direct the North Carolina gunners while shells burst about him, killing two men near him.

When the sun set blood red on a bloody field, the Confederates still held their original positions. Fireflies seemed to swarm in the dark, but these yellow lights were really the bobbing lanterns of those who searched among the dead and wounded. Confederate casualties numbered 2,700 killed, 9,029 wounded; Union casualties, 2,108 killed, 9,549 wounded. No other day in the war had seen such losses. The Confederates had been outnumbered seven to four and had been deprived of all advantage of surprise. The fact that the men in gray held their ground was evidence not only of the superb fighting qualities of a great army, but also the magnificent talents for extemporaneous tactics of its commander and his chief lieutenants. McClellan still had unused reserves. Lee's army was badly battered and it had lost three generals. Lee's principal officers urged him to retreat to Virginia at once.

Instead, Lee posted his artillery in new positions and awaited the morrow. The next day, the opposing armies stirred only to bury their dead and then watched each other warily in the shimmering heat. That night, Lee began the retreat back to Virginia. McClellan was apparently receiving reinforcements.

No time must be lost in gaining the protection of the Potomac barrier.

Early on September 19, Lee sat on horseback, silhouetted against the pre-dawn glow of the Eastern sky. So seen, in immobile dignity in that moment of danger and torturing suspense, he seemed more a monument than a man. But, when nearly all the troops had crossed, a passing officer heard him murmur, "Thank God."

Lee proudly told his men of their accomplishment, "History records few examples of greater fortitude." The praise was merited. But fortitude had not been enough. Inconclusive militarily, the Battle of Sharpsburg was most influential politically. The governments of Britain and France, almost persuaded to recognize the Confederacy and intervene as mediators, now indefinitely postponed the contemplated action. Lincoln deemed the moment psychologically right to issue on September 23 the Preliminary Emancipation Proclamation, which he had held ready through a series of Union reverses. The altruistic aspects of the document were somewhat darkened by the exclusion from emancipation of those slaves living in areas held by the Federal government, but the noble sound of the word "emancipation" was enough to win friends abroad and to inspire some Northerners with crusading fire.

Patriarch of an Army

The Army of Northern Virginia had come to regard Lee as its patriarch. Probably not even one of his generals would have thought of slapping him on the back, but privates cheered him to his face as "Marse Robert" and he was often called "Uncle Robert" or the "Old Man" behind his back.

Colonel Walter H. Taylor, a member of Lee's staff who had come to know the warmth of his chief's personality, was astonished by an incident of late October when Lee was in camp in Northern Virginia. Lee was handed a note telling of the death of his daughter Annie. No trace of emotion flickered across his face and he seemed to accord the note no more attention than the most ordinary message. But a few minutes later, Taylor returned to the tent when Lee did not expect him. The gray head was bowed and Lee's powerful frame was shaking with the force of his sobs.

Earlier in the month, Lee had sent Stuart on a raid deep into enemy territory, to Chambersburg, Pennsylvania. As a result, the

Confederacy gained information that a drive on Richmond was unlikely in the immediate future as well as the more concrete aid of 1,200 horses to revitalize the army's ailing transport. The raid, coupled with Lee's unmolested retreat from Sharpsburg, resulted in McClellan's removal from command of the Army of the Potomac. "I hate to part with McClellan," Lee said, "for we always understood each other so well. I fear they may continue to make these changes until they find someone I don't understand."

McClellan's successor was Major General Ambrose E. Burnside, a man less intelligent than McClellan, but one more difficult for Lee to understand. With his famous sideburns, his long double-breasted blue coat with its rows of brass buttons and his bread loaf helmet of a hat, he was surely the precursor of the Keystone Cop. He was animated by all the well-intentioned energy of that fabulous celluloid character and had the same predilection for chasing up blind alleys. Lee knew what an able commander would do in various situations, making due allowance for the caution or boldness of the individual. But he did not know what Burnside would consider to be the necessary military move.

In November, Lee learned that enemy flanking troops were withdrawing from the western hills and that Federal patrols had been seen near Fredericksburg. Lee proceeded to the historic town, which had been the boyhood home of his idol, George Washington. The city was located on the south bank of the Rappahannock at the fall line dividing Tidewater from the Piedmont. Lee decided to concentrate troops to repel any crossing of the river from the north. When Jackson arrived from the Valley with his corps on November 29, Lee sent him to the area, in the belief that Burnside would not challenge Confederate strength concentrated on the elevated south bank. Nevertheless, he began the energetic construction of earthworks and of timber defenses. His spies were busy on both flanks of Burnside's Army, but still he did not discover the Union general's intentions.

Colonel Garnet Wolseley, who afterwards became Commander-in-

Chief of the British army, had visited the Army of Northern Virginia. He reported: "General Lee is regarded in the light of infallible Jove, a man to be reverenced. The feeling of the soldiers for General Lee resembles that which Wellington's troops entertained for him, namely, a fixed and unshakable faith in all he did, and a calm confidence of victory when serving under him." That confidence was not shared by Lee himself in this time of uncertainty. He wrote his wife: "I tremble for my country when I hear of confidence expressed in me. I know too well my weakness, that our only hope is in God."

On the night of December 10, a woman's voice came from somewhere across the river through the chilling mist. She shouted a warning that the Yankees, not far away, were preparing to march.

Near 5 A.M. sounds of hammering and splashing told the Confederates that bridges were being built from the fog-wrapped opposite shore. Sporadic fire broke out from both armies. When the mid-morning sun burned away the white fog, the Federals began shelling the Confederate position and the town.

Lee looked down on Fredericksburg. Built in a basin in the hills, it still held the fog like a bowl of milk. Only the steeples of its churches showed. Above this strangely peaceful scene appeared the white puffs of bursting shells. Then startlingly black pillars of smoke rose straight up from the white fog several hundred feet into the still air.

Lee's neck reddened and his head jerked with anger. "Those people," he exclaimed, "delight to destroy the weak and those who can make no defense; it just suits them!"

When, later in the day, Lee became convinced that the blue host would attack the Confederate heights, he seemed to feel a fierce joy. "I shall try to do them all the damage in our power when they move forward," he said.

The next morning, both sides of the river were again enveloped in fog. Lee's army, 78,000 strong, awaited the assault of 100,000 Federals and possibly untold reinforcements. Battle opened in midmorning and Lee gloried in the courage of young John Pelham who, with two small artillery pieces, held back the enemy assault until the bringing up of 16 Federal guns made the duel unequal even for his courage and skill. When the Federals were within 800 yards, the Confederate artillery turned them back with great losses.

In the afternoon, the Yankees attacked with a courage and ferocity that the Confederates' heaviest artillery could not destroy. Hand-to-hand fighting, with splendid acts of courage on both sides, raged while the fate of the battle teetered in the balance. Then, just as the heaviest Federal assault on the heights reached its crest, the rebel yell sounded from the woods below and the Federals retreated.

Lee turned to one of his generals. "It is well that war is so terrible —we should grow too fond of it." Almost at that moment, an on-rushing wave of blue broke on the stone wall below Lee's observation post. The senseless loss of life was a reproach to the Union general-ship, but the magnificent valor of the Yankee soldiers themselves was an inspiration, even to their Confederate opponents. The futile slaughter went on until after dark.

That night was made weird by the unearthly lights of the aurora borealis, which shimmered and danced in the Northern sky like the watchfires of Walhalla. From the fields themselves rose the mingled cries and groans of dying Union soldiers. The wails and moans, as a Union colonel said, "flowed together into a keynote weird, un-earthly, terrible to hear."

Lee wrote Jackson: "I am truly grateful to the Giver of all Victory for having blessed us thus far in our terrible struggle. I pray He may continue."

Lee was out riding by dawn, anticipating another attack by Burn-side. But the clear light of morning revealed that the Union general had stolen back across the river. Lee wrote his wife: "They went as they came—in the night. They suffered heavily as far as the battle went, but it did not go far enough to satisfy me. . . . The contest will now have to be renewed, but on what field I cannot say."

Lee had reason to be grateful that he was still alive. Once in the previous day's battle, a shell had nosed into the earth beside him, but it had failed to explode. Later in the day, a huge Parrott gun had exploded near him, and a fragment weighing about a third of a ton had fallen just behind him. One of Lee's officers recorded that "he only looked upon the mass calmly for a moment, and then, without a syllable expressive of surprise or concern, continued the business occupying him at the time."

As might have been expected, Burnside was removed from command in January of 1863. His successor was Joseph Hooker. Some Federal officers had conceived an antipathy for General Lee, but they should have been grateful to him for making so many promotions possible. Seldom had there been so rapid a turnover in high command.

In winter camp along the Rappahannock, with ragged scarecrows huddled over small fires in the snow or dragging rag-wrapped, frostbitten feet in sentry march before snow-roofed huts, Lee must have been reminded of that other Virginian who had commanded a rebel army at Valley Forge. Even drearier were the days when drenching rain turned the snow to mud and the whole world seemed to be cold slush.

All the while, Lee waited for the first move from Hooker, one of the fiercest of the Union generals. Across the river, the great blue army crouched in waiting, growing in strength, growling in menace. And all the time Lee knew what so many in high posts refused to see: that the South was growing weaker, that so many of the South's bravest and ablest fighting men were in their graves and that there was no hope of adequate replacements. Victory after victory the Army of Northern Virginia had won. But so many gallant men, so many irreplacable officers had left the "invincible Army" to join the invisible Host. And some of the best officers that remained— Jackson, Trimble, and Stuart—were engaged in bitter controversies, quarrels exacerbated by the monotony of camp and the tension of waiting.

In February, Lee wrote his daughter Agnes:

The only place I am to be found is in camp, and I am so cross now that I am not worth seeing anyway. Here you will have to take me with the three stools—the snow, the rain, the mud. . . . We are now in a floating condition. . . . But here come, in all their wet, the adjutants general with the papers. I must stop and go to work. See how kind God is? We have plenty to do in good weather and bad.

Later, in a lighter mood, he wrote his wife: "I owe Mr. F. J. Hooker no thanks for keeping me here. He ought to have made up his mind long ago what to do."

Toward the end of March, the green mark of spring appeared on the land to match the red mark on the calendar. But the commander's heart was not lightened. With spring would come action in the field and the army was ill-prepared for it. Lee reported to the government:

The men are cheerful, and I receive but few complaints, still I don't consider [the reduced rations] enough to maintain them in health and vigor, and I fear they will be unable to endure the hardships of the approaching campaign. Symptoms of scurvy are appearing among them and, to supply the place of vegetables, each regiment is directed to send a daily detail to gather sassafras buds, wild onions, garlic, lamb's quarter and poke sprouts; but for so large an army, the supply obtained is very small.

About this time, Lee was seized with excruciating pains in his chest, back, and arm. Much against his wishes, he was forced to take to his bed for several days. Still he did not lose his sense of humor, reporting that the doctors were "tapping me all over like an old steam boiler before condemning it."

That sense of humor, as well as more Spartan qualities, stood him in good stead after he resumed active duty, for his burdens were heavy and he was still not well. When he learned that Hooker had ordered the preparation of eight days' rations, he knew that attack was imminent.

On the night of April 29, Lee was waked in his tent by a courier from Jackson. Lee quickly dropped his feet to the floor and sat on the side of his cot. He listened with perfect composure to the news.

His eyes twinkled as he looked up at the young man and said, "Well, I thought I heard firing, and was beginning to think it was time some of you young fellows were coming to tell me what it was all about. Tell your good general that I am sure he knows what to do. I will meet him at the front very soon."

In the afternoon, Lee learned that Federal infantry had crossed the Rappahannock far above Fredericksburg. It was obvious that Hooker was attempting to execute a massive flanking movement. He had 130,000 men. Lee had fewer than 60,000. The battle would be fought in the Wilderness: the great wooded area south of the Rapidan and the Upper Rappahannock in the vicinity of the cross-roads village of Chancellorsville. On the morning of May 1, the two armies groped toward each other through the tangled forest. Jackson was not far from Chancellorsville and two divisions of the Army of Northern Virginia were already engaged with the enemy when Lee rode out to confer with Stonewall. When the troops caught sight of that famous profile, they broke into spontaneous full-throated cheers. He lifted his hat as he galloped by, and someone exclaimed, "What a head, what a head! See that glorious head!" And others shouted in chorus, "God bless it, God bless it!"

Night closed on a battle distinguished more by tentative probing on the part of the combatants than by fierce fighting. The white-bearded Lee and the black-bearded Jackson, their faces ruddy in the firelight, sat on a log in the shadowy grove of giant pines, whose tops were black against the cold light of a full moon. The scene resembled some Germanic print of a Black Forest tableau. A third bearded figure joined them. Stuart had come to report that the Union flank in the woods near Wilderness Church might be vulnerable. Lee sent Stuart back to study the roads leading to that place. A lantern had been lit and, within the yellow circle of its light, the two remaining figures bent over a map. For a moment there was only the soft sighing of the pines and the crackle of the fire.

Then Lee spoke: "Jackson, how can we get at those people?"

"You know best," Jackson replied with unaccustomed humility.

"Show me what to do and we will try to do it."

With his finger, Lee described a bold arc extending around Hooker's right. The exact route would depend on what Stuart discovered about the roads, and Stuart would cover Jackson's movement with his cavalry. An evanescent smile crossed Jackson's face, and he unfolded his long frame to its full, ramrod-straight height. Touching his cap, he said, "My troops will move at 4 o'clock."

Lee spread out his cloak under a tree and fell asleep as though he had no greater responsibility than his humblest private. He was waked by the same eager young officer who had roused him in his tent to tell him that Hooker was crossing the river. Lee listened attentively to the detailed information about conditions on the enemy right. Then, with a mock gravity contrasting sharply with the young man's enthusiasm, Lee said, "The young men now are not what they were when I was a boy." As the courier turned away, he was surprised and relieved to hear the commander break into a hearty laugh. Lee's laughter was still ringing in his ears when the young man lay down on a saddle blanket to snatch a little sleep.

Who would suspect that that easy laughter boomed from a commander who, outnumbered more than two to one by an enemy force of 130,000, had elected to retain only 14,000 of his own men to withstand the enemy horde while he sent the greater part of his army on a long Wilderness march to make a flank attack of almost incredible daring?

Lee's outward calm was unshakable the next day, even when in the late afternoon there was no sound of battle to tell that Jackson had found and engaged the enemy. If the sun went down before a flank attack could be made, the campaign would be lost and Lee's army might be destroyed.

Suddenly a sweating, slobbering horse dashed into camp bearing a frenzied rider who blurted out the news that Union forces under General John Sedgwick had wrecked the defenses of Fredericksburg and were even then bearing down on the rear of Lee's force.

An eye witness wrote of that moment:

I have never seen anything more majestically calm than General Lee was. . . . Something very like a grave, sweet smile began to express itself on the General's face, but he checked it, and raising his left hand gently . . . he interrupted the excited speaker : "I thank you very much, but both you and your horse are fatigued and overheated. Take him to that shady tree yonder and you and he blow and rest a little."

A few minutes later, Lee called the officer over and smilingly asked, "Now, what were you telling us about Major Sedgwick?" Lee remembered Sedgwick from the old army, and to him the Union general was still a major. He also remembered him as a very decent sort of man, but not one likely to move with the speed of lightning. He therefore listened quietly while the officer, in calmer tones, recited his narrative of disaster, experienced and pending. He then said : "I am very much obliged to you. The Major is a gentleman; I don't think he would hurt us very badly, but we are going to see about him at once. I have just sent General McLaws to make a special call upon him."

A little later, the roar of battle, analyzed by Lee's sensitive ear, told him that Jackson had launched an effective attack on the Union flank. Lee ordered the attack to be pressed in his own immediate front.

Jackson had pounced on the unsuspecting Federals while they were getting their supper in the quiet dusk. His attack had become a rout. Not since Bull Run had he seen Federal soldiers fleeing in such utter panic. Before them rushed the deer of the forest in a panic to match their own. Only the brave stand of General Alfred Pleasanton, whose handful of Union soldiers stood like an island of blue in the confusion, prevented the almost complete destruction of a whole wing of Hooker's army.

When Lee dropped to sleep on the ground a little after midnight, the guns had been silent for several hours, but a ruddy glow in the sky showed that the woods were on fire in the area of the battle. After less than two hours of sleep, Lee was waked by the arrival of Jackson's aide, who told him of the enemy rout, but also brought the news that Jackson had accidentally been shot by his own men. The wound, however, was believed not to be critical.

Lee groaned and shook his head. "Ah, Captain, any victory is dearly bought that takes General Jackson from us, even for a short time."

Lee ordered that the Union forces be pressed back "with the utmost vigor" before they could rally from their defeat. The two wings of the numerically inferior Confederate Army must be united in the day that would soon break.

With Stuart commanding Jackson's corps, the Confederates after much hard fighting put the Federals to flight again. After the two wings were joined, Stuart sent his Prussian aide, Heros von Borcke, to Lee for final instructions. He found the commander "looking as calm and dignified as ever" while shells burst around him and solid shot plowed up the ground on both sides of him. Lee ordered a general attack with the combined forces of his army. The Confederates charged and the Federals were reduced to 'huddled masses fleeing across the landscape. Lee ordered his army to halt and then he rode out to the scene.

Colonel Charles Marshall had been on Lee's staff almost from the start of the General's field service in the War between the States. He had shared his tent and had seen him under the most informal circumstances. But he was awed by the Lee that he saw now sitting grandly astride the powerful gray horse, steed and rider standing in bold relief against the flames of the Chancellorsville House, with the blue hordes of the vanquished enemy dissolving in the distance. The Confederate soldiers, some standing atiptoe and some struggling to raise their shattered bodies from the ground, gave one long, mighty cheer for their chief. Marshall said, "As I looked on him in the complete fruition which his genius, courage, and confidence in his army had won, I thought that it must have been from some such scene that men in ancient days ascended to the dignity of gods."

Lee was not one to gloat, but any feeling of triumph that he might have experienced was quickly dashed by the arrival of a messenger with the news that one of Jackson's arms had been amputated.

Another distressing message followed. What Sedgwick had failed to accomplish earlier, the Union Army had now done by a strong flank attack. The Confederate defenders of Fredericksburg had been driven from their positions. Lee's army was now between Hooker and Sedgwick. The news of Stonewall had brought an expression of deep anguish to the commander's face, but he received this last bad news with an impassive countenance.

The next day Lee attacked Sedgwick, but, without Jackson and his "foot cavalry," the army did not move with its accustomed speed, and the attack was not mounted until six o'clock. The fighting was inconclusive then and on the following day.

On the morning of May 6, Lee's army was poised for attack. After frustrating delays, decisive action would be sweet. But up rode young General Dorsey Pender with the news that Sedgwick had safely stolen across the river. Lee's face flushed a brick red. "Why, General Pender," he exploded, "that is the way you young men always do! You allow those people to get away. I tell you what to do, but you don't do it!"

The next day Lee learned that Jackson had developed pneumonia and might die. He told Chaplain B. T. Lacy, who was returning to Stonewall's side: "Give Jackson my affectionate regards, and tell him to make haste and get well, and come back to me as soon as he can. He has lost his left arm, but I have lost my right."

The next day he sent an even more emotional message by the same man: "When a suitable occasion offers, give him my love, and tell him that I wrestled in prayer for him last night, as I never prayed, I believe, for myself." A few hours later, Lee learned that Jackson was dead.

No Right Arm

The victory at Chancellorsville was notable enough, entirely apart from any other achievements, to place both Lee and Jackson among the great captains of history. But, with Jackson dead, Lee had no corps commander who could almost intuitively grasp his strategy, amplify it if necessary, and quickly translate it into effective tactics to meet the conditions of the field. The communication between Lee and Jackson had been almost telepathic. The army had grown weaker while the enemy, with far greater resources of manpower, had multiplied in strength. Completely subordinating his own personal status to the welfare of the Confederacy, Lee suggested to President Davis that he order part of Beauregard's forces to join the Army of Northern Virginia and place the Creole general in command of the combined forces. Lee believed that the combination was necessary if the army was to attain the essential strength in Virginia, and he doubtless realized that Beauregard would not have taken kindly to a subordinate role.

But Davis believed that Lee's leadership was necessary to Southern success. Lee began the reorganization of his army. Longstreet remained as commander of the First Corps. Richard Stoddart Ewell succeeded to the command of Jackson's Second Corps. A Third Corps was organized under the command of A. P. Hill. The choices seemed sensible : one-legged Dick Ewell, for all his laughable eccentricities, was a stout-hearted fighting man who had proved himself Stonewall's most dependable lieutenant, and A. P. Hill, though high-strung and highly sensitive, was a gallant and high-minded officer. But the seeds of discord lay in these appointments. Longstreet was bitterly jealous of Ewell and Hill's being raised to his own status. He was particularly resentful because both were Virginians. The Georgian complained that Virginia officers were "advertised" more than those from other states.

Lee's army had been so reduced that he was hard put to find worthy replacements for lost regimental and brigade officers. He wrote : "Our army would be invincible if it could be properly organized and officered. There never were such men in an army before. They will go anywhere and do anything if properly led. But there is a difficulty—proper commanders—where can they be obtained?"

Despite the many problems of reorganization, Lee saw that the only hope for his army and the land which it defended lay in bold offensive action.

About the middle of May, conferring in Richmond with the President and his cabinet, Lee won support for another invasion of the North.

Longstreet urged Lee to conduct a campaign of defensive tactics. The assurance and persistence with which he pressed his views showed that he anticipated a co-equal relationship such as Jackson had enjoyed with Lee. Indeed, Longstreet's recent successes in the field and the attention accorded his views in Richmond had imbued him with so much confidence in his own judgment that he seemed to believe it necessary to instruct Lee in strategy.

Word came June 2 that Federal forces were being evacuated from the area below Richmond. With pressure lessened on the capital, Lee deemed the time for invasion at hand. He sent Ewell and the Second Corps to the Winchester area. He also moved a portion of his Fredericksburg forces toward Culpeper. Longstreet was sent to Culpeper and, leaving A. P. Hill's Third Corps to maintain his old line, Lee broke camp on June 6, joining Longstreet and Ewell at Culpeper the next day.

Longstreet still was not committed in his heart to Lee's strategy. Only five days before, at a council of war, he had said that "if we were ever going to make an offensive battle, it should be done south of the Potomac."

On June 8, there was a glittering cavalry review, followed by a grand ball. Some of the gallant young men were dancing for the last time. The next morning Union cavalrymen raided across the Rappahannock in force. The greatest cavalry clash of the war ensued. Only the infantry and artillery saved Stuart's hard-fighting horsemen. For dash, daring, and competence, Stuart's cavalrymen were probably unexcelled anywhere in the world. But many of them were now mounted on tired, bony nags. The Yankee cavalry, once the subject of many Confederate jokes, was now an efficient and superbly mounted force. On the eve of the invasion, Lee sadly noted that his cavalry superiority was gone.

A more personal sorrow tortured Lee the same day. His son, General W. H. F. Lee, known as "Rooney," had been severely wounded. But Lee proudly wrote home, "He seemed to be more concerned about his brave men and officers who had fallen in the battle than himself."

At this juncture, Lee was far from confident that his strategy would be successful. He would have to carry out his plans with a much smaller force than he had expected for the operation. He had told the President, "The best use that could be made of the troops in Carolina, and those . . . guarding Richmond" would be to concentrate them in Middle Virginia under Beauregard, poised as a threat toward Washington while Lee's army moved North. In answer to arguments that Richmond and points to the South must be defended, he had said, "It should never be forgotten that our concentration compels that of the enemy and . . . tends to relieve all other threatened localities."

Lee clearly saw that the invasion would be a desperate gamble. He would be outnumbered more than two to one by the foe. Furthermore, if the enemy were to lose every man in the field at the rate of two Union casualties for every Confederate loss, the Federal government had the resources to field another great army to invade the South. Lee told Davis that if the war lasted much longer, the Confederacy would not. He said that he did not think the Confederate States of America should "make nice distinctions between those who declare for peace unconditionally and those who advocate it as a means of restoring the Union, however much we may prefer the former."

Because of, rather than in spite of, the Confederacy's desperate plight, Lee resolved to prosecute the invasion with the forces available to him. Movement into the North might be a temporary solution for the problem of feeding the half-starved Army of Northern Virginia. Lee argued that operations north of the Potomac would relieve Virginia farms and storehouses from the depredations of the enemy while the Army of Northern Virginia subsisted on Northern resources. Then there was the overriding strategic consideration : "An invasion of the enemy's country breaks up all his preconceived plans of invasion." Lee's words were a variation of the trite but often sound maxim that "a good offense is the best defense."

In mid-June, Ewell soundly thrashed the Union garrison at Winchester and crossed the Potomac. A. P. Hill marched from Fredericksburg, also following a route west of the mountains. Longstreet marched northward by a route east of the Blue Ridge. Stuart was to screen the advance but he obtained Lee's permission to harass Hooker's rear. Lee, knowing Stuart's penchant for daring, independent action, had some misgivings about the cavalryman's part in the plan. He therefore admonished him in writing to keep in communication with General Ewell and to "be watchful and circumspect in all your movements."

The northward movement of Lee's three separate corps completely baffled Hooker. Much depended on his being kept baffled. In a level-headed appraisal, Lee wrote Davis, "It is plain that if all the Federal Army is concentrated upon this, it will result in our accomplishing nothing and being compelled to return to Virginia."

In his passage through Maryland, Lee was idolized by the women. He accepted their gifts of flowers but tactfully refused to part with locks of his hair, saying that it was thinning and suggesting that the ladies snip their souvenirs from the abundant blond curls of General George Pickett.

The women of Pennsylvania were in an entirely different mood. No enemy troops contested the Confederates' passage, but the females were skirted terrors. In contrast with some of the cursing harridans but sharing their sentiments was a pretty young girl, her face flushed with anger, who stood on the terraced lawn of a large house and waved a small American flag almost in the faces of the marching Confederates. Behind her and cheering her on was a chorus of richly attired women. She must have found the discipline of the troops infuriating, for they filed by as though unaware of her presence. Then, riding up on his great gray horse, came Robert E. Lee, looking like one of "the spear-carrying kings in the history books." He turned that magnificent, bearded visage toward the young woman and his great brown eyes looked directly into hers. She lowered her flag, then dropped it to the ground. Then she clasped her hands and fervently exclaimed, "Oh, I wish he was ours!"

Lee's army must have been one of the most gentlemanly invading forces in history. A British observer, Colonel A. J. L. Fremantle, reported : "I saw no straggling into the houses, nor were any of the inhabitants disturbed or annoyed by the soldiers. . . . I witnessed the singular good behavior of the troops."

But there were some cases of irregular "requisitioning," and these distressed Lee. In an order commending the troops on their generally good behavior, he admonished : "There have, however, been instances of forgetfulness on the part of some that they have in keeping the yet unsullied reputation of this Army, and that the duties exacted of us by civilization and Christianity are not less obligatory in the country of our enemy than in our own."

One woman went directly to Lee's tent to ask for flour, complaining that his army had taken the supplies available in the town. Lee told her that he had given the supplies to his men to keep them from ravaging homes. He added, "God help you if I permitted them to enter your houses. Your supplies depend upon the amount that is sent in to my men." He told her, too, that war was a cruel thing and that his only desire was to "go home and eat *his* bread there in peace." The woman's request had been formally denied, but before she left Lee's tent, she asked for his autograph.

The Confederate commander's tent was pitched near Chambersburg on the road to an obscure village called Gettysburg. It was at Chambersburg that Lee remarked to General John B. Hood, "Ah, General, the enemy is a long time finding us; if he doesn't succeed soon, we must go in search of him." Hood thought that Lee was in exceptionally buoyant spirits. He did not know that the commander was troubled because he had received no report from Stuart. The absence of news could mean that Hooker had not yet crossed the Potomac. If this assumption was correct, the prospect was most encouraging. "When they hear where we are," Lee told General Ike Trimble, "they will make forced marches to interpose their forces between us and Baltimore and Philadelphia. They will come up . . . broken down with hunger and hard marching, strung out on a long line and much demoralized, when they come into Pennsylvania. I shall throw an overwhelming force on their advance, crush it, follow up the success, drive one corps back on another."

At least, all this could be done, if Hooker had not yet crossed the Potomac. But had he? What had happened to Stuart?

On the night of June 28, with no word yet from Stuart, Lee learned from a scout that the Army of the Potomac had not only crossed into Maryland but was even then marching toward Gettysburg in great force. Hooker had been replaced (chalk another one up for Lee) by General George Meade. This news did not cheer Lee. He had great respect for Meade's competence.

Lee ordered A. P. Hill and Longstreet to march to Cashtown, a village near Gettysburg. He recalled Ewell, who was then nearing Carlisle, Pennsylvania, directing him to return by Gettysburg or Cashtown. Lee would have his forces concentrated, but he would not have the cavalry. Where could Stuart be?

On the 29th, Lee told his officers: "Tomorrow, gentlemen, we will not move to Harrisburg as we expected, but will go over to Gettysburg and see what General Meade is after."

Lee spent the next night at Cashtown with Longstreet's corps. There he received a disturbing report from A. P. Hill. Some North Carolina troops had hiked to Gettysburg in search of shoes and there had had a brief brush with Federal cavalry. The enemy was almost upon the Army of Northern Virginia.

July 1st dawned clear and quite cool for that time of year. The green, rolling country under a benign blue sky presented a scene of such pastoral peace that it was hard to believe that violence on a titanic scale might soon erupt. Lee was riding with Longstreet when he heard the sound of cannon. As it welled to a crescendo, he rode rapidly to the front.

By two o'clock in the afternoon, from an eminence three miles west of Gettysburg, he looked down on the village and its surrounding fields and woods. The men in gray were preparing to attack. Earlier, General Harry Heth of A. P. Hill's corps had succeeded in driving two Union brigades almost into the village, but then had been pushed back with heavy losses. The bluecoats now outflanked the Confederates, and more Federal troops were coming up to reinforce them.

General R. E. Rodes' division of Ewell's corps, arrived on the scene, rushed into battle on the Federal flank.

Heth appealed to Lee, "Rodes is heavily engaged; had I better not attack?"

"No!" Lee said, "I am not prepared to bring on a general engagement today. Longstreet isn't up."

But Early's division, fresh on the field, attacked the Federals on Rodes' left and a general engagement was on. As Heth said, the fight was "stumbled into," and "was without order or system."

The blue and the gray lines wavered in the shock of battle and then the Confederates routed the Federals. Lee called for A. P. Hill to press the fleeing Yankees, but he learned that Hill had been too ill to participate in the battle and that his corps was so scattered that it could not quickly be organized. So he then sent Ewell a message saying that pursuit of the enemy by his corps could secure possession of the heights which dominated the battlefield. With the courtesy which he customarily showed to subordinates, Lee said that he "wished" for Ewell to act accordingly "if possible."

Ewell understood that he was being given discretion in the matter, something he was seldom allowed as Jackson's lieutenant. Paralyzed by the unaccustomed privilege of choice, the usually aggressive Ewell ordered his troops to halt. When one of his subordinates, General John B. Gordon, realized that Ewell had no intention of storming the hills, he continued to move forward and halted only after receiving Ewell's fourth command to stop.

That night Longstreet renewed his insistence on defensive strategy. This persistence was too much for Lee's patience. The commander raised his fist in the air and rumbled, "No! If he is there tomorrow, I will attack him."

Previous experience with Lee had led the Georgian to believe that he could contradict his chief with impunity. Undismayed, he continued the argument: "If he is there tomorrow, it will be because he wants you to attack. If that height has become the objective, why not attack it at once?"

"No," Lee retorted, "they are there in position, and I am going to whip them or they are going to whip me."

As Lee pointed out, some Federal troops were already on the higher ground, and he had no troops with which to occupy it. Longstreet's troops still had not arrived. Lee pointedly asked him how far away they were and asked him to speed their movement. He began planning to "attack the enemy in the morning as early as practicable."

He asked Ewell if he could open the attack at daylight. An uncomfortable silence followed. It soon became apparent that Ewell, though fearless under fire, was afraid of responsibility. A. P. Hill's corps was near exhaustion and its commander was sick. There was only one thing Lee could do, and he was not happy about it. "Well," he said resignedly, "if I attack from my right, Longstreet will have to make the attack. Longstreet is a very good fighter when he gets in position and gets everything ready, but he is so *slow*."

That night Stuart was heard from, but he was too far away to be on hand for the next day's battle. Lee would have to attack without his cavalry. "If we do so," he told a member of his staff, "we will not, if successful, be able to reap the fruits of victory."

Lee was up before daylight. After dawn, he searched the horizon for the approach of Longstreet's corps. At length, fearing that Longstreet would not arrive in time, Lee sent a message to Ewell asking if he could shift his troops to take Longstreet's place. Then Longstreet arrived and stolidly resumed the argument of the night before.

Lee listened with great self-control until he saw the arrival of some Federal troops on the ridge beside the town. He then terminated the discussion by walking away. His coat buttoned to the throat, and his field glasses suspended at his side, he proceeded to a grove of trees, where he paced up and down, pausing occasionally to take another look at the enemy. Lee turned to General John B. Hood and said, "The enemy is here, and if we don't whip him, he will whip us."

A little later, Longstreet walked up, and he and Hood sat together under one of the trees. Longstreet told Hood: "The General is a little nervous this morning. He wishes me to attack. I do not wish to do so without Pickett. I never like to go into battle with one boot off."

Lee had every right to be nervous. While he waited for McLaws' division to take position, the bluecoated horde could be seen occupying some of the very posts which Lee had been trying for hours to fill with his own men.

As soon as McLaws arrived, Lee pointed to a place on his map and said: "General, I wish you to place your division across this road. And I want you to get there if possible without being seen by the enemy. Can you do it?"

McLaws said that he knew no reason why he could not. He said that he would "take a party of skirmishers and go in advance and reconnoiter."

Longstreet, who was now doing some pacing on his own, halted suddenly and turned to McLaws. "No, sir," he interrupted, "I do not want you to leave your division." Lee was either so absorbed in battle plans that he was unaware of Longstreet's remark or he chose to appear so. But he could not ignore Longstreet when the Georgian leaned across him, ran his finger parallel to the road on the map that the commander was holding, and told McLaws, "I wish your division placed so."

Lee lifted his head, and said quietly but firmly: "No, general, I wish it placed just perpendicular to that, or just the opposite." Longstreet turned away. McLaws then asked Longstreet's permission to go with the reconnoitering party. Longstreet denied the request. McLaws thought that there was irritation behind Longstreet's stolid, bearded countenance. But who could be sure?

Before 9 A.M., Lee told Longstreet, "I think you had better move on."

More than two hours passed in an agony of waiting, with Lee saying, "What can detain Longstreet?" About 11 A.M. Lee came upon Longstreet and his staff waiting in complete inactivity. The Georgian had made no move to hurry his corps forward. Lee then ordered him to move at once.

There is no report of the Virginian's exact words or manner at this time, but his face must have been flushed and his neck must have jerked as it usually did when his patience was exhausted.

Lee's principal objective was Cemetery Ridge, a rounded stretch of high ground. To gain it, he ordered the taking of two other eminences. Ewell attacked Culp's Hill and Longstreet charged the Round Top Hills on Meade's flank. Inadequate reconnaissance, resulting from Lee's lack of cavalry, led him to believe that Cemetery Ridge was not yet occupied by the Federal troops. Both of Lee's attacking forces gained ground, and the Union Third Corps was completely knocked out of action. But Cemetery Ridge, contrary to expectation, had been occupied by the Federals, and the Confederates failed to drive them from it.

When the second day's fighting ended, both armies remained overnight in the positions that they had held at sundown. The next day would almost certainly bring the climactic battle. In his tent that night, in the full loneliness of any man who has ultimate responsibility in time of crisis, Lee knew that the next twenty-four hours would probably determine the fate of his nation.

Lee himself was sick, suffering weakness and pain.

There was some comfort in the fact that Stuart's cavalry had arrived at last and would be available for the next day's operations. Lee had reprimanded Jeb for depriving the army of its "eyes and ears" while time was consumed in rounding up enemy wagons in a raid more spectacular than valuable. But, after the first flush of anger, Lee had found it impossible to be too hard on a general who was just thirty years old and had already made inestimable contributions to the success of Confederate arms.

It probably was harder for Lee to be charitable with Longstreet, who deliberately slowed his movements in rebellion against the commander's strategy. But "Old Pete," as half the army called the Georgia general, was the experienced and battle-tried soldier whom Lee had once called "my old warhorse." Longstreet was certainly insubordinate at times. But Lee did not doubt that Old Pete's opposition was rooted in sincerity. Furthermore, he could not remove Longstreet from command on the eve of battle because he had no one to replace him. Lee once again would have to subordinate his personal pride to the requirements of the task at hand. He would have to entrust the execution of his battle plan to a man who did not believe in it; to one who, for all his appearance of stolid simplicity, was an unknown quantity.

On the morning of July 3, Longstreet renewed his arguments against Lee's strategy. He resumed operations with obvious reluctance and great deliberation.

Heavy Federal fire from the Union right drove Ewell's corps down from Culp's Hill. Charging Little Round Top on the Union left, Longstreet drove back the Union corps commanded by General Daniel Sickles. Possession of Little Round Top would enable the Confederates to enfilade the entire Union position. But possession had not yet been gained.

Lee ordered Longstreet to conduct a direct attack on the strongest part of the enemy center with Pickett's, Pettigrew's, and Trimble's divisions.

Longstreet protested: "That will give me 15,000 men. I have been a soldier all my life, in pretty much all kinds of skirmishes. I think I can safely say there never was a body of 15,000 men who could make that attack successfully."

Noon came. The heat was intense. Pickett came up and saluted Longstreet.

Old Pete struggled for utterance. Tears glistened on his cheeks and beard. "Pickett," he said at last: "I am being crucified. I have instructed [Col. E. P.] Alexander to give you your orders, for I can't."

The hour arrived. Pickett shook his yellow mane and roared: "Up, men, and to your posts! Don't forget today that you are from Old Virginia!" General Pettigrew shouted to his North Carolinians: "For the sake of the good old North State, forward!" Two hundred yards they moved forward through a field of golden grain before a terrible fire was concentrated on them. Still they moved on inexorably and in unbroken line, firing as they advanced. When they reached the Emmitsburg road, blue coats fired from behind a stone fence and the enemy artillery was turned in full force upon the Confederates. Double quick, the men charged, closing the great gaps torn in their ranks. Whenever a regimental flag fell, another hand grasped it and flourished it in the enemy's face. With the rebel yell floating above them, they mounted the Yankee defenses, drove the gunners from their artillery pieces and planted their red banner over the enemy's works. The rebel yell melted into a shout of victory.

Then discipline replaced panic in the blue ranks. Blue and gray seemed to boil up in confusion on the crest. Slowly and begrudgingly at first, then with quickened pace, the Confederates fell back. Fifteen thousand men had marched unflinchingly uphill across three quarters of a mile of open space into a wall of fire in the longest charge of the war. A thousand men ran, limped, or stumbled over the shattered bodies of fallen comrades to make their way back to their lines. A few hundred more, some slipping in their own blood, attempted to crawl to shelter.

Lee hovered like a father over every wounded man that came his way: "All this will come right in the end," he was saying, or "We will talk it over afterward." For the only slightly hurt there were other words: "Bind up your hurts and take up muskets."

Brigadier General Cadmus Wilcox, who had made a futile effort to support Pickett's brigade, came up to Lee almost in tears. Noted for his coolness amid the most dreadful battle scenes, he was now almost distraught. Lee grasped his hand and said, "Never mind, General. All this has been my fault. It is I that have lost this fight."

A wounded Yankee lay on the ground nearby. Despite his pain, he was a defiant prisoner. Recognizing Lee, he shouted, "Hurrah for the Union!" Lee dismounted immediately and went directly to the man. A look of fright came on the prisoner's face. Was the General going to kill him? Lee shook the soldier's hand as though the boy had been one .of his own men and then looked at him with sad eyes. "My son," Lee said in a gentle tone, "I hope you will soon be well." Only hatred had sustained the soldier to this moment, and now that was gone. He sobbed himself to sleep.

Lee ordered General Pickett to place his division in position to repel a possible advance by the enemy.

Pickett replied, "General Lee, I have no division now." And he ticked off the names of his brigadiers, "Armistead is down, Garnett is down and Kemper is mortally wounded."

Instantly, Lee attempted to console him: "Come, General Pickett, the men and officers of your command have written the name of Virginia as high today as it has ever been written before."

Night came with no counterattack by the Federals.

Some of Lee's staff blamed Longstreet for not sending in the divisions of McLaws and Hood to support Pickett's charge. Orders directing Longstreet to send in the divisions had been sent. What had happened to them?

At 1 A.M. Brigadier General John Imboden of the Cavalry was waiting at Lee's headquarters where the commander had ordered him to report. In the bright moonlight, Lee came riding up slowly, alone, on Traveller. Reining in before his tent, Lee tried to dismount. The effort was so obviously painful that Imboden stepped up to help him. Lee's feet were on the ground before Imboden could assist him. For a moment, the commander threw his arm across the saddle and leaned against Traveller's gray bulk. A tide of sympathy swept over the cavalryman as he looked at Lee. "The moon," he said afterwards, "shone full upon his massive features and revealed an expression of sadness that I had never before seen upon his face. Awed by his appearance, I waited for him to speak, until the silence became embarrassing."

At length, Imboden said, "General, this has been a hard day for you."

"Yes," Lee said, it has been a sad, sad day to us."

Silence again. Then Lee suddenly pulled himself to his full height and, his bass voice choked with emotion, declared: "I never saw troops behave more magnificently than Pickett's division of Virginians did today in that grand charge upon the enemy. And if they had been supported as they were to have been—but, for some reason not yet explained to me, were not—we would have held the position and the day would have been ours." In a voice that was almost a groan wrung from him, he added: "Too bad! *Too bad! Oh, too bad!*"

He then went into his tent with Imboden and told him, "We must now return to Virginia." He ordered Imboden to cover the retreat with his horsemen.

The Long Retreat

Independence Day dawned as clouded as the South's own hopes for independence. Until four o'clock in the afternoon, Lee's army remained at Gettysburg, sickened by the stench from the swollen corpses that carpeted the battlefield.

The Union forces made no move to attack. As a Tarheel soldier observed with a truth independent of logic, "Both sides got the worst of the fight at Gettysburg." Lee's army had suffered about 20,000 casualties, but Meade's had suffered about 23,000 casualties. After waiting long enough to prove that the enemy had no taste for a renewal of hostilities, Lee's men with the wagons of wounded moved off slowly through the mud in a rain-drenched caravan of privation, suffering, and death.

The last units of the Army gained the Virginia bank of the Potomac on the rain-swept night of July 13 after only minor skirmishing with the Federals.

Early in August, from his camp at Orange, Lee wrote Davis:

I have seen and heard of expression of discontent in the public journals at the result of the expedition. I do not know how far this feeling extends in the army. My brother officers have been too kind to report it, and so far the troops have been too generous to exhibit it. It is fair, however, to suppose that it does exist, and success is so necessary to us that nothing should be risked to secure it. I therefore, in all sincerity, request Your Excellency to take measures to supply my place. I do this with the more earnestness because no one is more aware than myself of my inability for the duties of my position. I cannot even accomplish what I myself desire. How can I fulfill the expectations of others? In addition, I sensibly feel the growing failure of my bodily strength. I have not yet recovered from the attack I experienced the past spring. I am becoming more and more incapable of exertion, and am thus prevented from making the personal examinations and giving the personal supervision to the operations in the field which I feel to be necessary.

The President promptly replied: "Our country could not bear to lose you. To ask me to substitute you by someone in my judgment more fit to command, or who would possess more of the confidence of the army or of the reflecting men of the country, is to demand an impossibility."

After Gettysburg, Lee's army participated in no great battle until the spring of 1864. But, while Lee stood guard over Richmond, decisive defeats were being suffered by the Confederacy in the West. The fall of Vicksburg had been almost simultaneous with the Battle of Gettysburg. The Southern forces were defeated at Chattanooga after winning a costly victory at Chickamauga.

In March of 1864, Ulysses S. Grant was given supreme command of the Union armies. Tough-minded rather than brilliant, he was a man of great resolution. Realizing that the North's principal advantage over the South was in men and matériel, Grant determined upon a strategy of quantity rather than quality. He proposed to bury Lee's army under sheer weight of numbers.

He assembled the 100,000-man Army of the Potomac at Culpeper for a southward movement toward Richmond. Grant ordered General Benjamin F. Butler to march with his 36,000-man Army of the James up the south bank of that river and thus cut off Lee from the armies and supplies of the Lower South. Major General Franz Sigel was ordered to move southward through the Shenandoah Valley and take Lynchburg, Virginia.

To oppose these three forces converging on the Richmond area, Lee had 60,000 men in the Army of Northern Virginia and the support of 30,000 men commanded by Beauregard.

Grant, as supreme commander, and Meade, as commander of the Army of the Potomac, crossed the Rapidan with that 100,000-man force on May 4 and entered the Wilderness.

Lee was delighted to learn of the move and sent orders to Ewell to attack the enemy. To his own staff, on the morning of the 5th, Lee expressed pleasure that Grant "had not profited by General Hooker's Wilderness experiences, and that he seemed inclined to throw away . . . the immense advantage which his great superiority in numbers . . . gave him."

The armies clashed at noon. As one of the Federal soldiers later wrote, "It was a blind and bloody hunt to the death, in bewildering thickets, rather than a battle . . . ." Again and again, bluecoats rushed forward, only to be driven back by the murderous fire from concealed Confederate muskets. That night the brush caught fire. Some of the wounded on both sides were overtaken by the flames.

Lee looked to the next day with a worried mind. With only 30,000 troops, he had attacked a force of 100,000. He had counted upon the arrival of Longstreet's corps, but "Old Pete" had gone into camp six miles from the main army and had decided to rest his men until 1 A.M,

Could Lee's fragment of the army hold off the enemy until Longstreet arrived?

At dawn, Grant's army attacked in force. Soon the overpowered Confederates were streaming back in retreat. Lee rode up to one of his generals and exclaimed, "My God! Is this splendid brigade of yours running like a flock of geese?"

The officer replied: "General, the men are not whipped. They only want a place to form, and they will fight as well as ever they did."

Now only one small battery of artillery stood between the Confederates and disaster. Lee turned to an officer: "Longstreet must be here. Go bring him up!"

Suddenly the Texas brigade of Longstreet's corps burst upon the scene. Reinforcements had arrived. Lee waved his hat and shouted, "Hurrah for Texas! Hurrah for Texas!" He ordered their commander, General John Gregg, to charge the enemy. "When you go in there," he said, "I wish you to give those men the cold steel —they will stand and fire all day and never move unless you charge them."

Gregg shouted: "Attention, Texas Brigade! The eyes of General Lee are upon you. Forward march!"

Lee rode to the front of the brigade, stood in his stirrups, raised his hat from his head and boomed above the martial din, "Texans always move them."

An ear-splitting yell rose from the brigade. One of Gregg's couriers, with tears running down his cheeks, shouted, "I would charge hell itself for that old man!"

Forward Lee rode with the brigade. Five or six members of his staff urged him to go back, pleaded with him, but still he moved forward. Then they seized Traveller's reins and even laid hands on the commander himself to hold him back. But he shook them off and still rode forward.

The Texans, fearful for Uncle Robert's life, took up the chant: "Go back, General Lee! Go back!" Lee still moved forward. "We won't go on unless you go back," came the insistent cry. A sergeant grabbed Traveller's bridle. Gregg pleaded with Lee. Reluctantly, Lee turned back.

Heavy fighting followed. The Federals were checked.

Lee had devised strategy for turning the Federal left. He now ordered an advance. As the troops moved to the front, Lee, astride Traveller, watched the flight, his face "flushed and full of animation." An Alabama colonel, watching Lee, said afterward: "I thought him at that moment the grandest specimen of manhood I ever beheld. He looked as though he ought to have been and was the monarch of the World."

"What troops are these?" the commander asked as ragged regiments filed past.

"Law's Alabama brigade," answered a proud private.

"God bless the Alabamians!" Lee shouted. Whooping, the men rushed forward.

The bluecoats were fleeing when the wounding of Longstreet removed him from command. The advance slowed. One more Confederate sally drove back the Federal Corps. Night came and the fighting ceased. The morning of May 7 revealed that Grant had withdrawn. Lee had outmaneuvered his heavier opponent, exacting about 18,000 casualties for about 10,000 of his own.

Lee rode out with General John B. Gordon, a gallant Georgian high in his esteem. Gordon told Lee of reports that the commander had already heard—that Grant was retreating.

"General Grant isn't going to retreat," Lee said with quiet finality. "He will move his army to Spotsylvania."

Gordon was surprised. "Is there any information on that?"

Lee calmly replied: "Not at all. But that is the next point at which the Armies will meet. Spotsylvania is now General Grant's best strategic point. I am so sure of his next move that I have already made arrangements to march by the shortest practicable route, that we may meet him there."

On the night of May 6, Grant had begun the first of a series of "sliding movements," a gradual shifting, shifting, shifting south-easterly down a diagonal line toward Richmond. The two armies clashed twice on May 8 as Grant moved his army toward Spotsylvania Court House. When Grant's army reached its objective, Lee's army was already waiting for it behind breastworks. Thoroughly outguessed, Grant was frustrated in his efforts to flank the Army of Northern Virginia.

On May 10, with both armies in position, there were at least five separate bloody clashes. The Confederates were successful until late in the day when, with two Federal corps making a terrific assault on the Confederate left, Union Colonel Emory Upton led a bold and vigorous charge that penetrated the apex of the angle of Confederate entrenchments. Lee's skillful employment of artillery enabled his men to restore the line in the "Mule Shoe," as this angle was called because of its shape. But a strong Federal effort on the next day might penetrate the position again, cut Lee's army in two, and take the whole Confederate line from the rear.

The next day, however, brought little action at Spotsylvania. General Philip H. Sheridan, with 7,000 men, attempted a cavalry raid on Richmond, but was turned back by Stuart's force of 1,100. The Confederate victory, though, was infinitely costly, for Stuart was mortally wounded.

That same day, Grant made the famous statement, "I propose to fight it out along this line if it takes all summer." Grant could afford to wait. Time was on his side. He had two soldiers for every man Lee had, could call up reinforcements, and would be aided by simultaneous Union attacks in other areas, which would prevent reinforcement of Lee. Moreover, Grant's army was well fed, well clothed, and splendidly equipped, while Lee's was half-starved, ragged, and short of guns, ammunition and horses. In addition to all these advantages, the Union had command of the seas.

A massive Federal assault began at dawn of the 12th. Lee mounted and rode to the front. Soon a torrent of fleeing Confederates rushed past him on both sides.

"Shame on you men! Shame on you!" the general scolded. "Go back to your regiments. Go back to your regiments." But the tide of frightened humanity rushed on. A young officer from General Edward Johnson's staff rode up with the news that the Yankees had broken the line at the "Mule Shoe" and were rushing through the breach in incredible numbers.

Lee instantly called up General Gordon. He had already told Gordon to be prepared to lead an attack on the enemy in the event of such a break-through.

As the Georgian formed his lines, Lee, with his white head bared, rode out in front. Gordon would never forget that moment. Years later he recalled, "Lee looked a very god of war." Gordon instantly perceived that Lee intended to lead the charge in person, the very thing he had barely been restrained from doing in the Battle of the Wilderness. The Georgian blocked Traveller with his own horse and grasped the great charger's bridle. He raised his stentorian voice so that his words would carry to his men. "General Lee," he said, "you shall not lead my men in a charge. . . . Another is here for that purpose. These men behind you are Georgians, Virginians, and Carolinians. They have never failed you on any field. They will not fail you here. Will you, boys?"

"No, no, no!" swelled the answering chorus.

Gordon shouted to his chief, "You must go to the rear!"

The men took up a new chant, "General Lee to the rear! General Lee to the rear!" They turned Traveller around and began shoving him back. A colonel called out, "Three cheers for General Lee and Old Virginia!" Amid the lusty cheers, Traveller was led to the rear.

Gordon's men rushed forward with the fury of inspiration. The center of the line was restored. But the day still hung in a doubtful balance. Lee watched calmly while bullets whizzed past his head. Again the men yelled: "Go back, General Lee. Go back."

Lee shouted, "If you will promise to drive those people from our works, I will go back." Fighting for Lee, they drove the Yankees back.

Not until May 18 did Grant again attempt to storm the "Mule

Shoe," now called the "Bloody Angle." He was vigorously repulsed. The Union Army began to pull out on the night of May 19, once again with a sliding movement.

Understanding Grant's strategy as well as any member of the Union general's staff, Lee hurried his army along a roughly parallel line in an effort to reach the North Anna River before Grant.

Before leaving Spotsylvania, Lee's salvage crews collected 120,000 pounds of fired lead to be recast into bullets. The musketry fire at times in the battles just concluded was the heaviest thus far in military history. Lee's casualties had numbered about 20,000. Grant's casualties totaled more than 33,000. The Union general had lost an average of 2,000 men every 24 hours since crossing the Rappahannock.

Ill and in pain, Lee was forced to take to his bed on May 25. A battle must soon be fought and he could not bear the thought of being away from the field. Over and over he said, "We must strike them a blow." On May 31, Grant was reported in strength at Cold Harbor. Lee ordered an attack at that point as early as possible on June 1. Racked with pain, he rode toward the scene in a carriage.

The attack was made and failed. Despite his condition, Lee worked all night to strengthen his lines and he examined the defenses himself. There was only skirmishing on June 2. A full-scale battle opened about dawn of June 3. Lee's engineering genius had prepared the defenses with phenomenal success. Within the first hour, 7,000 Yankees fell. Again and again, Grant threw his men against the Confederate lines, and each time the bodies of the attackers provided a carpet for the next assaulting wave. Finally, when the Federal officers were ordered to renew the attack, they gave the command, but not a man stirred. Shortly after noon, Grant sent word to Meade: "You may direct a suspension of farther advance for the present."

In the days that followed, hundreds of wounded Yankees, stranded in the "no man's land" between the armies, groaned and screamed for water, but Grant, too proud to admit defeat, would not ask for a truce to aid them. Not until June 7, too late for many of the men, was there a truce. On the night of June 12, Grant's army abandoned the field.

In the month ending June 12, trading two Yankees for every Confederate put out of battle, Grant had lost 60,000 men : a number equal to Lee's total strength.

Colonel Upton, Union hero of the "Bloody Angle," and afterwards a renowned military expert, had written his sister from Cold Harbor :

"I am disgusted with the generalship displayed. Our men have, in many instances, been foolishly and wantonly sacrificed. . . . Thousands of lives might have been spared by the exercise of a little skill; but as it is, the courage of the poor men is expected to obviate all difficulties."

A day later he wrote his sister : "Twenty thousand of our killed and wounded should today be in our ranks. But I will cease faultfinding, and express the hope that mere numbers will yet enable us to enter Richmond."

The same hope animated Grant. The Wilderness Campaign had failed to achieve its two immediate objectives, destruction of Lee's army and capture of Richmond. Having failed to take the city by drives from north and east, the Union army might now attack from the south. If Lee's army could not be destroyed with dramatic rapidity by bold strategy, it could still be worn down by its far heavier antagonist.

Lee had guessed that Grant would cross to the south bank of the James and then move on Richmond. But Lee did not have the men and resources to make effective use of his own foresight. If he led his army across the James in anticipation of Grant's move, the Union general might then abruptly alter his strategy, sending only half of his army (a body equal to Lee's total force) to the south side to do battle with Lee while the other half remained north of the river for an assault on Richmond. Grant was aware that capture of Petersburg, the rail center linking Richmond and its hinterland with the South and West, could be the means of isolating the capital and its defending army from supplies and possible reinforcements. Equally aware of the importance of Petersburg but severely restricted by the smallness of his force, Lee had to leave the defense of that city to Beauregard's troops, gradually reinforcing them as Grant's deepening involvement in the Petersburg area made such action feasible.

Grant crossed the James on June 12. A few days later, after failing in assaults on Petersburg, he decided that the city would have to be taken by a siege.

Grant's strategy was simple but certain to succeed. Since his army was twice as large as Lee's, he could slowly push his line to the West, forcing Lee to extend the opposing line to match it. Before the Federal line was substantially weakened by attenuation, Lee's line would be thinned to the breaking point.

The siege of Petersburg became the longest of the entire war. Incredibly, its defenders, though weakened by disease and malnutrition as well as constant vigilance and frequent combat, held out for nine months.

An offensive conducted by Sheridan in the Valley made it necessary for Lee to detach part of his troops for service there.

Petersburg fell even then only when Sheridan rode down from the Valley to join his forces with Grant's. On March 25, Lee, cognizant of the heavy odds against success, gambled desperately in the attack on Ft. Stedman, Union fortification near Petersburg, which was the key to Grant's supply base. At first, the Confederates were successful. But eventually they fell back from a line manned by four men to their one.

The next day, Lee notified President Davis that the city of Richmond must fall. On April 1, Sheridan struck at the Confederates under Pickett and Fitzhugh Lee at the village of Five Forks, a few miles southwest of Petersburg. Under Sheridan, the Federals had an overwhelming combination of superior numbers and great skill. This disaster was the worst suffered by Lee's army.

The day after this defeat Lee lost General A. P. Hill. Jackson, Stuart, Hill—all were gone. The "iron lines of Petersburg," pressed ever thinner under the hammer strokes of Grant's army, cracked. On April 2, Lee evacuated both Petersburg and Richmond.

Besides the Army of Northern Virginia, there was only one other Confederate army in the field, the hard-pressed army of General Joseph Johnston, which Union General William Tecumseh Sherman had relentlessly pursued into North Carolina. In hopes of effecting a junction with this weakened force, Lee headed for Lynchburg, which still had rail communications with Carolina.

Grant was in hot pursuit. Sheridan seized Burkesville, a railway junction, and thus dashed Lee's hopes of joining Johnston. Grant extended his line to block westward routes of escape. Completely isolated from all reinforcements and supplies, with rations almost gone, and with his force reduced to fewer than 30,000 men opposed to an army several times that size, Lee had open to him only one humane and sensible course. To continue to fight under such conditions in a country almost completely occupied by the enemy would be to sacrifice many lives and bring untold suffering to the civilian population without in any way altering the final result.

On April 8, Lee vowed that he was "resolved to die" rather than surrender unconditionally. But he agreed to meet Grant to discuss terms of surrender. The meeting was set for April 9—Palm Sunday.

Appomattox

Searching for a conference room at Appomattox, Colonel Charles Marshall, Lee's aide, selected the brick farmhouse of Wilmer McLean. Ironically enough, McLean had moved from Manassas, scene of historic conflicts, to get away from the war. And now the war was to end, for all practical purposes, in his parlor.

As Grant prepared to enter the house to talk with Lee, Sheridan protested: "This is a trick. We will whip them now in five minutes, if only you will let us go in." Grant was contemptuous of such advice. He had "no doubt about the good faith of Lee."

General Lee, immaculate in full dress uniform of Confederate gray, with gleaming epaulets and glittering dress sword, was standing at the end of the room opposite the door. Through that door stepped Grant, his square forehead corrugated, the outline of his square jaws visible in the cut of his nutbrown beard, and a mud-spattered blue uniform hanging loosely on his slightly stooped figure. In after years, Grant said that he was deeply embarrassed at this moment. One of the Federal officers with Grant said later that all of them entered quietly and stood against the walls of the room "very much as people enter a sick chamber when they expect to find the patient dangerously ill."

Grant advanced toward Lee, and said courteously: "I met you once before, General Lee. In Mexico, when you came over from Scott's headquarters to visit Garland's brigade." Lee nodded in acknowledgment.

"I have always remembered your appearance," Grant began again, "and I think I'd have recognized you anywhere."

"Yes," said Lee, "I know I met you then, and I have often thought of it and tried to recollect how you looked, but have never been able to recall a single feature."

After a brief silence that seemed long, the two generals began reminiscing about adventures in Mexico. All Americans may be proud that at this moment Lee exhibited no trace of rancor, and Grant showed not a sign of gloating. Lee asked to meet a Union general who had thoughtfully sent him word that his son Custis Lee, who had been captured, was unhurt. Lee thanked the man.

Grant seemed loath to mention the business at hand. At length, Lee said: "General, I have come to meet you in accordance with my letter to you this morning, to treat about the surrender of my army, and I think the best way would be for you to put your terms in writing."

Grant wrote out the terms rapidly in the form of a letter. He then copy read it, making a few corrections, and passed it on to Lee, who was seated at a spool-legged table by the window. Lee drew a pair of steel-rimmed spectacles from his pocket, polished the lenses with his handkerchief, crossed his booted legs, slightly adjusted the glasses on his nose and began to read the letter with an expression of intense concentration.

Under Grant's terms each officer and man would be allowed "to return to his home, not to be disturbed by the United States authorities so long as they observe their paroles and the laws in force where they may reside." Officers would be permitted to retain their side-arms and their private horses.

After reading the section on paroles ("individual paroles not to take up arms against the government of the United States until properly . . . "), Lee looked up and said: "After the words 'until properly' the word 'exchanged' seems to be omitted. You doubtless intended to use that word."

"Why, yes, I thought I had put it in," said Grant.

"With your permission," said Lee, "I will mark where it should be inserted."

"Certainly," Grant agreed.

When Lee reached the generous provision regarding the sidearms and horses of officers, a surge of emotion melted his frosty reserve. Lee looked up at Grant who was standing near him now, and said with great feeling, "This will have a very happy effect upon my Army."

Grant then said, "Unless you have some suggestions to make in regard to the form, I will have a copy of the letter made in ink and sign it."

"There is one thing I would like to mention," Lee said. "The cavalrymen and artillerymen in our army own their own horses. . . . I would like to understand whether these men will be permitted to retain their horses."

"You will find that the terms as written do not allow this," Grant said. "Only the officers are allowed to take their private property."

"No, I see the terms do not allow it," Lee said. "That is clear." But his expectant look showed clearly that he did not view the matter as closed.

Instantly, Grant responded: "Well, the subject is quite new to me,

Of course, I did not know that any private soldiers owned their animals, but I think this will be the last battle of the war. I sincerely hope so. . . . I will arrange it in this way: I will not change the terms as they are written, but I will instruct the officers to let all the men who claim to own a horse or a mule take the animals home with them to work their little farms."

"This will have the best possible effect upon my men," Lee said. "It will be very gratifying and will do much toward conciliating our people."

Some of the Union officers seemed awestruck not only by their presence at a great moment of history, but also by the flesh-and-blood reality of Lee. The Virginian was as much a legend to the Army of the Potomac as to the Army of Northern Virginia. A colonel on Grant's staff was too nervous to copy the terms and another officer, a full-blooded Indian, Chief Ely Parker of the Six Nations, undertook the task.

Lee's aide prepared a letter of acceptance and passed it to his general. Lee read it and instructed the unhappy man: "Don't say, 'I have the honor to acknowledge the receipt of your letter of such a date'; he is here. Just say, 'I accept these terms.' "

Introductions followed. The Federal officers were eager to meet Lee. Courteous but unsmiling, he greeted them.

Grant was still embarrassed, partly because of his sensitivity to Lee's feelings, partly because his muddy attire contrasted sorely with Lee's crisp uniform.

"I was about four miles from the wagons where my arms and uniforms were," Grant explained, "and I thought you would rather receive me as I was than to be detained."

Instantly, Lee put him at ease: "I am much obliged to you. I'm very glad you did it in that way."

Then Lee stepped outside the door. A Northern reporter thought that "his demeanor was that of a thoroughly possessed gentleman." Those who knew Lee better noticed that his face and neck were flushed darker even than their customarily ruddy hue.

Union soldiers were standing outside for a glimpse of the defeated captain. Those nearby automatically saluted. Lee returned the compliment. He slowly drew on his gauntlets. Then he smote his hands together several times and, in a hoarse voice, called, "Orderly! Orderly!"

The man appeared with Traveller. Lee patted his old war horse on the forehead, then swung into the saddle. Grant was standing there. Both generals raised their hats.

Back in his own camp, Lee went off to himself and paced back and forth under an apple tree. But he was to be denied the blessing of privacy in this moment. Federal officers in groups of four or five, most of them impelled by sheer curiosity, sought him out. Lee gave none of them the privilege of shaking his hand. Colonel William Blackford, who witnessed the strange reception, wrote: "It was rather amusing to see the extreme deference shown by them to General Lee. When he would see Colonel Taylor coming with a party towards his tree, he would halt in his pacing and stand at attention and glare at them with a look which few men but he could assume. They would remove their hats entirely and stand bareheaded during the interview while General Lee sometimes gave a scant touch to his hat in return and sometimes did not even do that."

About sunset, Lee mounted Traveller and rode back toward his headquarters. The ragged veterans of the Army of Northern Virginia crowded both sides of the road. Waving their hats, they cheered Lee as few conquerors have been cheered. The rigidity of Lee's face was that of a man struggling for control. Suddenly tears welled up in his eyes and began to flow down his cheeks. The men ran up to him, sobbing and crying aloud, reaching out to touch in reverence the horse he rode. All down the line, there were cheers to which Traveller responded with a repeated toss of the head, and everywhere as the chieftain passed the cheers melted into tears. Officers astride their horses wept openly. And some of the men threw themselves on the ground and cried like babies.

When Lee dismounted, his soldiers crowded around him again.

He spoke to them quietly, so quietly that few of them heard what he said beyond the words, "I have done the best I could for you." But his affection was expressed more eloquently by his looks than it could have been by any words he might have used.

Though it was spring, there was a chill in the night air. Lee and several of his staff sat by a fire in front of his tent. He entrusted to Colonel Marshall the task of writing the final order to the troops. It has become celebrated as "Lee's Farewell," a document which, though not composed by Lee, bore the stamp of his personality as much as any of the original products of his pen.

Soon Lee rose from the fire and entered his tent. At last he could be alone. He lay in the quiet dark. Then rain began to drum on the canvas.

Patriarch of a People

Lee remained for several days in the vicinity of Appomattox, not shirking the many duties attendant upon surrender of his army which he might have assigned to a subordinate. Before Lee left Appomattox, Grant talked with him about the part that the Virginian could play in making the whole South more amenable to peaceful surrender. In his memoirs, Grant recalled the conversation and said, "I knew there was no use to urge him to do anything against his ideas of what was right."

Before Lee left Appomattox, he received a call from an old friend —General Meade, his companion in the old army, and his opponent in crucial days of the war. At first Lee did not recognize him, and then exclaimed, "What are you doing with all that gray in your beard?"

Meade smiled. "You have to answer for most of it."

When Lee joined his family in Richmond, a steady stream of callers from both armies poured through the house. During the war, Lee had dreamed of acquiring the old home at "Stratford" and living the life of a farmer in the Northern Neck. His aspirations were now more modest. He wrote one of his former generals : "I am looking for some little quiet house in the woods where I can procure shelter and my daily bread if permitted by the victor. I wish to get Mrs. Lee outside of the city as soon as is practicable."

One of Lee's visitors was General Meade, who urged him to apply for pardon and the opportunity to take the "oath of allegiance" that he might set an example of conciliation for other officers. Subordinating personal pride, he took the painful step. But his request was denied.

In many other ways Lee set an example of conciliation, both publicly and in conversation with individuals. Once, when a clergyman calling on him declaimed bitterly against the North, Lee said to him: "Doctor, there is a good old Book which I read and you preach from, which says, 'Love your enemies, bless them that curse you, do good to them that hate you, and pray for them which despitefully use you and persecute you.' Do you think your remarks this afternoon were quite in the spirit of that teaching?"

The minister apologized, and Lee told him, "I have fought against the people of the North because I believed they were seeking to wrest from the South dearest rights. But I have never cherished toward them bitter or vindictive feelings, and have never seen the day when I did not pray for them."

During these days when Lee, apart from receiving so many visitors, insisted on answering all his voluminous correspondence personally, many people were impressed with the calm of his demeanor. But those who shared his home, in quiet hours, heard the footfall, footfall, footfall of his pacing in his lonely room.

Lee and his family moved into the country, occupying a cottage in Powhatan County. Here Lee was freed from the pressure of visitors. Moreover, like most of his class in Virginia, he was a countryman at heart. He had always delighted in the beauties of nature, and he found peace of spirit in communion with growing things.

On August 4, the trustees of Washington College unanimously elected Lee to the presidency of the institution. After being assured that the trustees had no fears of animosity in the North as a result of Lee's connection with the college, he accepted the post. In the middle of September, he rode alone and on Traveller to Lexington, a journey of 108 miles. Some thought his choice of transportation strange in view of his age and health, but Mrs. Lee explained, "He prefers that way, and besides, does not like to part even for a time from his beloved steed, his companion in many a hard-fought battle."

Traveller, of course, was his favorite, but Lee loved all horses. Even in the heat of battle, he had found time to see to the welfare of mounts as well as men. When he first assumed full command in the War Between the States, and was still wearing civilian dress, he paid so much attention to the cavalry horses that an old stableman complained, "That durned old fool is always hanging around my horses like he is fixing to steal one of 'em."

Under Lee's administration, the college prospered even beyond expectations of its hopeful trustees. Lee's name, as was confidently forecast, was a powerful magnet to draw both students and funds. But Lee made many other contributions. He lent his weight to the movement within the faculty to broaden the curriculum, adding courses in agriculture and practical engineering that would prepare young men to rebuild the shattered economy of the South. By careful attention to individual needs and by the force of his example, he succeeded very largely in eliciting the best efforts of both faculty and students.

In reprimanding the erring, he could be stern or humorous, as the occasion demanded. Once he asked a lazy boy, "How is your mother?" The boy must have smiled when Lee said, "I am sure you must be devoted to her." But the smile must have faded when he added by way of explanation, "You are so careful of the health of her son."

Once Lee said: "I have a self-imposed task, which I must accomplish. I have led the young men of the South in battle; I have seen many of them fall under my standard. I shall devote all of my life now to training young men to do their duty in life."

He taught them to revere the Old South code of honor, courage, and chivalry and to eschew its one great fault, false pride. On being told that a former officer, who had known prosperity, was laboring as a porter because no other employment was available, he replied, "That becomes him more than anything he ever did in the army."

Two occurrences interrupted the quiet tenor of Lee's busy days at the college. One was when he was urged to run for governor of Virginia. He declined all proposals that he be a candidate. The second was when a lynch-mad mob surrounded the little jail in Lexington one night and demanded that the jailer hand over to them a prisoner who had aroused the hatred of the whole countryside. Lee strode into their midst, talking with small groups of the men at a time. By degrees, the howling mob vanished quietly into the night.

In these years, the spirituality always characteristic of him deepened. He once told a worried member of his faculty that there was no cause for self-reproach when a man was conscious that he had done his best. We could all only "do our best and leave the results to God." He said once, "If I could only know that all the young men in the college were good Christians, I should have nothing more to desire."

Lee's spirituality never smacked of fanaticism. He was a member of the Episcopal Church, and favored the Low Church. But he was never concerned with denominational issues. Some of the orthodox regretted his statement about Lent: "The best way for most of us is to fast from our sins and to eat what is good for us." He proselyted more by example than by preachment, saying, "I find it so hard to keep one poor sinner's heart in the right way that it seems presumptuous to try to keep others."

His faith called for action as well as prayer. When a minister regularly prayed so long in chapel that classes were delayed, Lee asked, "Would it be wrong for me to suggest that he confine his morning prayers to us poor sinners at the college, and pray for the Turks, the Jews, the Chinese, and the other heathen some other time?"

In those days tributes poured in to Lee from all over the South and even from some in the North who had fought against him in the great war of 1861–65. Sometimes the adulation was embarrassing for him as when, riding alone on a forest trail, he was recognized by one of his own veterans. "General Lee," the man declared, "I am powerful glad to see you. And I feel like cheering you." Lee politely protested that such a demonstration would be completely unnecessary with just the two of them there and only the trees as witnesses. But the man would not be deterred. "Hurrah for General Lee," he shouted at the top of his voice, "Hurrah for General Lee!" As the old commander rode away, the cheers were still echoing in the woods.

In the autumn of 1869 Lee began to suffer severe pains in his back and arms, similar to those that had incapacitated him for a time in 1863. His physicians apparently did not tell him that his heart was affected, but Lee diagnosed his own case with reasonable accuracy and confided to his son Custis that he believed he did not have long to live. For the sake of his health, and at the urging of solicitous associates at the college, he made a tour of the South. It was one of triumph for a man who had drunk the dregs of defeat. In city after city, there were fresh proofs that the South revered him as it had no other man since George Washington.

Lee rejoiced in reunion with those who had borne with him the shock of battle and had known the camaraderie of the campfire. But there were so many missing. In a letter of condolence, he wrote, "Death in its silent, sure march is fast gathering those whom I have longest loved, so that when he shall knock at my door, I will more willingly follow."

In September, Lee returned to Lexington and plunged into the duties of the new college session. He was pale and haggard.

On the evening of September 28, he walked home in the rain from a vestry meeting. Removing his wet coat and hat, he entered the dining room, where Mrs. Lee awaited him in her wheelchair.

He had often teased her for her tardiness, and now she had an opportunity to turn the jest. "You have kept us waiting a long time," she began with a mischievous smile. "Where have you been?"

He did not answer, but sat down in his chair at the head of the table and, with his lips, formed the opening words of his customary grace. But no intelligible sound came. Lee was placed on a couch and two physicians were immediately summoned.

As days passed, the doctors talked hopefully of his recovery. But Mrs. Lee thought that she had seen a look of resignation in her husband's eyes. As the aurora borealis danced in the sky for several nights, the superstitious took it for a sign that the great man would pass from their midst.

Custis spoke to his father about recovery, but Lee shook his great gray head from side to side and pointed upward.

By the night of October 10, it was apparent to the physicians that he did not have long to live. One of his professors sat in the room when the night was coming on. He later recalled the experience with awe :

As the old hero lay in the darkened room, with the lamp and hearth fire casting shadows upon his calm and noble front, all the massive grandeur of his form, face and brow remained : and death seemed to lose its terrors, and to borrow a grace and dignity in sublime keeping with the life that was ebbing away. The great mind sank to its last repose, almost with the equal poise of health.

On October 12, as the gray light of dawn began to contend with the yellow glow of hearth and lamp, the watchers in the room were startled to hear the old familiar bass voice speak out distinctly: "Strike the tent."* Silence followed. There was no more labored breathing: only the measured, unmoved ticking of the clock.

*   *   *

In his person and in his character, Lee had epitomized the highest ideals of the Old South with its traditions of noblesse oblige. After the War Between the States, he symbolized the spirit of reconciliation, industry and union upon which the rise of the new South would depend.

But he has become far more than a regional symbol. Speaking in Lee's native state in January of 1959, Bruce Catton, foremost historian of the Union armies, said :

---

*William Preston Johnston is the only witness to this quotation, a fact that has troubled some historians, e.g. Marvin P. Rozear et al., "R. E. Lee's Last Stroke," *Virginia Magazine of History and Biography,* Vol. 98 (April 1990), pp. 271–308. But others have testified that his mind wandered over battlefields toward the end, and Charles Bracelen Flood, *Lee: The Last Years,* Boston, 1981, p. 292, says, "Although Johnston refers to them as 'those last significant words,' his phrase can also be taken to mean the last comprehensible words."

His people, in the end—the end which he did not live to see—were not just the people of Virginia, or even the people of the Southland. They are all of us who today rejoice in the name of Americans. You in Virginia can no longer keep Lee as your private possession. The whole country wants its share in him, wants it because, of all the men this nation has bred, he is one of the very small handful who best show us the noble heights our manhood can reach.

In placing his portrait on a postage stamp, the United States recognized the fact that Lee had become a national hero. Indeed, his status as a national hero is probably higher today than it would be if he had accepted command of the Union Armies in 1861 and then, after triumphs in the field, been boosted to the Presidency as was Grant. And his example is more instructive, for it may remind a young nation that has moved from triumph to triumph that greatness and success are not always synonymous.

But to speak of Lee's reputation in purely national terms is to impose false limitations on it. In 1958, Sir Winston Churchill published the fourth volume of his *History of the English-Speaking Peoples,* the one devoted to the nineteenth-century achievements of all countries speaking the English tongue. A distinguished British critic correctly observed that the hero of this volume was not an Englishman, not even a resident of the Empire, but an American : Robert E. Lee.

Thus the memory of Lee is an international heritage. It is a heritage of genius, but even more one of character, and hence in combination a heritage of wisdom. Lee, contrary to common belief, did not proceed throughout life from abstract motives of Aristotelian objectivity. Instead, he was a man of disciplined fire. This discipline was not dependent upon the consolations of easy optimism. Near the end of his life, he expressed the essence of the faith that sustained him :

My experience of men has never disposed me to think worse of them, nor indisposed me to serve them; nor, in spite of failures which I lament, of errors which I only now see and acknowledge, or of the present aspect of affairs, do I despair of the future. The truth is this : The march of Providence is so slow and our desires so impatient : the work of progress is so immense and our means of aiding it so feeble; the life of humanity is so long, that of the individual so brief, that we often see only the ebb of the advancing wave and are thus discouraged. It is history that teaches us to hope.

ROBERT E. LEE

Bibliography

Freeman, Douglas S. *R. E. Lee,* Vols. I–IV. New York, 1934–1935. The definitive biography of Lee and one of the great monuments of American historical scholarship. The work is so thorough, so well organized, and so honestly written that it even affords a basis for the scholarship of those who disagree with Dr. Freeman's interpretations.

Freeman, Douglas S. *Lee's Lieutenants,* Vols. I–III. New York, 1942–1944. Another great work. Important to an understanding of Lee's relations with his officers.

Lee, Capt. Robert E. [Jr.]. *Recollections and Letters of General Robert E. Lee.* New York, 1924. General Lee as a family man described by his son; also revelatory letters by the General himself.

Battles and Leaders of the Civil War, Vols. I–IV. New York, 1887–1888. These volumes are so filled with valuable accounts of Lee that the citing of particular articles is impractical. The narratives, whether colorful anecdotes such as those of Henry A. Wise or scholarly analyses such as those of D. H. Hill, have the force and authority of eyewitness accounts.

Dowdey, Clifford, and Manarin, Louis H. *The Wartime Papers of Robert E. Lee.* New York, 1987.

Thomas, Emory M. *Robert E. Lee: A Biography.* New York and London, 1995. Professor Thomas assumes that he was a pioneer in disagreeing with Douglas S. Freeman's presentation of Lee as an uncomplicated character while at the same time respecting Dr. Freeman's excellent biography. In the first edition of *Frock Coats and Epaulets,* in 1963, I expressed gratitude to Dr. Freeman for encouraging me to write my first book, *The Virginia Experiment,* but said, "Honesty has caused us to depart from Dr. Freeman's concept of Lee as a 'simple man.' But it has no way lessened our recognition of his vastly superior knowledge of Lee and the whole field of Confederate operations, and in no instance have we been truer to our mentor's example than in obeying the dictates of our own integrity." Nevertheless, I certainly cannot quarrel with Professor Thomas for presenting much more fully the thesis which I have maintained for 33 years, and in the process producing what I consider the best single volume Lee biography available.

Connelly, Thomas L. *The Marble Man: Robert E. Lee and His Image in American Society.* New York, 1977. Professor Connelly seems to think that he is the first person to discover that Lee had fierce emotions that burned behind a facade of reserve. Others have been aware of this fact, and the Lee chapter in the first edition of *Frock Coats and Epaulets* (1963) bore the subtitle that it has in this one, "Man of Disciplined Fire." Exaggerated claims aside, Connelly's book is second only to Emory M. Thomas's *Robert E. Lee* as a single volume work on the subject.

Nagel, Paul C. *The Lees of Virginia: Seven Generations of an American Family.* New York, 1990. Places Robert E. Lee in the context of his family. The book benefits from the perspective gained by the author in his chronicle of another great American clan, *Descent from Glory: Four Generations of the Adams Family.* Both works are highly readable.

Southern Historical Society Papers. Richmond, Va., 1876–1930, 47 vols. Nuggets of important Lee material are scattered through these volumes, most heavily in Vols. 4–7.

Maurice, Maj. Gen. Sir Frederick. *Robert E. Lee, the Soldier.* Boston and New York, 1925. Valuable appraisal by British military expert. Particularly interesting is Chapter XI, "Lee's place in History," pp. 274–294.

Lee, Fitzhugh. *General Lee.* New York, 1894. Not so intimate a portrait as one might wish, but, as the work of R. E. Lee's nephew who moreover was an officer in the field under the general, it contains family reminiscences and eyewitness accounts of value.

White, Henry Alexander. *Robert E. Lee and the Southern Confederacy.* New York, 1897. This volume affords more insights into Lee's personality than many more recent works. Though intensely subjective, and of course not including some of the findings of recent scholarship, it contains much valuable information that the author gained through close association with General G. W. Custis Lee, president of Washington and Lee University and son of Robert E. Lee.

Davis, Burke. *Gray Fox.* New York, 1956. The most readable one-volume account of Lee's activities in the War of 1861–65.

Bradford, Gamaliel, Jr. *Lee the American.* Boston and New York, 1912. Gracefully written, with good psychological insights.

Jones, J. William. *Christ in the Camp.* Richmond, 1887. Insights into Lee's spiritual interests.

Freeman, Douglas S., and McWhiney, Grady (eds.). *Lee's Dispatches: Unpublished Letters of General Robert E. Lee, C. S. A., to Jefferson Davis and the War Department of the Confederate States of America.* New York, 1957. Includes 10 dispatches discovered after publication of Freeman's *R. E. Lee.* They provide no new revelation but some additional illumination.

Commager, Henry Steele. *The Blue and the Gray, the Story of the Civil War as Told by Participants.* Indianapolis, 1950. Contains firsthand descriptions of Lee with valuable commentary by the editor. Of particular interest are pp. 251–255, 514–515, 591–593, 640–641, 1024–1027, 1060–1079. These accounts are available in other volumes less accessible to the general reader.

Catton, Bruce. *This Hallowed Ground, the Story of the Union Side of the Civil War.* Garden City, 1956. Informative about Lee's opponents and the respect in which they held him. See particularly pp. 166–169, 238–244 and 316.

Catton, Bruce. *A Stillness at Appomattox.* Garden City, 1954. Valuable for same reasons as *This Hallowed Ground.* See particularly pp. 42–43.

Henry, Robert S. *The Story of the Confederacy.* New York, 1936. Helpful to an understanding of Lee's strategy and its significance in the general framework of the war.

Richmond Dispatch, Richmond Enquirer, and *Richmond Examiner* for appropriate dates (microfilms in Virginia State Library). The pages of the *Richmond Examiner* for September and October 1861 abound in evidence of the low esteem in which Lee was then held both by many public men and by many private citizens.

Rister, Carl Coke. *Robert E. Lee in Texas.* Norman, Oklahoma, 1946. Description of Lee's 25 months of cavalry service in Texas. Detailed picture of him as a refined gentleman who could "rough it."

Long, A. L. *Memoirs of Robert E. Lee.* New York, 1886. Research suffers from the late author's blindness, but his personal recollections are valuable as are his quotations from Northern appraisals of Lee.

Blackford, W. W. *War Years with Jeb Stuart.* New York, 1945. Especially interesting is Blackford's account of Lee's reception of Federal officers under an apple tree at Appomattox and of the general's emotional farewell to his own men.

Taylor, Richard. *Destruction and Reconstruction.* New York, 1955. Especially pp. 111–113. Taylor's estimate derives interest from the fact that he was not only a Confederate lieutenant general but also a brilliant and articulate observer of unusual perception.

Dowdey, Clifford, *Death of a Nation: The Story of Lee and His Men at Gettysburg,* New York, 1958. An effective reconstruction of the Battle of Gettysburg characterized by fresh and provocative insights.

Flood, Charles Bracelen. *Lee: The Last Years.* Boston, 1981.

Churchill, Sir Winston. *A History of the English-Speaking Peoples,* Vol. IV. New York, 1958. English historian's high estimate of Lee is indicative of the General's international stature. See especially pp. 169–170, 210–213.

Nolan, Alan T. *Lee Considered: General Robert E. Lee and Civil War History.* Chapel Hill, N.C., 1991. Among the Lee biographies, the most conspicuous example of the debunking school. The attorney author has subordinated objectivity to prosecutorial zeal.

NOTE: There are more than 50 Lee biographies in print, and more biographies of his lieutenants, and general histories of the War Between the States, besides countless monographs on subjects of smaller scope, all containing information on the general. But the volumes listed above contain virtually all the most important facts about Lee generally accepted by scholars.

Important manuscript collections are available to the serious student at the Virginia Historical Society Library, the Virginia State Library, and the Confederate Museum, all in Richmond; at Washington and Lee University in Lexington, Va.; at the Library of Congress, Washington, D.C.; and at the Duke University Library, Durham, N.C. However, most of this material is reprinted or abstracted in J. William Jones' *Life and Letters,* and the *Calendar of Virginia State Papers.*

III

THOMAS J. (STONEWALL) JACKSON :
Joshua in Gray

(Virginia Historical Society)

III

THOMAS J. (STONEWALL) JACKSON:
Joshua in Gray

"What in Hell . . . "?

"WHAT IN HELL are you riding over my oats for? Don't you know it's against orders?"

Swollen with indignation and red-faced with rage, the stout little man brandished his cane in the face of the abashed cavalryman.

The soldier, caught riding his horse through the farmer's oats, fumbled with the bridle of his sorrel mount. He seemed to wish that he could completely withdraw his lanky frame into the dusty Confederate uniform and disappear. Not much face showed between the brim of his low-pulled kepi and the luxuriance of a heavy black beard, but the visible flesh was suffused with a ruddy blush.

"Damn it!" shouted the farmer. "Don't you know it's against orders? I intend to have every damned one of you arrested! What's your name, anyhow?"

The response was humble and muffled in the beard. "My name is Jackson."

"Jackson! Jackson!" The farmer vibrated with indignation. Too full for utterance, he spat on the ground like a volcano spitting lava. By this time, other riders in gray had drawn alongside the chief offender. "Jackson, I intend to report every one of you and have you every one arrested. Yes, I'd report you if you were old 'Stonewall' himself instead of a set of damned quartermasters and commissaries riding through my oats! Yes, I'll report you to 'Stonewall' Jackson myself, that's what I'll do."

The first cavalryman shifted uneasily in the saddle. "They call me that name sometimes."

"What name?"

" 'Stonewall.' "

The farmer was incredulous. His eyes roved over the unprepossessing figure on horseback. "You don't mean to say *you* are *'Stonewall'* Jackson, do you?"

The soldier was as contrite as a schoolboy. "Yes, sir, I am."

For a moment, the farmer only stared. Then, waving his cane aloft in a wild salute, he yelled: "Hurrah for 'Stonewall' Jackson! Hell, general, do me the honor to ride all over my damned old oats!"

This Piedmont Virginia farmer, who encountered "Stonewall" Jackson riding through the field of oats on July 13, 1862, was not alone in failing to recognize in the humble figure before him the lightning-eyed avenger of the battlefields. A year before he emerged as one of the great captains of history, Jackson was derided by his V.M.I. students as an inept disciplinarian. His air of other-worldliness, of complete abstraction from the practical concerns of daily life, had earned him the nickname of "Fool Tom Jackson." What voices did he hear in these ridiculed reveries that transformed him, at the sound of a trumpet, into a black-bearded, Old Testament warrior answering the call to Armageddon?

There was little in Jackson's childhood to suggest his later emergence as a flaming genius of war. Even after he attained fame, those who had known him in his early years were hard put to dredge up recollections of happenings that had infallibly marked him as destiny's child.

As with Patrick Henry, the effort has sometimes been made to dramatize Jackson's rise to eminence by portraying him as climbing up from the ranks of the underprivileged. The picture is as false in the case of Jackson as of Henry. Both were sons of the Virginia hills, but neither was by any stretch of the imagination a hillbilly.

Jackson was born January 21, 1824 in Clarksburg, Virginia (now West Virginia), a small town whose bustling optimism no less than its dirt streets and rough buildings marked it as only one generation removed from the frontier. His father was Jonathan Jackson, an attorney and former Federal Collector of the Internal Revenue for the District of Western Virginia. The mother, Julia Beckwith Neale Jackson, was related to some of the Commonwealth's most prominent families. She had an uncommon amount of education for a woman of her day—and not just in terms of frontier society, either. Jackson's lineage was not humble enough to give him the democratic appeal of a Lincoln, nor distinguished enough to invest him with the aristocratic glamor of a Lee. It was a background from which one might reasonably have anticipated a progeny of worthy citizens with some of them earning a claim to local fame.

When Tom Jackson was two years old, an older sister and his father died of typhoid fever. In that month of tragedy, Julia Neale Jackson gave birth to a daughter, Laura Ann. The young widow had the responsibility of three children : the new-born baby, five-year-old Warren, and little Tom.

Jonathan Jackson had put virtually all his money into long-term investments whose success was dependent upon continuation of his earning capacity. The house had to be sold. A small cottage for the family was provided by the local Masonic Lodge, which Jonathan had helped to organize. The widow became a schoolteacher, and soon was managing her meager income so resourcefully that she could decline offers of help from both Neale and Jackson relatives.

After four years of widowhood, she was married to Captain Blake B. Woodson, an impecunious lawyer, and moved with him to Fayette County, newly carved from the frontier, where he had secured the post of county clerk. Financial opportunities for professional men were small and, when Julia Jackson Woodson's health went into a sharp decline during another pregnancy, family resources did not permit the hiring of adequate help. The mother had to part with her children. Warren was sent off to an uncle in Petersburg. Laura and six-year-old Tom were sent to their Grandmother Jackson. The little boy left with a heavy heart.

A few months later, the mother was on her death bed. Her overwhelming desire was to see her children again before she died. Tom and Laura were rushed back to Fayette County in the care of a Negro servant. The little boy arrived just before the end came. The mother that he adored looked wasted and there was an unaccustomed sadness in the familiar gray eyes. She gave the little fellow her dying blessing and prayed that Providence would watch over him.

The parting had a profound effect on Tom. He always remembered vividly the fervent faith with which his mother had committed him to God's care.

Back Tom and Laura went to Grandmother Jackson's. Her death several years later caused Laura to be sent to one aunt while Tom was sent to another. He had not been long at her home when he showed up one day at the door of some Clarksburg relatives. His rosy-cheeked face unusually earnest, he told them that he had left his Aunt Polly and Uncle Brake.

"You ought to go back," one of the women told him. Tom's blue eyes stared unblinking from under the mop of brown hair. "Maybe I ought to, ma'am, but I am not going to."

Other relatives were brought in to persuade the little boy. But he told them with firm dignity : "No. Uncle Brake and I can't agree. I have quit and shall not go back anymore."

He walked back to Jackson's Mill, where Grandmother Jackson had lived, and where his Uncle Cummins Jackson now made his home. The doorway at which the small boy knocked was soon filled by two hundred pounds of solidly built man. The man had to stoop to avoid hitting his head on the lintel. His sharp, steel-blue eyes stared down at the boy. But as soon as he knew who Tom was, Uncle Cummins—for he was the big man—gave him a hearty, man-to-man welcome and swept him into the house on a flood of joviality. The prosperous proprietor of a sawmill and grist mill, Uncle Cummins was a bachelor who loved good talk, the cup that cheers, fast horses, and children.

Cummins Jackson took his responsibilities as guardian with the intense, all-encompassing seriousness of the fun-loving, large-hearted bachelor who suddenly finds himself with a foster son of his own flesh and blood. This man who might have seemed happy-go-lucky at the race track worried greatly when Tom did not grow rapidly. When the boy ate little and complained of what was diagnosed as dyspepsia, the burly uncle was as upset as a young mother. Outdoor exercise was prescribed as a remedy, and it fitted in perfectly with Uncle Cummins' ideas of what a boy should be doing.

There was one sport in which Tom's light weight should be an asset. He ought to make a first-class jockey for Uncle Cummins' horses. Tom trained earnestly and conscientiously and he rode in a few local races, but he was always an awkward figure in the saddle. Yet, there was something about the actual race, something about the sense of competition, that stirred the boy's blood.

Uncle Cummins was not a conspicuously pious man, but he adhered faithfully to a rigid code of honor. The honesty of his nephew became proverbial in the community. One story that has outlived Jackson himself tells of his experiences as a commercial fisherman. The boy used to fish in the West Fork of the Monongahela, selling his catch regularly to a Mr. Kester at the rate of fifty cents a fish. Once, when Tom was returning with a particularly fine specimen, a three-foot pike, he was stopped by a Colonel Talbott, who called out: "Tom, that is a fine fish you have there. What will you take for it?"

Tom said, "This fish is sold, Colonel Talbott." The colonel then offered him a dollar.

"I can't take it," the boy protested. "This fish is sold to Mr. Kester."

"But, Tom," the colonel insisted, "I will give you a dollar and a quarter. Surely he will not give you more than that."

Tom now spoke with finality. "Colonel Talbott, I have an agreement with Mr. Kester to furnish him fish of a certain length for fifty cents each. He has taken some from me a little shorter than that. Now he is going to get this big fish for fifty cents."

Tom brought the same firm resolve to his studies. He was not one of the quick learners in the little country school, but he had a tremendous hunger for knowledge. Even after an aura of fame brightened the name of Jackson, his old schoolteacher recalled with uncompromising honesty : "He was not what is now termed brilliant, but he was one of those untiring, matter-of-fact persons who never would give up an undertaking until he accomplished his object. He learned slowly, but what he got in his head he never forgot."

By the time he was sixteen, he had laboriously acquired enough knowledge to be a schoolmaster himself. In those days and in that place, a teacher did not have to be more than a jump ahead of his students on the road to learning.

Now a new interest entered his life. He would walk three miles to the Methodist Church to sit listening with a quiet intensity to the long sermons. He began studying the Bible zealously.

Infant Constable

Not even Uncle Cummins knew what went on inside the boy's head. Was it a turmoil of thought that kept his stomach stirred up most of the time? Did the quiet, controlled exterior hide a hair-trigger nervous system? Tom had started growing; in fact, he was tall enough now. But he still had a lean and hungry look. For what did he hunger?

Uncle Cummins thought that outdoor exercise was a good cure for most of man's ills. When someone suggested that Tom would be a good choice to fill the post of district constable, Uncle Cummins happily seized upon the idea as a means of keeping the boy outdoors. Some citizens protested that a seventeen-year-old, an infant under Virginia law, was too young for so responsible a post. But Uncle Cummins used his influence and Tom's reputation for honesty and determination helped. He got the job and rode all over the district serving processes on elusive debtors.

The task was an unpleasant one, but did not constitute as many problems for Jackson as it would have for many other people. His duties were clearly defined; they would be fulfilled without deviation.

One of the most stubborn debtors with whom he had to deal was a man who owed a widow. The proper procedure in such cases was to put a lien on the debtor's property. In this case, the logical item would be the man's horse, his means of transportation. Tom saw the man astride his horse just outside a stable. The only difficulty was that a man could not legally be deprived of possession of his horse so long as he remained in the saddle.

Tom seized the reins, and led the horse toward the stable door, an opening so low that the rider could not remain in the saddle if his mount entered. In vain, the man tried to turn his horse around or hold him back. Tom led the animal on as inexorably as those bronze figures of victory that used to lead on the horses' of generals in the monuments in court house squares. The man's expostulations might as well have been addressed to a bronze figure. Then he raised his whip and brought it squarely down on the boy's back. Still Tom led the horse on without faltering. The rider lashed out in fury, raining blows on the boy. But the youngster walked on, unresisting but un-yielding, like a stone-faced Christian martyr running the gauntlet of the flagellants. At the door, the rider dismounted.

Tom took formal possession of the animal. The owner knew it was useless to argue with this uncanny stripling. He paid the bill.

"Come to Stay"

Tom was still constable nearly two years later when he had a chance to become another kind of officer. The congressman from his district announced a competitive examination for appointment to the United States Military Academy. Tom apparently had no great thirst for military glory, but he was still hungry for knowledge.

Seeking a college education, he took the examination and lost to a friend. But the winner found life at West Point too rigorous and quit. Tom applied to his congressman for the vacancy.

He did not find it easy to get the kind of recommendations he wanted. Plenty of prominent citizens would testify to his character, but the reservation in many minds was voiced by one of them who asked the boy whether he himself believed that he had enough educational background to survive at the Point. Tom's blue eyes were steady under his mop of brown hair. "I am very ignorant," he said, "but I can make it up in study. I know I have the energy and I think I have the intellect."

Tom got the appointment. He entered upon his military education as an eccentric and unprepossessing figure. His huge feet and ham-like hands protruded from a gray homespun suit and his coarse felt hat was so big that he seemed to be hiding under it. Worse still, because he was replacing a boy who had quit, he was entering late upon his course of study. A group of plebes chuckled quietly at sight of him. But a fellow Virginian, Dabney H. Maury, took a long look at Tom Jackson's jawline and at the determined way he planted his feet as he walked. Maury pronounced to his comrades : "That fellow looks as if he had come to stay."

Tom Jackson needed all his determination. Only by the greatest effort was he able to make enough of his work to remain at the Point. Whenever he was sent to the blackboard to work out a problem, he sweated profusely and wiped his brow and tugged at his face and smeared his wet palms on his uniform so that he returned to his seat covered with chalk. His classmates used to say that, if he got a really difficult problem some day, his sweat glands would surely flood the room.

Just before the "lights out" signal, he would fill up the grate in his room with anthracite coal. Then, with the lamp extinguished, he would stretch out on the floor and study his books by the ruddy light of the fireplace. He would not move on to a new lesson until he had thoroughly mastered the preceding one. As a result, despite his long hours of study, he fell so far behind in his classes that he was often totally unprepared for the daily lesson.

His difficulties were not confined to the classroom. Only by strong determination did he eventually learn to keep step in marching. As a child, he had been effective on horseback but never graceful. Try as he might, at the Point he never learned to maintain the regulation seat of the dragoon.

Meantime, he was acquiring a considerable reputation for eccentricity. His life was dominated by serious purpose. His only recreation was walking, and he usually walked alone and at a rapid pace. He made few efforts to win friends, and then only in instances where he thought he would have an opportunity to learn something of value. His study habits were unusual, aside from his remarkable assiduity. He always sat bolt upright at his table with his book open before him. When he was not reading or writing, he fixed his eyes on the wall or ceiling, and external noises impinged upon his concentration at little as upon the meditations of a Hindu in Nirvana. His explanation of his ramrod posture when studying increased his reputation for peculiarity. He feared that, in any other position, his internal organs would be cramped and therefore subject to disease.

The boys soon learned that, however unsociable Tom might be, his word could be depended upon. And many whom he had treated with cool indifference were surprised by the extreme solicitude that Jackson showed when they were sick, even to the extent of taking time from his studies to act as nurse. Because he shared the patronym of the hero of New Orleans, he was jokingly called "the general." In time, the nickname assumed a connotation of respect and something akin to affection. Eventually, he became "Old Jack," not sought after as a companion but prized as a campus institution.

Tom Jackson's sense of duty not only made him hold himself to strict account but also to exact the same unyielding rectitude from his associates. This trait was a bar to intimacy and even to strong friendship. Once a slovenly cadet exchanged his dirty rifle for Jackson's clean one before inspection. When the culprit was discovered, he attempted to defend himself by a lie. The shy, withdrawn Jackson suddenly became an imperious avenger. His fellow cadets could not restrain him as he vowed that so low a creature should not be permitted to stay at the Point and demanded that the offender be court-martialed and expelled.

In his four years at the Academy, Jackson never became an officer or even sergeant of the cadet battalion. Given the handicaps with which he entered the school, to survive was itself an achievement. But he did much more. At first, he was near the very bottom of the class and more conspicuous in his ineptness than the few who were below him. At the end of the first twelve months, like a man going hand over hand up a precipice, he had climbed to fifty-first position in a class of seventy-two. By the end of the second year, his general standing was greatly improved and he stood eighteenth in mathematics. By the end of the third year, he was eleventh in natural philosophy. By the end of the fourth year, he was fifth in his favorite course, ethics. Interestingly enough, his record in infantry tactics was much less impressive. In this subject, in which he would do considerable postgraduate field research, he stood twenty-first. On graduation day, when twenty-two-year-old Tom Jackson stepped up in his brass-buttoned gray coatee and spotless white trousers to receive his diploma, he stood seventeenth in his class. The achievement is especially remarkable in view of the fact that his standing was based on his four-year record, and therefore included the miserable first year. Some of his colleagues said that, if the course had been one year longer, "Old Jack" would have finished first.

During the years of struggle at the Point, Jackson had written as a reminder to himself, "You may be whatever you resolve to be." Then he had resolved to be a West Point graduate of creditable standing. What did he want to be now? Less than a year before graduation he had written his sister, Laura, that he thought the practice of law would be "most congenial." Consequently, he wrote, "I expect to adopt it, after spending a few years in pursuing the . . . profession of arms."

Determined to avoid the infantry, Jackson sought and got an artillery commission. The United States had already been at war with Mexico more than a month. On furlough, Jackson visited his sister, Laura, and then Uncle Cummins. The young officer was asked to command a company of Lewis County militia in a muster parade. The whole community was eager to see its own new army officer on parade, but the effect was somewhat spoiled by Jackson's literal-minded obedience. Following without hesitation an incorrect order from the militia colonel, he led his company off the grounds to the astonishment of the disappointed spectators and through a deserted street. Would he expect such blind obedience from subordinates?

A Strange Fear

By the circuitous route of Fort Columbus in New York, Pittsburgh, New Orleans, and Texas, Lieutenant Jackson rode ashore in a small surfboat with the third assault group of Winfield Scott's invasion force at Vera Cruz. No enemy resistance was encountered and Jackson, lusting for battle, feared the war would end before he could get a taste of combat. He saw action with advanced batteries during the siege of the city, but his thirst for glory remained unslaked. Nevertheless, the possibility of dangerous action excited him. He wrote Laura, "I am in better health than usual." She would discover that her brother's ailments always receded under the pressure of battle.

Jackson did his duty inconspicuously at Cerro Gordo, Churubusco, and Molino del Rey. At Chapultepec came the opportunity he coveted. Frowning down from the hill of Chapultepec was the ancient castle of Montezuma , now the strongest fortress of the Mexican Republic. Its heavy guns commanded every approach. General Worth's division attacked from the north while General Pillow's division, to which Jackson's battery was attached, made a frontal attack. Linking the two attacking forces was the 14th infantry, which moved along a road skirting the base of the hill. A section of Jackson's battery was detached to support the infantry, and Jackson was placed in command.

He had to move up with his guns along a narrow causeway flanked by marshes. He and his men were like tenpins in a bowling alley and, from behind a breastwork, a Mexican fieldpiece threw ball after ball at them, while the great guns of Chapultepec poured down a murderous fire. Nearly every horse was killed or wounded, and Jackson's guns had to be moved forward by hand. When these field pieces were almost near enough to reply to the enemy's fire, the attempt to roll forward was frustrated by a ditch across the road. While cannonballs bounced around them, Jackson and his men, straining and tugging, lifted one gun across. No sooner was this accomplished than the lieutenant discovered his soldiers were fleeing to the rear. Jackson walked up and down the road in the hail of shot, a strange light in his eyes, a peculiar look of exaltation on his animated face, and exclaimed : "There is no danger ! See ! I am not hit."

They marveled, but they did not follow. Even the infantry he had been ordered to support had vanished from the field.

A courier dashed up with orders from General Worth to retire. Jackson sent back word that withdrawal would be more dangerous than remaining. He asked for fifty veterans to storm the breastwork that shielded the Mexican field piece.

By now, the ditch behind Jackson was filled with wounded and dead Americans and a few soldiers cowering for shelter. The only man standing on his side of the ditch was a faithful sergeant. With the aid of this one soldier and a single gun, Jackson defied the guns of Chapultepec. His spirits soared as he fired shot after shot at the enemy citadel. To him, the shower of shot falling all about him was as invigorating as a rain shower to a desert traveler. This was war, and he had thirsted for it.

His madness was contagious. Another gun was carried across the ditch and added its fire power to Jackson's lone weapon.

General Pillow's troops drove the Mexicans from their entrenchments at the base of the hill. The enemy artillery was overpowered. Scaling ladders were thrown against the walls of the fortress, and blue uniforms soon were swarming over the parapets like hordes of insects.

Jackson pursued the fleeing. Mexicans with his guns. By eight o'clock that night, the suburbs of the city had been cleared of snipers. The next day, September 14, the city of Chapultepec, a community of 180,000 inhabitants defended by an army of 30,000, surrendered to the United States force of fewer than 7,000 men.

All who had seen Jackson in action marveled at his intrepidity. Yet he afterward confessed that he had known a kind of fear: "a fear lest I should not meet danger enough to make my conduct conspicuous."

He had been conspicuous enough to gratify the most demanding ambition. In the most exciting part of the battle, he had held the stage alone except for one supporting player, with a gun to speak his lines and an army to chorus his praise.

At a levee after the capture of Chapultepec, Lieutenant Jackson was presented to the commander-in-chief, General Winfield Scott. The bulky old general drew himself up to his full height, glared down at the lieutenant from beneath fiercely bristling brows, and placed his hands behind his back. "I don't know that I shall shake hands with Mr. Jackson," he said in an angry voice that drew all eyes to the commander and the furiously blushing lieutenant standing before him.

"If you can forgive yourself," said the general, "for the way in which you slaughtered those poor Mexicans with your guns, I am not sure that I can." Then the general's broad face broke into a smile, laughter shook his massive frame, and he extended his hand to Jackson.

More conventional commendation for the young artilleryman came in the general's official report, and Jackson was breveted to captain. Within eighteen months after joining his regiment, he was breveted to major. In trial by combat, he had outdistanced all of his West Point colleagues.

Heart and Soul

Jackson spent nine months in Mexico City while peace negotiations were conducted. This period was largely unmarred by suspicion and hostility between the populace and the army of occupation. Before the coming of the North Americans, the city had been ravaged by a succession of revolutionary armies. As G. F. R. Henderson observed, "The capital, itself, had enjoyed but few brief intervals of peace, and now, although the bayonets of an alien race were the pledge of their repose, the citizens reveled in the unaccustomed luxury." The beautiful, elevated city with its substantial, Spanish-style, stone buildings soon assumed a festive atmosphere. The liquid notes of the guitar and the ring and snap of castanets floated from many a courtyard on moonlight nights while firelight struck sparks from dark eyes and umbered the slim legs revealed by whirling petticoats.

Jackson was captivated by a pair of flashing eyes. The young officer who had had so much difficulty in learning to keep in step on parade now disciplined his wilful feet until he became a passable dancer. He began learning Spanish. Even years afterward, the words in that tongue that came most easily to his lips and pen were the tender diminutives of courtship. Jackson never revealed the identity of the girl, though he readily confessed to fascination.

After a while, either a concern for spiritual things interrupted Jackson's romance or termination of his romance caused him to seek spiritual consolation. In any event, he was soon reading the Bible instead of a senorita's dark eyes.

Colonel Frank Taylor, commander of the first artillery, was a deeply religious man. According to the later testimony of Jackson's Civil War Chief of Staff, the Rev. R. L. Dabney, this officer's conversation and prayers awaked "an abiding anxiety and spirit of inquiry in Jackson's mind." Probably, it would be more accurate to say "reawaked," for Jackson was now returning to the interest that had made him so diligent a student of the Bible in adolescent years. He became friendly with Catholic priests in the area, and was invited to share their quarters. It is not surprising that Jackson, with his thirst for explicit knowledge and his habit of implicit obedience to duly constituted authority, should have found Catholic doctrines appealing. He went so far as to obtain several interviews with the Archbishop of Mexico. Jackson was impressed with the prelate's learning and was convinced of his genuine goodness. But he had not yet found an answer that satisfied him.

In the summer of 1848, with the Mexican peace secure, Jackson's battery was sent to Fort Hamilton on Long Island. Here, with his outward life attuned to the quiet routine of garrison duty, he fought many an engagement on the hidden battlefield of the spirit. When he felt that he was irrevocably committed to Christianity, he wanted to signify that adherence. Not knowing whether he had been baptized in childhood, he arranged to be baptized in an Episcopal service in 1849. But he insisted on one proviso, that the sacrament be such that he was committed only to Christianity, not to any particular sect.

A Female Leg?

In October of 1850, Jackson was ordered to duty in Florida. At first, the prospects seemed good. A Florida winter would be a welcome change from a New York one, and Jackson's commanding officer would be Brevet Major William Henry French, a friend of long standing. But the post, Fort Meade, was an isolated one. Consequently, French and Jackson were much dependent on each other for company. In the enforced intimacy of isolation, the hearty, extroverted personality of Major French, whose laughter matched his large frame, clashed with the ascetic, introverted personality of the reticent Major Jackson. Moreover, both men were extremely ambitious. Jackson apparently resented being subordinate to a man who outranked him only in seniority. French evidently became painfully aware of this resentment.

Jackson claimed the right, as quartermaster, to supervise the erection of new buildings on the post. When French insisted on assuming the responsibility himself, Jackson protested to department headquarters. The situation so deteriorated that at one time both French and Jackson were issuing orders to a confused and harassed crew of builders who probably would have liked to apply their hammers to both hard heads.

At last, Jackson stopped speaking to French. But one day Jackson broke the silence to ask French why he disliked him. French's manner softened immediately. He said that he had felt it his duty to limit Jackson's independence of action, but that he did not dislike him. He offered to forward to higher authority a full statement of Jackson's complaints.

Jackson accepted the offer and stated his case in regard to construction on the post. In his covering letter, French complained that Jackson had been trying to "assume to himself more importance than the Commandant of the Post."

The commanding general upheld French and gently rebuked Jackson. Jackson became physically ill, probably from "swamp fever," but his illness must have had psychosomatic aspects. His health was so impaired that he had to be taken off the active list. On rainy days in the spring of 1851, he remained in his quarters and brooded, sinking into an ever deeper depression. The wound to his ego was implicit in lines he wrote his sister, Laura: "You say that I must live on . . . [fame] for the present. I say not only for the present, but during life."

In this time of bitterness, Jackson heard that Major French had been seen walking in the company of a nurse in his employ. Disposed to believe ill of French in every respect, Jackson jumped to the conclusion that the major was having an affair with the girl. He convinced himself that it was his moral and professional duty to inquire into the situation.

One day, he called a number of the enlisted men to his tent, and asked them to tell all they knew about French's relations with his "servant girl." They produced no evidence prejudicial to the commandant. But Jackson persisted. One of the men had laughed one day as he looked into French's quarters on passing. Had he seen the major and Julia in bed? The answer was disappointing. The man had seen only a foot. But Jackson would not quit. Did the man perhaps see a bare leg? And could it have been female?

Loyal to French, the men went immediately to their sergeant with the story of Jackson's interrogation, and the sergeant went directly to the commandant.

French had Jackson arrested and confined to quarters for "conduct unbecoming an officer and a gentleman." Jackson immediately set to work compiling a voluminous collection of charges against French. His already weak eyes dimmed under the unremitting labor. He was so convinced of his own rectitude that, with no apparent embarrassment, he requested French's cooperation in preparing the complaints. In an extraordinary note to the commandant, he said :

I am desirous that additional accusations against you should be forwarded by the steamer which leaves Tampa Bay for N. Orleans on Thursday next, as in my opinion it is very important that they should accompany those already forwarded.

About twenty specifications which are for conduct unbecoming an officer & a gentleman, have been made out for some time, but owing to ill health have not been copied, and in their present condition ought not to be forwarded. . . . And as I have no other certain means of getting them copied [sic] and [sic] soon as I deem the interest of the public service requires, I respectfully request that you will permit me to employ Corpl. Bruning or such other person as you may designate for the purpose of transcribing them.

French complied with Jackson's request.

Assistant Surgeon Jonathan Letterman visited Jackson's tent to plead with him to drop the moral charges against the commandant on the grounds that they would occasion needless suffering for Mrs. French, whom Jackson admired and who had often been his hostess. Tears ran down Jackson's cheeks, but he said that "his conscience compelled him to prosecute the case."

French prepared his letter of defense, describing the girl in question as "a respectable white woman who has lived in my family for nearly nine years, has faithfully attended my wife and children in health and devotedly nursed them in sickness." He said, "The family is attached to her, and I know of nothing which should or shall prevent me from appearing in public as in private what I am, and ought to be, her friend and her protector." He had a simple explanation for why he had been seen walking with the girl on two occasions in the evening. "Being the only grown male person in the family, at much inconvenience to myself I accompanied my servant once to the commissaries store for candles and once to the beef contractors for milk."

Jackson had no evidence contravening French's statements. He therefore resorted to a request that a court of inquiry be called to investigate the administration of Fort Meade. French urged that Jackson be court-martialed and that the court convene at Fort Meade so that the members might appraise conditions for themselves.

Both Jackson and French directed so much correspondence to their superiors that those gentlemen grew heartily tired of the feud in the little Florida outpost. At length, the Secretary of War, apparently in the spirit of "A plague on both your houses," pronounced, "I perceive nothing in this case that calls for my interference."

Jackson felt that he had gained a victory in being released from arrest, and looked forward to spending leave in Europe.

But, before he could sail, he was appointed professor of artillery tactics and natural philosophy at the Virginia Military Institute, and resigned from the Army. He had been recommended for the post by a Mexican War comrade, Major D. H. Hill, who was a member of the faculty at another Lexington school, Washington College, the future Washington and Lee University.

"Fool Tom" Jackson

The pleasant college town, situated in the Valley of Virginia with its golden waves of wheat and green islands of forest against the cool, blue backdrop of the majestic Blue Ridge, was a welcome change from garrison life. But Jackson had not chosen the location to pamper himself. He believed, as he said, "that a man who had turned, with a good military reputation, to pursuits of a semi-civilian character, and had vigorously prosecuted his mental improvement, would have more chance of success in war than those who had remained in the treadmill of the garrison."

Certainly, in the years at V.M.I., Jackson "vigorously prosecuted his mental improvement." The institute, then just twelve years old, was modeled after West Point and was very nearly the equal of its archetype. Jackson found stimulus in faculty minds that roamed intellectual provinces far removed from the problems of drill and tactics. Access to the school's library was one of his great joys. His classes in natural philosophy embraced higher mathematics, optics, mechanics, and astronomy. He read in all these subjects so that he would have something to impart beyond the lessons printed in the prescribed textbooks. With far greater enjoyment, though, he read accounts of Napoleon's campaigns. These he studied over and over, becoming confirmed in the view that swiftness and daring were the keys to spectacular military success.

For all his industry, Jackson was not a popular teacher or even a particularly successful one. No humor leavened the heavy earnestness of his lectures. He expected from students the same almost incredible application that had advanced him at West Point.

An interesting key to Jackson's mental processes is afforded by the fact that, when his class would fail to follow the steps by which he solved a problem, he could only repeat word for word the solution that he had first advanced. For Jackson, there was only one truly correct approach to every problem.

He became a campus character at V.M.I., as he had been at West Point. His powers of concentration made him seem a caricature of the traditional college professor as he walked in spring-kneed awkwardness under arches and beneath barracks windows, oblivious to the objects falling around him from the hands of student pranksters. When classroom wags asked him absurd questions, he answered with grave courtesy. When cadets talked out of turn in class, his gentle, gray-blue eyes showed more hurt than anger. Even a full, dark, beard did not give a military appearance to this stoop-shouldered instructor. Many students doubted that their shy, soft-spoken teacher had really been a conspicuously daring hero at Chapultepec.

Discipline problems multiplied in Jackson's classes. Cadets talked back to him and several were court-martialed for disrespect. His exaggerated concern for picayune detail, in the opinion of some faculty members as well as most of the students, was symptomatic of a small mind. Some cadets began calling him "Fool Tom" Jackson.

To a few persons, though, he was a hero. Some professors discovered that, beneath his awkwardness and literal-mindedness, was an indomitable spirit and a brain of considerable energy. Tom Munford, the cadet adjutant, worked closely with Jackson when the major served as temporary commandant of cadets. With remarkably mature perception, the young man said, "I flatter myself to have had extraordinary advantages to learn to honor & to respect and to love . . . this grand, gloomy & peculiarly *good* man."

Jackson was hated by many cadets. He would have been hated by more if he had not been considered laughable. He was the subject of many campus anecdotes, some of which engendered a measure of respect even though they provoked laughter. For example, there was the experience of one cadet who, when summoned at his barracks on a bitter winter's night, was confronted by Professor Jackson's grim visage. The knowledge that the teacher had come some distance in the cold from his own quarters was more chilling to the student than the icy blast that had accompanied Jackson's entrance. The cadet found no comfort in the hard-frozen face and the frosty eyes. What could he have done to bring "Old Jack" out on a night like this? The boy's astonishment was unbounded when Jackson said that he had come to apologize. In that day's class, he had censured the boy for what he deemed an incorrect solution to a problem. Late that night in his own home Jackson had suddenly realized that the boy had been right. The professor would not wait until morning to rectify the injustice.

One of Jackson's few friends in his first months at Lexington was John Lyle, bookshop proprietor and leader of the Presbyterian Church choir. In visits to the shop, Jackson often discussed religion and Lyle became his informal tutor in Presbyterian theology.

Through Lyle, Jackson met the Rev. W. S. White, Presbyterian minister. The professor, avid for knowledge, plied the poor clergy-man with a host of questions, many of them dealing with fine points of theology to which the minister had given little or no thought.

After several conversations, Dr. White invited Jackson to join the church. The professor was eager to be admitted to the fellowship of the congregation, but he feared that he would be a hypocrite if he publicly professed faith in the Presbyterian creed when he had definite mental reservations about some of its elements. Still, devout Christian though he was, he had never found a denominational creed to which he could subscribe *in toto*. And Dr. White insisted that literal acceptance of all church doctrines was not a prerequisite of church membership. It is not surprising that Jackson should have joined the Presbyterian Church. In temperament and philosophy, he had been a Calvinist even before he was a Christian.

At first, Dr. White was baffled by Jackson's habit of reporting to him at regular intervals on the state of his soul. He soon learned that Jackson, who had derived most of his ideas of cooperative endeavor from his military training, conceived of Dr. White as his commanding officer in the church. He regarded every pronouncement by the pastor regarding obligations to the church as a command to be obeyed. Jackson was in truth a Christian soldier.

Once Dr. White said that lay members should share in the leading of prayers at the weekly prayer meetings. Of course, he never in-tended that every member should undertake the responsibility. But Jackson, painfully shy and totally inexperienced in public speaking, believed that he had received an order. "You are my pastor," he told Dr. White, "and the spiritual guide of the church; and if *you* think it my duty, then I shall waive my reluctance, and make the effort to lead in prayer, however painful it may be."

So earnest a volunteer could not be denied. Dr. White called on him one night to lead in prayer. When he rose, Jackson looked more awkward than usual in his loose-fitting V.M.I. uniform. He stam-mered as he had at the blackboard at West Point and sweat stood out on his high forehead. When he finally got through, the congregation breathed a fervent "Amen."

After a few weeks, Jackson asked why the minister had not requested him again to lead in prayer. Was Dr. White trying to spare him embarrassment? Dr. White acknowledged as much. Jackson then protested with great earnestness: "My comfort or discomfort is not the question; if it is my duty to lead my brethren in prayer, then I must persevere in it until I learn to do it aright; and I wish you to discard all consideration for my feelings in the matter."

After that conversation, Jackson often led in prayer. Apparently, he was completely unaware that, in performing what he conceived to be his Christian duty, he was making Christian martyrs of his fellow worshipers. But, in this duty, as in so many things that Jackson began ineptly, he gained proficiency through persistent effort.

In church, as in all other places, he sat bolt upright. At the start of a sermon, he would stare at the preacher with an intensity that must have been unnerving. But soon his eyelids would droop and then close and then his head would fall forward. He would slumber on, his spine still like a ramrod. With his sallow skin, he looked like a corpse in rigor mortis.

This foible in so rigid a model of propriety provoked considerable merriment in the congregation. When one member teasingly asked him why he didn't slump in his seat so he could really relax while sleeping, he replied with the most profound seriousness: "I will do nothing to superinduce sleep by putting myself at ease, or making myself more comfortable; but if in spite of my resistance I yield to my infirmity, then I accept as punishment the mortification I feel, because I deserve it."

The Professor's Secret

Jackson's chief confidant in many matters of embarrassment was Major Hill, who had helped him secure the post at V.M.I. One evening in 1853 Jackson called at Hill's office in a state of obvious agitation. Hill's glowing eyes, which comported so strangely with his generally cadaverous appearance, were riveted on the sweating major who, bolt upright in his chair, looked like a prisoner in the dock. Jackson was so painfully embarrassed in approaching the subject he had come to discuss that Hill attempted to divert him to another topic. He feared that Jackson might make some intensely personal disclosure that he would later regret. But Jackson persisted. Finally, it became clear that he had something to say about Elinor Junkin, daughter of the Rev. Dr. George Junkin, president of Washington College.

What could Jackson have to say about Elinor that was so embarrassing? Hill knew her as a discreet and winsome girl about twenty-eight years old. She had been courted by a number of young men, all of whom eventually had been discouraged by her coolness.

Jackson explained that he needed Hill's advice because of something connected with Elinor. Finally, he blurted out: "I don't know what has changed me. I used to think her plain, but her face now seems to me all sweetness."

Hill burst out laughing and laughed until Jackson's crimson face provoked him to pity. "You are in love," Hill said. "That's what is the matter!"

Jackson considered the matter carefully, as if it were a problem in physics. Hill might be right, he conceded objectively. "I have never previously been in love, but I certainly feel differently towards this lady from what I have ever felt before."

Hill could keep a secret well. Not even Elinor Junkin's family suspected that Jackson was in love with her. Elinor's sister, who had a distinctly literary turn of mind, discovered that the major had a far livelier intelligence than was generally suspected. But Ellie's parents wondered why she enjoyed the company of a decidedly eccentric man who seemed to have little to recommend him other than respectability and politeness.

Of course, Laura may have suspected that something was afoot when her normally staid brother wrote her a bantering letter requesting the return of a daguerreotype of himself which he had given her, and said in the same letter: "I am invited to a large party tonight, and among the scramble expect to come in for my share of fun."

And all doubts must have been removed when in April Jackson wrote : "I derive much pleasure from morning walks, in which is to be enjoyed the pure sweetness of carolling birds. The weather is delightful at present; our peach trees are beginning to bloom, and in the course of a few more weeks the forests will be clad with verdure." Only a dense person could have failed to guess at a change of climate in Jackson's heart when he wrote : "Now, for the first time, have I truly and fully appreciated . . . [Lexington.] Of all the places which have come under my observation in the United States, this little village is the most beautiful."

Jackson saw more and more of Ellie. His intentions became unmistakable. Then something drove them apart. Both were reticent about the rupture. In the months of spring and summer that followed, Jackson sought his comforts and joys beyond the earthly sphere. He wrote Laura : "I am cheered with an anticipated glorious and luminous tomorrow . . . . No earthly calamity can shake my hope in the future so long as God is my friend."

He was troubled by his sister's apparent immunity to the consolations of religion. He urged her to accept Christianity on the basis of his own findings. And, in so doing, he unconsciously revealed the hard core of almost incredible self-confidence that lay beneath the all too obvious layers of diffidence and embarrassment. "My Sister," he wrote, "do reflect upon my course of life; think and see if I have ever erred since arriving at mature age, and then consider how I could ever have been satisfied of the truth of the Gospel unless it is true. Have I ever erred in the affairs of this life?"

In July, Jackson visited his sister, who was ill, and continued his efforts to convert her. While in her home town of Beverley, Virginia (now West Virginia), he delivered a series of lectures on Christianity. Zeal had carried him a long way since his first, stumbling prayers in public.

On returning to Lexington, he resumed his frequent visits to the Hill home, and appeared to be assuaging the pain of separation from Ellie by squiring Mrs. Hill's two lively sisters, who were spending the summer with her. But outward appearances were deceiving. One midnight, a determined knocking on the door roused Hill from his bed. On his doorstep stood a distraught Jackson, who insisted on seeing Mrs. Hill alone. In private conference with her, he told her of his and Ellie's disagreement and begged her to intercede for him. When she agreed, he pleaded with her to go over to Dr. Junkin's at that very hour, rouse Ellie from her slumbers and talk to the girl then. She compromised with the excited man and agreed to go the next day.

One morning early in August, Jackson called on the Hills. Except for his confirmed reputation as a teetotaler, they might have suspected he had been drinking. He laughed and joked and called on the ladies of the family to sing his favorite songs. After an hour or more of this unwonted frivolity, he took his leave. The next morning the Hills were astonished to learn that Jackson and Ellie had been quietly married at her home by her father, and had already left town on their honeymoon.

The honeymoon was an unusual one. Ellie and her sister Maggie were extremely close, and Jackson had always enjoyed Maggie's conversation, so Maggie went with the couple. The tour included the traditional trip to Niagara Falls, but also took them to famous battlefields.

On the Plains of Abraham at Quebec, Maggie first saw an unsuspected side of her mild-mannered brother-in-law. At the foot of the monument erected to General Wolfe, he removed his cap and a "dilating enthusiasm . . . seemed to take possession of the whole man." He stood atiptoe and seemed to grow taller. His eyes flashed blue fire and his nostrils literally quivered. Turning his bearded face toward the setting sun, and including most of the field in a sweeping gesture of his long right arm, he quoted Wolfe's dying words, "I die content." Then, his voice throbbing with emotion, he exclaimed, "To die as he died, who would not die content!"

While stopping in Boston on the return trip, Jackson took time to write a note to Dr. Lowry Barney, a New York physician who had treated him for dyspepsia and nervous tension just before the major joined the V.M.I. faculty. The doctor had prescribed diet and exercise, and had told Jackson to sandwich in more play with his work. But the most important prescription, the doctor said, was marriage. Now, a little more than two years later, Jackson reported to the physician : "I was married on the 4th instant to an intellectual, pure and lovely lady. . . . So you observe that I continue to carry out your advice."

The ensuing months revealed that the bridegroom had not misjudged the effectiveness of the prescription. Because of the difficulty of finding adequate quarters, he and Ellie moved in with the Junkins. Jackson enjoyed immensely being part of a family again. And the Junkins, deeply concerned with learning and religion, were just the sort of family he liked best. To these estimable proclivities was added the leavening of a sense of humor. Gay, laughing Ellie, her face alive with merriment beneath its cap of chestnut hair, taught Jackson that life could be a matter of fun as well as of duties done and successes won. And the whole Junkin household grew fond of Ellie's major. His habits seemed less eccentric than before, and even his eccentricities acquired a certain charm.

Though Ellie's father was an ordained minister, he was amazed by the way in which faith permeated his son-in-law's life. Once, during a family discussion of St. Paul's phrase "instant in prayer," Jackson illustrated his definition with his own experience. "I have so fixed the habit in my own mind," he said, "that I never raise a glass of water to my lips without a moment's asking of God's blessing. I never seal a letter without putting a word of prayer under the seal. I never take a letter from the post without a brief sending of my thoughts heavenward. I never change my classes in the section room without a minute's petition on the cadets who go out and those who come in."

Jackson needed the refuge of a happy home. Dissatisfaction with his teaching, always widespread among the students, was increasing among alumni. He thought he saw a chance for a fresh start when the University of Virginia invited applications for its mathematics chair. Jackson applied, garnering recommendations from his colleagues at V.M.I. (some of whom were interested for the sake of the institution as well as for the applicant) and from the loyal Major Hill and another Mexican War comrade, Colonel Robert E. Lee, superintendent of the United States Military Academy.

But Jackson did not get the job. So he went on with the Lexington grind, sustained by his happy marriage.

Tragedy struck the Junkin household. Ellie's mother became ill. Her condition suddenly worsened, and the Rev. Dr. Junkin broke to her the news that she had only two or three hours to live. With every appearance of perfect resignation, she called her children to her and kissed them. She kissed Jackson, too. She then told them all to "live near to Jesus and . . . be kind to one another." The scene made a profound impression on Jackson. Perhaps he was reminded of his own mother's deathbed prayers and injunctions. With unaccustomed eloquence, he wrote Laura : "Her death was no leaping into the dark. She died in the bright hope of an unending immortality of happiness."

Before long, there was the promise of new life in the family. Ellie was pregnant. What mattered classroom troubles when a man could come home to Ellie and soon would have a little son or daughter besides?

The baby was due in October. On Sunday, October 22, 1854, the nervous father was told that Ellie had been delivered of her child. But both she and the baby were dead.

Ellie had grown infinitely more precious to Jackson than she had been even on the night when, half crazed with seemingly unrequited love, he had begged Mrs. Hill to intercede in his behalf. A little more than three months after his wife's death, Jackson wrote to her sister Maggie : "I cannot realize that . . . my wife will no more cheer the rugged and dark way of life. The thought rushes in upon me that it is insupportable—insupportable !"

Jackson's friends and relatives became concerned for his physical and emotional health. His thoughts turned increasingly toward death until it seemed to become his chief preoccupation. Gaunt and haggard, the bearded figure roamed the cemetery like some prophet of doom. Once he said, "Ah, if it only might please God to let me go now!" He wrote his aunt, "Oh, do you not long to leave the flesh and go to God, and mingle with the just made perfect?" Even more disturbing was his confession to Major Hill that when he visited Ellie's grave he had to fight down the urge to dig up the coffin, tear off the lid, and look once more upon her mortal remains.

Life Calls

Jackson continued to live with the Junkins. Slowly but surely, under the steadying influence of his sister-in-law Maggie, he regained perspective. Warmed by her affection, his reticence thawed and floods of emotion found release. A new ritual helped restore the tenor of his life. Before the clock struck nine each night Jackson would be seated bolt upright at his desk, his eyes closed as he concentrated on a review of the day's reading. To judge from his fixed posture and expression, the first stroke would not even permeate his consciousness. Nor would the second, nor any of its successors until the ninth. But, on the ninth stroke, he would wheel around in his chair as though released from a spell by the chiming of the hour. And he would smile at Maggie, who would be waiting to talk for an hour or two. Sometimes they talked of his studies, sometimes of her writings. Often they talked of simple things that brought amusement. The joint study of Spanish became part of the evening program. Once, with a reminiscent look, Jackson observed that Spanish was a mellifluous tongue for lovers.

Maggie was deeply touched when Jackson invited her: "Come to me with every joy, and every sorrow, and let me share them with you." She amused her father by asserting with a firmness defying ridicule that Jackson was "the very stuff out of which to make a stirring hero." Whatever others might think, she knew that she had never "known just such another man." To Jackson, she was his favorite companion : sister of his lost Ellie, and therefore a doubly precious sister to him.

Jackson's grief was not forgotten, but sublimated. As so many times before in his life, he was determined to learn from hard experience. On a clean page in a notebook, he wrote, "Objects to be effected by Ellie's death." Under this head, he wrote injunctions to himself. The most inclusive was : "If you desire to be more heavenly-minded, think more of the things of heaven, and less of the things of earth." One of the mundane things that he would strive to subordinate was personal ambition. Ambition had been the steel mainspring of Jackson's life. Was the iron will strong enough to hold it in check?

He sought opportunities for service in humble capacities. He organized a Sunday school class for Lexington Negroes and served as its teacher. He always opened the class by closing the doors, then stepping to the front and singing a hymn. Closing the doors was a merciful act toward the people outside, and probably a prudent one as regarded any back benchers who might hope to slip quietly away. From the throat of the ram-rod stiff major who stood before the class in his baggy uniform emerged sounds that, however impressive in volume, were totally lacking in musical tone. And nearly every Sunday the hymn was the same : "Amazing grace, how sweet the sound that saved a wretch like me." Perhaps Jackson was aware of his musical shortcomings and, as in his first year at West Point, was determined to stick with his initial assignment until he had mastered it.

Jackson's class provided fodder for the grist mills of small-town humor. But soon it was observed that his efforts had a salutary effect on the behavior of his hundred pupils. Eventually religious education for Negroes became a matter of official concern in the Lexington Presbytery.

In October 1855, Jackson, who seemed to pay little attention to politics, revealed his awareness and deep concern over a national problem. His half-brother, Wirt Woodson, was eager to acquire land in free-soil territory. Jackson wrote Laura that he hoped Wirt would not move to the new lands. The major explained : "He would probably become an abolitionist; and then in the event of trouble between North and South he would stand on one side and we on the opposite."

But now, while the threatening cloud was no larger than a man's hand, this was the time to enjoy the sunlight of life. In the summer of 1856, Jackson toured Europe : England, Scotland, Belgium, France, Germany, Switzerland, and Italy. Except for Waterloo, which he could not resist, he visited no important battlefields. Perhaps he realized that, if he was to hold ambition in check, he must avoid scenes of martial triumph. He visited the celebrated cathedrals whose spires pointed heavenward, as he would have his thoughts inclined. And he visited, too, the famous art galleries. At first, the tour may have been perfunctory, part of his determined effort to acquire knowledge. But rich Italian colors fired his imagination and marble figures stimulated the imagery of his mind. After his return, he wrote a friend :

I would advise you never to name my European trip to me unless you are blest with a superabundance of patience, as its very mention is calculated to bring up with it an almost inexhaustible assemblage of grand and beautiful associations. . . . Well do I remember the influence of sculpture upon me during my short stay in Florence, and how there I began to realize the sentiment of the Florentine : "Take from me my liberty, take what you will, but leave me my statuary, leave me these entrancing productions of art." And similar to this is the influence of painting.

Behind the cold brow of the puritan was a passion that panted after the beautiful.

His friends noted a big change in him after his return from Europe. Enthusiasm had replaced gloom and a healthy tan had supplanted pallor. In general, he seemed far more robust than at his leavetaking. But there was a subtler change as well. There were a decisiveness in his manner and a fire in his eye that usually appeared only when he dreamed of martial glory. But Major Jackson was suppressing these visions now. Another conquest claimed his attention. He had determined to remarry and had selected the unsuspecting object of his next courtship.

Mary Anna Morrison, unaware that she was the subject of so much determined thought, pursued the even tenor of her ways in the North Carolina home of her father, the Rev. Robert Hall Morrison, a conservative Presbyterian divine who had been first president of Davidson College. She was startled, therefore, when she received a letter from Major Jackson expressing the delight which he had found in her company when she had visited her elder sister, Mrs. D. H. Hill, in Lexington. That visit had been about three years ago. Why was the major just getting around to writing about it now? She laughed off her sister Eugenia's prediction that the letter was a prelude to a visit and a courtship. She laughed until the day she looked out the window and saw the major approaching with purposeful stride. Her parents were soon as disconcerted as she was, for Jackson lost little time in asking for their daughter's hand in marriage. They wanted more time to appraise this strangely direct suitor, as did Anna herself. But Jackson explained that his Christmas holidays would soon be over and he must have an answer before returning to work. He waged a relentless, dogged campaign.

When he returned to Lexington, no one knew what had happened over the holidays, but the major laughed often in his curious way, clasping his hands below his knee and raising it almost to his chin while his whole frame shook convulsively in silent mirth.

The courtship continued by mail, and Anna must have discovered that the major was even more extraordinary than she had realized. His letters were frequent and ardent, but she soon learned that hers to him would not be opened until the following day if they arrived on a Sunday. Anything that gave that much pleasure was a violation of the Sabbath,

As so often before, he was convinced that the thing he most desired was ordained of God. He told Anna it was "a great satisfaction to feel that our Heavenly Father has so manifestly ordered our union." And, like everything else that mattered greatly to him, his love for Anna was inextricably entwined with religious sentiment and the occasion for searching self-analysis. "When in prayer for you last Sabbath," he wrote, "the tears came to my eyes, and I realized an unusual degree of emotional tenderness. I have not yet fully analyzed my feelings to my satisfaction, so as to arrive at the cause of such emotions; but I am disposed to think that it consisted in the idea of the intimate relation existing between you, as the object of my tender affection, and God, to whom I looked up as my Heavenly Father."

On July 16, 1857, the predestined was made manifest. Waiting in an upstairs room at the Morrisons, Jackson sweated as he had at the blackboards of West Point and in his first attempts at public prayer. But he removed his sadly wilted collar and, with a groomsman's help, replaced it in time to descend to the parlor in his neat V.M.I. uniform and stand grimly beside bright-eyed Anna Morrison to repeat the marriage vows in tones of solemn asseveration.

The bride was soon popular in Lexington. The faithful Maggie, who had suddenly married a widower with seven children, told Anna, "You are taking the place that my sister had, and so you shall be a sister to me."

Life was pleasant in their own little home with its delightful garden. Jackson's idea of Sunday afternoon recreation was reading the *Shorter Catechism* with his wife, but there were many less serious diversions. Playful as a child, the major delighted in surprising her by jumping out from behind doors to kiss her resoundingly. She even appreciated his sense of humor when he flourished his saber over her head. In respites from Saxon austerity, he would court her daily in the liquid syllables of Spain. Sometimes Anna must have wondered how he had learned Spanish baby talk. Behind closed doors (one must avoid the appearance of evil), the major and his bride danced the spirited dances of old Mexico, he always vowing afterward that his inspiration was therapeutic rather than terpsichorean.

But there was as well a daily regimen of exercise prompted solely by a sense of duty. Each morning he took a brisk walk. At home, he practiced with gymnastic equipment. Plain brown bread became the staple of his diet. Cold water was the only liquid that passed his lips. But, despite these precautions and the domestic bliss he found in what he called his house with "golden hinges," Jackson continued to suffer dyspepsia and his nerves were often bow-string tight. He adhered to his old rule about not reading by artificial light, but his eyes pained him and the application of cold water and of a patent medicine brought no relief. Did Jackson still believe, as he had some years before, that his physical afflictions "were decreed by Heaven's sovereign as a punishment for . . . offences against His *Holy Laws*?" Did he feel that he had to pay for undeserved moments of domestic bliss?

Soon new suffering was added to his usual burden of psychosomatic illnesses. A severe inflammation seared his throat and right ear, and the pangs of neuralgia stabbed his face. The ministrations of local physicians were unavailing. He rapidly grew deaf in his right ear. When his left was threatened, in July of 1858, he went to New York for treatment. Tonsillectomies were popular that year and Jackson submitted to surgery, but the relief obtained was only temporary. He resorted to hydropathy, but was an ill man when he returned to the Institute in September. At least one of his colleagues believed that the major's health had been "worsted by his new system of treatment."

Anna had her own hard struggle that year. At the end of February, she had given birth to a beautiful baby girl. Jackson's delight had been inordinate. But, before summer, the child was dead. Jackson preserved a stoic front, but he showed increased tenderness for all children. An overnight visitor in the Jackson home had his small daughter with him. In the night, a sound woke him. The major was leaning over the child, drawing the covering closer around her.

The void in their hearts was partially filled when, at Jackson's instance, Thomas Arnold, Laura's twelve-year-old son, joined their household. Lexington offered educational advantages unobtainable in the lad's mountain home. The major gave the boy fatherly affection. Uncle and nephew had long, happy walks together.

But Tom left Lexington in the summer of 1859, and Jackson again became deeply concerned over his own health. His throat still pained him and, regardless of what the doctors might say, he was sure that he was seriously afflicted with some vague disorder of the liver. He tried the waters at White Sulphur Springs. Anna was convinced that his vigorous program of hydropathy worsened his condition but he claimed, on returning to the Institute in September, that he was "under the blessing of Providence . . . much improved."

Who Is This Major . . . ?

There was a festering in the nation that could be cured only by the knife. Jackson was reminded of that in October when John Brown seized the arsenal at Harper's Ferry. In November, the bearded fanatic was sentenced to be hanged on December 2. New England abolitionists compared the approaching execution with the crucifixion of Christ. In Lexington, as in other American communities, there were predictions that a desperate attempt would be made to rescue Brown, that his hanging at Charles Town would precipitate civil war. Militia were ordered to the scene. So was the V.M.I. cadet corps.

Jackson was in charge of the artillery detachment. Standing with the red-shirted cadets between two howitzers, he had a clear view of the scaffold on the fateful morning. In a letter to Anna, he provided a circumstantial account of the hanging which is the most detailed and vivid description of the event:

The gibbet was erected in a large field, southeast of the town. Brown rode on the head of his coffin from his prison to the place of execution.

. . . He was dressed in a black frock-coat, black pantaloons, black vest, black slouch hat, white socks, and slippers of predominating red. There was nothing around his neck but his shirt collar. . . . Brown had his arms tied behind him, and ascended the scaffold with apparent cheerfulness. After reaching the top of the platform, he shook hands with several who were standing around him. The sheriff placed the rope around his neck, then threw a white cap over his head, and asked him if he wished a signal when all should be ready. He replied that it made no difference, provided he was not kept waiting long. In this condition he stood for about ten minutes on the trap door, which was supported on one side by hinges and on the other (the south side) by a rope. Colonel Smith then announced to the sheriff "All ready"—which apparently was not comprehended by him, and the colonel had to repeat the order, when the rope was cut by a single blow, and Brown fell through about five inches, his knees falling on a level with the position occupied by his feet before the rope was cut. With the fall his arms, below the elbows, flew up horizontally, his hands clinched; and his arms gradually fell, but by spasmodic motions. There was very little motion of his person for several moments, and soon the wind blew his lifeless body to and fro.

So objective is this account of what the man in epaulets saw when he watched the man in the frock coat die that we are startled by the intrusion of personality in the addendum:

I was much impressed with the thought that before me stood a man in the full vigor of health, who must in a few moments enter eternity.

I sent up a petition that he might be saved. Awful was the thought that he might in a few minutes receive the sentence, "Depart ye wicked, into everlasting fire!"

Every detail of the scene had been burned into Jackson's brain. The lifeless body, blown to and fro by the wind, was the awful pendulum of a time running out. "What do you think of the state of the country?" he wrote a relative. "Viewing things at Washington from human appearances, I think we have great reason for alarm, but my trust is in God; and I cannot think that he will permit the madness of men to interfere so materially with the Christian labors of this country at home and abroad."

In the summer of 1860, Jackson made his annual pilgrimage in search of health, first to the baths at Brattleboro, Vermont, and then to the celebrated waters of Round Hill, in Northampton, Massachusetts. A stay among scenes of natural beauty was marred by sneering references to the South, encountered among almost any large group.

When he returned to Lexington in the fall, some people were openly advocating secession. Jackson usually remained quiet while the hotheads ranted. Sometimes one, offended by his silence, would demand, "Don't you think the South ought to fight for its rights?" Jackson would fix the questioner with a steady eye. "Yes, sir, but it can make a better fight in the Union than out."

The major was one of twelve Lexington citizens who met, hoping "by the expression of our opinion [to] contribute our mite to arrest, if possible, the impending calamity—and if that is impossible to consult together as to what is the safest course for us to pursue in the event of a dissolution of the Federal Government."

As the old year drew to a close in 1860, with South Carolina already out of the Union, he still permitted himself a glimmer of hope. He wrote his sister: "I am looking forward with great interest to the 4th of January when the Christian people of this land will lift their united prayer as incense to the Throne of God in supplication for our unhappy country." But the same head that bowed so eagerly in prayer was bent more than ever over ordnance reports and volumes on heavy artillery. There was no inconsistency in this Cromwellian attitude. Jackson made his position perfectly clear in a letter of January 26, 1861 to his nephew Tom:

I am in favor of making a thorough trial for peace, and if we fail in this, and the state is invaded, to defend it with a terrific resistance. . . . I desire to see the state use every influence she possesses in order to produce an honorable adjustment of our troubles, but if after having done so the free states, instead of permitting us to enjoy the rights guaranteed to us by the Constitution of our country, should endeavour to subjugate us, and thus excite our slaves to servile insurrection in which our families will be murdered without quarter or mercy, it becomes us to wage such a war as will bring hostilities to a speedy close.

On the very day that the major wrote, Louisiana—following the example of South Carolina, Mississippi, Florida, Alabama, and Georgia—seceded from the Union.

Jackson was among the vast majority of white Southerners who had little or no vested interest in slavery and no passionate attachment to the institution and yet who feared the consequences of a sudden freeing of the Negro even more than they dreaded war. They believed that the Negro was potentially dangerous as a slave but would be utterly destructive when freed from white surveillance.

Nevertheless, the major was no saber rattler. He told Tom:

"People who are anxious to bring on war don't know what they are bargaining for; they don't see all the horrors that must accompany such an event."

But he was hopeful:

"For myself I have never as yet been induced to believe that Virginia will even have to leave the Union. I feel pretty well satisfied that the Northern people love the Union more than they do their peculiar notions of slavery, and that they will prove it to us when satisfied that we are in earnest about leaving the Confederacy [i.e., Union] unless they do us justice."

Jackson echoed the hopes of many Southerners. Their optimism was matched by that of the many Northerners who argued that Southerners must be more devoted to the Union than to their "peculiar institution" and would evidence that fact when forced by Northern firmness to make a choice. In the absurd hopes nurtured North and South was the seed of miscalculation. From it grew the rankling weeds of war.

Texas seceded on February 1. In Virginia, as in Arkansas, Tennessee, and North Carolina, there was a growing body of secessionist sentiment, but the attitude of the dominant majority in each of the four states was voiced by an administration that expressed reluctance to secede while warning that any federal attempt to coerce a state would be opposed.

On April 12, Fort Sumter was fired on. The next day was a Saturday. While Major Robert Anderson, within the fort, debated how long honor required him to hold out under the intense bombardment, an hour of decision approached silently but swiftly for another major in faraway Lexington. About the time that the United States flag was lowered over Sumter that afternoon, a Union standard and a secession flag were raised by rival factions in the Virginia town. V.M.I. cadets, trained for action and restless for it, milled among the excited citizens. Tempers flared. Cadets, spotting a schoolmate in a fight with a townsman, rushed to the boy's aid. Citizens attacked the cadets. The outnumbered students sent a plea for help back to their fellows at the Institute. Shouldering muskets, the reinforcements dashed toward town. Quick-moving officers of the Institute headed them off and led them to a section room. There the superintendent reprimanded them for insubordination and lectured them on their responsibility to preserve law and order.

The boys were not indifferent to the issues of Union and secession, but their riot had been inspired at least as much by the traditional spring restlessness of college youths as by the excitement of political convictions. When Jackson entered the room with his usual spring-kneed awkwardness and other-world stare, tension broke in laughter. "Jackson, Jackson, Old Jack!" the cadets yelled. Jackson shook his head. But the superintendent turned to him in all seriousness. "I have driven in the nail, but it needs clinching. Speak with them."

Cadets looking on as Old Jack mounted the rostrum suddenly beheld a stranger. The mild-eyed major was transformed into an electric figure whose fierce gaze singed the smile off every face. There was a strange note of authority in his clipped speech:

"Military men make short speeches, and as for myself I am no hand at speaking, anyhow. The time for war has not yet come, but it will come and that soon. And when it does come, my advice is to draw the sword and throw away the scabbard."

Three days later, in response to Lincoln's call for 75,000 volunteers to invade the seceding states, Virginia withdrew from the Union. The superintendent of V.M.I. tendered the services of the cadets to the Commonwealth. On April 18, a Sunday, they were ordered to move at 12:30 P.M. for Richmond under Major Jackson's command.

Before he would sit down for breakfast, Jackson checked on two necessities: the supply of ammunition and the availability of the Rev. Mr. White to lead the young soldiers in prayer. Then he hurried home, swallowed a little food and spent a few minutes alone with Anna. He read aloud from the Bible: "For we know that if our earthly house of this tabernacle be dissolved, we have a building of God, a house not made with hands, eternal in the heavens." He knelt with his wife and prayed that the "earthly house" of the Union might yet be preserved in peace. Then he rose, clasped her to him, pressed his bearded lips to hers with a fierce ardor, and abruptly strode out of the house.

Dinner began promptly at noon. But the cadets were hungrier for adventure than for food. So they had finished eating and had listened to Mr. White's prayers before the marching hour of 12:30 arrived. "Let's go, Let's go!" they called out. But Major Jackson, sitting on his camp stool, seemed not to hear. The orders did not say that the men should be formed to march after 12:30 or before 12:30, but precisely at 12:30. And, precisely at the moment that the hands of Old Jack's watch formed one vertical line, he stood up, forming another equally straight, and shouted: "Right face! By file, left march!"

That night, after a train ride enlivened by derailment in a Blue Ridge tunnel, the Corps arrived in Richmond and bivouacked on the fairgrounds with a host of volunteers. In ensuing days, the cadets were much in demand as drillmasters for volunteer units.

But Major Jackson himself received no immediate assignment. He volunteered to serve as drillmaster and helped around the camp in humble capacities, awaiting an assignment in keeping with his military record.

But when his commission in the Virginia forces arrived April 25, it was only as a major in the Engineering Corps. Jackson hated engineering. But, above all, the rank was an insult to the man who had won the plaudits of an army at Chapultepec and who had confessed to his sister that he lived for fame. Higher commissions were going to civilian soldiers who wore uniforms with a soldierly grace that put the awkward Major Jackson to shame.

Friends of Jackson protested to Governor Letcher and acquainted the chief executive with the mountaineer soldier's accomplishments. Jackson himself may have enlisted their aid. He was seldom hesitant about mustering the influence of well-placed friends and relatives. Ten days later Jackson was commissioned a colonel of the line.

When the name was submitted to the State Convention, it stirred few memories. One delegate asked, "Who is this Major Jackson?" A member from the nominee's own Rockbridge County replied, "He is one who, if you order him to hold a post, will never leave it alive to be occupied by the enemy."

Harper's Ferry

On the very day that Jackson was commissioned a colonel, he was ordered to one of the most challenging posts that could be offered any officer of his rank. He was placed in command of Harper's Ferry. Its arsenal was vital to the defense of a state with no surplus of arms and ammunition. Moreover, because of its situation at the confluence of the Potomac and Shenandoah rivers and the junction of two important railroads, together with its proximity to the Maryland border, the town was popularly regarded as the gateway to the Valley of Virginia. But the town was far from being the natural fortress that most Valley residents supposed it to be. Those who boasted that Harper's Ferry was secure in its mountain fastnesses overlooked the elementary fact that soldiers stationed there would be trapped in a bowl in the hills if an enemy gained control of the surrounding heights.

With the aid of two V.M.I. cadets, Jackson would have to fashion an army to defend this spot. His materials would be raw volunteers and untrained officers. General Lee had informed Jackson that machinery for arms manufacture must be shipped at once from Harper's Ferry to Richmond. Arms in process of manufacture might be finished at the arsenal if Jackson deemed that course expedient, but the new colonel would be held responsible for any resulting loss.

Jackson gloried in the challenge. He had, he wrote Anna, "the post which I prefer above all others . . . and you must not expect to hear from me very often, as I expect to have more work than I have ever had in the same length of time before."

And work he did! The hours he kept were prodigious. After a few hours' sleep, he would be up at dawn, examining every phase of the defenses, putting the men through military exercises, studying reports, and finally getting to bed for a few hours, only to rise for another day of equal labor. But he flourished under this regimen. When he snatched opportunities to write to Anna, his letters were free of any references to his health except reports on his vigor and exuberance.

And the work was showing results. The transformation in the post was equal to that in its commander. Gone was the undisciplined, holiday mood of the volunteers. Most of the militia officers above the rank of captain, indignant over decommissioning orders from Richmond, had hurried off to the capital trailing clouds of sulphur. The men had stopped playing soldier and begun working at the job in earnest. They grumbled, but they responded to a man who seemed to know what he was doing.

Jackson, for his part, was intent on learning what the enemy was doing. His small cavalry forces were busily employed in scouting. They were commanded by two of the most colorful young soldiers in the army : Turner Ashby, swarthy-skinned, black-bearded, fiercely mustachioed, who rode like an Arab and looked like one, and Jeb Stuart, of the lush chestnut beard, jingling spurs and flying cape. Behind their theatrical appearance was a vast reservoir of energy and resourcefulness. Such was Jackson's confidence in them that he could inform Lee, "Have no fear of this place being surprised."

Jackson placed detachments on the heights around Harper's Ferry. He did not scruple to station soldiers on Maryland Heights, on the soil of a state still in the Union though manifesting sympathy with the Confederacy. Anticipating Richmond's sensitivity on this point, Jackson reported to Lee that he had not yet erected works in Maryland. But he added ominously that, if a federal threat from that area should appear imminent, he would "no longer stand on ceremony." A day later, the sober student of predestination wrote like a man of destiny : "This place should be defended with the spirit which actuated the defenders of Thermopylae, and, if left to myself, such is my determination."

The florid heroism of Jackson's declaration, coupled with his activity on Maryland soil, must have given the well-balanced Lee some anxiety. The general wrote the colonel : "I am concerned at the feeling evinced in Maryland . . . it will be necessary, in order to allay it, that you confine yourself to a strictly defensive course." This was Lee's second gentle warning on the subject. Jackson withdrew from Maryland Heights.

There were no more heroic pronouncements or gestures for a while. Jackson was involved in the prosaic but harassing business of securing supplies for his soldiers and transport for the ordnance. For both, he resorted to impressment. He was fortunate in finding a resourceful quartermaster in the unmilitary but thoroughly proficient John A. Harman.

Jackson, in the impressment of a B & O train, acquired a small sorrel horse, for which he paid a fair price out of his own pocket. Later he would conclude that Little Sorrel was priceless. Henry Kyd Douglas, who served under Jackson, called the horse "a plebeian looking little beast." But he also wrote of the "boundless endurance" of this "natural pacer with . . . no style," and said, "It would have been impossible to have found another horse that would have suited his new owner so exactly—he was made for him." The soldiers at Harper's Ferry soon grew accustomed to the sight of their commander, still in his old blue major's coat, his cap pulled down over his eyes, his angular knees raised to ludicrous heights by the shortness of the stirrups into which his huge boots were thrust, as he rode his stocky little mount from one detachment to another.

Jackson still dreamed of dramatic action. When Lee invited his opinion on the problem posed by strong Unionist sentiment in Northwestern Virginia, Jackson urged a swift and secret expedition to "crush out opposition." The move was not deemed feasible at the time, but Lee had Jackson's recipe for military success: speed, secrecy, and relentless purpose.

Just when Jackson had visions of a larger theater, he found he was expected to quit the small stage he occupied. On May 24, Joseph E. Johnston, as immaculately neat as when Jackson had known him in the old army days but now wearing an iron-gray beard, appeared at Harper's Ferry without warning. He carried the Confederate rank of brigadier general. He had come to assume command of the post. Would Colonel Jackson publish an order announcing that fact?

Jackson quietly but firmly stated that he would be glad to show Johnston and his staff around but that, in the absence of orders from Richmond, he could not turn over his command. Johnston made a hurried search of his luggage and produced a letter of confirmation from Robert E. Lee. Jackson immediately relinquished command.

The Stonewall Brigade

Disappointment was soon assuaged. Johnston reorganized the Harper's Ferry forces into three brigades and made the colonel commander of the one composed largely of men from his beloved Valley of Virginia. Jackson wrote Anna, "I am very thankful to our Heavenly Father for having given me such a fine brigade." Jackson still saw himself as a soldier anointed of the Lord.

But, though he was thankful, not all his hopes were fulfilled. He wanted to be a brigadier general and he enlisted the aid of friends who could exert political influence in his behalf.

Meanwhile, he longed for action. When Johnston began evacuating Harper's Ferry, Jackson rejoiced that they might be bound on an aggressive expedition. Jackson readied his First Brigade for an attack on Patterson, only to learn that Johnston intended a genuine retreat. The normally reticent colonel must have been near frustration when he confided in a letter to Anna, "I hope the general will do something soon."

When Jackson was ordered to establish a base of operations at Martinsburg and destroy the rolling stock of the Baltimore and Ohio Railroad in that area, he hoped to encounter Federal opposition. When cavalry scouts brought word that some of Patterson's men were not far away, Jackson prepared to attack. But Johnston vetoed the move.

The colonel's hunger for battle was rewarded on July 2 when a reconnaissance in force became a rear-guard action with a stiff fight at Falling Waters. Jackson's men acquitted themselves well. He was happy with their performance and his own. He wrote Anna that he had learned indirectly that Johnston had recommended him for a brigadier general's commission. He tried to write modestly, but implicit in his words of humility was the faith that he was one of the chosen of God. "I am very thankful," he said, "that an ever-kind Providence made me an instrument in carrying out General Johnston's orders so successfully."

The promotion came. Despite all his energetic pulling of strings to get it, Jackson convinced himself that it had come to him through the invisible motions of a favoring Providence. He also minimized the motivation of personal ambition. He wrote Anna :

My promotion was beyond what I anticipated, as I only expected it to be in the volunteer forces of the State. One of my greatest desires for advancement is the gratification it will give my darling, and [the opportunity] of serving my country more efficiently. I have had all that I ought to desire in the line of promotion. I should be very ungrateful if I were not contented, and exceedingly thankful to our kind Heavenly Father.

Another blessing came his way soon : the chance to participate in the first great battle of the war. In mid-July, two major Federal armies were in Virginia—the one under Patterson assigned to oppose Johnston in the Valley and another under McDowell, poised in the Washington and Alexandria area of Northern Virginia for a drive on Richmond. Patterson was ordered to hold Johnston in the Valley while McDowell moved against Beauregard, sixty miles east of Johnston and across the Blue Ridge at the little railroad junction of Manassas.

On the night of July 17, the Confederate government, in response to Beauregard's urgent solicitations, authorized Johnston to slip away from Patterson in order to join forces with the Creole to repel an imminent attack on Manassas. By forced marches and by use of the railroad, Jackson's brigade and its artillery and cavalry were on the field at Manassas by the 20th. There Beauregard's 25,000 men were drawn up along an eight-mile line south of a stream known as Bull Run. McDowell, with about 54,000 men, was at Centerville, three miles north. Both McDowell and Beauregard had elaborate plans for the battle that they expected to fight on the 21st. Because of many factors, not least of which was the rawness of the troops on both sides, neither general got a chance to execute his complicated schemes. First Manassas, or Bull Run, has been called "the best planned and worst fought" battle of the war.

The battle began, as it was to end, in confusion. Firing began about 5 A.M. After four hours of abortive efforts to launch a large-scale attack on the right, the Confederates learned that they had been outflanked and their left was imperiled. This development took place before Johnston and Beauregard could reach the scene.

On the left, General N. G. Evans fought valiantly with his half brigade until help arrived from General Barnard E. Bee's brigade and a Georgia unit. But heavy Federal reinforcements led by McDowell himself drove the Confederates back. South Carolina's Wade Hampton, a magnificent embodiment of manhood, arrived on the scene with his spirited legion. But the resulting lift to Confederate morale was shortlived. As the Yankees poured upon the Southerners in an engulfing flood, threatening to turn both ends of their line, the Confederates broke. Their confused flight carried them across a shallow branch and to a plateau—Henry House Hill.

Waiting for them there was a man who had no orders to be there and who apparently had not even bothered to inform his superiors that he would be there : that stubborn professor from V.M.I. His powers of perception intensified by the excitement of battle, Jackson had grasped the situation before the fleeing troops reached him. Instead of rushing forward to make contact with the enemy, he began to dispose his troops along the ridge of the hill to provide a rallying point. He had unerringly selected the ideal position, the higher of two edges, a line covered by pine thickets. Through the late morning and early afternoon, Jackson, after placing his own artillery with great care, continued to take charge of any guns available, even if they had not been assigned to his command. When Captain Imboden's battery of Bee's brigade began retiring from the field under heavy Federal assaults, Jackson took over and moved up the guns to join the batteries he had already concentrated.

By now, Bee was behind Henry House Hill, striving desperately to rally his men. He came face to face with Jackson, riding up with Imboden's guns. Bee's eyes were misty with tears or sweat, or maybe both. He waved his sword in frustration. "General," he said, "they are beating us back." A strange light burned in Jackson's eyes as he stared at the South Carolinian. "Sir," he said, "we'll give them the bayonet."

Once again, Bee rode among his men, exhorting them at the top of his voice. Still they milled in confusion or hesitated. Then, pointing to Jackson's steady line on the crest of the plateau, he shouted : "There is Jackson standing like a stone wall. Let us determine to die here, and we will conquer. Follow me." Beauregard came up. Darkly handsome, Napoleonic in command, he shouted to Bee's men to rally behind Jackson.

Minie balls sprayed the Stonewall Brigade. Whistling shells exploded all around them. The men might have wavered, except for the example of Jackson himself. He rode up and down in front of the line, careless of bullets. One passed through his coat, but he rode on undaunted. Another bullet found the middle finger of his left hand. Jackson raised the wounded member aloft to check the bleeding.

To his men, he appeared to be invoking the blessing of Jehovah. There was a strange, contagious exaltation in this bearded figure with the upraised arm. A wild, unreasoning excitement passed down the line. Gideon and Joshua—all those stern, bearded men who battled for the Lord—must have been something like Old Jack.

During the time bought by Jackson, Confederate reinforcements under E. Kirby Smith arrived by railroad. They could turn the blue tide beating relentlessly against the Stonewall Brigade. Another wave of Yankees was sweeping forward. Jackson shouted: "Reserve your fire till they come within fifty yards. Then fire and give them the bayonet. And when you charge, yell like furies!"

The muskets fired. The First Brigade pushed forward with cold steel. The Federal center wavered, then reeled. The retreat became a rout.

As night closed on Manassas, General Bee lay dead. But his name was linked with an immortal phrase born in the battle that cost him his life: "There is Jackson standing like a stone wall." The First Brigade and its commander had gained a new name. Soon, in Bee's native South Carolina, gentlemen planters were drinking "Stonewalls," potent concoctions guaranteed to produce courage. The teetotaling Jackson, if he knew of it, must have disapproved. But he had experienced his own intoxication, the heady whiff of battle-smoke. It was still with him on the following day when he wrote Anna: "Whilst great credit is due to other parts of our gallant army, God made my brigade more instrumental than any other in repulsing the main attack."

The name of "Stonewall" Jackson was joined with those of Beauregard and Johnston in extravagant celebrations throughout the South. Nowhere—not even in Richmond—was news of Jackson's exploits more eagerly awaited than in Lexington. The Valley community was not only Jackson's home, but also the home of many men in his brigade. And V.M.I. and Washington College had been fully represented at Manassas. While a Lexington crowd milled and murmured at mail time, the Rev. Mr. White suddenly yelled out in excitement: "Jackson has written. Now we shall know all the facts."

A hush fell. Mr. White began reading in a clear pulpit voice that carried through the crowd. "My dear Pastor, In my tent last night after a fatiguing day's service"—the people leaned forward eagerly— "I remembered that I had failed to send you my contribution for our colored Sunday school. Enclosed you will find my check for that object, which please acknowledge at your earliest convenience, and oblige Yours faithfully, T. J. Jackson."

Frostbitten Laurels

Months of inaction followed the Battle of Manassas. The North, realizing at last the magnitude of the task before it, buckled down to laborious preparation. The Southern people, too confident as a result of their victory, indulged in premature celebration.

Loyal little Anna Jackson, despite the recognition gained by her husband, was disturbed that he did not receive as much credit as Johnston and Beauregard. Jackson, with more accuracy than modesty, wrote her a letter of reassurance:

I know that the First Brigade was the first to meet and pass our retreating forces—to push on with no other aid than the smiles of God; to boldly take its position with the artillery that was under my command —to arrest the victorious foe in his onward progress—to hold him in check until reinforcements arrived—and finally to charge bayonets, and, thus advancing, pierce the enemy's centre. . . . It is not to be expected that I should receive the credit that Generals Beauregard and Johnston would, because I was under them; but I am thankful to my ever-kind Heavenly Father that He makes me content to await His own good time and pleasure for commendation—knowing all things work together for my good.

After boring but hard-working months of drill, enlivened by a visit from Anna, Jackson received fresh confirmation that all things worked together for his good. On October 7, he was promoted to major general in the Provisional Army of the Confederate States,

He wrote Anna: "I am very thankful to that God who withholds no good thing from me (though I am so utterly unworthy and ungrateful) for making me a major-general."

His joy was great, but not unmitigated. The promotion meant parting with his beloved brigade. He would be charged with defense of the Shenandoah Valley. He, Beauregard, and Theophilus Holmes would each be in charge of a newly created military district under Johnston.

President Davis and Secretary of War Benjamin both had some misgivings about the appointment. Benjamin, in his letter of instruction to Jackson, made no bones of the fact that the officer's ability had not been the predominant determinant. There were "other weighty considerations—Your intimate knowledge of the country, of its population and resources. . . . Nor is this all. . . . The people of that District with one voice have made constant and urgent appeals that to you, in whom they have confidence, should their defense be assigned."

The confidence of his own people may have been even more gratifying to Jackson than high praise from Richmond politicians. He was a happy man—and yet, there was the necessity of saying goodbye to the old brigade.

They awaited him on the morning of May 4. Gray lines against a forest whose autumnal gonfalons matched the blood red of their own shredded pennants, they stood rigidly at attention. Old Jack loved spit and polish even if he himself sometimes seemed to have less polish than spit. And then appeared Little Sorrel and her master, merged into one awkward and oddly congruous unit of angular flesh. Old Jack paused. He looked all down the line. Each soldier was sure that the general had looked at him. Stonewall was struggling with strong emotions. He seemed unable to find his voice.

At last he choked out the opening words of a stilted farewell:

"Officers and men of the First Brigade, I am not here to make a speech, but simply to say farewell. I first met you at Harper's Ferry in the commencement of the war, and I cannot take leave of you

without giving expression to my admiration of your conduct . . . ."
The speech went on slowly, a painful experience for both speaker
and audience. The phrases were so conventional, yet both the general
and his men felt that the occasion had a unique poignance. Nevertheless, Old Jack plowed on to the final sentence : "I shall look with
great anxiety to your future movements, and I trust whenever I shall
hear of the First Brigade on the field of battle it will be of still nobler
deeds achieved and higher reputation won."

Jackson just sat in the saddle looking at the men, and they looked
back at him with the same silent concentration. Abruptly, the general
stood in the stirrups and stretched out his gauntleted right hand.
Lightning was in his eye and it crackled, too, in his voice.

"In the Army of the Shenandoah," he shouted, "you were the
First Brigade. In the Army of the Potomac you were the First
Brigade. In the Second Corps of this army you are the First Brigade.
You are the First Brigade in the affections of your General. And I
hope by your future deeds and daring you will be handed down to
posterity as the First Brigade in our second War of Independence.
Farewell !"

He "gently settled into his saddle," caught up the reins with his
left hand, and turned his horse's head. From hundreds of throats
burst the rebel yell with which the brigade had charged the enemy
at Manassas. Jackson pulled off his weatherbeaten cap, waved it in
farewell, and galloped along the line and out of sight. That savage
chorus of tribute, echoing among the trees, followed him as he went.

Before another dawn, Jackson was in Winchester. In the morning,
he officially established headquarters for the Valley District. He had
altogether about 1,650 men, consisting of parts of three militia
brigades and some unpromising cavalry units. There were some guns,
but their usefulness was considerably impaired by the fact that
there were no gunners to man them. Federal troops were not far
away in Romney and about 6,000 were within striking distance
of Winchester.

Jackson appealed to the War Department for disciplined troops.

The answer was better than he could have expected. The old Stonewall Brigade was being detached for service with him. He could have his cake and eat it, too.

Still Jackson's position was perilous. From the Ohio River to the Shenandoah Valley, Virginia was occupied by Federal troops. Other Federal troops were massing north of the Potomac for invasion of Virginia. Jackson's force seemed almost insignificant by comparison.

The only hope, as he saw it, was in attack before the Federal forces concentrated. On November 20, he proposed in a letter to the Secretary of War that the Confederacy lure McClellan into an attack on Johnston before the Federal general completed the training of the force assembling north of the Potomac. An expedition to the Northwest, Jackson argued, might lead McClellan to suspect a far greater diversion of force from the main body of Johnston's army than would actually be the case. Raw Federal recruits thrown against Johnston might produce another Manassas. Jackson proposed an attack on Romney. Besides achieving deception of the enemy, successful occupation of the town would give the Confederates control of the whole northwest portion of the Valley. Jackson was confident that, if McClellan moved against Johnston, the Valley force could be on hand for the battle.

Jackson realized that he would need reinforcements for an expedition against Romney. He suggested that General William W. Loring's Army of the Northwest, about 6,000 men, might be more profitably employed in union with Jackson's own army in an attack on Romney than in guarding the Staunton-Parkersburg Road. With Loring's aid, Jackson's force should be definitely superior to the Romney garrison, estimated at about 5,000 men.

Wisely, the general omitted from his letter to the Secretary of War, a shrewd lawyer, any high-flown rhetoric about Thermopylae. Instead, he mustered logical reasons to support his contention that "Northwestern Virginia must be occupied by Confederate troops this winter." He said:

"At present it is to be presumed that the enemy are not expecting an attack there, and the resources of that region necessary for the subsistence of our troops are in greater abundance than in almost any other season of the year. Postpone the occupation of that section until spring, and we may expect to find the enemy prepared for us and the resources to which I have referred greatly exhausted."

He knew what Valley winters were like. "I know that what I have proposed will be an arduous undertaking and cannot be accomplished without the sacrifice of much personal comfort; but I feel that the troops will be prepared to make this sacrifice when animated by the prospects of important results to our cause and distinction to themselves."

Jackson adhered to Napoleonic opinion that "an active winter's campaign is less likely to produce disease than a sedentary life by campfires in winter quarters." He seems to have given little thought to Napoleon's possible reflections on the same point while crossing the snow-covered steppes of Russia.

Loring himself was unenthusiastic about the idea, as was Lee. Benjamin would not order Loring to participate in Jackson's plan, but recommended that he cooperate. Loring consented.

Early on New Year's morning, 1862, Jackson's army marched northwestward out of Winchester. The sun shone brightly, and there was a deceptive springtime warmth to the air. As Old Jack rode along on Little Sorrel, he must have thought again, "All things work together for good. . . . "

But the balminess of the air was an enemy to his expedition. Some of the men rashly threw away their heavy overcoats. Others, only a little more cautious, stored their heavy blankets in the regimental baggage wagons.

Before many hours, skies began to darken and then to turn ashen. The temperature plummeted. A searching wind made the men remember discarded overcoats. A few snowflakes were blasted by the icy winds, and then needle-sharp sleet stung their faces. The men looked toward the head of the column for some sign from Jackson. The word from him was, "Press on!"

Late in the day, Jackson himself was cold enough to seek warmth in a bottle of wine. Only, what the teetotaling general believed to be a mild wine was actually aged whisky provided by a Winchester admirer. He uncorked the bottle and, while young Kyd Douglas and others of his staff looked on in fascination, "tilted it to his mouth and without stopping to taste, swallowed about as much of that old whisky as if it had been light domestic wine." As they rode on, with the snow thickening, Old Jack complained of being very warm. Soon he unbuttoned his overcoat. A little later he began unbuttoning his uniform. Gone was his thinlipped reticence. He talked on and on at a great rate. A short while ago the Valley had been frigid. Now it was positively hot. These sudden changes in temperature, gentlemen, were a phenomenon worthy of investigation.

That night the army bivouacked near Pughtown. The wagons with the heavy blankets were far behind, impeded by the icy road. The men had been ordered to take rations with them, but they had either long since eaten them or ignored the order from the start. Hungry, cold, and miserable, they lay down on the frozen ground, pulling their thin blankets tightly around them. A squad from the Stonewall Brigade were huddled around a large fire, some standing hunch-shouldered, others lying down. The keening wind, honed on the frozen ridges, cut deep. Whirling sparks and smoke assailed the men's rheumy eyes. One unhappy fellow, clutching his flapping blanket about him, "stood nodding and staggering over the flames." His blanket caught afire. He sprang awake in time to fling it to the ground, shouting, "I wish the Yankees were in Hell!"

A "drowsy growl of approbation" came from his fellow sufferers. "I don't," dissented a shivering figure stretched out behind the partial shelter of a fallen tree. "Old Jack would follow them there with our brigade in front."

Not all the grumbling was as good-natured as that from Jackson's old brigade. As the second day of marching dragged toward a close with most of the men still without food, Jackson pushed on and picked up reinforcements. His force now numbered about 8,500.

Perhaps the attitude of the officers would have been a little different if Jackson had confided to them that he was pressing on in hopes of attacking Bath, destroying communications between Federal General Kelley in Romney and the body of Federal troops under General Banks. If he succeeded, Kelley might evacuate Romney without a fight.

Jackson's subordinate officers knew little more than the men. All -the men knew was that they were cold and hungry and weary. They suspected they were led by a maniac. A few days ago Jackson had climbed into a persimmon tree after some of the fruit and then had been unable to get down until rescued by some of his staff. He might now be leading the army into some inescapable plight.

By January 7, suspicion that Jackson might be insane had become conviction. He was forced to halt the march on that day of snow and sleet so that the horses, slipping and sliding on the ice, injuring the men as well as themselves, might be provided with the winter shoes which had been forgotten.

The men and animals could not be driven on before January 13. Riding along the struggling line that day, Jackson heard something he probably had not heard since the days at V.M.I., certainly not since Manassas. More than once there came the murmur, "Fool Tom Jackson."

The next night, Jackson and his vanguard reached Romney. The town had been deserted by the Yankees.

The following day, the general was excited about pushing farther west, destroying bridges, rails, and telegraph communications. But the men were near the breaking point. Some were near mutiny. The horses were scarcely alive. From the knees of one hung icicles of blood that almost dragged the ground. Even Jackson realized that he could not push on.

Leaving Loring and his men to hold Romney, Jackson rode back to Winchester with his old brigade, now spitefully denominated "Jackson's pets."

Jackson reported to the Secretary of War that the enemy had been driven from Romney and the surrounding territory "without the firing of a gun" and "had been forced from the offensive to the defensive." All had been accomplished "through the blessing of God."

The blessing was not obvious to everybody. On the last day of the month, the general received a telegram from the Secretary of War : "Our news indicates that a movement is being made to cut off General Loring's command. Order him back to Winchester immediately."

Jackson wrote Benjamin that the secretary's order had been complied with, but added :

"With such interference in my command I cannot expect to be of much service in the field, and accordingly respectfully request to be ordered to report for duty to the superintendent of the Virginia Military Institute at Lexington . . . . Should this application not be granted, I respectfully request that the President will accept my resignation from the Army."

Jackson sent that letter through Johnston's headquarters and dispatched an account of what had happened to another Valley man, Governor Letcher. Johnston first delayed sending Jackson's letter to Richmond, then endorsed it : "Respectfully forwarded, with great regret. I don't know how the loss of this officer can be supplied."

Jackson's political friends got busy. Soon the general was informed that Governor Letcher feared the resignation would lower the people's morale.

On February 6, Jackson wrote the Governor :

"If my retiring from the Army would produce that effect upon our country that you have named . . . you are authorized to withdraw my resignation, unless the Secretary of War desires that it should be accepted."

The Secretary had no such desire.

Officially, the incident was closed. But from the Romney operation there was a residue of ill will. Jackson had preferred charges of "neglect of duty" against a V.M.I. faculty colleague serving under Loring. Against Loring himself he had preferred charges of neglect

of duty and "conduct subversive of good order and discipline."
Nothing came of the charges against either officer. Indeed, Loring
was soon promoted to major general. Eleven officers of Loring's
command had signed a petition implying that Jackson was inept
and dangerously unreliable in judgment. The petition had been
handed to President Davis himself by Brigadier General William B.
Taliaferro. Some friends of Jackson maintained that the Romney
campaign was justified by its psychological effect on the enemy.
Others less friendly argued that the psychological and physical effect
on the Confederacy's own troops had been horrible.

At West Point, Jackson had demanded the court-martial of a fellow
cadet. In the U.S. Army he had demanded the court-martial of his
commanding officer. Now he had preferred charges against a fellow
general and said that he should be cashiered. When Jackson had
taught at V.M.I., the administration had been plagued with discipline problems originating in his lecture room. Now a near mutinous
spirit had appeared among officers serving under him. Was Jackson
a failure in human relations?

Some people would even take away from him a large measure of
the glory of Manassas. His courage then, they said, was born of
madness. The Romney campaign, they insisted, proved his insanity.
This extreme view was not universally held; it certainly did not
prevail in the Valley. But the laurels won at Manassas had been frostbitten, cold-hurt, on the road to Romney.

The Artful Dodger

Nobody in the Confederacy was winning new laurels. In that
gloomy February, North Carolina's Roanoke Island fell to the
Federals. The Yankees won control of Southern Kentucky and
Middle Tennessee. Fort Henry and Fort Donelson had been captured by the enemy.

In Winchester, Jackson, shorn of Loring's troops, had only about
4,600 men. He was menaced by an enemy force of 38,000. In these
circumstances, he advocated attack. He asked Johnston for reinforce-

ments, arguing : "If we cannot be successful in defeating the enemy should he advance, a kind Providence may enable us to inflict a terrible wound and effect a safe retreat in the event of having to fall back."

Johnston's own appraisal of the military situation was very different from Jackson's. On March 8 and 9, Johnston evacuated Manassas, beginning a retreat to the Rappahannock River. No reinforcements would be sent to Jackson. He would have to evacuate Winchester. But the decision went hard against the grain. Even on the morning of the 11th, with Banks' Federal army poised for seizure of the city, Jackson had hopes of wresting victory from the evacuation. His strategy was daring almost to the point of madness. He proposed to march only a short distance out of Winchester and then to double back so that, after dark, when Banks' troops would be entering the town, the Confederates could pounce on them. In the resulting confusion, the Federals might panic.

Secretive and dogmatic though he was, even Jackson hesitated to attempt so risky a move without first presenting it to his subordinate commanders in a council of war. While the council was assembling, he went to the home of the Presbyterian minister and, booted and spurred, his saber at his side, knelt in prayer to the God of Battles.

The council of war was held in a headquarters barer than a barracks. The officers stood around. Most of the chairs had already been removed. Jackson soon learned that his hope had been barren. During the preparations for the conference, his infantry had continued to march farther and farther from Winchester. They were now too far to the south to return for a surprise attack after nightfall.

Jackson himself quit Winchester a little after dark. He was accompanied by Dr. Hunter H. McGuire, the able young medical director of his army. From a hill, the two men paused to look down on the lights of the little town. For McGuire, the moment was a peculiarly poignant one. Winchester was his home town. He could picture familiar faces, drawn with anxiety, as the citizens sat in the lamplight behind those shining windows, listening for the hoofbeats of invading cavalry. He looked at Jackson. Even in the dim light, the general's face was the personification of rage. In a hoarse, fiercely primitive voice, he shouted : "That is the last council of war I will ever hold !"

Jackson's anger did not subside into despair. A few days earlier, he had written to a friend in the Confederate Congress : "If this Valley is lost, Virginia is lost." He was determined that the Valley should be saved. He went into camp at Mount Jackson, about forty-two miles south-southwest of Winchester. He subjected the men to the most rugged drilling, but he himself was at the greatest pains to see that they had good tents and adequate rations. Perhaps Romney had taught him that the mass of men did not thrive on martyrdom. Morale improved.

Jackson himself had time to study the topography of the Valley. He already knew its basic peculiarity : the middle portion of the great Valley between the Allegheny Mountains and the Blue Ridge was for practical purposes two valleys, since it was divided down the center by a short range, the Massanuttons. Indeed, the area west of the Massanuttons was often called the Shenandoah Valley, while that east of the range was called the Luray Valley. On this peculiarity must hinge the strategical and tactical ingenuity to compensate for the enemy's overwhelming superiority in numbers. A knowledge of the mountain passes could enable the Confederate general to play a fascinating game of fox and hounds. Secrecy and celerity could enable him to lead his enemies on many a bootless chase up blind alleys.

Preparation was interrupted on March 21 by a report from Colonel Ashby that General Shields' Union division had moved northward out of Strasburg. Ashby's cavalry was in pursuit. McClellan was drawing men from the Valley to cooperate in the long-awaited pincers movement on Richmond. Jackson's primary assignment was to prevent the movement of Banks' army from the Valley.

Jackson broke camp for the march toward Strasburg. Up and down the column he rode on Little Sorrel, calling out mercilessly in his clipped tones, "Press on, press on !" Stragglers fell by the wayside, but the bulk of the infantry covered nearly forty miles in forty-odd hours.

As they approached the village of Kernstown on the afternoon of the 23d, artillery firing could be heard. Ashby rode up to report that his cavalry was in contact with the rear guard of withdrawing Federals. The Yankees, he said, had only four regiments of infantry and a little cavalry and artillery left in Winchester.

Old Jack's eyes lit at "the Arab's" excited report. The 3,000 men he had at hand should be sufficient to deal with a force of that size.

But then the fire in his eyes died. Could a Christian soldier battle for the Lord on a Sunday? For this raw, most unspringlike day that presented such a tempting opportunity for the general presented also an agonizing dilemma. If even the letter opener must remain unused on the Sabbath, would it not be heinously sinful to use the bayonet?

As Jackson explained in a letter to Anna : "Arms is a profession that, if its principles are adhered to for success, requires an officer to do what he fears may be wrong . . . if success is to be attained. And this fact of its being necessary to success, and being accompanied with success, and that a departure from it is accompanied with disaster, suggests that it must be right." Deacon Jackson kept a discreet silence. General Jackson ordered an attack.

From a hill, Jackson watched with satisfaction as Brigadier General Richard B. Garnett led the old First Brigade into battle while a gray-clad regiment behind a stone wall brought the bluecoats under effective fire. The tempo and volume of firing increased in the center. Then, while the Federal fire swelled toward a crescendo, that from the Confederates abruptly diminished. Here and there, Confederate soldiers began to slip to the rear.

Jackson rode down from his perch and toward the front. The first man to fall under his baleful eye was a soldier hurrying from the line of battle. "Where are you going?" the general barked.

The soldier explained that he was out of cartridges and so were his comrades. Jackson's face flushed and he rose in the stirrups. "Then go back and give them the bayonet!"

A flood of Federal soldiers rushed toward the First Brigade. Garnett realized that his men could not withstand this assault with empty guns. With the bitterness of a brave man thwarted, he ordered a retreat.

Jackson galloped up to Garnett. He shouted to him to halt the withdrawal. Spying a drummer boy, he seized him by the shoulder and dragged him to a little knoll. "Beat the rally!" he shouted. "Beat the rally!" The boy beat bravely, more awed by Jackson than by the enemy. But the sound was drowned in the mingled shots and shouts.

Reserve regiments that Jackson had counted on were already in line of battle in the rear, covering the retreat of the infantry and artillery.

Even Jackson saw it was useless to persist. The most he could do was to ensure an orderly withdrawal, yielding ground slowly enough to save supplies, equipment and wounded. Every wounded man whose life would not be endangered by removal must be taken from the field.

"But that requires time," said Dr. McGuire. "Can you stay to protect us?"

Jackson looked solemnly at the doctor. "Make yourself easy about that. This army stays here until the last wounded man is removed. Before I will leave them to the enemy I will lose many more men."

The general made good his word. The enemy abandoned the pursuit after a mile and a half. The Confederates camped that night at Newtown, four and a half miles south of the battlefield.

As the general stood by a campfire, his sharp features umbered by the leaping flames, he was an object of derision to some of the troopers. One young man was bold enough to taunt him.

"The Yankees don't seem willing to quit Winchester, General."

"Winchester is a very pleasant place to stay in, sir."

The trooper persisted. "It was reported that they were retreating, but I guess they're retreating after us."

"I think"—there was a cutting edge to the general's voice—"I may say I am satisfied, sir."

Jackson's words were not mere bravado. The battle of Kernstown would add to the legend of his insanity, but it had accomplished something. His main purpose was to keep Banks in the Valley. There was every reason to believe that the battle of Kernstown would awaken enough anxiety among the Federals to accomplish that purpose.

Jackson's attack, in retrospect, seemed incredibly rash. But it had been based on inaccurate information furnished by Ashby, a most trustworthy scout. Shields had very cleverly concealed the fact that his force numbered 9,000.

The only unsoundness with which Jackson could fairly be charged was in insisting that Garnett continue the fight against enemy rifles and artillery after his ammunition was gone. But, after the battle was over, Jackson still adhered to his condemnation of the brigade commander. Perhaps Jackson's wrath was greater than it would otherwise have been because of his continuing identification with his old brigade. On April 1, Jackson relieved Garnett of command, put him under arrest and demanded that he be court-martialed. Garnett had an impressive reputation for bravery and competency. Jackson's action angered many of Garnett's men and shocked officials in Richmond. The Adjutant General suggested that Garnett be released from arrest and assigned to command. Jackson answered: "I have only to say that I have no desire to see the case pressed any further; but that I regard Gen. Garnett as so incompetent a Brigade commander, that, instead of building up a Brigade, a good one, if turned over to him, would actually deteriorate under the command." Garnett never served again in Jackson's army.

Jackson determined to bring superior numbers against the enemy when next he met him. He could not count on sufficient reinforcements to gain numerical superiority. He must use cunning to make the enemy divide his forces. Then he could attack the small units separately. Again, speed and secrecy were the essentials. Luray Gap in the Massanuttons would be vital in moving quickly from one part of the Valley to the other. Passes in the Blue Ridge leading out of the Valley to Confederate concentrations in Eastern Virginia would also be important. With the invaluable aid of maps prepared by an expert engineer, Major Jed Hotchkiss, Jackson continued to familiarize himself with the Valley's many topographical peculiarities.

In ensuing weeks, Jackson slowly fell back up the Valley (Up was south, since the Shenandoah River flows roughly northward to its junction with the Potomac). Once again, he went into camp at Mount Jackson with Ashby screening his lines. Reorganization was necessary. Charles S. Winder was appointed to command of the First Brigade. As he rode past, he drew hisses from the men, who bitterly resented Garnett's fate. Jackson needed another brigadier to succeed a commander on sick leave. Johnston, trying to be helpful, sent General Taliaferro. Jackson could not forget that Taliaferro had carried the petition of the dissidents to President Davis during the Loring affair. Jackson protested to Adjutant General Cooper: "Through God's blessing my command, though small, is efficient and I respectfully request its efficiency may not be injured by assigning to it inefficient Officers." Richmond had become accustomed to Jackson's complaints about officers. Taliaferro stayed on, determined to prove his effectiveness.

Meanwhile, Jackson had other troubles in human relations. One colonel, whose ability was generally acknowledged, relinquished his rank to avoid direct responsibility to the general. Another swore that, because of Jackson's rudeness, he would never again darken the door of headquarters unless specifically ordered to report there.

With one officer, Jackson dealt more gingerly. Ashby's cavalry was spirited, resourceful, and intelligent, as was Ashby himself. But its formal organization was almost nonexistent, a matter that had troubled Richmond. Jackson ordered the 1200-man cavalry divided into two regiments, one to be assigned to Winder's brigade, the other to Taliaferro's. Ashby resigned. Winder interceded to arrange a conference between Jackson and Ashby. The day after the conference, Jackson issued a general order leaving the cavalry assigned to the two brigades but detailing it to Ashby.

Some militiamen in Jackson's district hid in the hills around Swift Run Gap to avoid the rigors of service under the general. Jackson had his own way of dealing with the A.W.O.L. They were shelled out of their nest. The report : one killed, twenty-four captured.

The usefulness of the Kernstown battle in keeping Banks from adding to Johnston's troubles in the Richmond area was receiving recognition in the capital. Congress voted its thanks. But, among Jackson's own officers and men, opinion was different. Major Harman, the capable quartermaster, confided in a letter to his brother, "We are in great danger from our crack-brained General."

The suspicion must have been strengthened when the general invited a new man to join his staff : a man with no previous military experience, the Rev. Robert L. Dabney, a Presbyterian minister from Lexington. Dr. Dabney was distinguished in his profession, but when he rode about in a Prince Albert coat and beaver hat instead of a uniform and carried an umbrella instead of a sword, it was difficult for the men to take him seriously in the role of Assistant Adjutant General. One day when, in ministerial attire and carrying a raised umbrella, he rode in the rain with Jackson and the rest of the staff, the incongruity provoked rude jests. There were sarcastic cheers and cries of "Come out from that umbrella !" Jackson sought to rescue his Assistant Adjutant General from ridicule by turning off the road and trotting through the woods. The umbrella and the beaver hat did not survive the contest with low-hanging boughs. Afterwards, Major Dabney appeared in uniform and at times looked almost military.

After Kernstown, Johnston had promised reinforcements if Jackson should be too heavily pressed by his Federal antagonist. Jackson was eager for reinforcements for offensive use. Reports from Ashby indicated that the enemy was about ready for an advance toward the Confederate Army. Johnston hoped that he would be able to release to Jackson a division of about 6,500 infantry and 500 cavalry commanded by General Richard S. Ewell. Johnston was aware that his own withdrawal south to protect Richmond left Jackson painfully exposed to attack by numerically superior forces. The primary function of Jackson's corps, as Johnston now saw it, was to prevent Banks from reaching Staunton, a depot town perilously close to Richmond's principal supply line. Johnston suggested what must already have occurred to Jackson—the attachment of Ewell's division in the upper (or southern) part of the Valley for a combined attack on Banks. Staunton was some twenty miles south of the rough parallelogram of roads that enclosed the Massanuttons. Jackson's plans hinged on retaining control of the road from New Market to Luray, the only road across the Massanutton Mountains, and therefore the sole link for a space of forty miles between the western and eastern divisions of the Valley. He could strike at the Federals as they moved southward up the Valley on the Valley Pike, west of the Massanuttons, and then, if too heavily opposed, could move over the road from New Market to Luray on the other side of the mountains. Such a move would leave two possibilities for Banks; either to pursue the escaping Jackson or to ignore the Confederates and proceed along the Valley Pike toward Staunton. If Banks attempted pursuit, Jackson could either turn upon him in the Massanuttons or lure him farther east into the Blue Ridge. In either case, the Confederate general would utilize natural features to afford maximum protection for his own army. If Banks chose to ignore an escaping Jackson and proceed toward Staunton along the Valley Pike, Jackson could use the road from Luray to New Market to place a fast-moving army in Banks' rear.

By now, Lee, under the direction of President Davis, was in charge of operations beyond the Richmond area. Without meeting face to face, he and Jackson evolved bold strategy with such harmony and quick understanding that it is impossible to say one or the other was principally responsible for certain phases of it. The tactics by which it would be executed, however, were necessarily so dependent on the enemy's moves and on Confederate quickness in combating them that the major tactical responsibility would be Jackson's.

Both Lee and Jackson knew that Union strategy called for McDowell to move southward from Fredericksburg to unite north of Richmond with McClellan. Then, with a combined force of 150,000,

McClellan would attack Johnston, whom he would outnumber about three to one. Two of McDowell's generals, Banks and Fremont, were threatening Jackson in the Valley. Why stop at detaining these men? Why not do more than hamper McClellan by preventing Banks and Fremont from joining him before Richmond? Why not really wreck Little Mac's plan by making such an effective feint against Washington that McDowell would not be permitted to leave the environs of the Federal capital?

Through Lee's intervention, Jackson soon had at his disposal about 19,000 men, the force of 8,000 under his personal command in the Valley proper being augmented by another 8,000 under Ewell and 3,000 under Edward (Allegheny) Johnson. Conferences between Jackson and these two generals did little to inspire new confidence in Jackson's camp. Allegheny was so ungainly and rough looking that Jackson's men, not knowing who he was, laughed at him openly when he rode up. Ewell—bald, beaked, and birdlike—would cock his head on one side, stare hard at those around him with his beady eyes, and then pipe out an astonishing succession of oaths.

What Allegheny Johnson thought of Jackson, we do not know. But Ewell made his opinion volubly clear. Jackson was chary about explaining his grand strategy to anyone, even another Confederate general. Changing his plans sometimes daily in order to meet new developments among the Federals, Jackson repeatedly altered his directions to Ewell without ever condescending to explain to him the reasons for the changes. On April 15, Jackson ordered Ewell to proceed to Swift Run Gap for a junction of forces, but the next morning he ordered him to Fisher's Gap instead. Before sunset, however, he ordered him back to Swift Run. On the 18th, he ordered him to proceed to neither Fisher's nor Swift Run, but to a third location east of the Blue Ridge. Ewell replied uncomplainingly to each of these diverse communications. But in the first week of May, ordered to watch Banks and having no intelligence system to help him, Ewell made bold under cover of a request for Jackson's advice to ask his general how he had determined what the enemy was doing. Jackson's reply seemed smugly secretive : "I have been relying on spies . . . ." Colonel James A. Walker, of Jackson's army, was about to ride off from Ewell's headquarters when Ewell called to him : "Colonel Walker, did it ever occur to you that General Jackson is crazy?"

"I don't know, General. We used to call him 'Fool Tom Jackson' at the Virginia Military Institute, but I do not suppose that he is really crazy."

Ewell's eyes were bulging with anger and the beard was trembling under his beak. "I tell you, sir, he is as crazy as a March hare. He has gone away, I don't know where, and left me here with instructions to stay until he returns. But Banks' whole army is advancing on me, and I have not the most remote idea where to communicate with General Jackson. I tell you, sir, he is crazy, and I will just march my Division away from here. I do not mean to have it cut to pieces at the behest of a crazy man."

But Ewell did not just march his division away. As the crisis neared, he stayed precisely where Jackson wanted him—east of the Blue Ridge near the railroad junction of Gordonsville and about forty-five miles almost exactly due east of Staunton, which was linked with it by the railroad through Rockfish Gap.

West of the Alleghenies, Allegheny Johnson observed the approach of Fremont's army of 15,000. Banks was in the lower (or Northern) Valley with about 19,000 men. Waiting at Fredericksburg, and available for use in either the Valley or the Richmond area, was McDowell's force of about 40,000. The potential of forces threatening Jackson's combined command of about 19,000 men totaled about 74,000.

Jackson himself was at Swift Run Gap, nearest of the Blue Ridge gaps to Ewell's camp at Gordonsville. From Swift Run Gap he marched down the Luray Valley to Port Republic, nearly ten miles south and slightly west of the Massanuttons. The word "marched" is deceptive. The army slogged through mud, pushed and pulled wagons, forded streams. Jackson spared neither himself nor his men. The general himself sometimes carried rocks to fill holes in the path of his wagons. Most of the time, he moved up and down the lines, often on foot, barking, "Close up, men, close up; push on, push on!" Sometimes his men dreamed they were stumbling along with Old Jack shouting to them "Push on, Push on!" and woke to find that they really were. A. R. Lawton, who served under Jackson and rose to brigadier general, recalled of his old commander:

He had . . . small sympathy with human infirmity. He was a one-idea-ed man. He looked upon the broken-down men and stragglers as the same thing. He classed all who were weak and weary, who fainted by the wayside, as men wanting in patriotism. If a man's face was as white as cotton and his pulse so low you scarce could feel it, he looked upon him merely as an inefficient soldier and rode off impatiently. Like the successful warriors of the world, he did not value human life when he had an object to accomplish. He could order men to their death as a matter of course.

Of course, no one took Jackson's blood pressure at these moments. Mrs. Jackson knew from her husband's confession that he found the hanging of John Brown an "awful" sight, but those who saw Jackson on that occasion thought he accepted the event "as a matter of course."

Anyway, on May 3, 1862, most of the speculation about Jackson regarded his destination. And there was speculation aplenty! For, on that day, having marched westward to Port Republic, he turned eastward, crossing the Blue Ridge at Brown's Gap. This was the day on which Yorktown fell, bringing the Federal menace closer to the Confederate capital. Jackson must be headed for Richmond. So thought his subordinates, and so thought the enemy. When the troops found trains waiting for them at Mechum River Station, they boarded them in the expectation of getting off in Richmond a few hours later. They were surprised to discover that they had re-crossed the Blue Ridge by rail and were back in the Valley, this time in Staunton, which commanded the upper Valley. Meanwhile, pursuant to Jackson's instructions but still a stranger to his commander's grand design, Ewell had occupied the position at Swift Run Gap evacuated by Jackson. He was still charged with keeping an eye on Banks, who was still in the lower Valley. Jackson marched westward from Staunton to a junction with Allegheny Johnson, and the combined forces marched westward in the mountains for two days to the village of McDowell.

There they met and repulsed Fremont's advance, commanded by Union General R. H. Milroy. Part of Jackson's force followed the retreating Federals to Franklin, where two days of indecisive skirmishing began. On May 13, having thus paralyzed Fremont's advance, Jackson marched back to the village of McDowell, and from there to the Valley town of Harrisonburg.

Jackson inaugurated a new marching system. His men marched fifty minutes of every hour and rested ten. In the middle of the day, there was an hour's pause for lunch and rest. They covered ground at a rate that earned them the name of "foot cavalry."

Meanwhile, General Ewell was made even more miserable by his enforced inaction when he heard from a deserter that Major General James Shields' Division of Banks' Army was going to leave the Valley to join McDowell. Ewell sent the report to Jackson and ordered Col. T. T. Munford to harass Shields with a cavalry detachment. About midnight, Munford took leave of Ewell, who had already gone to bed. Suddenly, Ewell leaped from the sheets in his nightshirt, spread out a map in the lamplight on the bare floor, and got down on his knees. According to Munford, "his bones fairly rattled; his bald head and long beard made him look more like a witch than a Major General. He became much excited, pointed out Jackson's position, General Shields' and General McDowell's . . . ."

"Why, I could crush Shields before night if I could move from here," Ewell agonized. "This man Jackson is certainly a crazy fool, an idiot. Now look at this."

He showed Munford a message from Jackson announcing victory at McDowell and the capture of Milroy's wagon train through the blessings of Providence.

"What has Providence to do with Milroy's wagon train?" Ewell demanded.

"Mark my words, if this old fool keeps this thing up and Shields joins McDowell, we will go up at Richmond!"

Before long, Ewell was somewhat reassured by a personal meeting with Jackson. He apparently was impressed by the Valley man's aggressive fire and concluded that, though he might be a fool, he was at least a fighting fool.

Jackson marched northward in the Shenandoah Valley along the Valley Pike. On the 20th, he halted near New Market to await, according to plan, the advance of Ewell's division.

First of Ewell's men to arrive were the jauntily marching, nattily uniformed men of Richard Taylor's Louisiana Brigade, their white-gaitered legs moving with rhythmic precision to the spirited strains of bands with gleaming instruments. General Taylor, the son of President Zachary Taylor, had his father's courage plus a brilliant mind and the polish of a well-educated, well-traveled man of the world. He looked eagerly for Jackson, whom he had never met. He didn't see anyone who looked like a commanding general. Finally someone pointed out an unprepossessing figure perched on a rail fence. Taylor saw, in his own words, "a pair of cavalry boots covering feet of a gigantic size, a mangy cap with visor drawn low, a heavy, dark beard and weary eyes . . . ."

A model of military etiquette, Taylor saluted and declared his name and rank. After a lengthy silence, Jackson asked in "a low, gentle voice" about the road and distance traveled that day.

"Keezletown road, six and twenty miles."

"You seem to have no stragglers."

"Never allow stragglers," Taylor replied.

"You must teach my people. They straggle badly." There was no accent of irony in Jackson's words.

The Creole band with Taylor's brigade struck up a waltz. Jackson listened, sucking hard on a lemon. Finally, he spoke again: "Thoughtless fellows for serious work."

Jackson had a much more disturbing experience the same day. A courier arrived from Ewell with news that Johnston had forbidden an attack on Banks and had ordered Ewell to leave the Valley.

Jackson would not permit his plans to be ruined now. For days he had been receiving orders directly from Lee. He now appealed directly to him and, after a little military red tape, received instructions from Richmond to proceed with his original scheme.

Old Jack was jubilant. At dawn, with Taylor's brigade in the lead, he marched a little way north up the Valley Pike, then abruptly turned east, crossing the Massanuttons through Luray Gap. In the Luray Valley, he joined the main body of Ewell's forces.

The Louisianans, like other men that Jackson had commanded, began to think that he was crazy. Why had he ordered them to leave the Luray Valley to meet him on the west side of the Massanuttons, only to march back with them across the Massanuttons and into the Luray Valley again? Taylor himself could only suggest that perhaps "Jackson was an unconscious poet, and, as an ardent lover of nature, desired to give strangers an opportunity to admire the beauties of his Valley."

Jackson's passion was for the poetry of war. His delight in a well executed movement was positively aesthetic. At this moment, it was hard for him to guard against unbecoming exultation. He had succeeded in concentrating his entire force between Banks and Richmond. With Allegheny Johnson's and Ewell's men, he now had 16,000 soldiers. He had 48 guns. He commanded the Blue Ridge passes vital for communication with the East. In the Shenandoah Valley, Ashby's Cavalry preserved the illusion that Jackson was still in that area. Banks was not sure that Jackson would advance, but he was confident that if the Confederate general did advance, it would be along the Valley Pike. That was precisely what Old Jack wanted him to think.

Jackson marched northward in the Luray Valley toward Front Royal. Ewell's information about Shields' movement out of the Valley to General McDowell had been correct. The Federal command had acted in the confused belief that Jackson had left the Valley. Thus Banks, with his force reduced to 10,000, was nearing Front Royal from the north while Jackson, with his 16,000, approached it from the south.

After a remarkably swift march, Jackson surprised Banks' advanced force at Front Royal on the afternoon of May 23. The short, bitter fight was literally brother against brother. It pitted the First Maryland Regiment of the Confederacy against the First Maryland Regiment of the Union. The outnumbered and outflanked Federals were driven from the field.

Jackson pursued a retreating Banks northward to Strasburg, then to Winchester. There the Union general made a stand. On the morning of the 25th, Jackson fell upon him, flanked him and drove the Yankees northward in disorder. As the bluecoats fled, Old Jack waved his cap in the air, shouted "Let's holler!" and gave the wildest of yells. A presumptuous subordinate reminded him of the need for preserving his dignity. The general, in too good a humor to explode, told the officer: "Go back and tell the whole Army to press forward to the Potomac."

Outside the town, Jackson met Taylor. Just as the battle for Winchester was beginning, Taylor had shouted to some of his men: "What the hell are you dodging for? If there is any more of it, you will be halted under this fire for an hour!" Jackson had looked at him in "reproachful surprise," placed a hand on the younger man's shoulder, and, in a tone of gentle remorse, had said, "I am afraid you are a wicked fellow." In the hours since then, Taylor's men had been the first to sweep into Winchester. Now Jackson rode up to Taylor, reached over from the saddle, gripped his hand. Then, without having spoken a word, he rode off.

Banks, some distance ahead, rode on, too. He didn't stop very long anywhere until he reached the Potomac.

The day before Winchester, Jackson's pursuit of Banks had caused United States Secretary of War Stanton to order McDowell to halt his advance on Richmond and detach a force of 20,000 for service in the Valley. On the day of the battle, the Federal government seized all railroads within its territory. The governor of every State in the Union received an alarming message from the War Department : "Intelligence from various quarters leaves no doubt that the enemy in great force are advancing on Washington. You will please organize and forward immediately all the volunteer and militia force in your State."

When effective pursuit of Banks proved impossible, Jackson let his men rest for two days. Then wagon trains of captured supplies, literally filling the road from fence to fence, were started southward. Jackson protected this tortuously slow caravan by a spirited feint at Harper's Ferry.

On May 29, he began his retreat. In some ways, it was as masterly as his advance. He escaped through a narrow corridor between two armies—Banks' and Fremont's. Again, speed and secrecy were the keys to success. At the start of the southward movement, a lieutenant in Jackson's own Army rode up to him and asked : "General, are the troops going back?"

"Don't you see them going?"

"Are they all going?" the lieutenant asked.

Jackson looked hard at the man, then turned to a nearby colonel. "Colonel, arrest that man as a spy." Only Ashby's intervention on a plea that the young officer "hasn't much sense" caused the general to revoke his order.

At one stage of the retreat, Jackson's escape depended upon reaching Strasburg before the Federals. He had to cover forty-four miles; they had to cover eleven. But Jackson won the race. He fought two savage engagements, one at Cross Keys, the other at Port Republic. He held off Fremont. He drove Shields back. Both Union generals fell back to the upper Valley as Jackson found security in the lower.

Near the end of the long retreat, Colonel J. M. Patton reported that all but one of a Union force making a last desperate attack on Jackson's rearguard had been killed or captured. The colonel said he regretted the necessity of slaying so many brave men.

"No," said Jackson. "Shoot them all. I do not wish them to be brave."

But the general was stunned by the death of one of his own cavalrymen. Ashby, the gallant "Arab," had been shot down while charging the enemy. When Jackson learned of the loss, he told his staff that he must not be disturbed except in emergency, even by a general. Then he closed the door. The boards creaked for a long time under his pacing feet.

The Valley campaign was quickly recognized as historic. Jackson's performance had not been perfect. He had needlessly antagonized some of his officers and thus injured morale. Perhaps a little more thorough planning would have provided a more adequate concentration of batteries at Front Royal. But such faults fade before the glowing record of his achievement. With about 17,000 men, he had kept 40,000 enemy troops from being employed in the major objective of Federal strategy: the taking of Richmond. Despite his over-all numerical inferiority, he had so skillfully deployed his forces that he had enjoyed the numerical advantage on all but two battlefields. He had moved his troops with a speed that had astonished Confederates, Federals, and military observers in foreign capitals. In retreat, he had led 16,000 men to safety, though they were threatened on both sides by forces totaling 62,000. He had forced Lincoln to revise his strategy. Small wonder that, as Douglas S. Freeman has said, "many critics regard [the Valley campaign of 1862] as the most remarkable display of strategic science, based on accurate reasoning, correct anticipation of the enemy's plans, rapid marches, and judicious disposition of an inferior force, in all American military history."

Lee wrote Jackson: "Your recent successes have been the cause of the liveliest joy in this army as well as in the country." A victory-starved people yelled themselves hoarse for Stonewall. The newspapers printed so many columns of tribute to him that he stopped reading them for fear that he would fall victim to the sin of vanity. The foot soldiers that he had driven so hard had come, as much to their own surprise as to anybody's, to love this stern warrior who sucked on lemons as other men would on sweets. Wild rabbits were much prized by the men as a variation from the monotony of army fare. It became proverbial in the army that a particularly lusty cheer meant that the soldiers had sighted one of two things : a jack rabbit or Old Jack.

Even now, however, in this June of 1862, when most of the civilized world was marveling at Jackson's achievement, some of his general officers were unwilling to concede his greatness. They were nearer than either the public or the enlisted men to Jackson's eccentricities and stinging rebukes. In conversation one night, four of them agreed that he had simply been unusually lucky and that he would probably yet meet with some great disaster.

Ewell was not in that group. He gave his opinion in a private conversation with Colonel Munford. "Look here, Munford, do you remember a conversation we had one day at Conrad's Store?"

"To what do you allude?" asked Munford, as if he could forget the sight of Ewell on his knees in his nightshirt.

"Why, . . . to General Jackson . . . ."

"Very well."

"I take it all back," said Ewell, his eyes bulging with earnestness, "and will never prejudge another man. Old Jackson is no fool; he knows how to keep his own counsel, and does curious things; but he has method in his madness. He has disappointed me entirely."

Merely Human

While Jackson was winding up the Valley campaign, Lee succeeded the badly wounded Joseph E. Johnston as commander of the forces around Richmond, now known as the Army of Northern Virginia. Jackson's brilliant successes in the Valley awakened in Lee the hope that, if reinforced by troops from the Carolinas and Georgia, Stonewall would be strong enough to march into Pennsylvania, drawing the Federal armies away from Richmond. But the states south of Virginia would not agree to the use of their troops so far from home, so the militarily feasible was politically impracticable. Lee then produced a compromise plan calling for a limited offensive in the Valley to keep the Federals occupied there, followed by one of Jackson's lightning movements out of the Valley, this time to Richmond.

During the campaign just completed, Jackson had sometimes been reported simultaneously in three or four different places. If he could delude the enemy into thinking that he was still a menace in the Valley while reinforcing Lee before the Confederate capital, a great victory might be won.

In accordance with this scheme, A. R. Lawton's brigade from Georgia and eight Army of Northern Virginia regiments under W. H. C. Whiting were sent to Jackson by June 11.

Whiting had earned one of the most brilliant records in the history of West Point. He was generally conceded to be handsome and impeccably military, but was also quite obviously undersized. Behind his back, his troops called him Little Billy. This proud and sensitive man was ill-prepared for condescension from a rawboned, mangy-capped commander who was ten years his junior. He was in a sputtering rage when he came away from his first conference with Jackson. Stonewall, as usual, had refused to confide any of his plans to a subordinate. He had even refused as of the moment to tell Whiting what his orders to him would be for the next day. "He simply told me," Whiting protested to Colonel John Imboden, "to go back to Staunton and he would send me orders tomorrow. I haven't the slightest idea what they will be. I believe he hasn't any more sense than my horse."

When the orders arrived, they left Whiting almost apoplectic. Jackson was instructing him to put his troops at once on the train for Gordonsville. "Didn't I tell you he was a fool?" Whiting exploded, "And doesn't this prove it? Why, I just came through Gordonsville day before yesterday."

Other officers were riled with Jackson. Stonewall was unusually bad tempered these days. General Charles S. Winder, the battle-proved commander of the First Brigade, became so angry in a face-to-face encounter with Jackson that he resigned on the spot. General Taylor pleaded with Jackson to make up the quarrel, saying that Winder was badly needed and that the Valley commander could afford "magnanimity" after "the rich harvest of glory he had reaped in his brilliant campaign." Taylor afterwards wrote : "Observing him closely, I caught a glimpse of the man's inner nature. It was but a glimpse. The curtain closed, and he was absorbed in prayer. Yet in that moment I saw an ambition boundless as Cromwell's, and as merciless." Jackson talked privately with Winder, and the resignation was withdrawn.

Taylor meditated much on the insight he had received into Jackson's character. He thought of it in terms of the many other occasions on which he had observed "Old Jack." And he concluded that

His ambition was vast, all-absorbing. Like the unhappy wretch from whose shoulders sprang the foul serpent, he loathed it, perhaps feared it; but he could not escape it—it was himself—nor rend it—it was his own flesh. He fought it with prayer, constant and earnest—Apollyon and Christian in ceaseless combat. What limit to set to his ability, I know not, for he was ever superior to occasion. Under ordinary circumstances it was difficult to estimate him because of his peculiarities—peculiarities that would have made a lesser man absurd, but that served to enhance his martial fame, as those of Samuel Johnson did his literary eminence.

What was this strange man planning now? Even the valiant Ewell, who by this time enjoyed General Jackson's admiration, did not know. He said that every time one of Stonewall's couriers approached him, he expected to be ordered to assault the North Pole. At last, Jackson, alone in a hotel room with the Reverend Mr. Dabney, confided to him that the army's destination was Richmond. The General must go ahead for a conference in the Confederate capital. In the General's absence, the preacher would be in charge of the march.

The minister, though a brave and highly intelligent man, had no training to qualify him for the assigned task. When he fell ill, another complication was added, and the march was further slowed.

Jackson sat down to a council of war on June 23 with Lee, Longstreet, D. H. Hill (his old friend) and A. P. Hill. Lee's plans for what came to be known as the Seven Days' campaign called for turning and driving the right flank of McClellan's army, which then straddled the Chickahominy River. Jackson's specific assignment was to clear the bridges of the Chickahominy so that other generals, coming up for the attack on the north side of the river, would not have to cross under fire.

Obviously, with the other divisions already within striking distance, the timing of the attack was dependent on Jackson. How long would it take his command to reach its assigned destination on the Court House road? When Jackson had left his troops the day before, they had been about fifty miles from Richmond, but he confidently answered that he could be in position "tomorrow." Longstreet, understandably incredulous, persuaded Jackson to give himself another day. It was agreed, then, that the battle would open on the 26th.

Jackson rode all night to rejoin his command. A steady rain was falling and the Piedmont roads, a far cry from the limestone of the Valley Pike, must have reminded the Bible-conscious general of the bottomless pit. His topographer, Jed Hotchkiss, was back in the Valley. Jackson was frankly puzzled by a terrain not only unfamiliar but also devoid of the prominent identifying features to which he was accustomed in more rugged country.

Jackson had another problem that he did not know about. On the afternoon of the 24th, a deserter from his army told Union officers that Stonewall was moving via Frederickshall to an attack on McClellan. The carefully guarded advantage of secrecy was lost.

The day of battle dawned on the 26th. Night closed on a field of slaughter with the Confederates completely repulsed. Infantry fire persisted uselessly until nine o'clock. The artillery gave up an hour or so later. Jackson had not appeared on the scene in time to carry out Lee's plan to turn Beaver Dam Creek. Hours had passed with no word from Jackson and no sign of his whereabouts. Fearing that further delay would wreck Lee's entire plan and hoping that something might yet be salvaged from a day gone wrong, A. P. Hill had thrown his troops into an assault on Fitzjohn Porter. One regiment, the 44th Georgia, had lost 335 of its 514 men. Its casualties almost equaled those for McClellan's entire army. Gross casualties of the Confederates totaled about 1,400. Jackson had arrived only after the scene was hopelessly confused. Taking no part in the attack, he had bivouacked with the sounds of battle still coming to him on the warm night air.

How can such apparent dereliction be explained? If Jackson had not been a teetotaler, most people would have assumed that he was drunk. And in one sense he was drunk, drunk for want of sleep, muddled from sheer exhaustion. Following close upon the strains of the Valley campaign he had plunged furiously into the preparations for the attack on McClellan. He had experienced all the nerve pressure of a taxing march under conditions of uncertainty in a strange environment. He had spent two nights in the saddle. During ninety-six hours of labor, thought, and anxiety, he had snatched at most a total of ten hours' sleep.

Before daylight, Jackson, a day late, moved beyond McClellan's right flank. The Federals fell back to another prepared position on a ridge east of Powhite Creek. There was fought the battle of Gaines' Mill on the 27th. The Confederate attack began at 2 P.M. with an assault by A. P. Hill, followed two hours later by Longstreet. Jackson, with D. H. Hill's force joined to his own, moved down from the north. The density of the woods and the serpentine twisting of the road so delayed him that his men arrived late on the scene and were badly scattered besides. Jackson's secretiveness had contributed to the delay because the General had declined until very late in the march to tell his guide precisely where he wanted to go. After five o'clock, with the Confederates hard-pressed and their general officers in an agony of doubt and suspense over Stonewall's failure to appear, Old Jack, sucking on a lemon, rode up to Lee as though nothing had happened. He made no apologies. Lee gave one of his gentle rebukes: "Ah, general, I am very glad to see you. I had hoped to be with you before."

Jackson mumbled something unintelligible and jerked his head in an enigmatic gesture.

"That fire is very heavy," Lee said. "Do you think your men can stand it?"

"They can stand almost anything. They can stand that!"

After listening to instructions from Lee, Jackson rode off to the left, where he was to play his part. It was nearly seven o'clock before, with the aid of reinforcements from Jackson, the front was complete. The Army of Northern Virginia moved forward in a general assault. Soon men of the Stonewall Brigade had pushed so far ahead that they were well in advance of their compatriots, but they held fast under a withering fire. Major Dabney was amazed when he looked at his general. Stonewall's face was crimson and in his eyes burned a fierce, frightening light. He barked out : "Tell them this affair must hang in suspense no longer. Sweep the field with the bayonet!"

Soon the Union front cracked. Many men played a part in the victory. Longstreet said that "there was more individual gallantry displayed upon this field" than he had ever seen before. Jackson's men, though almost disastrously late in arriving, had played as noble a role as any.

On the 29th, Jackson was ordered to pursue McClellan, who was retreating (or, as the Union general euphemistically reported, "changing his base" from the Pamunkey to the James).

McClellan's immediate problem was to get past the ten-mile-long semicircle of White Oak Swamp and then, with that morass between him and the pursuing Confederates, to put up a stiff fight.

Jackson's specific assignment was to repair Grapevine Bridge and cross over it rapidly so as to sweep down on McClellan. A dilatory crew made an all-day job of it. Finally, ordering an artillery barrage, Jackson crossed the swamp, fighting a touch-and-go battle with mosquitoes and the heat before facing the enemy. With a barrage from a well-placed battery, Jackson tried to soften up the Federals. Then, riding with his troopers, he galloped down hill and through the morass.

To his shock, he spied bluecoats on a hill dominating the Confederate right and center and barring passage of the swamp road. Jackson ordered his men to take cover in the woods. This last frustration was too much. He had not had a regular meal for four days. He had had very little sleep. Now he dropped down under a tree and slept. When he woke, he sat on a fallen tree trunk. He stared at the ground and said nothing.

A new and unattached brigadier reported to Jackson and asked for orders. Jackson simply suggested that the officer rejoin his division.

A courier arrived from Colonel Munford with the news that a feasible crossing had been found and that the colonel awaited orders. Jackson sent none.

A little later, General Wade Hampton rode up to Jackson and reported that he had found a good crossing which would bring Confederate troops in sight of open ground on the Union side. He had also discovered Federal infantry in a deep ravine commanding the ground along which the Confederates would have to advance if they used the existing bridge.

Jackson roused enough to ask Hampton if he could construct a bridge over the stream at the crossing which he had discovered.

The South Carolinian said that he could easily build a bridge for infantry, but the felling of trees to permit passage of artillery would be heard by the enemy.

Jackson told him to build a bridge.

When Hampton returned, Jackson was still sitting on a log. He seemed almost inanimate. Hampton reported that an adequate bridge for the infantry had been built. With characteristic thoroughness, he had checked personally to make sure that the Federals had not been alerted.

During Hampton's report, Jackson listened with closed eyes and even pulled his cap down over them. When Hampton finished, Jackson gave him no orders and no thanks. He simply said nothing, but got to his feet and walked away.

The sound of battle swelled loud and louder as the Confederates fought on in desperate need of reinforcements. Meanwhile, the 18,000 infantry under Jackson's command lay or crouched or walked idly about in the thickets. Longstreet's and A. P. Hill's men had fought their hearts out, hoping for the help that never came.

Night closed out the Confederate assault. Jackson sat down to eat with his staff. Suddenly his head dropped forward on his chest. With a biscuit in his mouth, he had fallen asleep. In a moment, he opened his eyes, raised his head and stared at those around him like a man coming out of a hypnotic trance. "Now, gentlemen," he said, "let us at once to bed, and rise with the dawn and see if tomorrow we cannot do something."

The next day Jackson tried earnestly to do something. In the Battle of Malvern Hill, he checked personally on the condition of his batteries. He kept on about his self-assigned task, even when his figure on horseback drew fire from the Federals, even when a shell exploded in front of his horse and brought the frightened animal almost to its knees. One of Lee's staff officers came riding up. "General," the man called out, "General Lee presents his compliments and directs that you return at once." He returned.

A little before noon, with shot falling all around him, he sat at the foot of a tree and scrawled a note to Jeb Stuart, whose cavalry was guarding his left flank. A shell exploded near him, blasting some passing infantry into eternity. Jackson shook off the dirt that had been showered on his paper and finished the note. It read : "I am engaged with the enemy. I trust that God will give our army a glorious victory. . . . "

Later, perceiving that D. H. Hill was in serious trouble on the right, Jackson ordered his own and Ewell's divisions to double-time to their aid. But they were too late.

The confused fighting ended about ten o'clock that night. A storm came up, bringing a driving rain that drenched the torches of soldiers hunting for wounded companions on the field, causing them to slip again and again in mud or blood as they picked their way among the groaning and the silent. In the day's action just closed, Jackson had been neither conspicuously better nor worse than most of Lee's subordinates. Despite the failures of coordination that had plagued the Army of Northern Virginia in seven days of fighting, the principal purpose of the campaign had been achieved. McClellan had been forced to retreat from the outskirts of the Confederate capital. But in no measure was this success attributable to Jackson's efforts. Indeed, Jackson's inactivity in White Oak Swamp had cost the lives of many brave soldiers and had nearly wrecked Lee's campaign. About a fortnight after that battle, Jackson overheard some of his aides speculating on the reasons for his apparent apathy on that fatal day. Jackson broke in: "If General Lee had wanted me, he could have sent for me."

The answer does not conform to the spirit of the Jackson who so often before had shown bold initiative. Nor does there seem any need for the involved psychological explanations that have been offered by some twentieth-century writers. Jackson, a man so prone to sleep that to his mortification he dozed repeatedly in church, had gone without sleep for many days. He had also gone without adequate nourishment. Such conditions, even without the added strain of nervous excitement, induce either torpor or hallucinations in most people. Sometimes Old Jack appeared superhuman in determination and accomplishment. Sometimes he was laughably eccentric in his frailties. But, in the Seven Days' Campaign, he was merely human.

"Hurrah for Jackson"

Jackson had time to rest after the campaign. He did not know the strain of battle or of independent action again until July 13, when he was detached and sent to Gordonsville. With his slightly more than 23,000 men, he advanced to Cedar Run, with the hope of surprising his old adversary, General Nathaniel P. Banks. Old Jack was gleeful. Banks, he said, "is always ready to fight . . . and . . . generally gets whipped."

On August 9, Jackson rushed into battle too soon. The number of his own hot, dusty, road-weary infantry actually engaged in the beginning of the battle barely exceeded Banks' force of nearly 9,000. Just when things seemed to be going well for the Confederates, General Winder was felled by an exploding shell. In the resulting confusion, Banks outflanked Jackson. The Confederates began falling back.

The withdrawal was becoming a rout. Some gray units were completely surrounded. In the center of what had been the line, Confederates and Federals bayoneted each other in a hopeless melee.

Into the very center of the churning mass galloped a crimson-faced, fire-eyed officer with the bearded glory of an avenging prophet. In one hand he waved a sword. In the other, he flourished the red, white and blue battle flag of the Confederacy. "Rally, men!" he shouted. "Remember Winder! Where's my Stonewall Brigade? Forward, men, forward!"

He seemed invincible. Instantly, the Confederates rallied. A hatless Yankee officer, heedless of his own peril amid the rallying graycoats, stood entranced with his broken sword in his hand. When he recovered his voice, he asked a Confederate captain, "What officer is that?"

The captain answered with a thrill of pride, "Stonewall Jackson."

"Hurrah for General Jackson!" the Yankee yelled. "Follow your general, boys!"

When the dazed Federal began to recollect his situation and walk away, the Confederate captain let him go. You just couldn't shoot a man like that, or even take him prisoner.

Everywhere, the Union Army was rolled back. But, as night fell, Jackson had to abandon hopes of pursuit. Highly effective Federal artillery lurked in the darkness.

Jackson himself rode from farmhouse to farmhouse in the neighborhood, seeking a bed. Everywhere, the beds were filled with wounded. He could have ridden on to another house, but any available bed there might soon be needed by a wounded man. The general dismounted, dropped down on the grass and said he was going to sleep. A member of his staff urged him to eat first. "No," he said, "I want *rest,* nothing but *rest!*"

Two days later, Jackson, the victor by a narrow margin, began falling back. He knew that his force was too small for an attack on General Pope's large army. He hoped to draw Pope farther from his base, but the Union general could not be induced to follow the Confederate.

Jackson's army knew that something big was imminent, but had no idea what it was. Jed Hotchkiss had a better idea than most. Old Jack had instructed him to map as thoroughly as possible the part of Virginia between Gordonsville and the Potomac. How many maps should he make? The answer: "Do not be afraid of making too many."

On August 13, General Longstreet, dignified and ponderously impressive, arrived at Gordonsville with heavy reinforcements for the Army of the Valley. Despite the fact that the Georgian was the senior of the two major generals and had little confidence in Jackson's ability, he declined to take command because of Jackson's familiarity with the area of operations and because of the knowledge that Lee would soon assume command in person.

Lee arrived on the 15th. He quickly revealed his plan of action. There was every indication that McClellan's army would be shifted to Northern Virginia to reinforce Pope for his attack on vital lines of Confederate supply and communication. The Army of Northern Virginia could strike hard at Pope while the barrier of the James still remained between him and McClellan. Lee had hopes of virtually destroying Pope's army. The Union general's force of some 52,000 to 70,000 men was encamped a little more than twenty miles away in the narrow area between the Rappahannock and Rapidan rivers. A great victory was in prospect if the Army of the Valley could attack Pope before he received reinforcements or corrected his tactical error.

Jackson set his foot cavalry on the march that very day. The attack was scheduled for the 18th.

But the old troubles of the Seven Days' Campaign reappeared. By the night of the 17th, problems of coordination and failures of logistics forced Lee to postpone the attack until the 19th. Later that date was postponed.

The army knew nothing of plans or changes of plan. Many of Jackson's old troops had learned to accept him on faith. But to Longstreet's men, unaccustomed to his eccentric and mysterious ways, following Old Jack was a disturbing experience. One of Longstreet's men prophesied that, if Jackson were not brought under control within a month, "he would destroy himself and all under him." Some of these same doubts began to infect even those who had been with Stonewall when he so dramatically rallied his panicked soldiers at Cedar Mountain.

Even Captain C. S. Blackford, the Confederate officer who had let the Yankee escape because he had shouted, "Hurrah for General Jackson," had his doubts on the dark night of August 19th. Blackford and some troopers followed the General, knowing only that they were in for a long ride. Old Jack led them through underbrush and along sinuous trails where the branches and briars drew blood. Hour after hour they rode on, now this way, now that, with no discernible pattern, the same lone, dark, mysterious figure in the lead. At last, the weary Blackford fell asleep in the saddle. When he opened his eyes, the expedition was still jogging along. As he struggled into wakefulness, he wondered whether the General was suffering from one of the temporary fits of derangement to which rumor said he was subject. He asked the rider by his side, "Where is the old fool taking us?"

"What?" his companion barked.

It was the voice of the "old fool" himself.

Blackford could be thankful that Old Jack was both introspective and a little deaf.

Shortly after dawn, from the top of Clark's Mountain, the riders looked down on the white tents of Pope's army.

Lee started across the Rapidan the next day, but there was to be no battle yet. Pope had fled.

Lee wanted a battle and he did not give up easily. On the 20th, the army was reorganized into two corps, the left wing commanded by Jackson and the right by Longstreet. Both corps moved northward toward the Rappahannock with the idea of crossing that river and turning Pope's right flank.

Jackson sighted the Union Army on the 22d as he approached Beverly Ford. In an indecisive engagement, Early's brigade became separated by a freshet from Jackson's main army and came near destruction. Helpless to aid his subordinate, Jackson prayed in agony. Early's valiant efforts and Pope's hesitation made it possible for the Confederates to escape.

Lee rode up to Jackson's headquarters on Sunday, the 24th. The commanding general had conceived a daring plan that might still defeat Pope before the arrival of the bulk of reinforcements from McClellan. In effect, Lee was proposing a coordinate campaign between the two of them and one which called for the most extraordinary qualities of generalship on Jackson's part. Stonewall was to move far around Pope's right, circling behind him and severing his communications with Washington. This move was calculated to scare Pope into racing to the city's defense and thus moving rapidly farther from the reinforcements on the way to him from McClellan. Lee would then bring up the rest of the army for a killing blow.

Much was left to Jackson's discretion. To him was left selection of the point at which to strike the enemy's railroad line and the point for the junction with Lee.

The reticent Jackson simply replied that he would move at once, but he was bound to be deeply touched by his commander's faith in him. Not long before, he had declared that he would follow Lee blindfolded. He was not enthusiastic about following other men with his eyes open.

Jackson began the march with his 20,000 men at dawn on August 25, a morning with a premature touch of autumn chill. They did not know that they were going to cross the Rappahannock at the upper fords. They did not dream that they were part of one of the boldest schemes in military history. But they knew that something important was afoot. They had been ordered to cook three days' rations and then had been ordered to march before the task could be completed. Old Jack again expected the impossible, and his excitement traveled like electricity through the entire corps. Probably few of the men would have believed that, just before springing into the saddle, the unrelenting warrior had dashed off a note to his *esposita* : "I have only time to tell you how much I love my little pet dove."

As they marched on in route step, Jackson riding alongside calling out, "Close up, men, close up," the August sun burned the chill out of the air and clouds of dust powdered the men's sweaty faces. The raw beef in their knapsacks spoiled and had to be thrown away.

Toward sunset, Old Jack rode ahead of his men. A marching column came upon him standing like some eagle of the heights atop a huge rock, bare-headed, the familiar sharp profile etched against the glow of the dying sun. The men cheered. Old Jack signaled for silence; noise might alarm the enemy.

"No cheering, boys," the word went down the line. The cheering ceased, but the men removed their hats in silent salute. Stonewall smiled. He turned to his staff. "Who could not conquer with such troops as these?"

That night they slept on the ground near the village of Salem, to the right of Pope's army and behind the Federal flank. Many dropped off to sleep without supper. That day they had marched twenty-five miles.

At dawn they were on the march again, headed southeast toward the Bull Run Mountains. Through Thoroughfare Gap they marched. Now they were east of the mountains, well behind Pope's army and moving toward his principal supply line, the Orange and Alexandria Railroad. At Gainesville, on the highway to Washington, they were joined by Jeb Stuart, who had skirmished with the Federals along the Rappahannock and could assure Jackson that his right flank was secure. Jackson pushed on to Bristoe Station, driving off the small Union force there and at Manassas Junction seven miles away, capturing such a store of supplies as Confederates seldom saw and wrecking two trains by opening a derail switch. But one locomotive escaped to Washington and another to Pope, to give warning. That night, Jackson's men set fire to the base at Manassas Junction and marched away in the red glare of the giant fires.

The next day, Pope abandoned the line of the Rappahannock and began falling back toward Washington. The Union General marched his men to Manassas with the idea of concentrating a considerable force against Jackson there. But, when the Federals arrived on the morning of the 28th, their quarry had escaped. Jackson was bivouacking on or near ground that the Union soldiers had occupied at the Battle of Manassas the year before. Having covered more than fifty miles in two days, the Confederates were taking a well-earned rest. Now they awaited the arrival of Lee and Longstreet for a massive assault on Pope. Jackson's position, on a ridge north of the Warrenton-Alexandria Pike, was on Pope's flank, was excellent for both defense and offense, and had a covered escape route.

About noon a special courier found Stonewall and two of his division commanders asleep within an angle of one of the snake fences that rickracked across the landscape. Old Jack was wide awake as soon as he heard the news. One of his cavalry pickets had captured McDowell's orders providing for concentration at Manassas.

Within minutes, Jackson's corps was on the march to Groveton, a point from which it could spring from the woods onto Pope's divisions marching up the turnpike. Late in the afternoon, Stonewall attacked. For more than two hours, Confederates and Federals fired at each other at almost point blank range. About 9 P.M. the Federals disengaged. Jackson had bought the field with many gallons of blood. Among the severely wounded were two division commanders, Ewell and Taliaferro.

Jackson may not have shown tactical skill in the battle, but his strategy was sound. Pope would now try to crush him before Lee and Longstreet arrived. Confident of Confederate speed, Jackson wanted his adversary to do just that.

That night, while Pope issued a confused series of orders based on the supposition that Jackson was fleeing from him toward the Bull Run Mountains, Lee bivouacked east of Thoroughfare Gap, ready to march toward a junction with Stonewall the next day.

Pope attacked on the afternoon of the 29th, with Jackson seeking protection behind a railway embankment. When Pope sent a force to attack Jackson's "exposed right flank," they found themselves facing Longstreet instead. The battle continued on the 30th, with Jackson sustaining severe and repeated enemy attacks until Longstreet's artillery swung into action, enfilading the advancing bluecoats.

Pope had 30,000 reinforcements nearing him, but the skill and activity of Lee and Jackson had convinced him that he had to deal with "overwhelmingly superior numbers." In a dismal rain that night, he began retreating to Washington. Jackson's brilliant cooperation with Lee had helped to make the name Bull Run, or Manassas, doubly offensive in the North. His conduct in this campaign alone was enough to insure Stonewall a shining place in the military history of the world. Few critics have found cause to dispute G. F. R. Henderson's dictum that, in the course of the entire campaign, Jackson did not make a single strategical mistake. Seldom in history has a campaign so daring had the crowning virtue of perfection.

In September, Jackson followed Lee in another daring move—the invasion—or, as Old Jack thought of it, the liberation—of Maryland. Jackson's corps was in the lead as the Army of Northern Virginia forded the Potomac. From a distance, the sight was an inspiring one, for the men preserved their column of fours and close order even as they waded. Up close the view was more homely. The men had removed their shoes and trousers and were crossing with these articles of clothing tied around their necks.

The first Confederate base of operation in Maryland was Frederick. Jackson's entrance into this prosperous community gave rise to a legend inspiring one of John Greenleaf Whittier's poorest and most popular poetic effusions. The poem "Barbara Frietchie" was as devoid of factual basis as it was of literary merit. There was a Barbara Frietchie in Frederick when Jackson entered, but she apparently remained unobtrusively silent on that occasion. She did come out on her front porch and wave the American flag, but only while the Federals were marching through after the Confederates had left.

There was, however, at least one genuine act of defiance on the part of a civilian while Jackson and his troops occupied the town. A minister, while Stonewall Jackson sat in his congregation, prayed for the President of the United States. Jackson did not reprimand the man; the general's face did not even show indignation; as so often when in church, he was fast asleep.

Frederick was but a stepping stone in Lee's plans for invasion of Pennsylvania. His line of communication and supply ran westward through the Shenandoah Valley, passing between Union garrisons at Martinsburg and Harper's Ferry. Lee boldly decided to divide his force of about 55,000, sending 12,000 under Jackson to knock out the two Union garrisons and using the rest to delay McClellan until Jackson's work was done and the whole army could be united again. This plan involved the gravest risks, since McClellan was moving against him from Washington with 80,000 men, backed by 70,000 more.

On the 14th, Jackson's well-placed artillery blasted the defenses of Harper's Ferry from three sides. On the 15th the Union garrison surrendered. Leaving A. P. Hill to complete details, take care of 11,000 prisoners, and collect the spoils, Jackson marched rapidly to rejoin Lee at Sharpsburg.

On the way, Jackson was astonished to learn that McClellan, casting aside indecision, had purposefully marched to a confrontation with Lee. Of course, once arrived on the scene, McClellan had delayed the opening of hostilities. Even so, the Union general had acted far more promptly than either Lee or Jackson had expected. "I thought I knew McClellan," Jackson said to a fellow officer, "but this movement of his puzzles me." What Jackson did not know was that someone in Maryland had used the most expensive cigar wrapper in the world—a copy of Lee's "Special Order No. 191," detailing his plan for dividing his force, which thus found its way into McClellan's hands.

Outnumbered three to one by the enemy and with the Potomac at his back, Lee elected to stand and fight. The sounds of the horrible slaughter were borne miles away to General Ewell, who had lost a leg while fighting under the man he once called crazy and was now confined to bed. In the most acute misery, he kept wondering what was happening to Jackson, not just Jackson's corps, but especially Jackson himself. If Stonewall fell, he said in his earnest, pop-eyed way, the Confederacy might fall with him.

If Ewell could have seen Stonewall in those fateful hours, he would not have been comforted. Utterly oblivious to shot and shell, Jackson rode up and down his line, ordering, cheering, commanding and —almost miraculously—surviving.

At the end of the day, Lee had lost 8,000 to 10,000 of his 40,000 men. McClellan, who had had 70,000 men actually on the scene, lost more than 12,000. That night and the next morning, the Union general received reinforcements exceeding the number of his losses. After remaining on the field another day facing the enemy, Lee asked Jackson if he did not think retreat was the course of wisdom. Even Jackson, with daring bordering on madness and his exalted sense of destiny, had to agree. But, in a spirit of warm comradeship, he added that it "was better to have fought in Maryland than to have left it without a struggle."

When the Army of Northern Virginia forded the Potomac in retreat on the night of September 18, Jackson was by Lee's side. Shortly after midnight, when Jackson had established headquarters about four miles south of the river, he received the alarming report that all the army's reserve guns had been taken by the enemy and that a Union beachhead had been established on the south bank of the river. Even if the report about the guns was exaggerated, as it proved to be, the beachhead was still an intolerable threat. Without waiting to consult with Lee, Jackson ordered A. P. Hill's Light Division to charge the Federals. Straight they rode into the massed fire of powerful artillery, losing 261 of their number but saving the reserve artillery and driving the Yankees from their beachhead. D. H. Hill, whose division had been sent to A. P. Hill's support, later wrote: "I have sometimes thought that the Army of Northern Virginia would almost have ceased to have an organized existence but for this splendid movement."

Ten days after the retreat across the Potomac, President Davis, acting on authority granted him by Congress, asked Lee to submit the names of officers for promotion to the newly created rank of lieutenant general. The administration's plan to divide the Army of Northern Virginia into two wings or corps simply formalized the arrangements under which the commanding general had recently been operating with Jackson and Longstreet as his chief lieutenants. Lee, therefore, submitted the names of these two men and the nominations were duly confirmed.

It is odd that, although Jackson's reputation with the public and the politicians was far greater than Longstreet's, the commander simply recommended the Georgian's name without comment but deemed it necessary to explain the choice of his fellow Virginian. Lee wrote: "My opinion of the merits of General Jackson has been greatly enhanced during this expedition. He is true, honest and brave; has a single eye to the good of the service, and spares no exertion to accomplish his object."

Lee's words implied that at one time he had had definite reservations about Jackson's fitness for high command. Had doubts been aroused about his military capacity or willingness to cooperate by the unfortunate performance in the Seven Days' Campaign? If so, Lee would hardly have entrusted to Jackson the difficult role which he assigned him in the offensive against Pope. It is quite possible that the commanding general had had doubts about Jackson's character because of the Valley man's continued clashes with general officers. Still unsettled was the matter of honor growing out of a quarrel between Jackson and A. P. Hill so intense that Hill had presented Stonewall his sword in resignation of command and had promptly been placed under arrest by Old Jack. Hill was high-strung and sensitive, but he was among the bravest and most honored soldiers in the Confederacy.

But Jackson's command of the heart of the common soldier was now indisputable. Lee doubtless had had evidence of that fact during the advance into Maryland, in the action at Sharpsburg, and on the retreat into Virginia. He received additional evidence in December at Fredericksburg. On December 1, when Jackson's corps filed into their new positions about three and one-half miles southeast of the city, many of them wore only rags to keep out the bitter cold and marched barefoot in the snow. But their spirits were irrepressible. When Old Jack rode down the lines on December 18 in a brand new lieutenant general's uniform—"resplendent with gold lace and marks of rank," a new cap with a half-inch gilt band, and shining boots— these same men, not at all envious of the disparity, cheered him lustily. "Come here, boys," an Alabama infantryman alerted his companions, "Stonewall has drawed his bounty and has bought himself some new clothes." They looked, admired, and took vicarious delight. Somehow, when Old Jack put on finery, they all had a share in the glory.

A member of Jackson's staff, Henry Kyd Douglas, afterwards wrote : "There was nothing interesting about the battle of Fredericksburg, either in maneuver or action, in initiative or execution. Without strategy or tactics to speak of, it was a series of gallant attacks with little hope, disastrous repulses with little effort." Doubtless, many of his fellow soldiers would have quarreled with so cavalier a dismissal of a battle that cost so many lives and ended in so signal a victory for the Confederacy. And yet this battle, which in so many quarters demanded the supreme sacrifice of so many, had its quiet pockets in surprising places. Behind the stone wall from which the graycoats directed their withering fire, at least one group of soldiers kept a brisk card game going. Jackson was where there was action and, though the operations furnished no scope for the exercise of genius, he did serve with distinction.

Jackson spent the rest of the winter at Moss Neck, eleven miles from Fredericksburg. Here, with no battles to occupy him, he tightened the administration of his corps and enforced discipline with a heavy hand. He advocated punishment not only for unsoldierly conduct, but also for such vices as gambling. Kyd Douglas said : "Jackson was as hard as nails; in the performance of his duty he always was. I never knew him in such a case to temper justice with mercy; his very words were merciless." Jackson disciplined himself even more rigorously than he did his subordinates. Knowing that Old

Jack himself never took leave, but hoping that a staff member could get a little time off during a peaceful period, Douglas approached the general gingerly: "I have not been out of the army, since I entered it, for a day."

"Very good," Jackson interrupted. "I hope you will be able to say so after the war is over."

April brought a softening to the bleak landscape and to the frigid face of the commander. His beloved Anna visited him, bringing with her the infant daughter Julia whom he had never seen.

The brief idyll ended April 29 with the news that a Federal army of 130,000 was fording the Rappahannock both above and below Fredericksburg to double up both flanks of Lee's army, less than half the size of the aggressor.

On April 30, Jackson moved to Lee's aid with 37,000 men, leaving 10,000 behind to hold off the Federal left wing under Sedgwick. Sedgwick was making a strong demonstration against Lee's right wing while the main body of the Union army, under Hooker, was advancing toward its concentration point of Chancellorsville, ten miles west of Fredericksburg on Lee's left flank and rear. On May 1, Hooker exulted: "I have got Lee just where I want him; he must fight me on my own ground."

After midnight, two much less talkative generals, Lee and Jackson, rose quietly from a bed of pine needles in a thicket only a mile and a half from Hooker's headquarters. Over a small fire of twigs, they reviewed their strategy.

Once again Lee was going to divide a numerically inferior force, this time into three parts. One would remain in Fredericksburg, facing east toward Sedgwick; the second would face west toward Hooker at Chancellorsville; and the third, led by Jackson, would march westward by obscure roads before and around Hooker's army, coming out on the turnpike west of the Federal positions. Jackson would then turn abruptly eastward and press through the woods by two separate roads to hit Hooker's right flank while the Confederate forces remaining near Chancellorsville struck at his left.

Jackson began before daylight the great march that has been described by Douglas Southall Freeman as "one of the most effective operations of its kind in the history of war."

Barking, "Press on, press on!" Jackson moved his column at record speed. In the afternoon, stout Fitz Lee galloped into sight. He could show Jackson the Union's exposed flank. The two men rode up to the crest of a hill. With an expansive gesture, young Lee indicated the plain below. Stretching into the distance was the Federal camp. Bluecoats sat at ease around campfires, in expectation of the beeves being slaughtered within sight. Fitz Lee was startled by the way Jackson's eyes "burned with a brilliant glow." The thin lips began to move, but no sound issued from them. Was Stonewall praying?

Returning to his column, Jackson turned to Colonel Munford, who had been cadet adjutant when Stonewall was a professor at V.M.I. and who earlier in the war had recalled to Ewell that Old Jack had been known in those days as "Fool Tom Jackson." The general said : "The Virginia Military Institute will be heard from today." Many V.M.I. men, some former students, some faculty associates of Jackson's, were in key posts that day.

Near sunset, Jackson's men, giving the rebel yell that he called "the sweetest music," fell upon the rear of the Union right, completely routing the surprised eleventh corps. At every wild ululation, Stonewall would lift his head in thanks. When he passed his army's dead, he raised his arm in supplication for their souls. A wild exhilaration seemed to possess him as never before.

As dusk thickened, reinforcements came from the Federal left and the Union army rallied. But by that time the Federal right had been chased for two miles, crowding the bluecoats into so small a space on the Chancellorsville plateau that they were deprived of room to maneuver.

By now, Jackson, in that state of excitement in which his faculties operated with extraordinary acuteness, must have been reasonably sure that his threat to Hooker's line would make it necessary for the Union general to retreat across the Rappahannock. But it was essential to know precisely what was happening if the full benefits of the victory were to be reaped. With a few members of his staff, Jackson rode forward in the deepening twilight to make a personal reconnaissance of the Union line.

When only moonlight filtering through the trees relieved the darkness of the night, a staff member asked, "General, don't you think this is the wrong place for you?"

Jackson was impatient. "The danger is all over—the enemy is routed!—Go back and tell A. P. Hill to press right on."

Leaning forward in his eagerness, the general moved ahead on Little Sorrel. Presently he drew rein and listened. Though a little deaf, Jackson was close enough to the Union lines to hear the ring of axes and voices issuing commands.

He listened for a few minutes, then turned back to his own lines. The attack against the enemy must be pressed at once and he must see to it in person.

Suddenly, as the little cavalcade rode out of the darkness toward A. P. Hill's division, a shot split the night. Scattered shots followed— then a volley.

"Cease firing, cease firing!" That was Hill's voice. Little Sorrel swerved abruptly and raced into the woods. Jackson checked his horse with his left hand while he raised his right to protect his face from the tree branches.

A lieutenant with Jackson ran toward the shooting, yelling: "Cease firing! You are firing into your own men!"

"Who gave that order?" came an indignant voice. "It's a lie! Pour it into them, boys!"

There was a long, low, horizontal flash from the Confederate lines —a volley by kneeling soldiers. Jackson's left arm fell limply to his side. His right hand was bleeding from a bullet. Little Sorrel turned again and ran toward the Union lines, striking his master's head against a low limb.

With his wounded right hand, Jackson once more turned the horse toward the Confederate lines. Two of his officers seized the bridle.

"They certainly must be our troops," one said. A moment later, the general said, "You had better take me down."

He almost fainted as they lifted him from the horse.

Soon A. P. Hill, past differences swept aside, was kneeling by Jackson, gently removing the general's gauntlets and sword, holding his head.

Jackson insisted on walking instead of being carried. Half stumbling, half supported on either side, he made his way through the dark.

"Who is that?" his companions were asked every few steps.

They gave the answer ordered by the general himself : "A Confederate officer."

One soldier stared closely at the moon-dappled features of the wounded man. "Great God," he screamed, "that is General Jackson !"

As they struggled on, Jackson asked for whisky. His officers knew then that his pain must be almost unbearable. They carried him the rest of the way on a stretcher.

General Dorsey Pender, wounded himself, bent over his chief. "The lines here are so much broken that I fear we will have to fall back."

Jackson raised his head and barked out with the old spirit : "You must hold your ground, General Pender; you must hold your ground, sir !"

Stonewall found himself on a cot in a tent. The familiar face of Dr. McGuire was near his own. Though Jackson did not know it, it was now past midnight. A deathly silence reigned except for the persistent call of a whippoorwill, and now and then the shriller cry of a man under the surgeon's knife. McGuire was telling Jackson that his arm might have to be amputated. The general's voice was low but firm : "Yes, certainly, Dr. McGuire. Do for me whatever you think best."

The next day, Jackson, lying in bed minus his left arm, was told that the enemy's defeat had been completed by a brave charge by the Stonewall Brigade. Tears came into the general's eyes : "It was just like them to do so; just like them ! They are a noble body of men !"

A courier arrived with a message from Lee : "Could I have directed events, I should have chosen for the good of the country to be disabled in your stead. I congratulate you upon the victory, which is due to your skill and energy."

"General Lee is very kind," Jackson said, "but he should give the praise to God."

In the days that followed, Jackson bore his fate stoically, saying as so often in the past, "All things work together for good."

A great comfort to him at this time was the companionship of Lieutenant James Power Smith, a Presbyterian thinking seriously of the ministry. Jackson loved to test the young man's knowledge of the Bible. Once the general asked him, "Can you tell me where the Bible gives generals a model for their official reports of battles?"

Smith said he knew of no such models in the Bible.

"Nevertheless," Jackson said, "there are such : and excellent models, too. Look, for instance, at the narrative of Joshua's battle with the Amalekites; there you have one. It had clearness, brevity, fairness, modesty; and it traces the victory to its right source, the blessing of God."

Pneumonia set in and, as the hours passed, the general's breathing became labored.

Under the influence of morphia, Jackson faded into a semiconscious state in which one day slid imperceptibly into another. In one moment of clarity, he asked for a glass of lemonade. When Smith brought it to him, he tasted it, then said reproachfully : "You did not mix this; it is too sweet; take it back." Old Jack still liked his lemons sour and still expected his orders to be followed precisely.

He did not know that his words had saddened one dear to him. His wife had mixed the lemonade. Now she was by his side, quiet and pale. He smiled at her and dropped off to sleep. When he waked, he told her, "My darling, you must cheer up and not wear a long face. I love cheerfulness and brightness in a sick room." Another time he waked to tell her, "You are one of the most precious little wives in the world."

On May 10, Anna told him that the doctor said that he had not long to live. "I prefer it," he said. "I prefer it."

Afraid that he might not have understood, she rephrased her statement. This time he answered deliberately and clearly, "I will be an infinite gainer to be translated."

At 1:30 P.M., Dr. McGuire told the general that perhaps only two hours of life remained to him.

"Very good," Jackson reassured him. "It is all right."

He muttered indistinctly, and then the long silence was broken only by the sound of his labored breathing and finally the rattle in his throat. Then at 3:15 he spoke his last words, clearly and with assurance: "Let us cross over the river and rest in the shade of the trees."

Who had spoken, the general or the deacon?

Lee, who had once had doubts about Jackson's capacity for high command, said in his grief, "Such an executive officer the sun never shone on."

President Davis, who had once questioned his fitness as a brigade commander, declared, "A great national calamity has befallen us . . . ."

In the funeral escort was the cadet battalion from V.M.I. where he had been called "Fool Tom."

One of the attendant mourners in the procession to the capitol in Richmond was Ewell, who many months ago had called him crazy. Another was Garnett, who had pronounced him unjust. On this day, Garnett said: "I wish here to assure you that no man can lament his death more sincerely than I do. I believe he did me great injustice, but I believe also he acted from the purest motives. He is dead. Who can fill his place!"

Secretary of War James A. Seddon summed up the words of mourning: "Without disparagement to others, it may be safely said he has become, in the estimation of the Confederacy, emphatically 'the hero of the war.' Around him clustered with peculiar warmth their gratitude, their affections and their hopes."

By the end of the war, Lee was first in the hearts of the South, but Old Jack was never dislodged from his priority in the affections of many of his old soldiers. Years later, the morning after the unveiling of Richmond's equestrian statue of Lee, white-haired men were discovered sleeping around the statue of Jackson in Capitol Square. As they yawned and stretched, a shocked citizen exclaimed : "Heavens, men, could you find no other beds in Richmond last night?"

"Oh, yes, there was plenty of places," said one old man. "All Richmond was open to us." Then he looked up at the statue of Old Jack and said, "But we were his boys and we wanted to sleep with the old man just once more."

How could a man who once had inspired such burning hatred later inspire such lasting love? Above all, to return to the question posed in the beginning, how could the ridiculed professor so troubled with discipline be transformed within two years into one of the great captains of military history?

In some ways, the transformation was more apparent than real. Threads of consistency run through Jackson's entire career, civil and military.

His determination was evidenced as strongly in the heroic efforts by which he raised himself near the top of his class at West Point as in any of the celebrated instances of the war. "Press on!" had been his own motto long before it became a command to his troops.

His powers of concentration were always proverbial. The laughable professor who walked under arches at V.M.I. oblivious to the objects dropped about him by pranksters was not radically different from the general who, absorbed in writing a note to Stuart, seemed unaware of the shells exploding around him.

The general called Stonewall was not a whit more conscientious than the boy who refused a substantial profit on a fish rather than break a promise, or the young teacher who walked through a cold night to the cadet barracks to correct an error he had made in class.

The professor troubled with rebellious students but earning the deepest respect of a few serious-minded cadets was not a stranger to the general who, though he won the affection and admiration of some subordinates, was plagued through his command with problems of human relations.

The self-righteous commander who demanded courts-martial right and left and arrested one of the South's ablest generals was the same Jackson who could not be restrained from demanding punishment of a fellow cadet at West Point, who initiated an investigation of his superior officer in Florida, and who once in all seriousness asked his sister Laura if she had ever known him to be mistaken about anything since he had reached maturity.

The literal-minded, direct approach for which he was famous as a general had been evident long before in his career as a student at West Point, in his application to his minister for instructions in religious duty, in his habit of repeating to questioning students word for word the same explanations that he had originally offered.

The dogged courage that became so celebrated had been demonstrated long ago by a teen-aged constable leading an offender's horse to the stable while the blows of a whip rained on his back.

His zeal in battle had been evidenced at Chapultepec and as a soldier of the Cross. He saw himself serving Christ both on the college parade ground and the field of battle. In his mind, religion and fighting were inextricably entwined. As he explained shortly before his death, he sought in Holy Writ instruction in every phase of life from domestic activities to the preparation of a battle report.

How did Jackson's long-suffering constitution survive, and even flourish, under the shocks and strains of war? A careful review of his life suggests an answer. Jackson's nerves, eyes, and digestion suffered in peacetime from the conflict of desires and inhibitions within him. War gave him the opportunity to fight on an exterior battlefield, to oppose a concrete enemy in a conflict transferred from the microcosm of self to the macrocosm of a war theater.

Some people have suggested that, if Jackson had lived, the Confederacy might have won the war. Numerical inferiority, economic disparity, and the ineffectiveness of a decentralized government argue strongly against the possibility. However, Jackson's presence might have meant victory for Lee at Gettysburg. And a triumph on that field might have brought European intervention, if not to insure a victory for Confederate arms, at least to facilitate the writing of a peace not entirely inconsistent with Southern ideas of sovereignty. But the chain of events is like a molecular reaction. You cannot change one molecule and forecast the result on the assumption that the experiment is proceeding in the original milieu.

But speculation as to Jackson's personal fate if he had outlived the war is not entirely futile. The Valley Campaign, Groveton, and Chancellorsville had already made his place secure in military annals and there is every reason to believe that he would have continued to conduct himself with distinction. He doubtless always would have been regarded as a great man, but postwar years of peace might have robbed him of some of his heroic stature as the martyred hero of a lost cause. Nothing that we know of his temperament leads us to believe that he could have proceeded with Lee's outward serenity to heal the breach between North and South. There is only a chance that he could have forgiven his enemies by reason of seeing defeat of the South as an expression of God's will. Away from the pressure and excitement of battle, his psychosomatic illnesses and hypochondria would probably have reappeared. His self-righteousness would have made it necessary on many occasions for him to justify his wartime conduct, sometimes to the incidental disparagement of fellow soldiers. A shining record might have been tarnished by dispute and recrimination.

But, if Taliaferro, A. P. Hill, and Garnett could forgive the querulousness and unconscious injustice of the man and learn to value even his eccentricities as the peculiar trademarks of a great and enduring personality, those of us who merely read about him should be able to do the same. Jackson's achievements are studied today not only at his beloved Virginia Military Institute, which learned to love him, but also at West Point, Sandhurst, and Saint-Cyr. The man behind those achievements repays study too. He was peculiar in his foibles, but he also seems nearly unique in unconquerable spirit and unswerving devotion to his concept of duty.

THOMAS J. (STONEWALL) JACKSON
Bibliography

Vandiver, Frank E. *Mighty Stonewall.* New York, 1957. A readable volume and one of the most useful of all Jackson biographies.

Henderson, Col. G. F. R. *Stonewall Jackson and the American Civil War.* New York, 1949. A masterpiece of military biography.

Freeman, Douglas Southall. *Lee's Lieutenants,* 3 vols. New York, 1942–1944. Vols. I and II include beautifully written and penetrating analyses of Jackson's role in the Civil War; Vol. III contains interesting speculation concerning the effort of Jackson's death on Confederate fortunes.

Cook, Roy Bird. *The Family and Early Life of Stonewall Jackson.* Charleston, W. Va., 1948. The source of virtually all the anecdotes of Jackson's boyhood which appear in *Frock Coats and Epaulets.* One who reads Cook's book and the preceding volumes in this bibliography will be acquainted with most of the important facts of Jackson's life.

Douglas, Henry Kyd. *I Rode with Stonewall.* Chapel Hill, 1940. A delightful volume of personal reminiscence and the source of many anecdotes illustrative of Jackson's personality and the attitude of his soldiers toward him. The reader of *Frock Coats and Epaulets* may notice that Douglas is frequently mentioned as present at some scene described. In most such cases, he is the source.

Joseph E. Johnston Papers, Library of the College of William and Mary, Williamsburg, Va. This manuscript collection includes valuable information on Jackson at Harpers Ferry and in the beginning of the Valley Campaign, as well as on his relations with Johnston.

William B. Taliaferro Papers, Library of the College of William and Mary, Williamsburg, Va. A most interesting and not yet fully utilized collection of letters and documents shedding light on Jackson's difficulties with human relations. Interesting material on the John Brown raid and especially on the Romney expedition.

Taylor, Richard. *Destruction and Reconstruction.* New York, 1955. Interesting portraits of Jackson by a discerning observer. Information in *Frock Coats and Epaulets* on Taylor's conversations with Jackson is taken from this book.

Borcke, Heros von. *Memoirs of the Confederate War for Independence,* 2 vols. London, 1866. Information on Jackson in the operations in which Stuart cooperated with him. Accounts must be analyzed in light of the fact that Borcke was highly imaginative.

Jones, J. B. *A Rebel War Clerk's Diary at the Confederate States Capital,* 2 vols. New York, 1935. Intimate view of the War Department, with which Jackson had his troubles.

Kean, Garlick Hill. *Inside the Confederate Government: the Diary of Robert Garlick Hill Kean,* (ed. Edward Younger). New York, 1957. Valuable for the same reasons as *A Rebel War Clerk's Diary.*

Jackson, Mrs. Mary Anna. *Memoirs of Stonewall Jackson.* Louisville, 1895. Narrative and anecdotes by a worshiping widow.

Farwell, Byron. *Stonewall: A Biography of General Thomas J. Jackson.* New York, 1992. One of the best Jackson biographies.

Freeman, Douglas Southall. *R. E. Lee,* 4 vols. New York, 1934–1935. Masterly exposition of the way in which Lee and Jackson worked together.

Johnston, Joseph E. *Narrative of Military Operations Directed During the Late War Between the States.* New York, 1874. Information on Jackson from a man who had been his superior officer.

Tanner, Robert G. *Stonewall in the Valley: Thomas J. "Stonewall" Jackson's Shenandoah Valley Campaign.* Garden City, 1976.

Johnson, R. U., and Buell, C. C. (eds.). *Battles and Leaders of the Civil War.* New York, 1887–1888. Many personal reminiscences.

Henry, R. S. *Story of the Confederacy.* Indianapolis, 1936. Jackson's military role in perspective.

Govan, Gilbert E., and Livingood, James W. *A Different Valor, the Story of General Joseph E. Johnston, C. S. A.* Indianapolis, 1956. Jackson's relations with Johnston.

Williams, T. Harry. *P. G. T. Beauregard: Napoleon in Gray.* Baton Rouge, 1955. Information on First Manassas.

Chambers, Lenoir. *Stonewall Jackson,* 2 vols. New York, 1959. The most detailed life of Jackson, this biography is the work of a painstaking craftsman who seems to share his hero's belief in predestination.

Davis, Burke. *They Called Him Stonewall.* New York, 1954. This sprightly narrative includes an interesting collection of Jackson anecdotes. Though the book is well written, it makes the subject's eccentricities more apparent than his greatness.

Robertson, James I., Jr. *General A. P. Hill: The Story of a Confederate Warrior.* New York, 1987.

NOTE: Many more works relating to Jackson are available, but they contain little not available in the printed and manuscript sources listed above.

IV

JUDAH P. BENJAMIN : The Smiling Lion

IV

JUDAH P. BENJAMIN : The Smiling Lion

JUDAH P. BENJAMIN had a mocking smile. To the public, it must often have seemed that the smile was indelibly stamped upon the Hebrew features of his smooth, full face.

But what did the smile mock? Was it a wry comment on his associates and their confidence in a cause which he early saw to be lost? Was it his own anomalous position as a pillar of a government dedicated to the defense of an Anglo-Saxon culture alien to his forebears?

Benjamin's personal life was enough to account for the wry smile on the face of a man capable of viewing himself and his fortunes with sardonic honesty.

His background assured that he would be both a citizen of the world and an alien in any nation where he made his home. He was born of a race of wanderers. Both parents were Jewish. Judah was born on the 6th of August 1811 in the town of Christiansted on Saint Croix, one of the Virgin Islands. By virtue of conquest the year before, the Union Jack flew over these polyglot islands where blond Danes moved with the proud impatience of erstwhile rulers, Frenchmen spoke with nasal nostalgia of Paris, half-naked mulattoes rippled their shoulders in sinuous dance and rich, dark laughter, and an industrious colony of Jews, uninspired by hope and unfretted by despair, contrived to make a living through all the changes of flag and fortune.

Judah was only about two years old when his family left the island home to seek an easier life in Wilmington, North Carolina. Though the boy could have no vivid recollections of Christiansted, the cosmopolitan Caribbean was part of the background that the Benjamins brought with them to the United States. And Judah, living for four years in Wilmington with its Anglo-Saxon prejudices, for five years among the Scots of Fayetteville, and later in aristocratic Charleston where wealthy Hebrews scorned the society of their less successful co-religionists, must have been stirred as his small, dark father recalled long past days of glory when the Benjamins had been among the proud Sephardic Jews of Spain.

But Judah was learning other things that were a comfort. For one thing, he learned that a smile and a friendly manner could not only procure him such forbidden delights as slices of ham from Gentile friends, but also the genuine regard of highly respected persons.

The family income, despite the fact that Judah's mother shocked friends by working in the shop even on the Jewish Sabbath, was insufficient to provide the boy with a private school education. Public school in Charleston was what proper Charlestonians believed anything designed for the masses must inevitably be : unrelievedly common. But the boy's quick intelligence and faculty for being agreeable had attracted the attention of Moses Lopez, President of the Hebrew Orphan Society. Under the auspices of this organization, Judah was educated in a good academy. He took to learning so enthusiastically that he is said to have quoted Shakespeare even when on his knees shooting marbles with his little playmates.

At the age of fourteen, he entered Yale with the aid of others who had found him agreeable. Not surprisingly, he was the youngest student at the university, and his youth was emphasized by his small stature. Nevertheless, he was soon at or near the head of his class and excelled in debate and oratory. He was popular with his classmates and joined them in numerous pranks. At least one of his instructors admitted that he was inclined to wink at Judah's participation because of the boy's cleverness and general agreeableness.

Early in his junior year, Judah suddenly left the University. To this day, the reasons for his hurried departure are uncertain, but while not expelled, he certainly left under a cloud. In after years, a classmate said somewhat enigmatically that the boy's fondness for gambling was responsible for his troubles.

From New Haven, he went to Rochester, New York, where increasing indebtedness multiplied his difficulties. Some classmates followed him there and persuaded him to return to Charleston. But, embarrassed before his parents and perhaps before the many Yale alumni in that city, he left in a few weeks for New Orleans.

When seventeen-year-old Judah arrived in New Orleans in 1828, he found himself in what was then probably the most exciting city in America. Moreover, it was a community in which the doors of opportunity were not closed to any alien if he had brains, daring, and verve. The city could hardly afford to be other than hospitable to foreigners and wanderers, for the community itself seemed almost an alien on the American scene. The traditional first families were the Creoles, proud aristocrats, usually of pure French blood, sometimes with an admixture of Spanish. Only twenty-five years before, the tricolor of France had been lowered while the tear-dimmed eyes of its old citizens saw the Stars and Stripes run up the mast to flutter in token of United States acquisition. Newspapers were bilingual and so was commerce. But, in the warm, languorous nights, lanterns winked from perfumed dens in the French Quarter in a language understandable alike to sensation-weary Creoles, flesh-hungry sailors and lusty Mississippi flatboatmen. Wharves were crowded with freightage of steamboats from Cincinnati and Louisville, New York and Boston, Liverpool and Le Havre, St. Thomas and Havana. There were cotton and sugar from the dusky bayous and, of course, black slaves. The population of the city multiplied in number and variety at an incredible rate. To some of the newcomers the city was an opiate, to others a catalyst. It left no man unchanged.

Benjamin was a pleasure lover. Except for the goad of ambition, he might have become a sybarite. But he had come to New Orleans with a wounded ego, and he was determined to build a new reputation. He quickly got a job in a mercantile house, and on the side began private tutoring and the study of French and law. No wonder that Judah, with this crowded schedule, seems to have found little or no time for the winking lights.

His lively intelligence and agreeableness earned him many tutoring assignments. But his winning personality is said to have cost him at least one. A proud Creole was afraid for the young Jew to tutor his daughter lest she fall in love with him.

Another proud Creole, Auguste St. Martin, was undeterred by such apprehensions. At the age of twenty, Judah was tutor to Mlle. Natalie St. Martin, whose dark liquid eyes seemed so much older and wiser than the delicate sixteen-year-old face framed by smooth hair with the gleam of polished mahogany. Even when Judah was poring over his law books in the loneliness of his private room, her flashing glance, the arch tilt of her head, and the expressive grace of her slender hands intruded upon his studies and lured him into reverie. In February 1833, the two were married. By then, Benjamin had attained his majority and had been admitted to the bar of New Orleans.

Short though he was, Benjamin had a sort of swarthy glamor, compounded partly of smooth cosmopolitanism and a melodic voice and partly of genuine good humor. This smiling son-in-law quickly ingratiated himself with his in-laws, if indeed he had not fully done so before his marriage. They found him so agreeable and he was so pleased with them that the couple apparently spent their honeymoon in her parents' home and continued to stay with them as the months passed. Before the end of the year, the St. Martins moved to another house in New Orleans. Benjamin was delighted with this three-story mansion in the French Quarter and he and Natalie moved in with her parents.

But soon Benjamin, who had always been able to make himself

agreeable to anyone if he tried hard enough, found himself disagreeable in the eyes of the one whose love he cherished most. Natalie had led a pampered life and she was irritated by a husband who would sacrifice an evening in brilliant society in order to earn a legal fee. She was bored with Benjamin's bookish interests and increasingly seemed to care only for his money, which she nevertheless parted with quite freely. When Judah talked to her about extravagance, she replied in her stilted English, "Oh, talk not to me of economy! It is so fatiguing." Another issue strained their marriage. For all of her frivolity, Natalie was a devout Catholic. Judah, though not an ardent Jew, nor even of a spiritual cast, had no intention of embracing Catholicism. Increasingly, Judah turned to his growing law practice as a respite from discord at home.

Soon he was practicing before the Louisiana Supreme Court. He had formed a strong friendship with John Slidell, a brilliant Yankee lawyer who had found a new life in New Orleans after being graduated from Columbia at seventeen, taking a master's degree and then complicating a promising career by fighting a duel over an actress. Together they published in 1834 a *Digest of the Reported Decisions of the Superior Court of the Late Territory of Orleans and the Supreme Court of Louisiana.* The text of the digest, which was largely Benjamin's work, was written with a simplicity that contrasted happily with the forbidding title. It contained citations for more than 6,000 cases with references to Spanish law as well as the French civil code and State laws. The digest was recognized almost overnight as a standard work in its field and, at the age of twenty-three, Benjamin could boast a considerable reputation as a legal scholar.

Within a few more years, Benjamin was recognized as one of the ablest lawyers in a city that boasted several attorneys of national reputation. He took in a law partner, but the volume of his growing commercial practice kept him working night and day. In 1842, he crowned years of successful drudgery in the law by winning the "*Creole* cases" in which he represented an insurance company in litigation arising from a slave mutiny aboard the brig *Creole*. The cases were discussed in Congress and even gained international fame.

Benjamin's labors were lightened by the reflection that he was coming nearer to the distinction which he craved. But there was a short-term prospect that he dreamed of all through every fall, winter, and spring. When summer came to New Orleans, with a heat almost unbearable and a mugginess so great that mildew would cover articles left overnight on the floor, he would quit the city to visit his mother and sisters, who now lived in Beaufort, South Carolina. Benjamin's parents had separated, but his devotion to his mother had long exceeded any affection he might feel for his father. Upon arrival, the plump Benjamin, whose round head was now rimmed by a fringe of beard from one sideburn to the other, looked like a Hebrew Santa Claus. A slender cigar would protrude from his beaming countenance and his bags would be loaded with a great variety of presents, ranging from novelties to books, which his female relatives received with exclamations of delight. His pleasure probably exceeded theirs.

Far removed from these domestic scenes was the tough world of Louisiana politics in which Benjamin gained a foothold. Failing at the age of thirty in a race for alderman, he cheerfully returned to the fray the next year and won a seat in the State legislature. He was credited or blamed, depending upon the political preferences and squeamishness of the appraisers, for many of the clever tactics used by the young and growing Whig party. His oratorical abilities brought him more attention than any freshman legislator had a right to expect.

In 1844 he was elected a Whig delegate to the Louisiana Constitutional Convention and, when his election was contested, resigned and was re-elected by an even larger margin. Benjamin's persuasive powers were credited with getting the convention moved from Jackson, a country town, to New Orleans where French wines wrought a persuasive power of their own in obtaining the adoption of resolutions favorable to the big city. In the urban-rural conflict that threatened to rip the convention apart, Benjamin became the leader of the city forces. His brilliance, industry, and eloquence made him indispensable to his faction, but he proceeded with such smiling diplomacy that the leader of the opposition lauded his "spirit of conciliation and harmony." Benjamin's views on some questions brought charges of opportunism, but there could be no doubt about the sincerity of his convictions in regard to public education. In and out of the convention, he campaigned hard for more and better public schools, asserting, "With public education, you may extend democratic principles without danger."

This enthusiastic champion of urban privileges was rapidly becoming a country gentleman. He became part owner of Belle Chasse, a large sugar plantation across the Mississippi and six miles downstream from New Orleans. Here he installed his wife and little daughter Ninette. In this romantic setting, Natalie could entertain lavishly.

But Benjamin was often kept in town by business interests, and his wife tired of plantation life. In the summer of 1845, with her brother Jules de St. Martin, little Ninette, and a Negro nurse, she sailed for Europe. She told Benjamin that she was going because Ninette should be educated in France. But he was too shrewd a realist to accept the explanation at face value. His smiling good humor gave no indication that he missed his wife or daughter at all, but from now on he found it necessary to make a trip to France about once a year. Apparently, Natalie received her husband cheerfully on these occasions. She certainly received cheerfully enough the ample checks that he sent her between visits.

But Benjamin had to have a family—not just an ocean away, but near enough for him to enjoy the little smiles of delight and appreciation that acts of thoughtfulness and generosity could win. He brought his mother, his widowed sister, Rebecca Levy, and her young daughter to live with him at Belle Chasse. Soon a new plantation house was rising above its fields. Twenty-eight columns supported the double balconies from which Benjamin could look out on the river highway where white steamboats passed : by day, their gilt decorations flashing in the sun; by night, torrents of sparks swarming like fireflies from the tall smokestacks. The boy who had known scorn and condescension could now stride with a sort of elephantine majesty through the twenty rooms of his mansion. On party nights, he could stand on the great spiral mahogany staircase and see billowing skirts of blue and rose and emerald swirling to the rhythm of the strings while coruscating jewels and flashing eyes reflected the brilliance of gaslit chandeliers.

Even this retreat was not secure from misfortune. Benjamin's mother soon died. About the same time, his eyesight began to fail. To a lawyer whose success depended in large measure on the thoroughness of his research and to a lifelong student, this failing was an even greater loss than it would have been to many other men. He abandoned his law practice and made sugar planting his vocation. He did not play the role grudgingly, but threw himself into it wholeheartedly. He became such a student of sugar culture that, with his inventive turn of mind, he earned State and then national recognition as a pioneer of the industry. He also began to be known as a writer on agricultural subjects.

Benjamin found compensation in this way of life. The devotion of his slaves was pleasing to a man with his tremendous hunger for affection. He delighted in the presence of his sister Rebecca, whom he said he always regarded as "a sort of superior being." He was the special confidant of his young niece, who said he seemed "her own age, only more wise and gentle." And on weekends the boat from New Orleans would bring guests and a holiday spirit to Belle Chasse. A favorite guest, almost a regular occupant of the house, was Auguste St. Martin.

Gradually, Benjamin's eyesight improved and he returned to his law practice, quickly regaining lost ground and earning new fame in cases attracting national attention.

During this period, he was also active as a railroad promoter. In his interest in mechanical advances and industrial empires, Benjamin was more akin to businessmen of the Northeast than to leaders of the planter society he loved. Believing that strong national unity would mean greater prosperity for all, he told a railroad convention : "Let us ask ourselves how we can bind the South and the West and the Southwest in common bonds; how we can unite them indissolubly with the Northeastern and Atlantic States. Some great lines of inter-communication we all agree upon."

Liberal laws for railways were sought by the Whigs, whose convention to nominate two candidates for the State Senate met in New Orleans October 1851. Benjamin had not yet returned from one of his European trips to visit Natalie and Ninette, but he was nominated. His friends had told the convention of Benjamin's supposed views on current questions of policy. The opposition was quick to point out that these views contrasted sharply with some that Benjamin had expressed earlier, but he nevertheless enjoyed an easy triumph in the general election.

Shortly after this victory, Benjamin's name was mentioned with increasing frequency when Louisianans talked of the United States Senate seat to be filled by vote of the State legislature. Some wiseacres insisted that he did not have a chance. Many said that he was too "boyish" and some thought that he responded like a barometer to political pressure. But the powerful planters whose influence still counted heavily in Louisiana knew him as a member of the exclusive Boston Club, named for the popular game of cards which Benjamin played with such skill, and they wished him well. Wherever he talked in the State, he won other friends. The mellow voice, the winning smile had an almost magical effect on some audiences. An opposition newspaper admitted that old men would "stretch their eyes and mouths with wonder, whispering to one another, 'This is a devilish smart little fellow.' " Eager-eyed women would exclaim, "What a love of a man!"

To the astonishment of prognosticators, Benjamin was elected over two powerful opponents. The *Delta,* one of the newspapers that had predicted his defeat, now made a shrewd analysis of his victory. It said :

"He not only rendered himself very agreeable to the members of the legislature, but he manifested a zeal, industry and capacity in the preparation of business for the legislature—digesting and framing bills, and drawing up reports, etc.—which produced a most favorable impression as to his great practical talent and usefulness."

Benjamin's smiling face must have been the most cheerful thing in Washington on a gray Friday in March of 1853 when he entered the capitol, shaking the wet snow from his collar, and swaggered to the Senate chamber to take the oath of office with other freshman solons, among them Stephen A. Douglas of Illinois and Sam Houston of Texas. The swagger was pardonable. He was the only Jew in Congress at the time and the second to sit in the Senate in the history of that body.

In that day, eloquence was still a powerful factor in the Senate, and Benjamin's oratorical gifts won him quick recognition. He became a Southern hero when, in debates on popular sovereignty in the Kansas-Nebraska territory, he bearded the formidable Senator Charles Sumner of Massachusetts.

Benjamin was soon among Southerners moving into the Democratic Party and, at the Democratic National Convention in Cincinnati in June 1856, he helped his friend Slidell to defeat Franklin Pierce for renomination and to nominate James Buchanan of Pennsylvania. In the course of the campaign that followed, Benjamin made stump speeches for Buchanan as far north as Portland, Maine. Slidell was the power behind the Buchanan administration and, as one of his chief lieutenants, Benjamin was a potent factor in national politics.

Benjamin's love of variety was gratified by his life in Washington. He could be a prominent statesman on the national scene while making the most of the political patronage which he commanded in Louisiana, enhancing in repeated appearances before the Supreme Court of the United States his already great reputation as a lawyer, pursuing scholarly studies through the facilities of the Library of Congress, and making himself a general favorite in Washington society.

Oddly enough, Benjamin, despite his ingratiating ways, came near shooting, or being shot by, one of his most prominent Southern colleagues. The near-tragic sequence of events began with an inter-change on the Senate floor between Benjamin and Senator Jefferson Davis of Mississippi. The pain-drawn face of the ascetic-looking Mississippi senator was an index to his tortured nervous system on that June day in 1858. Probably only strong will power enabled him to stay at his desk. Benjamin asked a question, which Davis answered in his nervous manner. Benjamin accused Davis of sneering and Davis retorted with a charge of misrepresentation. Before the exchange of heated words was over, Benjamin felt that his honor had been impugned. Because he was a Jew and because of his unhappy experi-ence at Yale, the insult, if such it was, bit deep. Benjamin sent Davis a note challenging him to a duel. The Mississippian, whose physical courage had been proved beyond doubt in the Mexican War, had the moral courage to tear up the note, saying, "I will make this all right at once. I have been wholly wrong." The next day, he apolo-gised in the Senate chamber and Benjamin replied in a way that won him Davis's lasting friendship. If the threatened duel had been fought it might have had a profound effect on a far vaster shooting match, which would begin in 1861.

When Benjamin ran for re-election in 1859, he faced strong oppo-sition because of his position as chief lieutenant to Slidell, whose political machine was involved in public scandals. After more than 40 ballots in the Louisiana State Senate, Benjamin was re-elected by one vote more than a majority.

His optimism undiminished by his near defeat, he prepared to make Washington his true home. Belle Chasse was sold and Benjamin provided a house in a New Orleans suburb for his three sisters. He had been living in rented rooms and eating at a boarding house. Again he missed family life. A bold hope entered his head. He would lease a mansion in Washington. A handsome residence, capital society, and his own national prominence might be enough to lure back Natalie and Ninette. He leased Decatur House, the three-story brick residence which the eminent architect Benjamin Latrobe had designed for Stephen Decatur. The house had lost none of its elegance subsequently as the residence of a French and later a Russian baron, ministers from their respective countries to the United States, as well as of Sir Charles Vaughn, the British minister.

Natalie agreed to come to Washington. Benjamin was as excited as a schoolboy. Happily he surveyed the stocks of Washington shops. But the silver and china that they could offer were not enough. He imported silver, china, objets d'art, and other furnishings at staggering cost. Benjamin was spending recklessly, knowing that he could not match the elegance of European palaces, but hoping that in the elaborate surroundings he was providing Natalie would not miss Paris too much.

Natalie's arrival was preceded by rumors of indiscretions during her long stay in Europe. In fact, except for Benjamin's own personal popularity and prestige and the widespread curiosity about Natalie herself, the feminine leaders of Washington society would not have called upon Mrs. Benjamin. When they did call, they found a woman of forty-five with a beauty that defied the encroachments of time. Benjamin hung around her like an obedient courtier, but she seemed to scorn as her social inferior this man who was so highly respected in Washington. Nevertheless, Benjamin seemed to think it was far better to have her on these terms than not at all. And he could scarcely believe his good fortune in being able to see her every day, even if she did not smile on him.

She gave dinners to several of the diplomatic corps and frequently entertained members of the French legation.

Then, one day, Washington society woke to find that Mrs. Benjamin had silently fled the city the night before. She was last seen, it was reported, in the company of a handsome German officer.

For once, Benjamin's optimism deserted him. Distraught, he told a close friend that he must leave Washington and never return. He arranged for an auction to be held to dispose of all the rich furnishings which he had bought in such eager hope. He felt that he could never live again in the elegant mansion that was now the sepulcher of his most cherished dreams.

After a while, Benjamin did return to the capital. Those who searched his face for signs of suffering saw a smooth, smiling countenance.

About this time, a land title case, *United States* vs. *Castillero,* took Benjamin to California. Though on the losing side, he captured big newspaper headlines. A *New York Times* correspondent said that the Louisiana senator had made a "terribly tedious case interesting." Spectators crowded the court to hear him and he was begged to lecture in California. In one speech he declared that he could not look "with aught but kindling eyes and glowing heart . . . at the majestic march of our Union."

From June of 1860 until December, Benjamin had been away from Washington and from Louisiana because of his activities in California. Soon after his return to New Orleans, he realized that such Unionist sentiments as he had voiced on the West Coast, even when tempered by his strong stand for States' rights, would make many of his constituents see red. Lincoln had been elected President of the United States as the result of a campaign that had rung the changes on abolitionism and States' rights until the clamor of politics was threatened with replacement by the clangor of war. In common with other citizens of the South, Louisianans felt that they were in danger of being crushed by the might of a federal government dominated by the great cities and industrial interests of the North. They feared that constitutional law would be twisted to become their enemy instead of their protector. A prominent Presbyterian minister in New Orleans had advocated secession from his pulpit in November. A mounting cry for secession was rising from all parts of the State and many politicians were finding it expedient to echo what now seemed to be the majority sentiment. Fears of sudden emancipation of the Negroes and its consequences to society were so rampant that even a Yankee soldier, William Tecumseh Sherman, then in Louisiana as superintendent of the State Military Academy, wrote: "All the Congresses on earth can't make the Negro anything else than what he is. He must be subject to the white man, or he must amalgamate or be destroyed. Mexico shows the result of general equality and amalgamation, and the Indians give a fair illustration of the fate of Negroes if they are released from the control of the whites."

On December 11, Benjamin was quoted as being opposed to secession except as a last resort. Three days later, he was one of thirty Southern senators and representatives who in a joint address to their constituents declared :

The argument is exhausted. All hope of relief in the Union through the agency of committees, Congressional legislation, or constitutional amendment is extinguished. . . . We are satisfied the honor, safety, and independence of the Southern people require the organization of a Southern confederacy—a result to be obtained only by separate State action . . . .

On the twentieth of December, South Carolina seceded from the Union. A few days later, word went around Washington that Benjamin would make an address in the Senate on South Carolina's action. On the last day of the year, he rose to speak. The galleries were packed and the senators themselves were excited. Dispassionately, Benjamin stated the case. The question was whether South Carolina should be permitted to secede peacefully from the Union or should be coerced into returning to it. As usual, when he was on sound legal ground, Benjamin quietly and simply stated the precedents and opinions supporting the legality of South Carolina's move. He quoted not only Virginia's Madison, "Father of the Constitution," but also New England's idol, Daniel Webster. From a discussion of constitutional principles, Benjamin proceeded to a review of the economic plight of the South and its aggravation by Northern legislation. In deciding what to do about secession, the Southern States, he said, should consider not only what the North had done, but what she was likely to do. He compared the South to a tree which the Northern legislators did not intend to fell, but "merely proposed to girdle . . . so that it would die." Smilingly, he drew humorous analogies that dissolved hostility in laughter.

Then, lowering his melodious voice, he looked solemnly about the chamber.

And now, Senators, within a few weeks we part to meet as Senators in one common council chamber of the nation no more forever. We desire, we beseech you, let this parting be in peace. I conjure you to indulge in no vain delusion that duty or conscience, interest or honor imposes upon you the necessity of invading our States or shedding the blood of our people. . . . If, however, . . . you are resolved to pervert the government framed by our fathers for the protection of our rights into an instrument for subjugating and enslaving us, then appealing to the Supreme Judge of the universe for the rectitude of our intentions, we must meet the issue that you force upon us as best becomes freemen defending all that is dear to man.

What may be the fate of this horrible contest, no man can tell, none pretend to foresee; but this much I will say.

Without raising his voice, Benjamin now spoke with a quiet earnestness that excelled in effect any flights of elocution.

This much I will say: the fortunes of war may be adverse to our arms; you may carry desolation into our peaceful land, and with torch and fire you may set our cities in flames. . . . you may do all this—and more, too, if more there be—but you can never subject us; you can never convert the free sons of the soil into vassals, paying tribute to your power; and you never, never, can degrade them to the level of an inferior and servile race. Never! Never!

Benjamin sat down. From the galleries came thunderous applause, shouts, and screams.

On January 26, 1861, Louisiana seceded from the Union. On February 4, Benjamin rose in the Senate with his pistol at his side. But his words were peaceful. "To my brother Senators, on all sides of this chamber," he said, "I do bid a respectful farewell. With many of those from whom I have been radically separated in political sentiment, my personal relations have been kindly and have inspired me with a respect and esteem that I shall not willingly forget." Tears rolled down the cheeks of some of the senators. A federal officer of

Unionist sympathies later declared that he did not believe any Northern man in the chamber at that moment felt animosity toward Benjamin. "I was transported out of myself," he said. "There was neither violence in his action nor anger in his tone, but a pathos that lulled my senses. . . ."

On February 18, 1861, Jefferson Davis was inaugurated at Montgomery, Alabama as provisional President of the Confederacy. Soon after, he sent for Benjamin. Some who knew Davis best thought afterward that the respect which caused the President to seek the Louisianan's counsel at this time dated from their reconciliation after the threatened duel. A few days later, the public knew what the conference was about. By unanimous vote, the Confederate Congress confirmed Benjamin's nomination as Attorney General.

Benjamin's legal learning was highly respected, but in one of the early cabinet meetings he drew the ridicule of some of his fellow members. "We are entering on a contest that must be long and costly," he said. He urged that the government purchase a huge amount of cotton, ship it to England and use the proceeds to purchase arms and ammunition. The scheme seemed laughable to some of the men. How could the war be very long, or even very serious?

Before long, the Confederate government was rejecting thousands of volunteers because it could not furnish them with arms.

On May 21, the Confederate Congress voted to move the capital to Richmond, Virginia. Benjamin had no desire to spend a hot summer in Montgomery, but he opposed the move. Perhaps he thought that Richmond was too near the concentration of Federal military power at Washington and too vulnerable to attack by water, since the Confederate States had hardly more than a token navy.

Some elements of Richmond society seemed almost as worried about the invasion of Confederate statesmen from the Deep South as they were about Federal forces. The society of the Virginia city had been tightly knit for generations. The most exotic of all the newcomers was Benjamin, but nevertheless, he was one of the first to win acceptance. Thomas De Leon, Richmond's social chronicler, reported :

One ubiquitous and most acceptable social factor of the official circle [was that] polished and smooth brevet bachelor, Honorable Judah P. Benjamin. . . . There was no circle, official or otherwise, that missed his soft, purring presence, or had not regretted so doing. He was always expected, almost always found time to respond, and was invariably compensating. He moved into and through the most elegant or the simplest assemblage on natural rubber tires and well-oiled bearings, a smile of recognition for the mere acquaintance, a reminiscent word for the intimate, and a general diffusion of *bon ami*.

The industrious Benjamin must have felt at times that his responsibilities were not commensurate with his abilities. The attorney generalship offered no challenge comparable to that of the War Department over which Leroy P. Walker, inexperienced in administration, attempted to preside. In the bulletins from generals in the field, in the "note of dreadful preparation" that ran through all the department's activities, Benjamin found excitement to stir his blood. On the night of July 21, it was Benjamin, his eyes glowing "something like Daniel Webster's after taking a pint of brandy," who swaggered into the War Department office to tell an anxious group of cabinet officers that the Confederacy had routed the Yankees at Bull Run. Mrs. Davis had entrusted to him the contents of a private dispatch from President Davis himself and he recited the news of victory in the chief executive's own words. Early in August, an astute War Department clerk, J. B. Jones, confided to his diary:

Mr. Benjamin is a frequent visitor at the department, and is very sociable; some intimations have been thrown out that he aspires to become, some day, Secretary of War. Mr. Benjamin, unquestionably, will have great influence with the President, for he has studied his character most carefully. He will be familiar not only with his "likes," but especially with his "dislikes."

Nine days after making this entry, Jones found himself in a War Department without a head. Secretary Walker had gone to Orange Courthouse to see a dying officer. Pondering the problem, the clerk saw, just outside the door, the portly and assured figure of Benjamin.

Jones asked him if he did not think someone should act as Secretary of War in Mr. Walker's absence. Benjamin "replied quickly, and with interest, in the affirmative." Jones later recalled : "I asked him if he would not speak to the President on the subject. He assented; but, hesitating a moment, said it would be better for me to see him." Jones's reluctance was overcome by one of Benjamin's famous smiles and by the cabinet officer's granting the clerk the privilege of using his name in approaching Davis. Davis ordered Walker's assistant to be acting Secretary. Walker returned that night, and some thought he seemed a little disgruntled over what had happened. On September 14, he resigned to become a brigadier general in the Confederate States Army. Davis, ill and harassed, chose the serene and competent Benjamin for his next Secretary of War.

Benjamin had played the assiduous courtier to the President and his lady. To this fact, as much as to brilliant intellect and capacity for hard work, he owed his new position. He was about as ignorant of military affairs as a man of his intelligence and cultivation could be. He would be serving a President who preferred the field to the forum, one who coveted personal direction of the new nation's armies. Davis, Benjamin surely knew, would be in every practical sense his own Secretary of War. To retain the title of that office, Benjamin must maintain the courtier's role. So the same proud man who three years before had challenged the Mississippian to a duel on a point of honor now cheerfully accepted a position little short of subservience. Why? Expediency, obviously, was the chief reason. But it was not a strong enough one to keep Benjamin subservient to a man he did not respect. Subsequent events proved that Benjamin felt no shame in subordination to Davis. Benjamin did not share what some might have considered the President's quixotic view of life. But the Louisianan, so accustomed to smiling at men's foibles, found nothing amusing in Davis's "fine steel courage," his "magnificent folly of honor."

There was, in this stage of the war, too much folly not in any way connected with honor. Early Confederate success in the field had shocked the North into strenuous exertions for vast mobilization, but had lulled the South into a complacency that Benjamin and other leaders could not shake. The inefficiency of the Confederate commissariat and Quartermaster General's Department was a disgrace aired in the press as well as around campfires, but Benjamin was powerless to rectify the situation without stepping on extremely sensitive toes, including those of some of the President's old West Point colleagues.

Of paper work, Benjamin was a past master. Into this phase of his duties, he plunged with enormous energy. The *Charleston* (S.C.) *Courier* commented:

> He dispatches more business in one hour than most men could accomplish in a day. . . . Mr. Benjamin is one of the most extraordinary men in America, and is almost indispensable to the Confederacy. No public man has a larger share of the confidence of the President. . . .

Before the dawn of 1862, the genteel city of Richmond had become a rip-roaring boom town with shouting, drunken revelers staggering down once-quiet streets after prostitutes in tawdry satin. Far too many of the revelers wore whisky-soaked Confederate uniforms.

A connoisseur of wines, Benjamin could appreciate a thirst, but he also knew what liquor could do to demoralize an army. When the Commissary General proposed a whisky ration to the troops, Benjamin declared that he had "an invincible objection." He explained, "The deleterious effects of a ration of spirits, issued regularly to our volunteers, . . . many of whom are very young and totally unaccustomed to the use of liquor, would in our opinion be very great." Benjamin soon let it be known, and with some effect, that his recommendations for the promotion of officers would be strongly influenced by their reputations for sobriety.

Some wanted Benjamin to wage war on gambling, but this he never consented to do. In fact, after hours of labor at the War Office, he often found his chief recreation at the green baize tables of gaslit backrooms. There, as elsewhere, his enigmatic smile was an asset.

It is not surprising that Benjamin needed recreation. His difficulties

were multiplied by the fact that the Confederate States, having gone
to war for States' rights, guarded those prerogatives with a jealousy
that frequently precluded cooperation with the War Department.
Calls for aid from the various sovereign States could not be ignored
and the Davis administration found itself supporting a diffusive
defensive effort rather than waging offensive war with a mass of
maneuver. In these decisions, almost forced upon him, Davis had
Benjamin's unflagging support.

As Davis's faithful champion, Benjamin inherited quarrels with
two popular generals, Joseph E. Johnston and P. G. T. Beauregard.
Moreover, Benjamin's own ignorance of military protocol gave
offense in some cases.

Nevertheless, he was quite generally recognised as the ablest member of the cabinet. On November 6, Jefferson Davis, who had been
provisional president of the Confederacy, was unanimously elected
President. About two weeks later, he signed for Benjamin a full
appointment as Secretary of War.

In that very month, Benjamin received reports of sabotage and
armed assemblies in East Tennessee, which had opposed secession in
the first place. When some of the leading Unionists were captured,
the smiling lion showed his claws. Benjamin ordered that those who
had helped to burn bridges "be tried summarily by drum-head court-
martial, and, if found guilty, executed on the spot by hanging." He
coolly added, "It would be well to leave their bodies hanging in the
vicinity of the burned bridges."

Yet Benjamin used all the force of his office to free one of those
implicated in the burnings, because the man had been promised safe
conduct through Confederate lines. It was better, he wrote a Confederate district attorney, for "the most dangerous enemy" to escape
than for the good faith of the Confederate government to be
"impugned or even suspected."

The New Year began auspiciously for the Confederacy with
"Stonewall" Jackson recovering three western Virginia counties, and
throwing the Union on the defensive in a swift campaign ending

with capture of the village of Romney. He left a division in winter quarters at that settlement and returned to Winchester.

Eleven officers of the division, arguing that Romney was not worth the hardships involved in retaining it, petitioned the Secretary of War for abandonment of the position. Presumably doing what he thought Davis would wish, Benjamin telegraphed Jackson: "Order . . . [the division] back to Winchester immediately."

Jackson followed orders, but replied, "With such interference in my command I cannot expect to be of much service in the field; and accordingly respectfully request to be ordered to report for duty to the superintendent of the Virginia Military Institute. . . . Should this application not be granted, I respectfully request that the President will accept my resignation from the Army."

The letter was forwarded by General Joseph E. Johnston with the comment, "I don't know how the loss of this officer can be supplied." Johnston, who had no love for the administration anyway, was doubly incensed that Benjamin had gone over his head to give direct orders to Jackson.

Nobody in the South wanted to trade Jackson for Benjamin. Before the dispute was smoothed over enough for Jackson to remain in the field, Virginia's political leaders, from Governor Letcher down, had displayed their sympathy for the soldier. Benjamin was roundly abused for "indiscretion, lack of judgment, and disregard of the courtesies." At least one high official made an unfortunate reference to the war minister's Semitic ancestry.

In February, North Carolina's Roanoke Island, an important bastion of the Confederacy, fell to Federal forces superior in numbers and supplies. Brigadier General Henry A. Wise had made a personal plea for re-enforcements and more ammunition almost on the eve of the attack. Benjamin had given him an "easy-spoken, cool, suave reception," but had relied on a West Pointer's too-optimistic estimate of the situation. When disaster came, the public vented on Benjamin all of the fury of its grief and frustration. He saw hatred in the eyes of the bereaved when he walked the streets of Richmond. Confederate senators and representatives demanded his scalp. In the end, Davis reluctantly removed Benjamin from the War Department, nominating him for Secretary of State. The Senate gave grudging approval. Benjamin's six months' service as war minister could not be described as a success, but he did leave his successors a well-organized department, something that he had not found.

Assuming his new duties on March 17, Benjamin felt quite at home in the State Department. He was a master of French, the language of diplomacy, and a student of many aspects of international law. Furthermore, he was a true cosmopolite and delighted in intrigue.

In that spring of 1862 Richmond was a beleaguered city. Once General George B. McClellan's forces came so close that they could see the church steeples and tell time by the chiming of clocks in the Confederate capital. Summer saw the gray forces shove back the blue in the Seven Days' Battle, but the fearful spring had already cost the Confederacy Shiloh and New Orleans.

During these anxious days, Benjamin labored to obtain foreign recognition for the Confederacy. Britain and France, of course, were the chief objects of his wooing. The Confederate ambassador to Paris was Benjamin's old political colleague, John Slidell. Working through Slidell, Benjamin appealed to Louis Napoleon on an undisguised basis of material interest. He offered the Emperor the right of introducing French products into the Confederacy "free of a duty for a certain defined period." He frankly admitted that the offer was made because "it becomes of primary importance to neglect no means of opening our ports, and thereby obtaining the articles most needed for the supply of the army." In July, Slidell offered Confederate assistance in Mexico, where France was having her troubles with Juarez, who enjoyed United States support.

In the fall, the Emperor, swayed by Benjamin's arguments, tried to get Britain and Russia to join France in proposing a six months' armistice and suspension of the blockade.

It became apparent that France, whatever the inducements, would not risk recognition of the Confederacy without British support.

Lincoln had issued his Emancipation Proclamation, excepting from its provisions certain specific areas where slaves were held by Union sympathizers. As a stroke of domestic policy, the move was a huge political success, but there was no reason as yet to think that it might prejudice Confederate fortunes in Europe. December brought Southern triumph at Fredericksburg, and Benjamin's hopes for British recognition soared.

What Benjamin failed to realize was that, though the English aristocracy for the most part seemed to sympathize with the Confederacy, their sympathy was not enough. Rapid extension of the suffrage had given a leverage of power to laboring classes who identified the fate of the slaves with their own in former times.

But England, and France with her, might yet be influenced by a successful Confederate offensive. For Benjamin, these hopes died on July 4, 1863, when Lee was defeated at Gettysburg and Vicksburg surrendered to the Federal troops. Benjamin was an optimist, but he was also a realist. After this day of double doom, he could not delude himself.

Nevertheless, Benjamin's smile was unchanged as he walked to work every morning. He continued to labor diligently at his office where, however much calumny the public might heap upon him, he was popular with his subordinates. More and more, he was Davis's chief confidant in the government. Mrs. Davis later said:

"Mr. Benjamin was always ready for work. Sometimes, with half an hour's recess, he remained with the executive from ten in the morning until nine at night, and together they traversed all the difficulties which encompassed our beleaguered land."

After these sessions, she said, the President "came home fasting, a mere mass of throbbing nerves and perfectly exhausted." Benjamin "was always fresh and buoyant."

Amazed at the contrast, the First Lady asked Benjamin the secret of his endurance. His answer was almost as puzzling as the circumstance itself: "I always carry to these cabinet meetings a small cake which I eat when I begin to feel fatigued and it freshens me up at once."

In a more confiding mood, he told her that it was useless to disturb oneself and thus weaken one's energy to bear trials that were fore-ordained. Accordingly, he was not depressed by reversals when he believed that he had done all in his power to prevent them.

It was a time of privation for many residents of Richmond, of want sufficient to provoke a riot in 1863. Yet, occasionally Benjamin would be among favored dinner guests of a hostess who could boast, "We succeeded in running the blockade this week." He then could count on such rarities as good coffee and tea, preserved fruits, loaf sugar, and McHenry sherry. On these occasions, Benjamin maintained, "a man's patriotism became rampant."

Benjamin still found satisfaction, too, in bringing pleasure to others in innumerable small ways. After a banquet at the Confederate White House, he jubilantly brought some of the delicacies home in a napkin to Jules, his young brother-in-law, who now made his home with him. He delighted equally in showering attentions on a wallflower at a dance.

Even at the office, he seems to have found a boyish pleasure in communicating with diplomats by secret code and in devouring the reports of secret agents operating in enemy territory.

In December 1864, Benjamin sent an envoy to Europe to offer emancipation of the slaves in exchange for recognition. But the move was too late.

In the spring of 1865, the scent of death was in the air. It seemed to permeate like a fog almost every nook of Confederate officialdom. But a visitor to Benjamin's neat brick home at 9 West Main Street reported that there "blazing fires and an absolutely immaculate interior banished surface gloom and despondency." And yet the smiling host had sent his chief clerk southward in March with boxes and trunks of state papers. By April 5, they were stored in Charlotte, North Carolina, variously marked "W.J.B.," "J.P.B.," "G.O.," "D. F. Kenner," and "St. Martin" so as not to excite suspicion. Benjamin, for all his air of smiling complacency, had been preparing for evacuation of Richmond long before April 1 when Lee notified the President that the Confederate position on the James must be abandoned "at once."

A little after 11 P.M., Benjamin and other cabinet officers, together with President Davis, left Richmond for Danville on a slow-moving train. The near-sixteen-hour ride to the temporary capital, which promised to be so very temporary, was an ordeal of nerves. But the strain on his fellow passengers was relieved by Benjamin, who was still a gourmet even on the slender resources available to a refugee. He discussed the merits of a sandwich as cheerfully as he might have discoursed on the peculiar properties of an imported delicacy. He talked, too, Secretary of the Navy Mallory later recalled, of "other great national causes which had been redeemed from far gloomier reverses." Probably no one was more aware than Benjamin that the Confederacy was already near the end of the road to surrender. He was acting according to a habit ingrained since boyhood: keeping a cheerful countenance and making himself agreeable to his companions.

His Danville hosts found him a delightful and adaptable guest who even fitted perfectly into their custom of Christian prayers in the morning. Dr. Moses Hoge, a scholarly fellow refugee who was Benjamin's roommate, afterwards recalled those perilous times with pleasure. The cabinet officer's humor had been irresistible and he had "seemed to be as familiar with literature as with law."

When Benjamin returned from a walk one day in April, the ladies found him every whit as cheerful as usual. Then he casually left the room, motioning to Dr. Hoge to follow him. Behind the closed door of their bedroom, he told him, "I did not have the heart to tell those good ladies what I have just learned. General Lee has surrendered and the Confederate cause is lost."

What would Benjamin do? Accompany President Davis and other officials to Greensboro. After that, he did not know. "But how will it be possible to escape capture?" Dr. Hoge asked. Later, Dr. Hoge recalled, "I will never forget the expression of his countenance or the pitiless smile which accompanied his words when he said, 'I will never be taken alive.'"

There followed the overnight flight by train, with the Presidential party crossing a bridge just before Federal troops burned it. Greensboro, partly Unionist in sentiment and fearful of harboring refugees sought by the Federal invaders, allowed the cabinet the hospitality of a leaky boxcar. Benjamin cheered his colleagues with his talents as a raconteur. At a hastily called cabinet meeting, Generals Johnston and Beauregard said that further resistance was useless. Indeed, Johnston declared that it would be a crime. All the cabinet concurred with the exception of Benjamin. Although he knew the hard realities of a situation in which the Confederacy could field an estimated 25,000 men as compared with 350,000 in Federal uniforms, Benjamin seemed loath to destroy Davis's illusion that the South could still fight on.

There was no question about the fact that the Confederate officials must get out of Greensboro. The railroad tracks had been cut by the Federal troops. Davis, his staff, and some of the cabinet officials, accompanied by a cavalry guard, set out on horseback over muddy roads to Charlotte. The comfort-loving Benjamin, who had never liked unnecessary physical exercise, and whose ponderous weight was enough to discourage any horse, vowed that he would not sit in a saddle until forced to. So he, two other officials, and his brother-in-law rode in a horse-drawn ambulance like a caboose to the long train of horses.

A horseman who rode back to check on the rear of the column found the ambulance mired in a hole. But, even before reaching the vehicle, he could "see from afar the occasional bright glow of Benjamin's cigar." The Secretary of State's spirits glowed no less brightly. He was still seated in the ambulance, and, for the benefit of his companions, who were wrapped in a silence as deep as the gloom of night, he was intoning Tennyson's lines:

Lead out the pageant : sad and slow,
As fits an universal woe,

Let the long, long procession go,
And let the sorrowing crowd about it grow,
And let the mournful martial music blow. . . .

Arrived in Charlotte, Benjamin, who had already pronounced the requiem of the Confederacy in the English laureate's verses, supported his views by logical argument. Davis had requested his written opinion as to whether the Confederate States should accept the terms of surrender which Sherman had offered Johnston. Benjamin wrote that the fight could be pursued further only in guerrilla warfare, which "would entail far more suffering on our own people than it would cause damage to the enemy."

Through South Carolina and into Georgia, the Presidential party fled. On May 3, when they were about twenty miles from Washington, Georgia, Benjamin told Davis that he would part from him now to rejoin him later in the Trans-Mississippi District. Like other cabinet members, Benjamin knew that they must all flee for their lives and that there was no hope of a revitalized campaign west of the Mississippi. But he couldn't bear to tell Davis so.

The military escort knew what he had in mind and were saddened. They had enjoyed Benjamin's seemingly inexhaustible good humor. They knew that he was unaccustomed to "roughing it," and were sure that, of all the top officials, he was most likely to be caught.

But the smiling lion, for all his soft purring and feline guile, was no parlor cat. In a series of exciting adventures, he proved that fact. Wearing a cloak and goggles (almost too classic a disguise), he drove a horse and buggy across the Florida border as "Monsieur Bonfals." In Florida, attired in homespun clothes, he rode a mule and pretended to be a farmer looking for a place to settle. He was often hard put to discover whether he was among Unionists or Confederates. Once he was relieved to come upon admirers of Jefferson Davis by following a parrot that squawked, "Hi for Jeff!" He knew that escape, if at all possible, must be by the Gulf Coast rather than the well-patrolled Atlantic Coast of Florida.

With the help of a friendly guide, he reached the massive-columned Gamble mansion, near the Manatee River. For several weeks, he stayed in this setting of tropical beauty reminiscent of Belle Chasse and the plantation life which now was over for him, and for so many other Southerners. Once Federal troops raided the place and Benjamin and another occupant of the house had to dash out the kitchen door, followed unfortunately by an excited small dog. While the two fugitives crouched in the bushes, the troops came close enough for Benjamin to have reached out and touched their blue uniforms. But he remained very still, the dog made no sound and the soldiers did not persist in their search.

The mansion was no longer a dependable refuge. But the world outside seemed to offer threats almost as great. Nevertheless, Benjamin's leavetaking was jaunty. Clad in a blue denim suit made for him by the ladies of the mansion, he clowned for the children before saying goodbye. He crossed the Manatee to the home of Captain Fred Tresca, a native of France with a longtime knowledge of Florida's West Coast waterways. Staying with the Trescas two weeks, he endeared himself to the family, especially the children.

From here on, Benjamin's adventures were sheer melodrama. In a yawl raised from a creek bottom and manned by Captain Tresca and others, he made his way down the coast of Florida. Soon after they set out on June 23, a Federal gunboat spotted them but their shallow-draft boat hid in Gasparilla Pass and eluded the enemy, though the searchers were near enough once for Benjamin to hear their Yankee twang borne on the warm Florida air. Later, another gunboat overhauled them and searchers boarded the yawl. They saw Benjamin, but his round face was smeared with grease and soot and he was wearing a cook's apron and skull cap. The Yankees were not interested.

About July 7, Benjamin reached Knight's Key and embarked in a large sailboat, this one rakishly named the *Blonde*. The black fury of a tropical storm struck and two waterspouts narrowly missed the boat. Bailing with his hat, Benjamin turned to the skipper, smiled, and said, "This is not like being Secretary of State." True, but it was not unlike being Secretary of War.

On July 10, they reached the British-owned Bimini Islands. Benjamin, thinking that his perils were over, took passage for Nassau. But the next morning, thirty-five miles from shore, the sloop began sinking so fast that he barely had time to take to a rowboat.

Benjamin later wrote his sister :

> In the skiff, leaky, with but a single oar, with no provisions save a pot of rice that had just been cooked for breakfast, and a small keg of water, I found myself at eight o'clock in the morning, with three Negroes for my companions in disaster, only five inches of the boat out of water, on the broad ocean, with the certainty that we could not survive five minutes if the sea became the least rough.

Benjamin entertained while his three companions sculled with the single oar. A lighthouse yacht rescued them and carried them back to the Biminis. From there, he sailed again for Nassau, professing to be a "contented and cheerful" man. After safe arrival, he sent words of cheer to his relatives in the South and presents to those who had helped him escape.

He embarked for England via Havana. This time the ship was almost destroyed by fire and barely made the port of St. Thomas. But on August 30, Benjamin—no doubt smiling as blandly as usual— arrived in Southampton, England. He was technically a British citizen by virtue of his birth in a British possession, and he was determined to begin a new career at the English bar.

Eight months after he settled in London, a bank failed, carrying with it a huge part of his savings. But he supplemented his income by writing editorials on foreign affairs for the London *Daily Telegraph*. He was reduced to subsisting sometimes on bread and cheese, but he probably appraised each with a gourmet's perception.

Only a year after his flight to England, Benjamin won admission to the English bar. Within a few more years, he was one of the leading barristers in the realm and was the author of a treatise on the law of sales that was the foremost authority in its field. By 1870, he was Queen's Counsel for Lancashire. He was presented a patent of precedence by the Lord Chancellor. He enjoyed this prestige and, despite off-handedly humorous references in letters to his relatives, probably relished his presentation at a royal levee to which he wore a full-bottomed, shoulder-length wig, knee breeches, buckled shoes, silk judicial robes, and the same old smile.

Those who saw him savoring his after-dinner wine and fine cigars could scarcely conceive of his stupendous labors in the day. His earnings were growing apace, but he was dispensing them liberally among his blood relatives and Natalie, who was living in Paris with Ninette.

When increasing infirmity forced his retirement from the bar in 1883, he was a national figure. The London *Times* said that he had been "almost the leader of the English bar in all heavy appeal cases." The London *Telegraph,* reflecting general amazement over Benjamin's rapid mastery of English practice, observed, "The history of the English bar will hereafter have no prouder story to tell than that of the marvelous advance of Mr. Benjamin from the humble position he occupied as a junior in 1866 to the front rank of his profession in 1883." Many of the most prominent men in the kingdom honored him with a farewell banquet. Benjamin had made himself agreeable as well as respected.

Now seventy-two years old, suffering from diabetes and heart trouble, Benjamin moved to France and made his home in the French-speaking household that he had provided for Natalie. When it was necessary for her to have an operation, he sat by her side and held her hand the entire time.

But there were no operations or other medical treatments then known to save Benjamin. He died May 6, 1884.

In the years that followed, men forgot many things about Benjamin, but the memory of his smile survived. Indeed, historically, Benjamin has been in danger of becoming like the Cheshire cat in *Alice in Wonderland* who faded away until all had vanished but the grin,

To what extent was the smile a genuine reflection of Benjamin's feelings, particularly after he had to flee the Confederacy? Whether or not he missed sunny days on the lower Mississippi, he became a lion again in the fogs of London.

The last pen portrait of Benjamin seen by many Americans was published in the *New York Times* in 1879. A correspondent of that newspaper had interviewed him at the start of the new year. "Rarely," said the reporter, "have I met a smile so genial as that which welcomed me from the little gentleman whom Abraham Lincoln considered the 'smartest' of all the Richmond Revolutionary Junta. . . . Mr. Benjamin's physique is eminently Southern, of that jolly, well-fed Southern type which so nearly resembles the traditional John Bull. . . ."

"Nobody will call you a Yankee, anyway," the reporter said.

Benjamin laughed. Then, smiling, he replied, "I was born what I am—an Englishman."

JUDAH P. BENJAMIN

Bibliography

Butler, Pierce. *Judah P. Benjamin*. Philadelphia, 1906. All subsequent biographers of Judah P. Benjamin are indebted to Butler for the preservation and organization of the basic data on Benjamin's life. As a source book on Benjamin, it is still unsurpassed.

Evans, Eli N. *Judah P. Benjamin, the Jewish Confederate*. New York, 1989.

Meade, Robert Douthat. *Judah P. Benjamin, Confederate Statesman*. New York, 1943. The most readable book-length biography of Benjamin and the work of a sound scholar.

Davis, Varina Howell. *Jefferson Davis, a Memoir*, Vol. II. New York, 1890. Insights into Benjamin's relations with Davis and his informal manner in the company of friends. Especially worth noting are pp. 175–177, 207–208, 632.

Jones, J. B. *A Rebel War Clerk's Diary*, Vols. I and II. New York, 1935. Vol. I is especially valuable for its portraits of Benjamin as seen by an employee. Particularly informative are pp. 38, 64–65, 71, 73–75, 78–79, 84–181. In pp. 73–75 and 78–79, we have a firsthand account of the circumstances leading to Walker's resignation as Secretary of War and Benjamin's appointment to that office.

De Leon, Thomas C. *Four Years in Confederate Capitals*. Mobile, Ala., 1890. This volume is a source of anecdotes about Benjamin and of the gossip concerning him in his time. Particularly enlightening are pp. 34, 159–165, 277.

Dowdey, Clifford. *Experiment in Rebellion*. Garden City, 1950. Insights into Benjamin's relations with President Davis.

Hendrick, Burton J. *Statesmen of the Lost Cause: Jefferson Davis and His Cabinet*. Boston, 1939.

Patrick, Rembert W. *Jefferson Davis and His Cabinet*. Baton Rouge, 1944.

Wise, John S. *The End of an Era*. Boston, 1902. Firsthand portraits of Benjamin from a discerning but unfriendly source. Because the author was the son of Henry A. Wise, his account of the fall of Roanoke Island and the preliminary interview between the general and Benjamin, pp. 174–190, is especially interesting.

McElroy, Robert. *Jefferson Davis*, Vols. I and II. New York, 1937. Benjamin's role in the cabinet, Vol. I, p. 274; Vol. II, pp. 423–425, 432–433, 444–446, 471, 480–482, 492–493.

Goodhart, Arthur L. *Five Jewish Lawyers of the Common Law*. London, 1949. Benjamin discussed, pp. 4–15, 63–66. Of particular interest is the appraisal of Benjamin's legal scholarship by the author, professor of jurisprudence at Oxford.

Thomas J. Jackson Papers, Virginia Historical Society, Richmond, Va. Includes Jackson's letter of January 31, 1862 to Benjamin on Loring matter; also, Benjamin letter to Jackson in December 1864.

Southern Historical Society Papers, Vol. XXVI, ed. R. A. Brock. Richmond, 1898. "Retreat of the Confederate States Cabinet" by Capt. Micajah H. Clark, pp. 98–101.

(Confederate Museum, Richmond)

V

JOSEPH E. JOHNSTON: Bold Retreater

V

JOSEPH E. JOHNSTON: Bold Retreater

A Pair of Paradoxes

YOUNG LIEUTENANT F. Y. DABNEY was worried—and with reason. He was part of General Joseph E. Johnston's army retreating up the Peninsula toward Richmond. General George B. McClellan's Union forces were close on their heels—so close that, badly as the Confederacy needed guns and transport, Johnston had ordered "that any gun caisson or commissary wagon which might become set in the mud so as to impede the line of march must be destroyed at once." A cannon entrusted to the lieutenant's care had sunk over its axle in the soft Tidewater mud. The team of horses pulled to no avail. The drivers put their hands to the wheels, and still the gun did not budge. It remained stalled even when the lieutenant added his own strength and weight.

Long lines of men were now piling up in the blocked road. But, despite his anxiety about incurring a superior officer's wrath, the lieutenant was loath to part with his gun. Even when a party of officers appeared, he renewed his frantic efforts in hopes that the gun could be moved before they reached him. He and his men were still sweating and straining when the officers drew rein. Dabney looked up and was alarmed to see astride the lead horse an immaculately uniformed officer in spotless Confederate gray with bright gold

366

epaulets and the gold stars of a general on his collar. The piercing eyes under the domed forehead, the crisp cut of the iron gray mustache and goatee, even the way the white gauntleted hands held the reins, bespoke authority and decision. The man was General Johnston himself. Dabney saluted and "stood like a criminal awaiting sentence."

"Well, Lieutenant," the General said, "you seem to be in trouble." The lieutenant blushingly explained his plight. "Let me see what I can do," Johnston said. Almost in one motion, he swung down from his horse, waded into the mire, seized one of the muddy wheel spokes with his gloved hands, and shouted, "Now, boys, all together!" The men lunged forward and the gun jumped clear of the mudhole.

Years later, this incident on the road to Richmond was one of Dabney's most vivid memories of the war. "After that," he would say, "our battery used to swear by 'Old Joe!'"

This same man who was "Old Joe" to his devoted soldiers, and who did not hesitate to lend a hand in dirty labor, was regarded by President Jefferson Davis, Secretary of War Benjamin, and less prejudiced civil authorities as an officer intensely jealous of the prerogatives of his rank. This paradox is not the most conspicuous one of his career. His contemporaries wondered, and posterity has continued the speculation, why a man whose personal courage in combat caused him to be compared to a gamecock should also be known as "the greatest retreater" in the Confederate armies.

A plausible explanation of both paradoxes seems implicit in the story of his life.

Joseph Eggleston Johnston was born February 3, 1807 at Cherry Grove, the family plantation in Prince Edward County, Virginia. His father, Judge Peter Johnston of the Virginia General Court, was a former Speaker of the House of Delegates. A hero of the Revolutionary War, while still in his teens he had been a lieutenant in the famed legion of "Light Horse Harry" Lee. Young Joseph's mother was a niece of Patrick Henry.

When Joe was fours years old, the family moved to Panicello, a country home near Abingdon in the blue-misted mountain country of

Southwest Virginia. Judge Johnston delighted in gunning for the wild game which abounded in the heavily wooded Wolf Hills and his sons early in life became his hunting companions. There were seven boys older than Joe. Like many another plantation lad of his class, Joe was brought up to shoot straight, ride well, and tell the truth.

In addition to these manly virtues, a number of cultural interests were inculcated in the boy. Family reading, with members taking turns at reading aloud, was a favorite recreation of the Johnstons. Little Joe's imagination was fired by Sir Walter Scott's tales of border warfare, which, emphasizing chivalry, loyalty to the clan, and regional patriotism, appealed strongly to Southerners. The boy must often have imagined himself a knightly defender of his native soil when he and his playmates, armed with cornstalks, sallied forth against the invading foe. Many a time he relived the adventures of the rebels of Kings Mountain. Some veterans of that Revolutionary engagement lived near him. He never tired of listening to their stories and then re-enacting the struggle with a troop of little boys at his command.

When ten years old, he charged on horseback an "infantry position" prepared under his directions. As a result of this realism, Joe's leg was broken, the bone tearing through the flesh. It was set crookedly. Then the stitches were removed and the limb was reset properly. Without benefit of anesthesia, the little boy endured the entire ordeal without a tear or a groan.

His first education was at home. Then he attended the Abingdon Academy. Throughout this period, his interest in his Revolutionary heritage and in military affairs continued, so that it became evident that his was more than the temporary enthusiasm of the average child who delights in playing soldier.

Though Joe was the eighth of nine sons, it was he to whom Judge Johnston presented the sword that he had wielded in the Revolution under "Light Horse Harry" Lee.

At the age of eighteen, with a good academy record behind him, Joe was appointed to West Point. Small but manly, he had a pride nourished by family tradition and possibly reinforced by the game-cock spirit that characterizes so many small men of large courage.

Robert E. Lee, son of Judge Johnston's old general, was also at the Academy, and the two became fast friends. Both were fun-loving, but both took little delight in the company of the hell raisers. Young Lee became Joe's idol and he said years later that at that time "everyone recognized his superiority." If Johnston was sensitive, he was not offended by Lee's teasing, even when his friend gently chided him for a fault.

The two Virginians vowed to uphold the honor of the Old Dominion at the Academy. They made good their promise. Johnston did not compile so spectacular a record as his friend but, like his, it was notable for excellent deportment. Moreover, despite eye trouble that prevented night study, Johnston was graduated 13th in a class of 46. More important than his class standing was the fact that he carried away from the Academy intellectual enthusiasms that insured continuation of his education in the years after graduation. Besides being interested in military history and biography, he delighted in astronomy and French.

He already was distinguished by dignity and a military bearing, attested to by his West Point nickname of "Colonel."

Commissioned a second lieutenant in the Fourth Artillery, he served at various Atlantic Seaboard posts from 1829 to 1836.

One of the most pleasant of these assignments was to Fort Monroe, where Lee was also stationed. The two were very nearly unique there for their continence and temperance. But they thoroughly enjoyed the friendship of fellow officers given to more uninhibited pleasures. As Dr. Douglas S. Freeman observed in his *R. E. Lee,* "If the pair walked not in the counsel of the ungodly, they had no compunctions about standing in the way of sinners, at least to see what the sinners were doing."

One of Johnston's few exciting assignments during this period came when South Carolina's adoption of the Ordinance of Nullification provoked a national crisis over States' rights. Ironically enough, in the light of his later life, Johnston was part of the Federal force sent to enforce the will of the national government. At this time, three of his brothers were members of a State force preparing to resist the Federal troops. The crisis receded, but was not forgotten.

Later, Johnston was sent to the Florida theater, where he served as aide to Major General Winfield Scott in a war against the Seminoles and their almost invincible ally, the water wilderness that was their home. Johnston was promoted to first lieutenant in 1836 but, when the war was thought to be over, he resigned early in 1837 and became a civil engineer. He probably left the service because of the feeling prevalent among so many young officers in his day that Congress had little interest in the army and that military advancement would be unconscionably slow.

In September it became evident that, whatever the Federal government may have assumed, the Seminoles did not consider the war over in Florida. Johnston immediately volunteered to serve without military rank. As adjutant and topographical engineer, he accompanied a party of civilians and service men commissioned to survey areas of South Florida to determine the best sites for forts and depots. On January 15, 1838, a detachment including Johnston was exploring near the head of an inlet of the Indian River when a band of Seminoles appeared. Fierce fighting began and, one by one, all the officers received incapacitating wounds. Johnston immediately assumed command. The little gamecock sprang into the fray with an enthusiasm whetted by the bullets that whistled through his uniform and riddled his streaming red sash. Even when he received a surface wound on his forehead, he fought on like a bloody-combed champion of the pit. Thanks to him, the retreat to the boats did not become a rout. A member of the expedition recorded, "The coolness, courage, and judgment he displayed at the most critical and trying emergency was the theme of praise of everyone who beheld him."

This day's work was exactly the sort of thing of which Johnston had dreamed as a boy and for which he had bargained on entering the service. Army life might not be so dull after all. In July, he secured reappointment as a first lieutenant in the Corps of Topographical Engineers. Simultaneously, "for gallantry on several occasions in the war against the Florida Indians," he was brevetted to captain.

Johnston was not to see such excitement again for a number of years. Routine engineering duties consumed most of his professional time. There were no opportunities for conquest of the Indians. In fact, the most notable event in Johnston's life at this time came July 10, 1845 when he himself became a conquest. He was married to Lydia McLane, the witty, animated sister of one of his closest army friends. She was the daughter of Louis McLane, president of the Baltimore and Ohio Railroad, a former United States Senator, minister to England, and Secretary of the Treasury under Jackson. She seems to have been as strong-minded as he and the two did not always see eye to eye, but they were obviously quite happy.

With the outbreak of war with Mexico in 1846, Johnston applied for active duty. He sailed with Scott's Vera Cruz expedition, sharing a cabin with Lee. Thus, in the school of war, he was in the distinguished class of Lee, Beauregard, McClellan, and Meade. He was soon transferred from the Topographical Engineers to a regiment of picked skirmishers, which he served as lieutenant colonel. For this duty, he put on a gray uniform. It doubtless seemed strange to him not to be wearing the traditional blue, but he would learn to fight in a gray uniform.

In daring reconnaissance, he pushed so close to enemy defenses at the mountain pass of Cerro Gordo that he was wounded twice by musket fire and had to be put on the sick list. He was cared for in a makeshift hospital with partitions of wattled reeds. One of Johnston's companions reported that another of the patients "uttered a stream of coarse wit" which flowed through the thin partitions hour after hour, arousing the Virginian's "great disgust." One day, Johnston heard the offender order his servant to seize a kid from a flock of goats passing the door. Johnston startled all around him by the eruption of his anger. "If you dare to do that," he vowed, "I'll have you court-martialed and cashiered or shot!"

Johnston's devoted nurse much of the time was his orphaned nephew, Preston Johnston, a lieutenant of artillery, to whom he had been almost a second father.

Johnston recovered in time to participate in the fighting at Churubusco as Scott's army closed in on Mexico City. In this same part of the campaign, Preston Johnston was killed. Lee came upon Johnston just after the old friend had learned of his nephew's death. Ordinarily, Johnston's proud carriage made him seem not quite so short as he actually was, but now his "frame [was] shrunk, and shivered in agony."

Johnston was a conspicuous participant in the battle of Molino Del Rey and the storming of Chapultepec. He was brevetted colonel for "gallant and meritorious conduct." With a grandiloquence typical of military citations in that period, General Gideon J. Pillow reported that the "very gallant and accomplished Lieutenant Colonel Johnston" had "received three wounds, but they were all slight and did not at all arrest his daring and onward movements." Old General Scott is supposed to have pronounced, in more practical fashion, "Johnston is a great soldier, but he has an unfortunate knack of getting himself shot in nearly every engagement."

After the conclusion of the Mexican War in 1848, Johnston returned to the rank of Captain in the Topographical Engineers. Once again came deadly routine, relieved by some opportunities for Western exploration.

A promise of adventure came in 1855 when Johnston was commissioned Lieutenant Colonel of the First Cavalry as Congress expanded that arm to meet the threat of Indian wars on the Great Plains.

The excitement did not come, but during this period Johnston developed a close friendship with an officer nineteen years his junior. In some ways, the younger man may have taken the place of the dead nephew. Johnston seems to have regarded him almost as a member of his family or as a protégé. He dearly loved to discuss army affairs with him and confided in him to an unusual degree. A common salutation in his letters to him was, "Beloved Mc." Interestingly enough, the young man's name was George B. McClellan.

When McClellan decided that he would quit the Federal service because he would not be happy in the United States Army, Johnston was also dissatisfied because of what he considered a paralyzing "old fogeyism" in the upper echelons. When Johnston learned that McClellan had resigned, he wrote him : "It has overturned a great many castles-in-the-air on the subject of professional daily talks— reading—fencing—marches and campfire talks—chases of buffalo, wolves, and Indians. There is no one left in the regiment or army to take your place. I wish I was young enough to resign too."

Johnston was transferred to Washington for detached duty in the late 1850's. Mrs. Johnston, as the daughter of a Washington luminary of earlier years and a wit in her own right, sailed through Washington society with a bright and sparkling wake. Some Washingtonians boasted that a female triumvirate of their number, including Mrs. Johnston and Mrs. Jefferson Davis, comprised "the cleverest women in the United States."

John B. Floyd, a Virginian and Johnston's cousin by marriage, was Secretary of War. Floyd fully appreciated Johnston's talents and had no hesitation about advancing merit when it occurred in his own family. The choice assignments that came Johnston's way drew suspicions of favoritism even from his friends. No one impugned his honor. No one close to him could imagine his cheating in any way to gain advantage. But he apparently was not a young man to leave any task unattempted or any influential relative uncultivated that might gain him advancement. He thirsted for reputation.

Ambition can lead even a conscientious man up strange paths, and Johnston apparently considered taking an exotic one in 1857. In that year the filibuster—the soldier of fortune, not the Congressional orator—bestrode the islands of the Caribbean and the banana republics, stirring the embers of revolt with his booted feet and cutting with his sword a broad and bloody swath across the imagination of the world. In every clime, men who hungered for glory, and some who hungered for spoils, had their appetites whetted by tales of adventure from south of the border. Some of the filibusterers were idealists, and even those who were not could tell themselves that they were fighting to advance the cause of liberty.

In this year, Johnston and McClellan corresponded with each other in mysterious terms concerning some Latin American project. Two years later, when Mexico was seething with internal conflict, Johnston wrote McClellan from Vera Cruz that he had "some faint hope of founding a Spanish castle upon the basis of last year. I shall write to you from Vera Cruz whatever I can learn from party leaders and conditions of affairs generally." Later Johnston wrote :

I am already convinced that there is no chance for anything like our schemes of last year. The leaders, both civil and military, are too jealous of us to adopt any such course—they had rather run the risk of being overthrown by the opposite party of their countrymen, than that of being supplanted in the control of their own party by us. . . . Our castles in the air, my dear Mc, are blown away. You'll have to consent to becoming a rich civilian, instead of a member of a small but select party of maintainers of human liberty.

So back to Washington. But better things awaited him there. He was sent to New Mexico as acting inspector general. In 1860 he was made quartermaster general with the rank of brigadier general. Even Lee, who rejoiced in the success of his old friend, confided to his own son, "In proportion to his services, he has been advanced beyond anyone in the army . . . ."

On December 20, South Carolina seceded. One by one, sister states followed : each act of secession, as one Virginian picturesquely observed, like the crack of a sail blown from the ship of state.

On March 15, 1861, Confederate Secretary of War Leroy P. Walker, not waiting for action by Johnston's native state, offered him an appointment as brigadier-general.

About the same time, General Scott, now General in Chief of the army, tried to persuade Johnston to remain in the Federal service. He even sought the aid of Johnston's strong-minded wife. "Get him to stay with us," Mrs. Johnston said he told her. "We will never disturb him in any way."

She replied very much as Johnston would have : "My husband cannot stay in an army which is about to invade his native country."

"Then let him leave our army," Scott urged, "but do not let him join theirs."

Mrs. Johnston's answer to this question was on a more mundane level than her husband's would have been. "This is all very well," she said, "but how is Joe Johnston to live? He has no private fortune, no profession but that of arms.'

The Virginia Convention to consider secession had already voted down, 88 to 45, a resolution to implement such an ordinance when President Lincoln appealed to the governor of Virginia for troops. Quickly the Convention reversed itself.

Johnston's dreams of glory had been bound up with the traditions of Virginia. When his state left the Union he must go with her, without weighing the professional advantages and disadvantages, which ordinarily loomed large in his ambitious mind.

Despite her defense of Johnston's views in her conversation with Scott, Mrs. Johnston tried hard to persuade her husband to remain in the United States Army. She was from Delaware and Maryland, and for her secession meant breaking cherished family ties. She used many arguments. She worried over the fact that Jefferson Davis, who had been Secretary of War, was provisional President of the Confederacy. She had come to have a low opinion of the Mississippian, whose wife had once been her "inseparable" friend. Harping on Davis, she insisted, "He hates you. He has power and he will ruin you."

To all these adjurations, Johnston replied with laconic finality, "He can't, I don't care, my country," and wrote his resignation.

He left for Richmond with his father's Revolutionary sword under his arm. Like Lee, who had resigned on the same date, April 20, Johnston was the sort of Virginian to draw inspiration from remembered stories of his father's heroic role in the birth of a nation. Johnston called upon Lee, who had been made Major General and

Commander in Chief of the Old Dominion's military and naval forces. On Lee's recommendation, Johnston was commissioned a major general, and Lee gave him the task of organizing the troops pouring into Richmond by the carload.

Lee and Johnston were both fifty-four years old. They had seen each other little since the Mexican War days. As is common among any separated companions, each must have been surprised at the aging of the other. Johnston's hair had receded still farther from his domelike forehead, and what remained was almost as gray as his beard. But the gray eyes still sparkled with youthful brightness, and the austerity of his face when in repose heightened the appealing good humor of his occasional smiles. His ramrod posture still stretched his small frame to the maximum number of inches.

What did fellow officers and leaders of the Confederacy other than Lee think of him? Senator James Chesnut of South Carolina declared that Johnston had "all the qualities which [could] attract men to him. . . . a gift of the gods." The devotion of his friends, young men as well as those his own age, testified to the truth of this judgment. Johnston inspired not only respect but love, even among those who acknowledged that he was "critical, controversial, and sometimes irritable by nature." Some considered him "the best-read soldier in America" and all thought he was highly ambitious. One of his associates revealed more than many paragraphs of description when he casually observed that Johnston hated "to be beaten even at a game of billiards."

Johnston was chagrined within a few weeks after his arrival in Richmond by the reduction of his rank from major general to brigadier general. This action was prompted by the belief that the commander of the state's military and naval forces should be the only major general. Confederate commissions independent of the separate states were being issued by the government in Montgomery. Johnston visited the provisional capital and secured the commission of Brigadier General, C.S.A. Johnston also took pains to renew his acquaintance with old friends in the civil government and to meet officials unknown to him.

Lee, at this time, had declined transfer to the Regular Army, preferring to retain his rank as an officer of the state troops. Nevertheless, Davis made Lee commander of all Confederate troops in Virginia. Thus Lee was still the superior of Johnston, who had outranked him in the United States Army.

Johnston was ordered to assume command at Harper's Ferry, Virginia. This town, site of a former Federal arsenal, stood at the confluence of the Shenandoah and Potomac rivers and commanded the Potomac crossing of the Baltimore and Ohio Railroad. Johnston relieved Thomas Jonathan Jackson, with whom he was already acquainted. Jackson remained to assist in continuation of the training program already begun with the 8,000 troops available.

On May 20, transfer of the Confederate capital from Montgomery to Richmond began. In April, Virginia's army had been transferred to the Confederacy. These changes precipitated near mutiny among some of the Union-minded troops from Western Virginia (soon to become the state of West Virginia) who refused to acknowledge the Confederate government. Many deserted. Johnston sent armed details after them. The effectiveness of his disciplinary measures prompted enthusiastic comment from a Northern correspondent on the scene. Nevertheless, Johnston knew that part of his force was unreliable and that it was stationed in the midst of a population in large part hostile. Across the Potomac, mighty armies were gathering with the capture of Harper's Ferry one of their aims. Johnston concluded that he could not hold the point against an equal force, much less a superior one, and that the location was not of great strategic importance anyway. He apprised Richmond officials of his findings.

Lee replied that the loss of Harper's Ferry would have a bad effect on public morale. Johnston answered that loss of its garrison would give the people just as big a jolt and would be a much more serious military blow.

Early in June, Lee reminded Johnston that President Davis placed "great value upon our retention of the command of the Shenandoah Valley and the position at Harper's Ferry."

Johnston now besieged Richmond with requests for more specific orders. Adjutant General Samuel Cooper replied. After prefacing his instructions with a polite expression of confidence in Johnston's "sound judgment and soldierly qualifications," he said :

As you seem to desire . . . that the responsibility of your retirement should be assumed here, and as no reluctance is felt to bear any burden which the public interests should require, you will consider yourself authorized, whenever the position of the enemy shall convince you that he is about to turn your position and thus deprive the country of the use of yourself and the troops under your command, to destroy everything at Harper's Ferry . . . and retire upon the railroad towards Winchester. . . .

Johnston replied at once in graceless prose, revealing that Cooper had probed a sensitive spot : "I know myself to be a careless writer, and will not, therefore, pretend to have expressed clearly the opinions I wished to have put before the government. I am confident, however, that nothing in my correspondence with my military superiors makes me obnoxious [sic] to the charge of desiring that the responsibility of my official acts should be borne by any other than myself."

A Union army under General Robert Patterson already was moving south from Chambersburg, Pa. A few days later, Johnston learned that the entire Union Army was on the march toward Romney, about 60 miles west of Harper's Ferry. Ironically enough, it was commanded by McClellan, the "beloved Mc" of happier days.

Johnston sent two regiments toward Romney to deter the Yankees, and began a hurried evacuation of Harper's Ferry. The bridges over the Potomac and the railroad were destroyed. When Johnston's army left the town on June 15, it looked as though it had already been sacked by an invading host.

Word arrived that Patterson had crossed the Potomac and was marching on Martinsburg. Johnston changed his line of march to move on Bunker Hill, which commanded the Martinsburg-Winchester turnpike, believed to be Patterson's route.

With his troops aligned for battle at Bunker Hill, Johnston discovered that the Federal commanders did not share his ideas of their conquering might. Patterson withdrew across the Potomac. Johnston then withdrew to Winchester.

As reinforcements continued to come to Johnston, he reorganized his Army of the Shenandoah. Jeb Stuart, who had won his high esteem, was commander of the First Virginia Cavalry. To Jackson, who stood equally high in Johnston's favor, he entrusted the first of four brigades. The others were commanded by Francis S. Bartow, Barnard E. Bee, and Arnold Elzey.

Patterson recrossed the Potomac on July 2 and resumed his march toward Winchester. Johnston formed a line of battle to receive a Union attack. Patterson encamped at Martinsburg. Johnston waited four days, and then marched back to Winchester.

A storm of public criticism burst about Johnston's head. Many persons feared that retreating might be a habit with him. Some of Johnston's defenders shared his view that the preservation of a fighting force was more important than the holding of a plot of ground. At this difficult time, Johnston enjoyed the understanding sympathy of President Davis. The chief executive wrote him, "Follow the dictates of your own good judgment and true patriotism."

On July 17, Johnston received a telegram from General P. G. T. Beauregard, the handsome Creole hero of Ft. Sumter who commanded Confederate forces at Manassas. "War Department has ordered you to join me," the message read. "Do so immediately, if possible, and we will crush the enemy."

The strategic importance of Manassas was beyond dispute. It was in Northern Virginia at the junction of Virginia's main North–South Railroad with one leading westward into the Shenandoah Valley. Also obvious was the fact that either Beauregard or Johnston would be in great peril if forced to meet separately a mass attack by the united armies of Patterson, still menacing the Winchester area, and Major

General Irvin McDowell, then less than ten miles from Manassas. Nevertheless, not having yet received word from Richmond, Johnston made no movement. Instead, he sent Beauregard the question, "Is the enemy upon you in force?"

Shortly after midnight, Johnston received a message from Adjutant General Cooper: "General Beauregard is attacked. To strike the enemy a decisive blow, a junction of all your effective force will be needed. . . . In all the arrangements, exercise your discretion."

On the 18th, Johnston began the march to Manassas, with Stuart screening the movement. The army must move fast enough to reach Manassas before an alarm set Patterson's army in motion to join McDowell. Outside Winchester, Johnston halted his men to hear an order read by his officers. "Our gallant army under General Beauregard," said the document, "is now being attacked by overwhelming numbers. The commanding general hopes that his army will step out like men and make a forced march to save the country."

Until that moment, the troops had thought that they were retreating again. Now they shouted in their zest for battle, and marched with quickened step.

That night Johnston received a message from Beauregard embodying a grandiose plan for cooperation between Johnston and himself. The Louisianan wanted Johnston to abandon the plan to join forces at Manassas, and instead to proceed to Centerville and attack the right rear of McDowell's army. Beauregard would make a simultaneous attack on the enemy from the front. Johnston knew that raw troops could not be counted on for such precise maneuvers, and he rejected the plan.

A march begun at dawn brought the infantry to the railroad by 6 A.M. They then entrained for Manassas, leaving the cavalry and artillery to come up under their own power.

About midday on the 20th, Johnston, the circles under his eyes more conspicuous after the loss of nearly two nights' sleep, stepped off the train at Manassas Junction. Only about two fifths of his troops were at hand, drawn almost entirely from Bee's and Bartow's brigades. These he organized temporarily under Bee. He then conferred with Beauregard. Johnston had now been made a full general, a promotion long expected by him but one which apparently had not yet been officially announced. Johnston wired the President a request for the announcement "to prevent the possibility of a doubt of the relative rank of General Beauregard and myself in the eyes of the former."

The prompt reply was: "You are a General in the Confederate Army, possessed of the power attaching to that rank. You will know how to make the exact knowledge of Brigadier General Beauregard, as well of the ground as of the troops and preparation, avail for the success of the object in which you cooperate. The zeal of both assures me of harmonious action."

Beauregard explained that his own army, consisting of seven brigades and reinforced by an eighth from General Theophilus H. Holmes, was strung out in a seven-mile line extending from the stone bridge over Bull Run on the left to a railroad crossing on the right. Troops at the center of the line, under command of the iron-nerved Brigadier General James Longstreet, had repelled a Federal attack two days before. An ominous silence had followed. Both Johnston and Beauregard deemed it quite possible that McDowell awaited the arrival of Patterson, intending to crush Confederate forces at Manassas with the combined weight of the two Union armies. The two Confederate generals realized that they must strike before their opponents could join forces. McDowell's army was concentrated in the vicinity of Centerville, about three miles north of the center of the Confederate line. Beauregard already had prepared plans for an offensive in that area early the next day. Johnston assented. He then retired to get some sleep.

He was waked at dawn to read the battle orders which Beauregard and his staff had just finished preparing. He was disgruntled by the vagueness of the orders, but there was no time now for corrections. Reluctantly, he signed them, and dispatched them to the unit commanders.

The artillery and cavalry of Johnston's Army of the Shenandoah had arrived in the night, but the greater part of the infantry had not been heard from.

About 5 A.M., the Confederate generals learned that Federal troops were moving down the Warrenton Turnpike with the probable object of turning the Confederate left at the stone bridge. Immediately, the carefully prepared battle orders with all their resonant obscurities were thrown out the window. Orders were issued for a diversion and preparations to meet an attack on the left.

About an hour later, the Confederate generals heard the sound of firing from the direction of the stone bridge. Immediately they rode toward a hill from which they might observe the fighting. The sound of firing quickened Beauregard's martial ardor and he changed his mind again, this time calling for an offensive from the Confederate right. The message to the general whose brigade was supposed to lead the attack was never received. Consequently, there was no offensive.

The lightness of the Federal attack at the bridge made it evident that the effort there was a feint to divert attention from impending attack on another part of the Confederate line. Federal troops were soon spotted as they maneuvered to place themselves in the rear of the bridge's defenders. A little later, a large cloud of dust appeared on the horizon. It could be General Patterson coming to reinforce McDowell.

Johnston and Beauregard, from their post on Lookout Hill, awaited the Confederate advance, which had been ordered on the right, not knowing that those orders had not reached the brigadier. Johnston did not know what had stalled the attack, but he realized that it was now too late to execute it. More than ever, as the minutes passed into hours, he became convinced that the focal point of the struggle would be to the left. When the battle sounds suddenly reached a new crescendo, both commanders listened for a moment in dead silence. Then Johnston, obviously excited, exclaimed: "The battle is there! I am going." He strode briskly to his horse, shouted to his staff, "Mount and follow," and was off at a gallop before they were in the saddle. Beauregard, pausing only to order brigade commanders to move troops to the point of action, soon caught up with Johnston.

As the two generals rode on, they began to encounter stragglers in such numbers that it appeared possible the Confederates had already lost the day. Spurring their horses, they reached the plateau of Henry House Hill. Below them was a confused milling of Confederate troops like storm-roiled gray waters. A rock amid the turbulent waves was the well-placed brigade of General Jackson. Johnston had something to build on.

Nearby was a dispirited body of soldiers who did not know which way to turn. Johnston rode up to their color bearer and asked, "What regiment is this, and what are you doing here?"

"It is the 4th Alabama," was the answer. "Our officers have been disabled or killed, and there is no one left to command us."

Gripping the staff, Johnston called: "I will lead you. Follow me."

The color bearer retained his own grasp on the staff and walked quickly to keep pace with Johnston's horse. "General," he begged, "don't take my colors from me. Tell me where to carry them and I will place them there."

The General relinquished his hold and put a colonel in command of the men. They moved forward.

General Bee rode up. Tears rolled down his cheeks as he reported, "General, my command is scattered and I am alone."

Johnston replied, "I know it was not your fault, General Bee. But don't despair; the day isn't lost yet."

Exuding a confidence that proved contagious, Johnston welded scattered units into a new battalion under command of his ordnance officer. Amid the confusion of battle, he soon reduced chaos to order. At this point, Beauregard asked that Johnston, as over-all commander, retire to a more sheltered area to direct the battle while the Louisianan assumed command of the immediate front. With great reluctance, Johnston yielded to the logic of Beauregard's urging.

From a house about a mile to the rear, he sent orders to rush brigades from the center and right to the embattled left. A new report came of approaching Federal reinforcements. They might be Patterson's men. In any event the fate of the day was likely to be determined by the relative speed and efficiency with which the rival Federal and Confederate commanders brought up reinforcements and placed them in position.

Meanwhile, the bluecoats swarmed over the plateau and the gray lines swayed.

If only the troops Johnston had left behind in the railroad cars would arrive, the day might be saved. The Confederates would still be numerically inferior to their opponents, but the freshness of the new arrivals combined with the natural strength of the Confederate position might be sufficient to turn the tide.

These troops, commanded by General Kirby Smith, had been delayed by an engine failure and a collision. But a little after three o'clock, Smith got through with three regiments. Johnston ordered him to move to the left at once and attack the enemy in the flank. A fresh brigade of Beauregard's, commanded by Colonel Jubal A. Early, came up and Johnston sent it, too, to the left. As the new forces rushed forward into battle, Beauregard ordered a general advance all along the line.

The Federals fell back, then broke and ran.

Many distinguished citizens of Washington, including congressmen and government officials, had not suspected until now that the war literally would be no picnic. Ensconced in sleek carriages, and accompanied by their wives and daughters, they had ridden out from the city with basket lunches to encamp north of the battle ground. There they had expected the excitement of listening to the few volleys of shot necessary to disperse the rebels and then the pleasure of cheering the Yankee heroes!

They were panic-stricken when wild-eyed bluecoats plunged into their midst in headlong flight. Many of the carriages attempting to escape ahead of the fleeing soldiers jammed the roads, magnifying pandemonium. The pursuing Confederates were soon outdistanced by the Union soldiers who, in their alarm, threw aside their rifles and other impediments to fast running.

President Davis rode up to Johnston's headquarters just in time to learn that the battle had been won. He sent back to Richmond the message: "We have won a glorious though dear-bought victory. Night closed on the enemy in full flight and closely pursued."

That night, Johnston, Beauregard, and Davis assessed the victory and discussed possible future action. Both armies, Federal and Confederate, were composed of raw troops. As Johnston himself said, with only slight exaggeration, the Confederates were even more disorganized by victory than the Federals were by defeat. The pursuit by the Southerners had been as impulsive and disconnected as the Yankee flight. Efficient, organized pursuit would have to wait until the next day.

But, before daylight, a heavy rain began to fall. The streams rose and the roads were turned to mire. Pursuit seemed no longer practical. But there were compensations. The ordnance-poor Southerners found 28 artillery pieces, 4,500 muskets, and nearly half a million cartridges abandoned by the foe. When these gains were tallied some days later, Johnston wrote Davis in high spirits: "We hope to show you an efficient artillery soon—Northern matériel and Southern personnel."

The South was quick to idolize the two captains responsible for the first victory of the war. Both Johnston and Beauregard were extolled in a Senate resolution and in the editorial columns of many newspapers. As a professional soldier, Johnston was aware that his raw troops had shown less discipline than valor and thus probably had robbed the Confederacy of some of the fruits of triumph. But, in addition to his joy at Southern success, he could take professional pride in his early recognition of the need for concentration on the left and the skill with which he expedited the movement of troops to the vital sector. Also, there was satisfaction in being commander of the first victorious army to make extensive use of the telegraph and the railroad. He had helped to usher in a new era in military history.

Fighting Richmond

Three days after the Battle of Manassas, Johnston was surprised by the arrival of his old friend, Dabney Maury, a close companion of Mexican War days. He was shocked when he read the message which Maury handed him. It was an order from Lee appointing Maury Adjutant General to Johnston.

"This is an outrage!" the General exclaimed. "I rank General Lee, and he has no right to order officers into my army."

Quickly the gamecock reverted to the gentleman. Johnston put his arm around Maury's shoulder. He told him that he would rather have him for his Adjutant General than any other officer in the Army, but that he could not permit a flagrant infringement of his authority.

That day Johnston protested to General Cooper in Richmond:

I had already selected Major Rhett for the position in question who had entered upon its duties, and can admit the power of no officer of the Army to annul my order on the subject; nor can I admit the claim of any officer to the command of "The Forces," being myself the ranking General of the Confederate Army.

In the days that followed, Johnston's irritation mounted as he received orders from General Lee. Five days after his first letter to Cooper, Johnston wrote him again:

I had the honor to write you on the 24th inst. on the subject of my rank compared with that of other officers of the Confederate Army. Since then I have received daily orders purporting to come from "Headquarters of the Forces," some of them in relation to the internal affairs of this army. Such orders I cannot regard, because they are illegal. Permit me to suggest that orders should come from your office.

Johnston's complaints apparently received little attention. As summer passed into fall on an inactive front, Johnston had much time to meditate the injury he believed done him. About the middle of September he received news that turned his indignation to white-hot fury. He learned that the Confederate Congress had confirmed President Davis's five nominations for the rank of general. He learned that Davis had assigned different dates for the effectiveness of the appointments so that, in seniority, the officers ranked : Cooper, Albert Sidney Johnston, Lee, Joseph E. Johnston, Beauregard.

Joe Johnston poured out his anger in a letter to the President :

I will not affect to disguise the surprise and mortification produced in my mind by the action taken in this matter by the President and by Congress. I beg to state further, with the most profound respect for both branches of the Government, that I am deeply impressed with the conviction that these proceedings are in violation of my rights as an officer, of the plighted faith of the Confederacy, and of the constitution and laws of the land. . . . I now and here declare my claim that, notwithstanding these nominations made by the President, and their confirmation by Congress, I still rightfully hold the rank of first General in the Armies of the Southern Confederacy. . . .

The effect of the course pursued is this : it transfers me from the position of first rank to that of fourth. The relative rank of the others among themselves is unaltered. It is plain, then, that this is a blow aimed at me only. It reduces my rank in the grade I hold. This has never been done before in the regular service in America but by the sentence of a court-martial, as a punishment and a disgrace for some military offense. It seems to tarnish my fair fame as a soldier and as a man, earned by more than thirty years of laborious and perilous service. I had but this— the scar of many wounds, all honestly taken in my front and in the front of battle, and my father's Revolutionary sword. It was delivered to me from his venerated hand without a stain of dishonor. Its blade is still unblemished as when it passed from his hand to mine. I drew it in war, not for rank or fame, but to defend the sacred soil, the homes and hearths, the women and children; aye, and the men of my mother Virginia, my native South. It may hereafter be the sword of a general, leading armies, or of a private volunteer, but while I live and have an arm to wield it, it shall never be sheathed until the freedom, independence and full rights of the South are achieved. . . . I shall be satisfied if my country stands among the powers of the world—free, powerful and victorious, and that I, a general, a lieutenant or a volunteer soldier, have borne my part in the glorious strife and contributed to the final blessed consummation.

Johnston then set forth the legal arguments for his contentions.
He concluded :

If the action against which I have protested be legal, it is not for me
to question the expediency of degrading one who has served laboriously
from the commencement of the war on this frontier and borne a permanent part in the one great event of that war, for the benefit of persons
neither of whom has yet struck a blow for the Confederacy.

Johnston wisely reflected for two days before deciding whether to
dispatch the letter to Davis. At the end of that time, however, he
seemed to find nothing in it excessive or inconsistent with his own
character for dignity and restraint. He sent the letter.

The President's reply was prompt and brief : "I have just received
and read your letter of the 17th inst. Its language is, as you say,
unusual; its arguments and statements utterly one-sided, and its
insinuations as unfounded as they are unbecoming."

From that day on, Davis's letters to Johnston were signed "Very
respectfully yours" instead of "Your friend." Davis was as sensitive
as Johnston to considerations of personal dignity. Never again were
the relations between the President and the general on a basis of
easy informality.

They grew worse in that very month when Judah P. Benjamin
succeeded Leroy Pope Walker as Secretary of War. The bland, almost
perpetually smiling Benjamin was skilled in the art of pleasing. But
his endeavor was to please the President, not the generals. He acclim-
ated himself with readiness to Davis's likes and dislikes, and he was
quite willing to please his chief at the cost of displeasing the soldiers.
Though brilliant, and prodigiously industrious, he had no experience
in military affairs. Yet he immediately concerned himself with the
smallest details of command. He also proceeded in the most tactless
fashion to see that Johnston obeyed implicitly and promptly Davis's
slightest order.

One day Johnston exasperatedly exclaimed, "The Secretary of War
will probably establish his headquarters within this department soon."
Davis wanted the troops of the Confederacy reorganized on the basis

of States, believing that the cohesiveness of State units and their rivalry with units from other States would promote morale. When Johnston was slow about executing orders on the subject, Benjamin intervened to reassign two Mississippi regiments. Johnston protested that reorganization by States "would work a complete revolution in the organization of the Army" and thus make it highly vulnerable to enemy attack during the period of adjustment. Benjamin replied : "[The President] adheres to his order, and expects you to execute it."

In respectful terms, Johnston outlined his reasons for believing that the course ordered by the President would invite disaster and he appealed "for a continuance of the discretion [the President] has vested in me, merely to the time of executing the orders in question." Johnston went so far as to send, as an emissary to the President, General Richard Taylor, the brilliant brother of Davis's first wife. Taylor, who admired both Davis and Johnston, was saddened by the failure of his mission. But he found consolation in the thought that "the elevation of character of the two men, which made them listen to my appeals, justified hope."

General W. H. C. Whiting, to whom one of the Mississippi regiments had been assigned by Benjamin, joined Johnston in protesting the policy of grouping by States. As a result, Benjamin withdrew Whiting's commission as brigadier general, causing him to revert to major of engineers. In addition, he wrote a scolding letter to Johnston, saying,

The President requests me to say that he trusts you will hereafter decline to forward to him communications of your subordinates having so obvious a tendency to excite a mutinous and disorganizing spirit of the Army.

With great dignity and tact, Johnston replied to Benjamin on January 1, 1862. He must have written in the freshness of a New Year's resolution to control his temper. He said :

I beg to be allowed to intercede in this case, partly because this officer's services as a brigadier general are very important to this army, and partly because I also share the wrong. I am confident that he has in his heart neither insubordination nor disrespect. Had I returned the letter to him, pointing out the objectionable language in it, it would, I doubt not, have been promptly corrected. I regret very much that in my carelessness it was not done. No one is less disposed than I to be instrumental in putting before the President a paper offensive in its character.

No formal action was taken, but Whiting continued to command his brigade.

Meanwhile, the War Office continued to insist that Johnston reorganize his army on the basis of State units. Johnston now advanced a new argument, that the seasonal disruption of transportation made the proposed changes "physically impossible." The quarrel between Johnston and the administration still boiled, heated by tactlessness and lack of realism in Richmond and by Johnston's indisposition to confide in or even communicate with the capital.

One of the greatest points at issue was the government's policy of inducing re-enlistment of volunteers by granting of long furloughs. Under the law, final authority in such matters was vested in the Secretary of War, and Benjamin was quite willing to exercise it. Soon Johnston protested to Benjamin about the Secretary's practice of

. . . granting leaves of absence, furloughs, discharges, and acceptances of resignations upon applications made directly to yourself. . . . I have been informed that you have already granted furloughs to four entire companies, three belonging to the same regiment, but have received but one of the orders. . . . You will readily perceive that while you are granting furloughs on such a scale at Richmond, I cannot safely grant them at all. To execute these orders consistently and advisedly, there must be a system. If the War Department continues to grant these furloughs without reference to the plans determined on here, confusion and disorganizing collisions must be the result.

Johnston cited, as an example of picayune interference, the receipt of an order from Richmond detailing a particular private soldier for a working party. He commented, "I hazard nothing in saying that in time of war a Secretary of War never before made such a detail."

On March 1, Johnston protested directly to the President about Benjamin's interference, touching a sensitive chord by appealing to Davis's knowledge as a "trained soldier." Davis agreed that Johnston had suffered "some imposition" and assured him that his authority as a general would be upheld. But the President also reported that Benjamin had complained to him about Johnston's failure to execute orders. He added, "I regret that he was able to present to me many instances to justify that complaint, which were in no wise the invasion of your prerogatives as a commander in the field."

A new factor, in the winter of 1862, brought to a climax the quarrel between Benjamin and Johnston. Some officers under General W. W. Loring, commanding a brigade under Jackson, protested to politicians that Stonewall was exposing them unduly both to the enemy and to the elements by keeping them at Romney. Benjamin ordered Jackson to direct Loring to retire from Romney immediately. Jackson complied at once, but wrote Benjamin :

With such interference in my command, I cannot expect to be of much service in the field, and accordingly respectfully request to be ordered to report for duty to the Superintendent of the Virginia Military Institute at Lexington. . . . Should this application not be granted, I respectfully request that the President will accept my resignation from the army.

With a dignity and perspective contrasting favorably with the tone of the letter he had written to Davis regarding his own rank, Johnston wrote to Jackson :

Under ordinary circumstances, a due sense of one's dignity, as well as care for professional character and official rights would demand such a course as yours, but the character of this war, the great energy exhibited by the government of the United States, the danger in which our very existence as an independent people lies, requires sacrifices from us all who have been educated soldiers. . . .

I received my information of the order on which you have such cause to complain from your letter. Is not that as great an official wrong to me as the order itself to you? Let us dispassionately reason with the Government on this subject of command, and if we fail to influence its practice, then ask to be relieved from positions the authority of which is exercised by the War Department, while the responsibilities are left to us.

He told Jackson that he had withheld the letter of resignation "to make this appeal to your patriotism, not merely from warm feelings of personal regard, but from the official opinion which makes me regard you as necessary to the service of the country in your present position."

Afterward, Johnston wrote Davis another protest about interference from Benjamin. He said:

Permit me now to suggest the separation of the Valley District from my command, on the ground that it is necessary for the public interest. A collision of the authority of the Honorable Secretary of War with mine might occur at a critical moment. In such event disaster would be inevitable. The responsibility of the command has been imposed on me. Your Excellency's known sense of justice will not hold me to the responsibility while the corresponding control is not in my hands.

On February 7, having had no expression of a change of mind from Jackson, Johnston forwarded his subordinate's letter to Richmond, endorsing it: "Respectfully forwarded, with great regret. I don't know how the loss of this efficient officer can be supplied."

Most Congressmen were not willing to trade a "Stonewall" Jackson for a Judah P. Benjamin. Already existent displeasure with the Secretary of War attained new heights. Richmonders heard much talk of a dinner party at which Johnston and a number of Congressmen were present. Someone reportedly asked the general "whether he thought it even possible that the Confederate cause could succeed with Mr. Benjamin as War Minister." Johnston was said to have paused dramatically before answering, "No." That brief reply was cited in both houses of Congress and, according to a Tennessee representative, "was in the end fatal to Benjamin's hopes of remaining in the Department of War." Benjamin was kicked upstairs to the post of Secretary of State. Davis now had another reason for not liking Johnston.

Toward the end of February, with the Federals massing for a great spring offensive against Richmond, Johnston concluded that he would be wise to withdraw from his three Potomac River outposts and, indeed, from his whole Centerville line in Northern Virginia. A renewal of Federal activity on his flanks made him anxious to quit the area speedily. He wrote General Whiting on February 28, "We may indeed have to start before we are ready."

The retirement began on March 7. Great columns of smoke rose in the air as the flames devoured a mountain of meat that the troops could not take with them on their way to the Rappahannock. General Taylor said, "The movement was executed with the quiet precision characteristic of Johnston, unrivaled as a master of logistics." But a Federal officer who occupied Johnston's vacated post at Evansport said, "Everything left behind indicates that they left hastily and in great confusion."

McClellan, now in command of the Army of the Potomac, had converted that ramshackle fighting machine into an efficient engine of war. Its announced destination was Richmond. But the route still remained secret. Four possibilities were evident : through Manassas; through Fredericksburg; down the Potomac and the Chesapeake Bay by ship to a port of embarkation on the lower Rappahannock; by the same Potomac–Chesapeake route to a point of embarkation at Ft. Monroe. In view of these possibilities, Johnston left some infantry and Stuart's cavalry on the Rappahannock, but withdrew the bulk of his forces to a line behind the Rapidan River, thus bringing them closer to Richmond.

Unknown to Johnston at the time, this move completely frustrated a plan which McClellan was about to execute, that of transporting his men by water to the village of Urbanna on the south bank of the lower Rappahannock. McClellan's plan would no longer have placed him between Johnston and the capital the Confederate general was defending.

Exciting news came on March 24. Confederate Major General Benjamin Huger, commanding about 13,000 troops guarding Norfolk and Portsmouth with its nearby Gosport Navy Yard, reported that more than 20 steamers had sailed down the Chesapeake and that Federal troops in great numbers were disembarking near Ft. Monroe on the Peninsula. This neck of land between the James and York rivers could provide a route to Richmond, which stood at the fall line of the James. On this same Peninsula, at Yorktown, was the command of Confederate Brigadier General John E. Magruder, embracing about 12,000 men. Estimating that the enemy force on the Peninsula now numbered 35,000, Magruder asked for 10,000 men from Johnston.

Lee asked Johnston how many men he could send to Magruder or Huger. He suggested that Johnston organize his force so that part of it could be sent to the Richmond area while another portion held the line of the Rapidan.

Johnston made a counter proposal, that he lead 25,000 men to Richmond and leave only a skeleton force on the Rapidan. Not liking this idea, the government ordered him to send 10,000 men to the defense of the capital.

He complied, but under protest. "The division of the troops of this department made by the telegram of this afternoon," he said, "leaves on this line a force too weak to oppose an invasion, and furnishes to the threatened point a reinforcement too small to command success. . . . We cannot win without concentration." The Peninsula landings might be a feint.

On April 4, Lee notified Johnston that Federal forces were moving up the Peninsula. McClellan's intentions were clear. Johnston was asked to come to Richmond. Here Davis told him that the Yorktown and Norfolk-Portsmouth areas were now part of his command.

Johnston at once made an inspection tour of Magruder's defenses. Land batteries at Yorktown and on the opposite bank at Gloucester Point commanded the York River. The only notable impediment to the movement of Federal vessels up the James, however, was the

C.S.S. *Virginia,* the former Federal frigate *Merrimac,* now converted to a formidable but cumbersome ironclad. Near Yorktown rose the small Warwick River, which crossed the waist of the Peninsula to flow into the James. Magruder had dammed the river to make it a stronger moat and had constructed fieldworks along the river line.

At the narrowest part of the waist, at Williamsburg, Magruder had established a second line of defense.

On the morning of April 14, Johnston painted for Davis a gloomy picture of Confederate hopes in the Peninsula. He thought that the Warwick River line probably was not tenable. He believed that the Federals might force their way up the York and the James and trap the Confederates on the Peninsula by landing troops between them and Richmond.

In contrast to these dark possibilities, he held out the bright hope of ending the war by one great victory if all the troops available in North Carolina, South Carolina, and Georgia were brought to the Richmond area to join in offensive action. against McClellan after he moved up the Peninsula.

The President called in Lee and George W. Randolph, who had succeeded Benjamin as Secretary of War. At Johnston's request, two of his chief lieutenants, Gustavus W. Smith and James Longstreet, were also called in.

Johnston argued for abandonment of the Norfolk-Portsmouth area and of the Peninsula as a prelude to counterattack.

Randolph argued that giving up the Navy Yard at Portsmouth and the port of Norfolk would mean abandonment of the Confederacy's only hope for developing badly needed naval power. Backing up Randolph, Lee maintained that the Peninsula could be successfully defended. Smith, who had been a successful politician in New York City, argued forcefully in support of Johnston. Longstreet was silent most of the time. The argument lasted through the afternoon into the evening. After midnight, Davis said that he agreed with Lee and Randolph. The Peninsula must be defended. Johnston's state of mind is evidenced by the fact that, even after the passage of years, he wrote : "The belief that events on the Peninsula would soon compel the Confederate government to adopt my method of opposing the Federal army reconciled me somewhat to the necessity of obeying the President's order." The Peninsula campaign would be directed by a general who anticipated failure and who believed that in that failure would lie his own vindication.

Johnston assumed command at Yorktown and pressed the labor of finishing the field works begun by Magruder. Once again he was confronted with the necessity for reorganizing an army. Conscription became effective April 16. Confederate soldiers, members of what was probably the most democratic army in modern history, were busy electing their company and regimental commanders. In this balloting, "jolly good fellows" stood a much better chance than efficient disciplinarians. Johnston was under orders to brigade the men according to States. He wrote Lee : "The troops, in addition to the lax discipline of volunteers, are particularly discontented at the Conscription Act and demoralized by their recent elections. . . . Stragglers cover the country, and Richmond is no doubt filled with the absent without leave."

Davis had a worry of his own : an old one. Johnston was not grouping the troops by States. The President wrote the General :

While some have expressed surprise at my patience when orders to you were not observed, I have at least hoped that you would recognize the desire to aid and sustain you, and that it would produce the corresponding action on your part. The reasons formerly offered have one after another disappeared, and I hope you will, as you can, proceed to organize your troops as heretofore instructed.

Johnston did not contribute to the President's ease of mind by his reports to Richmond. On April 27 he said that a great artillery attack upon the Confederate lines at Yorktown might occur at any time, that Federal vessels were likely to proceed up the York and turn his flank, that the Peninsula would then have to be abandoned and that the evacuation of Norfolk should come soon. Two days later, in a spirit of "I told you so," he wrote Lee : "The fight for Yorktown, as I said in Richmond, must be one of artillery, in which we cannot win." He said that the Confederates would be able to hold out only a few hours and that the best policy was to retire from the field at once.

On the night of May 3, Johnston began a retreat up the Peninsula. Heavy artillery firing was kept up during the withdrawal to deceive the enemy and dummies were left in the front trenches. Incidentally, some of the Confederate soldiers seized the opportunity to inscribe these dummies with messages for the Yankees—writing more notable for vigor than for polish. As Johnston's army moved up the muddy road on the Peninsula, it left behind not only the laboriously constructed field fortifications of the Warwick River line, but also 56 big guns in good condition.

Yet all was not joy in McClellan's camp on May 4. He had been making careful preparations for a devastating artillery assault on May 6. He had gained ground and had deprived the Confederates of badly needed artillery, but had been cheated of a possible opportunity to destroy his opponent.

One of the most significant losses to the Confederates as a result of the withdrawal was the abandonment of Confederate positions commanding the York and consequently the opening of that river to Federal gunboats and transports.

About noon of May 4 Confederate troops moving up from Yorktown by two separate roads crowded onto a single road just south of Williamsburg at the junction of the two routes. The troops halted in the area of the town to rest and eat. Before the march was resumed, word arrived from Stuart, whose cavalry was screening the withdrawal, that the Federals were driving him. Johnston personally led a brigade toward the action, but only minor skirmishing resulted and that died with the day. A relentless rain beat down on the red clay roads through the night and subsided to a drizzle about dawn. The crack of rifles came sharply through the mist, but both Johnston and McClellan expected only minor skirmishing as the Confederates bought time for further withdrawal. Neither commander desired to fight a full-fledged battle at Williamsburg but Federal artillery, backing up the rifles and muskets, widened and intensified the action.

Confederate pickets were driven back to the Williamsburg line. Longstreet came to their assistance. As the conflict grew, and the Confederate left was severely threatened, Longstreet asked for a brigade from D. H. Hill. Soon Hill's entire division had come to Longstreet's assistance. Johnston, who had moved on from Williamsburg in the belief that only skirmishing would occur there, rode back to the town. He permitted Longstreet to conduct the battle. Though he assumed the role of a spectator, he was in more physical danger than some officers actively engaged. With unshaken calm, he sat his horse while bullets whizzed past him. The fighting was confused and was obscured by brush and trees. The battle sputtered out about sunset and the Confederates resumed their withdrawal.

Both sides claimed victory. The Confederates could boast that they had successfully frustrated McClellan's plan to engage the main part of Johnston's army. The Federals could brag that the Confederates were still in retreat. McClellan's army had suffered heavier casualties, 2,283 to the Confederates' 1,560. Johnston was reported to have ridden away from the scene humming "The Camptown Races."

Early the next morning Yankee transports moved up the York River with the object of placing Federal troops between Johnston and Richmond. Speed was vital in the Confederate retreat. Johnston had issued the order, so painful to Lt. F. Y. Dabney, "that any gun caisson or commissary wagon which might become set in the mud so as to impede the line of march must be destroyed at once."

Federal troops debarked at Eltham's landing on the York, but Johnston dispatched forces under Smith and Whiting to hold the Federal flanking threat until the main part of his army could be marched out of the lower Peninsula where McClellan sought to entrap them. This movement was so successfully executed that Johnston, nearly always generous in dealing with subordinates, was especially lavish in praise of those responsible. He urged promotion for Whiting and for Brigadier General John B. Hood and Colonel Wade Hampton.

On May 9, Norfolk was evacuated on Johnston's orders and Huger's troops moved toward Petersburg with the idea of joining Johnston. Loss of Norfolk and the Navy Yard at Portsmouth deprived the C.S.S. *Virginia* of a base. The ironclad drew too much water to be sent farther up the James, so it had to be destroyed. Thus the James, like the York, was now open to Federal ships.

By May 14, McClellan's army had reached its advance base at White House Landing on the Pamunkey River, a tributary of the York. This point was only 20 miles from Richmond. During this period of retreat, Johnston added greatly to the anxiety suffered by Davis and Lee by letting them know nothing definite about his plans. Appeals to him for information brought evasive answers and, even in personal conversation, Johnston confided in them about as much as he would have in a Federal courier.

A further complication arose from the fact that Johnston, whose command embraced the Valley District, was technically responsible for the direction of Jackson's efforts to draw some of McDowell's forces to that area and thus prevent that general from reinforcing McClellan on the Peninsula. Since Johnston could not readily keep in touch with Jackson and his problems while dealing with troubles of his own in the field, much of the responsibility for directing Jackson devolved upon Lee. Far from appreciating this work by Lee, Johnston viewed it as an encroachment on his own prerogatives. He wrote his old friend : "My authority does not extend beyond the troops immediately around me. I request therefore to be relieved of a merely nominal geographical command."

Lee diplomatically soothed Johnston's hurt pride, but at times it seemed that Johnston was more intent on fighting Davis than on battling with the Yankees.

Eventually, McClellan was within five miles of Richmond, so close that his men could tell the time of day by the chiming of clocks in the capital. Fear was widespread that Johnston might retreat through

Richmond and abandon the city to the enemy without a fight. During most of the campaign, Johnston's army had been outnumbered about 2 to 1 by McClellan's forces, and at best the ratio was 5 to 3. His artillery was almost incomparably weaker than his opponent's. The chiefs of government in Richmond knew that Johnston had believed that any battle fought between Yorktown and the Richmond area could result only in Confederate defeat. Did he believe that a battle fought at Richmond itself would have the same result? If so, would he fight to defend the city or simply retreat westward to effect a concentration of power for a spectacular campaign with the promise of victory and glory?

An anecdote circulating about Richmond brought no comfort. A gentleman from South Carolina who admired Johnston as "an accomplished soldier" and thought he was "as brave as Caesar," nevertheless had found him an unsatisfactory hunting companion. "We all liked him," he said, "but as to hunting, there he made a total failure. He was a capital shot . . . but with Colonel Johnston the bird flew too high or low, the dogs were too far or too near. Things never did suit exactly. He was too fussy, too hard to please, too cautious, too much afraid to miss and risk his fine reputation for a crack shot."

Johnston's anxiety about the possibility of McDowell's reinforcing McClellan was understandable. McDowell's men would add to McClellan's greatly superior army a force equal to Johnston's own. But Jackson's brilliant maneuvers in the Valley kept McDowell from moving to McClellan's aid.

On May 31, at Seven Pines on the outskirts of Richmond, Johnston attacked McClellan.

Johnston had placed Longstreet in tactical command. Movements by various brigades were to be keyed to those of Huger's division, but Johnston failed to inform Huger that Longstreet would direct the general operations. As a result there was some confusion. It was multiplied when Longstreet, possibly misunderstanding Johnston's orders, took a route different from the one assigned.

As the morning wore on amid blunder and confusion, Johnston was heard to exclaim that he wished the troops were back in their camps. But, by that time, the enemy was well aware of Confederate movements and it was too late to call off the attack. Turgid clouds hung over the field like the billowing, sable canvas of a funeral tent. Johnston's glower was equally dark. In the house that was his headquarters, he paced up and down, pausing again and again to listen in vain for the sound of fire from the south that would signify the attack had been launched at the appointed place. General Gustavus Smith, as nervous as Johnston, was there. Lee arrived from Richmond. The atmosphere was like that in a sick room where a family listens anxiously for a change in the patient's breathing.

About three o'clock the thunder of cannon announced that an artillery duel—and perhaps a full-scale battle—was under way.

Despite Confederate mistakes, the Southern forces quickly overran the first Union line. A little later, Longstreet sent word that he had "beaten the enemy after . . . severe fighting" and an attack "upon the right flank and rear" of the Federals would probably enable him to drive them into the Chickahominy

Johnston leaped on his horse and rode rapidly to the field of battle. Davis was riding up to headquarters to confer with Johnston. The fact that the general's hasty departure coincided with the President's arrival may have been only coincidence, but some observers assumed that Johnston had rather face enemy bullets than greet Davis.

Johnston found a fight of growing intensity with about 9,000 men engaged on each side. As twilight fell, deepening the darkness of the day, he realized that any further action before dawn would be inconclusive. He dispatched staff officers to the regiments with orders to bivouac in their positions in the field and be prepared for a renewal of fighting in the morning. The tempo of the firing was falling with the night. Johnston might as well ride back to headquarters.

Suddenly, searing pain struck his shoulder. He had been hit by a musket ball. He knew the sensation. He still sat his horse. Then something hit him in the chest and blackness engulfed him.

One of his couriers dashed to the general, who had fallen unconscious from his mount. A fragment of shell had struck him in the chest. The courier carried him back farther from the lines. Then excited men carried him to another spot to await the arrival of a stretcher.

Davis was bending over Johnston, all frigidity dissolved in the warmth of genuine concern. Johnston smiled and extended his hand. He said he "did not know how seriously he was hurt, but feared a fragment of shell had injured his spine." A few minutes later, Johnston became anxious, not for his life, but because his sword was missing. "That sword," he said, "was the one worn by my father in the Revolutionary War, and I would not lose it for $10,000. Will not someone please go back and get it and the pistols for me?"

There were several volunteers, despite the fact that the spot where Johnston had been wounded was still under fire. The courier dashed away and was soon back with sword and firearms. The grateful general gave him one of the pistols.

Davis offered to take Johnston to his own home, but a house was found for him not far away. Mrs. Johnston was soon at his side and stayed with him through the long days of bleedings and blisterings as the attending physicians fought with the customary weapons of their day a "constant tendency to pleurisy and an obstinate adhesion of the lungs as a result of the fracture of several ribs."

Lee succeeded Johnston in command of the army, which henceforth would be called by its historic name, the Army of Northern Virginia.

It soon became obvious that Seven Pines had not been a Southern victory. Confederate troops returned to the positions they had held before the battle. They had suffered 6,134 casualties to 5,031 for the Federals. Nevertheless, the wounding of Johnston brought a greater general appreciation of the man and the task that had confronted him. The *Richmond Examiner* eulogized him in an editorial that, if Johnston had not recovered, would have made any obituary anticlimactic. The newspaper said: "Time may yet produce another, but no living man in America is yet ascertained to possess a military knowledge so profound, or a decision of character so remarkable."

During the period of his convalescence, while compiling his report on Seven Pines, Johnston apparently took care to protect his reputation or Longstreet's, or both. There had been much unexplained confusion in troop movements before the battle. In his report, Longstreet made Huger the scapegoat. Gustavus Smith, in his report, shoved some of the responsibility onto Longstreet. Johnston returned Smith's report to him with a request for deletions. He explained that Smith's account touched upon "two subjects which I never intended to make known, which I have mentioned to no one but yourself, and mentioned to you as I have been in the habit of doing everything of interest in a military way." Johnston explained :

I refer to the mention of the misunderstanding between Longstreet and myself in regard to the direction of his division, and that of his note to me, received about four o'clock, complaining of my slowness, which note I showed to you. As it seems to me that both of these matters concern Longstreet and myself alone, I have no hesitation in asking you to strike them out of your report, as they in no manner concern your operations.

In his own report, Johnston was high in praise of Longstreet and omitted any reference to the Georgian's mistakes. Could Johnston have feared that a certain vagueness in his own orders—which may have been in large part oral—was responsible for Longstreet's blunders?

However much the preparation of Johnston's report might illustrate the influences of vanity and favoritism, his conduct was noble and free from evidence of petty jealousy when Lee began shoving McClellan down the Peninsula and back to the refuge of Yankee gunboats. When Johnston learned that Lee was receiving reinforcements, he commented : "Then, my wound was fortunate; it is the concentration which I earnestly recommended, but had not the influence to effect. Lee has made them do for him what they would not do for me."

Called to the West

On November 13, 1862, Johnston was well enough to report to the War Department for duty. The President had been urged by General Braxton Bragg and General Leonidas Polk, as well as lesser figures, to assign Johnston to command in the West. Bragg had met with repeated reverses in that theater. He had been preceded by Beauregard. The laurels that the Creole had won so easily at Charleston and Manassas had wilted under the Western sun. Johnston was assigned the command of all Confederate territory between the Blue Ridge Mountains and the Mississippi River.

This huge area was divided into military departments whose commanders could communicate directly with Richmond. Yet Johnston, operating from headquarters in Chattanooga or wherever his peregrinations might take him, must exercise over-all command. He was not, however, given field command. Persistent in his advocacy of concentration, he urged that Confederate forces east and west of the Mississippi be united for action against the enemy. The suggestion was not adopted. Johnston said it was not even "noticed." The prospect was not a cheering one.

Before Johnston left Richmond, he was given a farewell breakfast. On that occasion, Senator William Lowndes Yancey of Alabama raised a glass of champagne and proposed : "Gentlemen, let us drink to the only man who can save the Confederacy—General Joseph E. Johnston!" A burst of applause followed the toast, which was downed with enthusiasm. Johnston rose with glass in hand. "Mr. Yancey," he said, "the man you describe is now in the field in the person of General Robert E. Lee. I will drink to his health!"

Early in December, Johnston, accompanied by his wife, arrived in Chattanooga to assume command. Awaiting him was a telegram from Adjutant General Cooper reporting that Major General John C. Pemberton, commander of the Department of Mississippi and East Louisiana, was falling back in the direction of Vicksburg under heavy pressure.

On that very day, Johnston wrote his old friend Senator Louis T.

Wigfall of Texas: "Nobody ever assumed command under more unfavorable circumstances. If Rosecrans [the Federal commander] had disposed our troops himself, their disposition could not have been more unfavorable to us."

Mrs. Johnston deeply sympathized with her husband, but she must have done little to bolster his spirits. Not many days later, in a letter to Mrs. Wigfall, she professed to have the saddest heart in Chattanooga and exclaimed, "How ill and weary I feel in this desolate land and how dreary it all looks, and how little prospect there is of my poor husband doing ought than lose his army, truly a forlorn hope it is . . . ."

Johnston had been less than a week in his new post when President Davis arrived in Chattanooga. With Davis, Johnston reviewed troops and talked with commanders at Murfreesboro, Tennessee, and the two then made a tour of inspection in Mississippi.

Johnston argued with Davis that Tennessee and Mississippi, separated as they were by strong natural barriers, should not be components of the same command. Like Winfield Scott and Lincoln on the Union side, Johnston grasped the over-all importance of controlling the Mississippi. He therefore argued for the concentration of troops from both sides of the Mississippi in order to beat the numerically superior enemy. He was willing temporarily to sacrifice territory in order to beat an army.

He was as contemptuous of Confederate entrenchments in the Vicksburg area as he had been of those on the Peninsula in Virginia. All in all, Johnston was most unhappy about the resources at his command and about what he regarded as unrealistic determination of its geographical bounds. He told Davis that it was impracticable for him to attempt to command both Tennessee and Mississippi and he asked to be transferred from a "position so little to my taste." Davis replied that a high ranking officer was needed in a position where he could transfer troops between the Tennessee and Mississippi theaters in an emergency. Johnston did not relish the role of traffic manager for two armies. Though he rejoiced at news of Lee's great victory at Fredericksburg, it deepened his chagrin over the small prospects for success in his own area. "What luck some people have!" he wrote Senator Wigfall. "Nobody will ever come to attack me in such a place."

Johnston had not convinced the administration that it was wise to reduce to a minimum the garrisons at Vicksburg and Port Hudson, while maintaining a strong force in the field where it was free to maneuver and to relieve the garrisons by savage attacks on the enemy.

While Johnston pondered and fretted and was frustrated by the poor communications within his extensive command, the scales of battle were tipped momentarily in favor of the Confederates. But, just as suddenly, the scales dipped in favor of the Yankees on January 3, 1863 when Bragg, under heavy artillery fire from Rosecrans, withdrew his Army of Tennessee 35 miles south of Murfreesboro and went into winter quarters at Tullahoma. Johnston, who had sent a New Year's message of congratulations to Bragg, learned indirectly of the Confederate withdrawal three days after it had taken place. Johnston was then in Jackson, Mississippi. He protested to Davis, "The impossibility of my knowing the condition of things in Tennessee shows that I cannot direct both parts of my command at once." The President answered, "The difficulty arising from the separation of troops of your command is realized but cannot be avoided." In the persons of Johnston and Davis, two inflexible personalities confronted each other.

As Johnston learned that the enemy was moving "in full force" against Vicksburg, he was tortured by the thought that he would be blamed for failures which he deemed himself powerless to avoid. In great desperation, he wrote Wigfall, revealing his feeling of having been shelved and asking the Senator to use his influence in the capital to obtain for him release from so vexing a nominal command.

The bold-eyed, bristle-browed Texan was more forceful than subtle. But he was intensely loyal and went to work for Johnston with a ready will. Soon Johnston received a letter from J. A. Seddon, a fellow Virginian who had succeeded Randolph as Secretary of War.

In the friendliest and most complimentary terms, the secretary explained that, because of the remoteness of the Western theater from Richmond, Johnston's command had been created so that operations in that region would be subject to "the same guiding direction and control as was exercised nearer the capital by the [War] Department and the President." He explained that for this post the government had sought a general of the "largest experience and greatest ability." He confessed disappointment that Johnston had not so interpreted his instructions as to assume active command at Vicksburg or Murfreesboro when those points were endangered.

Toward the end of January, when Johnston was at Tullahoma with Bragg, he received a letter from President Davis informing him that there was reason to think Bragg did not command the confidence of his chief lieutenants. The President made it clear that he himself was sure of Bragg's ability but was afraid that distrust of Bragg by his subordinates could bring "disaster." Johnston was to investigate the situation and, if necessary, to assume command of the Army of Tennessee.

Bragg's generals had expressed, some without apparent malice and some viciously, a want of confidence in him. But Johnston wrote Davis a letter praising Bragg's "great vigor and skill." He said, "It would be very unfortunate to remove him at this juncture when he has just earned, if not won, the gratitude of the country." In this letter and in a later one, Johnston said that, because of his participation in the investigation, he thought it would be improper for him to replace Bragg if the General were removed.

Davis was convinced that Bragg's usefulness was impaired if not ended in the post he then occupied. He argued that Johnston need have no scruples about assuming active command of Bragg's army inasmuch as that army was already under his over-all command.

Johnston kept finding reasons why he could not replace Bragg, and finally, having exhausted these, reasons why the replacement should be deferred.

Wigfall wrote Johnston to ask what the general really wanted so that he might help him get it. Johnston replied: "My only official wish is to render service, my only ambition to please, to have work in which I may be useful—for more than three months I have been doing next to nothing. . . . I don't want to remain so. Anything else would be better."

But, besides Johnston's "official wish," there was another which he confided to Wigfall. "If the President and the Secretary of War really believed that the Western command was the most important," he said, "it should go to Lee." Then, Johnston said, he could "with great propriety" return to the place "where the Yankee missiles found me." As Johnston had hinted in his comment on Lee's victory at Fredericksburg, he really longed to command the Army of Northern Virginia.

The people of Chattanooga had no idea of the frustration that gnawed at Johnston from within. The *Chattanooga Rebel* told its readers: "He is one of those men for whom you cannot resist a personal impulse of kindness. Easy himself, he has the happy faculty of all men of good heart and graceful address of putting those with whom he is thrown also at ease." Residents of the city planned a *soirée* in the general's honor. But, before the affair was held, he was on his way south to confer with General Pemberton.

Stopping over in Mobile, he was besieged by an enthusiastic crowd. Someone called for cheers for the hero of Manassas. Always modest when the subject of adulation, Johnston protested that the hero of Manassas was at Charleston. The crowd understood that he was giving credit to Beauregard. A call went up for cheers for the hero of Seven Pines. The very model of military gallantry, the little general stood erect in his gray uniform and swept the crowd with his piercing eyes. "Gentlemen," he said, "No one man was ever the hero of Seven Pines. In that bloody battle, there were many heroes under our flag— and the very noblest of them were from Alabama." As the Alabama crowd cheered madly, Johnston bowed and disappeared.

But the general was not to resume his trip southward. There, in

Mobile, he received orders from the President and the Secretary of War to assume command of Bragg's army.

Though Johnston assumed command of the Army of Tennessee, he issued no official order about the change, and thus spared the feelings of Bragg, who was already worried over his wife's critical illness.

While working to strengthen the army in Tennessee, Johnston attempted to advise Pemberton regarding operations in beleaguered Vicksburg. He was hampered by the very difficulty of communication that he had so often emphasized in letters to Richmond authorities. Illness, probably related in part to his Peninsula wounds, drained his strength during much of this time.

On May 9, Seddon telegraphed Johnston to go at once to Mississippi and there assume "chief command of the forces, giving to those in the field, as far as practicable, the encouragement and benefit of your personal direction." He was to take with him 3,000 of the Tennessee troops. Johnston had been continuously ill for at least a month when the orders arrived. But he replied, "I shall go immediately, although unfit for field service." He left Tullahoma the next day in the company of his physician.

As Johnston moved toward a junction with Pemberton, his efforts to direct strategy were thwarted not only by inadequate physical communications, but also by a lack of rapport between the two generals. The reports reaching Johnston from Pemberton told of retreats and evacuations. Johnston, perceiving that it was now too late for Pemberton's army to practice that mobility which he had earlier urged, sent the Vicksburg commander word to stand firm. He was making every effort "to gather a force which may attempt to relieve you."

In Canton, Mississippi, Johnston awaited reinforcements. With the newly arriving troops was a shrewd British observer, Lieutenant Colonel A. J. L. Fremantle. Though finding Johnston gracious, he recorded that the general had the "power of keeping people at a distance when he chooses. His officers evidently stand in great awe of him." This initial observation little prepared Fremantle for what happened the next day when, with Johnston and a member of his staff, the British colonel boarded a locomotive for the rough ride to Jackson, Mississippi. When the engine stopped to refuel, Johnston grabbed a shovel and went to work. Outside Jackson, the locomotive was brought to an abrupt stop by a break in the track. The three dismounted to walk the rest of the way, Fremantle and the staff officer carrying baggage, and Johnston carrying his own cloak and the coats of his two companions.

By a series of five victories, climaxed by the Battle of Big Black River on May 17, Grant had succeeded in separating the armies of Johnston and Pemberton. Two days later, and again on May 22, he assaulted the Vicksburg entrenchments in vain. He then became resigned to siege operations. On July 4, General Pemberton surrendered the city and its garrison of 30,000 soldiers. On July 8, Port Hudson, Louisiana surrendered after a protracted siege by Union General Nathaniel P. Banks. Thus Johnston's efforts to protect the Mississippi were frustrated. The mighty river was now completely dominated by the Federal forces. The great North-South river highway of the Confederacy had become a moat separating the Eastern and Western parts of the young nation.

During the same period Lee's bold invasion of the North had culminated in bitter disappointment at Gettysburg. Gettysburg and Vicksburg were both symbols of Confederate frustration, but Jefferson Davis's confidence in Lee was unimpaired. His estimate of Johnston was quite different. General Gorgas, Confederate Chief of Ordnance, remarked to the President, "Vicksburg fell, apparently, from want of provisions." Davis's face was drawn with tension and irritation. "Yes," he said, "from want of provisions inside, and a general outside who wouldn't fight."

On the night of July 16, hard pressed by Sherman, Johnston evacuated Jackson, Mississippi. On his eastward march, Johnston was informed that his command no longer embraced Tennessee. He would now be responsible for territory bounded on the East by the Georgia-Alabama border, on the South by the Gulf of Mexico and on the

West by the Mississippi River. But his command would not extend north of the Tennessee River. This change could be interpreted either as acknowledgment of Johnston's correctness in asserting that his former command was too unwieldy, or as a rebuke for failure in the Vicksburg theater.

Johnston was not long kept in doubt about the Administration's attitude. On July 15, Davis wrote a 15-page letter to Johnston in reply to excuses which the general had made regarding his part in events leading to the fall of Vicksburg. Could some ill feeling between Mrs. Davis and Mrs. Johnston have aggravated the acrimony between their husbands? To Mrs. Wigfall, Mrs. Johnston wrote: "I feel now nothing can make me forgive either of [the Davises]. When I looked at my dear old husband's gray head and careworn face and felt how many of those tokens of trouble that man and woman planted there, I could almost have asked God to punish them." When Johnston, dissuaded by members of his staff from resigning, wrote a detailed reply to Davis's letter, he explained to Senator Wigfall that he had done so partly because of Mrs. Johnston, "who apprehends that the whole power of the government is preparing to overwhelm me."

The feud between Davis and Johnston soon broke into the press with missives being fired like missiles by adherents of the two proud men. A court of inquiry was called to investigate circumstances leading to the fall of Vicksburg, but the rapid deterioration of affairs in Tennessee made it impractical to bring witnesses from that theater and the court was never convened. On September 9, Yankee General William S. Rosecrans successfully maneuvered Bragg out of Chattanooga without even having to fight a battle. Alarmed at the loss of this "gateway to the East," Davis quickly dispatched the doughty Longstreet and 11,000 troops to reinforce the Army of Tennessee. Federal and Confederate forces met at Chickamauga, northeast of Chattanooga, and the Union line broke before the Confederate onslaught. But General George H. Thomas, a Virginian fighting for the Union, rallied the bluecoats until reserves arrived and thus saved Rosecrans' army. Grant was made commander of the Western armies of the Union in mid-October.

He replaced Rosecrans with Thomas and, with the aid of Generals Joseph Hooker and Sherman, drove Bragg from Lookout Mountain and then routed him from Missionary Ridge. The Union generals now prepared to march across Georgia to the sea. By seizing the Mississippi, the Federals had severed the Confederate East from the Confederate West as though by the swift, vertical stroke of a mighty saber. Now it seemed probable that, by a horizontal swipe, they could separate the upper part of the Confederacy from the lower. Sherman was to wield the naked blade of cold steel.

Bragg began the retreat toward Dalton, Georgia, and, on November 29, asked to be relieved of his command.

Lieutenant General W. J. Hardee succeeded to temporary command of the Army of Tennessee. The post was subsequently offered to Lee, though not necessarily on a permanent basis. He declined, believing that he was more useful as commander of the Army of Northern Virginia.

Officers who had fought in the West under Johnston boosted him for the post. One of Davis's most loyal friends, the shrewdly observant Mrs. James Chesnut, said of Johnston, "Whether advancing or retreating, [he] is magnetic . . . and draws the good will of those by whom he is surrounded."

Secretary of War Seddon, despite his dissatisfaction with Johnston in some particulars, advocated his appointment as commander of the Army of Tennessee. Secretary of State Benjamin, much closer to Davis than any other cabinet officer, opposed the selection. General Lee, for whom Davis had tremendous respect, urged the appointment. Davis named Johnston, in Seddon's words, "after doubt and with misgiving to the end." Wigfall wrote Johnston, "You owe your appointment to General Lee and doubtless fully appreciate his kindness."

After arrival in Dalton, a small, North Georgia rail center, Johnston learned that Davis's ideas about what should be done differed radically from his own. The President believed that the Army of Tennessee should again become in truth what it was in name. He wished Johnston to launch from Georgia an offensive carrying the Army once more into Tennessee. He wrote, "I assure you that nothing shall be wanting on the part of the government to aid you in your effort to regain possession of the territory from which we have been driven."

Johnston replied: "To assume the offensive from this point, we must move either into Middle or East Tennessee. To the first the obstacles are: Chattanooga, now a fortress, the Tennessee River, the Rugged Desert of the Cumberland Mountains, and an army outnumbering ours more than two to one. The second would leave the way into Georgia open. We have neither subsistence nor field transportation enough for either march."

Johnston said that he could undertake an offensive only after receiving and repulsing a Federal attack and then only with the aid of reinforcements.

Immediately he began to improve the organization of the army and lift its morale. He demanded the utmost efficiency from his officers and instituted a rugged training program. But he also knew that efficiency could sometimes be increased by well considered relaxations of discipline. He inaugurated a furlough system which would enable virtually every man in the Army to visit his home.

Though some of Johnston's generals found a large measure of reserve mixed with his affability, the privates and corporals were amazed at the free and easy way in which he mingled with them. The men grew to love and almost to worship the manly little general who galloped through the camps, reining in to speak to groups of soldiers along the way. Sometimes he would dismount and shake hands with every private in sight. This easy-going democracy was not just a carefully calculated part of the morale-building process. In private letters, Johnston evidenced suspicions of some of his high ranking officers, but he wrote with warm affection about the men in the ranks.

One division of the Army was so enthusiastic when Johnston returned it to the command of Frank Cheatam, who had been transferred by Bragg, that it marched to Johnston's headquarters behind a band to show its gratitude. When Johnston emerged from his tent, Cheatam placed his hand on the bare head of the game-looking little general and patted it two or three times, proclaiming to his men, "Boys, this is Old Joe."

As Johnston reviewed his military situation, the only comfort he found, by his own testimony, was the presence of Lieutenant General John B. Hood. This valiant fighter had been assigned by Davis to command of the second corps under Johnston. By the end of March, Johnston had fewer than 60,000 troops, who would have to withstand an offensive by nearly 100,000 Federals.

The shortage of transport was at least as bad as that of manpower. When the Confederacy's inspector general of field transport visited Dalton, he was alarmed to learn that the general, who despised details, had not tallied the transportation sources available and had no precise knowledge of what transport facilities would be necessary to conduct a campaign.

Hood urged an offensive, arguing that the ability of the army to attack would not improve with time.

In contrast, the North was mustering its vast industrial might and logistical resources for a two-pronged offensive against the Confederacy. Simultaneous drives would be mounted in Virginia and Georgia in May. Sherman was almost juvenile in his exuberance. "I am going to move on Joe Johnston," he exulted, "the day Grant telegraphs me he is going to hit Bobby Lee."

Grant, now commander of all the Union armies, had named Sherman commander of the Grand Army of the West. This army Sherman divided into three armies, commanded by Thomas, Schofield and McPherson.

Grant had warned Sherman that he would face in Johnston a wily antagonist. This estimate proved true. The Virginian was the greatest master of Fabian tactics—the retreat that costs the pursuer more dearly than the pursued—in either the Federal or Confederate armies.

In fact, he probably was the greatest master of retreat in American history.

With the skill and agility of an expert fencing master, Johnston parried with Sherman over the 85 miles of territory between Dalton and Atlanta and contrived to deliver three telling thrusts to his giant adversary. Johnston would straddle a railroad or a natural formation, inviting a flank attack from Sherman, and then be gone by the time the Union general was ready to deliver his blow. Twice Sherman brought Johnston to battle : at Resaca in the middle of May and at New Hope Church at the end of the month. But he had little cause to congratulate himself, for the engagements were fought on Johnston's own terms and the Confederate leader repulsed his enemy. In the first of these battles, Johnston brought lusty cheers from his troops by riding directly toward the enemy fire with a smile on his face and a jaunty black feather in his hat.

At Kennesaw Mountain June 27, Sherman abandoned his time-consuming flanking movements to make a direct assault on Johnston. The Confederate general was in his glory. He repulsed the enemy attack, suffering only 270 losses as compared with 2,000 enemy casualties. On July 17, Sherman's painful progress since the 7th of May left him still 8 miles from Atlanta. The Union general was tremendously impressed by the skill and resourcefulness of his opponent.

This admiration was not shared by the President of the Confederacy. Earlier experience with Johnston had convinced Davis that the General was likely to retreat in situations where a Lee or a Jackson would dare to attack. Johnston's habitual reticence and dislike. for making detailed reports had contributed to the President's suspicion of him. Besides, the running quarrel between the two had disposed Davis to believe many of the uncomplimentary things being said about Johnston. In his alarm over the nearness of the Federals to Atlanta, the President wondered if Johnston would give up the city without a fight. Davis believed that he could not afford the luxury of waiting to see.

A Confederate congressman visiting Johnston's headquarters told him that the President was displeased with the conduct of the campaign and was contemplating removal of the general. Davis was convinced, the politician said, that "if he were in your place, he could whip Sherman now." Johnston, harassed and vexed by impending defeat and misunderstanding critics, but at the same time at the height of his greatest military achievement, found this quotation too much to bear. His anger was increased by the fact that Braxton Bragg, to whom he had given so much support in Tennessee, was now, as Davis's military advisor, showing no comprehension whatever of Johnston's problems. The little general snapped that he was aware that the President believed himself capable of doing "a great many things that other men would hesitate to attempt." The vertical frown mark was deep between Johnston's eyebrows. "For instance, he tried to do what God failed to do. He tried to make a soldier of Braxton Bragg and you know the result. It could not be done."

Bragg had recently visited Johnston's headquarters and had reported to the President : "I cannot learn that he has any more plans for the future than he [had] in the past."

Bragg said that any change of command would be attended by "some serious evils," but added, "If any change is made, Lt. General Hood would give unlimited satisfaction, and my estimate of him, always high, has been raised by his conduct in this campaign."

Davis asked Johnston to reveal to him his specific plans. Johnston telegraphed : "As the enemy has double our number, we must be on the defensive. My plan of operation must, therefore, depend upon that of the enemy. We are trying to put Atlanta in condition to be held for a day or two by the Georgia militia, that army movements may be freer and wider."

The next night, while Johnston was conferring with his chief engineer about the defense of Atlanta, he received a message from Adjutant General Cooper :

I am directed by the Secretary of War to inform you that as you have failed to arrest the advance of the enemy to the vicinity of Atlanta, far in the interior of Georgia, and express no confidence that you can defeat or repel him, you are hereby relieved from the command of the Army and Department of Tennessee, which you will immediately turn over to General Hood.

Johnston lost no time in relinquishing command and congratulating his successor.

Hood joined with Generals Hardee and A. P. Stewart in a telegram begging Davis to postpone the change of command until after the approaching Battle of Atlanta. But Davis would not be dissuaded.

In the morning, Johnston informed Richmond authorities that he had obeyed the order to relinquish command. Stung by what he deemed the whiplash of injustice, he was goaded by a sense that he was not appreciated to the extent that Lee was. He wrote:

As to the alleged causes of my removal, I assert that Sherman's army is much stronger compared with that of the Tennessee than Grant's compared with that of Northern Virginia. Yet the enemy has been compelled to advance much more slowly to the vicinity of Atlanta than to that of Richmond and Petersburg, and has penetrated much deeper into Virginia than into Georgia. Confident language by a military commander is not usually regarded as evidence of competency.

This comparison was not fair to Lee. Like Johnston, Lee had been forced to retreat to the city he was responsible for defending. Johnston was entitled to glory for restricting to a mile and a quarter per day the advance of a well-equipped and skilfully led Northern Army twice the size of his own. But terrible as was Johnston's problem, it was still not so great as Lee's. Johnston was opposed to a great army supplied by a single railroad line. Lee was opposed by overwhelming numbers advancing as two separate armies from different directions and supplied by splendid water routes over which he had no control whatsoever.

In Johnston's farewell to his troops, which was read to them on the same day that he wrote Richmond in indignation, the general sounded a nobler strain. He said:

I cannot leave this noble army without expressing my admiration of the high military qualities it has displayed. A long and arduous campaign has made conspicuous every soldierly virtue, endurance of toil, obedience to orders, brilliant courage. The enemy has never attacked but to be repulsed and severely punished. You, soldiers, have never argued but from your courage, and never counted your foe. No longer your leader, I will still watch your career and will rejoice in your victories. To one and all I offer assurances of my friendship, and bid an affectionate farewell.

Troops that had just heard the reading of this message caught a glimpse of the erect, soldierly figure of Johnston as they marched past headquarters to their places in the line. They did not cheer. But they took off their hats and filed past as though in a funeral procession. Some of the officers broke ranks to grasp his hand as the tears streamed down their faces. Generals Hardee and W. W. Mackall asked to be relieved of their commands. Even General Taylor, Davis's devoted brother-in-law, said of Johnston's removal that "no more egregious blunder was possible."

Very different was the mood of a lanky, rust-bearded Yankee a few miles away when he learned of Johnston's fate. General Sherman wrote his wife, "I confess I was pleased at the change." General Hooker later candidly wrote, "The news that General Johnston had been removed from the command of the army opposed to us was received by our officers with universal rejoicing."

Curtain Call on a Flaming Stage

While General Hood prepared for an offensive against Sherman, Johnston and his wife settled down for a stay in Macon. He was without assignment and therefore free to participate in the social life of the town, which was not devoid of gayety despite the recognition of impending doom. The Georgians were delighted with the general's quick repartee. None of this wit, however, was indulged in at the expense of the government or of the man who had replaced him. Howell Cobb, a Georgian of national prominence, wrote his wife concerning Johnston, "He indulges in no spirit of complaint, speaks kindly of his successor and very hopefully of the prospect of holding Atlanta."

But Johnston was a subject of controversy throughout the Confederacy. Some people found it impossible to admire both the general and the President and were vociferous in their partisanship. Perhaps more significant than most of the editorials printed on the subject was the observation of Constance Cary, a Richmond belle with considerable intelligence and good pipelines to the executive mansion, who wrote, "People we met said outspokenly that the Executive's animus against Johnston was based upon a petty feud between their wives, who had been daily associates and friends in old Washington days."

Hood attacked the enemy on the 20th, 22nd, and 28th of July, suffering losses that caused Colonel B. S. Ewell to confide to his journal, "A more triumphal vindication of General Johnston's policy could not be offered."

Hood then was forced to limp back into the Atlanta entrenchments. On September 1 he had to evacuate the city. The next day Sherman took possession.

In November, Hood undertook a new offensive action, attempting to wipe out Sherman's tenuous line of communication with Tennessee. Sherman dispatched General Thomas to take care of this move and in mid-December, at the Battle of Nashville, Hood was resoundingly defeated by the combined forces of Thomas and John M. Schofield.

Meanwhile, Sherman had set out on his famous March to the Sea, tramping 300 miles from Atlanta to Savannah, through territory guarded almost entirely by aged men, women, little boys, and frightened slaves. His progress could be marked at night by the flames of burning plantation houses as he cut a 60-mile wide swath of destruction. Some of the Yankee officers were embarrassed by their mission, but they had explicit orders from Sherman and he had no less definite orders from Washington. So the pleas of lone women were of no avail as their houses were burned before their very eyes, the contents of their pantries devoured and destroyed, and their Negro servants led away, some joyful at the prospect of freedom, some reluctant to leave but prodded along by the bayonets of the bluecoats. Sherman had told the people of Atlanta on September 12, "You might as well appeal against the thunderstorm," and the conduct of his march to the sea proved that that warning was meant for other Georgians as well.

After resting his army for a month in Savannah, Sherman on February 1 began a northward march toward the South Carolina border, with the idea of moving through the Carolinas to Virginia and uniting his strength with Grant's. By this time the Johnstons were in Columbia, South Carolina, and Johnston placed his wife aboard a train loaded with refugees leaving the city. The march through Georgia had had, as Sherman himself implied, something of the emotionless quality of a natural force, but the flames lit in South Carolina were the tangible expression of burning hate. Here, in the minds of the Northern soldiers, was the State that had started the whole tragic war. The fires of vengeance must be fed.

Nevertheless, some of the more sensitive of the invaders lamented the destruction wrought everywhere. Captain Daniel Oakey, of the 2nd Massachusetts Volunteers, complained that independent foragers were "marauding through the country, committing every sort of outrage" and leaving the land a "howling waste." He went so far as to say that some of these "bummers" who "fell to the tender mercies of [Confederate General] Wheeler's cavalry and were never heard of again" earned "a fate richly deserved."

As Sherman neared Columbia, Governor A. J. McGrath asked Johnston to take command of the State troops defending the capital. But the general declined on the grounds that his acceptance would not promote harmony. Columbia fell on February 17 and became an inferno. The responsibility for the burning has never been definitely assigned to either the Yankee soldiers or the retreating Confederates. Johnston soon joined his wife in Charlotte, North Carolina, and together they traveled to Lincolnton which, despite its name, seemed a good place of refuge.

By this time Davis, yielding to Congressional pressure, had appointed a General-in-Chief of the Confederacy, Robert E. Lee. But the President still held out against Congressional pressure for the reappointment of Johnston.

General Longstreet, who believed that Johnston was the best general in the Confederacy, not excepting Lee himself, wrote the new General-in-Chief:

I learned from friends in the South that nothing but the restoration of General Johnston to the command of the Army of Tennessee will restore that army to organization, morale and efficiency. This is my opinion also. I hope, therefore, that you will not think it improper in me to beg that this may be one of your first acts as Commander-in-Chief.

When Davis had inspected Hood's troops toward the end of the previous September, he had been embarrassed by shouts from the men of "We want Johnston." The same cry was now reaching his ears from soldiers and politicians alike. On February 21, Lee asked that Johnston be recalled to duty. This voice Davis could not deny. Johnston was ordered to report to Lee, who immediately assigned him to command of the force opposing Sherman. In thanking Davis for this concession, Lee told him, "I know of no one who had so much the confidence of the troops and people as General Johnston, and believe he has capacity for the command."

Senator Wigfall, Johnston's consistent friend, was overjoyed, but in his letter to Johnston was implicit a fear that his friend's difficulty in getting along with his superiors might create a rift between him and Lee. As once before he had stressed how much Johnston owed Lee for his appointment to command of the Army of Tennessee in 1863, so now he told him that Lee's support of the move to return him to command had "given great offense" to the President. The Texas Senator emphasized the warmth of Lee's friendship for Johnston and pointedly expressed the hope that the two Virginia generals would be able to work together harmoniously.

The letter brought back memories of West Point and tapped a

fund of sentiment in Johnston. He wrote the senator of Lee :

In youth and early manhood I loved and admired him more than any man in the world. Since then we have had little intercourse and have become formal in our personal intercourse : a good deal, I think, for change of taste and habits in one or the other. When we are together former feelings always return. I have long thought that he had forgotten our early friendship. To be convinced that I was mistaken in so thinking would give me inexpressible pleasure. Be assured, however, that knight of old never fought under his king more loyally than I'll serve under General Lee.

But Johnston was not all sweet sentiment at this moment. Wigfall had written him concerning President and Mrs. Davis's unhappiness over his reappointment. He confided to the senator : "I have the most unchristian satisfaction in what you say of the state of mind in the leading occupants of the presidential mansion. To me it is sufficient revenge."

On February 23, 1865, Johnston received Lee's instructions to take command of the Army of Tennessee and of all troops in the Department of South Carolina, Georgia, and Florida. The Army of Tennessee was now commanded by Beauregard who thus, as once before at Manassas, was Johnston's subordinate. Lee ordered Johnston to "concentrate all available forces and drive back Sherman." Johnston replied : "It is too late to expect me to concentrate troops capable of driving back Sherman. The remnant of the Army of Tennessee is much divided. So are their troops."

Johnston set up headquarters in Charlotte with, as he later wrote, "a full consciousness . . . that we could have no other object, in continuing the war, than to obtain fair terms of peace."

Sherman had entered North Carolina, leaving "Sherman's sentinels," as the lone chimneys of burned houses were called, all through the countryside and in more than a dozen towns in South Carolina.

While Sherman moved on Fayetteville, Schofield, who had returned from Tennessee, moved toward Goldsboro. Obviously, Sher-

man and Schofield were to join forces for a march into Virginia and
a union with Grant. Johnston sent Bragg, once again his subordinate,
to hold Schofield. Bragg clashed sharply with Schofield and was
forced to retire to Goldsboro. Johnston now planned to attack the
vanguard of Sherman's attenuated columns before they could join
with Schofield. On March 19, he struck at Bentonville in what has
been called "the last chance of the Confederacy." As Alexander
McClung, chief of staff to one of Sherman's lieutenants, General J. C.
Davis, later wrote, "Johnston had massed his scattered troops across
the road with skillful strategy, and with wonderful celerity and
secrecy." The surprised Yankees were struck off balance and fell back,
but they rallied and won the day.

Even if Johnston had won this battle, the victory would only have
postponed defeat. Sherman and Schofield would eventually have
joined forces. To confront their united strength of 90,000, Johnston
had only 35,000 men.

Johnston reported to Lee: "Sherman's force cannot be hindered
by the small force I have. I can do no more than annoy him." Lee
and Johnston had been considering for some time the possibility of
uniting their forces even if it meant abandonment of a position held
by the Army of Northern Virginia. Johnston now said: "I respectfully suggest that it is no longer a question whether you leave present
position; you have only to decide where to meet Sherman. I will be
near him."

But the hour was too late even for this desperate expedient. Word
came on April 5 that the government had evacuated Richmond and
that Danville, Virginia was the temporary capital. Johnston led his
army to Raleigh, where he informed Governor Zebulon Vance that
his men would not be able to defend the city. Johnston then proceeded with Beauregard to Greensboro, North Carolina, where he
had been ordered to report to the President. The atmosphere of
defeat hung heavy over the town. No great sensitivity was required
to realize that the Confederate government was an unwelcome guest.
With the Confederacy crumbling into ruin before the approach of

mighty armies, the citizens of Greensboro did not want to be accused of harboring its leaders. Virtually alone, the President was optimistic.

That night, John C. Breckinridge, recently appointed Secretary of War after serving as a major general, arrived in Greensboro. Johnston hastened to him and told him that he and Beauregard agreed that there was no point in continuing the war. Breckinridge said that he would give Johnston an opportunity to explain the situation to Davis. The lack of confidence between Davis and Johnston made the presence of a respected third party desirable. The next day Davis called Beauregard and Johnston into conference. Surrounded by cabinet officers, Davis exhorted his generals to continue the war. "I think we can whip the enemy yet," he said, "if our people will turn out."

Silence followed. The President was the first to break it, by saying, "We should like to hear your views, General Johnston."

Johnston replied without hesitation :

My views are, sir, that our people are tired of war, feel themselves whipped and will not fight. Our country is overrun. . . . My men are daily deserting in large numbers, and are taking my artillery teams to aid their escape to their homes. Since Lee's defeat, they regard the war as at an end. . . . I shall expect to retain no man beyond the byroad or cow-path that leads to his home. . . . We may, perhaps, obtain terms which we ought to accept.

In a low but controlled voice, Davis asked, "What do you say, General Beauregard?"

"I concur," the Creole said, "in all General Johnston has said." On Johnston's confident assurance that he could deal with Sherman at the conference table, Davis reluctantly agreed to let him try. About noon on April 17, Johnston and Sherman met in a house near Durham, about midway between Confederate and Federal picket lines. Johnston was accompanied by General Wade Hampton. Large-framed, with curling mustachios and a luxuriant, dark, curly beard, he had a bold-featured handsomeness that would have inspired the best efforts of Velasquez. This great South Carolina planter looked like what he was, a magnificent embodiment of the aristocrat and the warrior. Much smaller, but just as neat in his gray uniform and carefully trimmed beard, Johnston was equally the patrician and the soldier. But with a difference : ˉmore of the kingly reserve of a Northern clime, less of the royal flamboyance of a Southern one.

General Sherman, who rode up to meet them, presented a contrast to both. He was the living reality of the lanky, stoop-shouldered Yankee farmer or storekeeper of the cartoons. He might have been the New England progenitor of Uncle Sam. And, where Johnston's beard and hair were silver, Sherman's had the look of rusty iron. Almost with the casualness of familiar friends, he and Johnston shook hands, and the Confederate and Federal officers rode off together to the meeting place, talking as they went.

As soon as the two opposing generals had entered the house and evaded prying eyes, Sherman drew from his pocket a telegram which he handed to Johnston. It revealed that Lincoln had been assassinated.

Johnston's look of horror left no doubt of his shock. He said that he hoped Sherman did not suspect the Confederate government of any part in the crime.

Sherman said, "I cannot believe that you or General Lee or the officers of the Confederate Army could possibly be privy to acts of assassination." But he was not prepared to say that the civil government of the Confederacy had had no part in it. He did not doubt the sincerity of Johnston's statement that the assassination was "the worst possible calamity to the South."

The two generals then agreed that further continuation of the struggle would be "murder." But they adjourned until the next morning without reaching agreement on details. Sherman, as magnanimous in triumph as he was ruthless in war, offered the same generous terms that Grant had given Lee at Appomattox. But Johnston was intent upon doing more than surrendering the army immediately under his command. He wished to make a settlement bringing peace to the whole ravaged Southland. Sherman was not prepared to discuss surrender on that basis until Johnston showed that he had the authority to participate in a settlement of such broad scope.

At Johnston's urgent request, Breckinridge arrived a little before dawn to take part in the second conference. As an official of the civil government, he would have broader authority than Johnston and could also relieve the general of a certain amount of responsibility, which was particularly onerous in view of his relations with the administration.

But this remarkable Kentuckian was no mere cipher of the Davis cabinet. He had been a United States senator, Vice President under Buchanan, and Southern Democratic candidate for the presidency in 1860. The scion of families long prominent in Virginia and Kentucky, he could delight polished society with his courtliness or convulse a tavern taproom with his rough and ready wit. Now in his forties, he had a personality as room-filling as his tremendous bulk. He had drunk almost as deeply of the Pierian spring as of good Kentucky bourbon, and in debate his logic was as unerring as his marksmanship with tobacco juice.

At first, Sherman objected to admitting Breckinridge to the conference, maintaining that the matter at hand was one for military men alone. Johnston explained that Breckinridge was a major general in the army as well as a government official, and Sherman withdrew his objections.

When he took his seat, Breckinridge owed all his impressiveness to sheer bulk. He was as devoid of animation as a sleepy hippopotamus in a mud wallow. Not only did his early arrival deprive him of morning sleep, but he had not had his customary quota of bourbon. His only solace was his tobacco quid, which his jaws attacked with a vigor which demonstrated that at least one reflex was not dormant.

Sherman asked the two Southerners to have a drink. Even in that moment of depression, Johnston noted that Breckinridge's expression instantly became positively "beatific." Throwing his quid into the fire, the Secretary of War "poured out a tremendous drink which he swallowed with great satisfaction." In a moment, he was arguing with the eloquence that had served him so well on the Kentucky hustings, marshaling facts, laws, and precedents with a facility that astonished both Johnston and Sherman. At length, the Union general pushed back his chair and protested : "See here, gentlemen, who is doing the surrendering anyhow? If this thing goes on, you'll have me sending a letter of apology to Jeff Davis."

After much argument over terms suggested in a memorandum prepared by Confederate Postmaster General J. H. Reagan, Sherman began writing terms that would be acceptable to him. In the course of this concentrated effort, he got up from his chair, walked over to his nearby saddlebags, and drew forth a bourbon bottle. Breckinridge's face brightened in anticipation and he threw away his second tobacco quid. But, much to the Kentuckian's chagrin, Sherman only poured himself a drink and then recorked the bourbon.

The Union general returned to his writing and, when finished, handed the draft to Johnston. It provided that the Armies of the Confederacy everywhere be disbanded and conducted to the various state capitals where they would deposit arms and equipment. Existing state governments then composing the Confederacy would continue in operation if the state officials took an oath of loyalty to the United States. Insofar as the President of the United States had authority in the matter, civilians in the Confederate states would be immune from punishment for participation in the war. Neither their political nor property rights would be abridged.

Johnston and Breckinridge read the terms and signed. Then, in the deepening twilight, they strode from the house to their horses, Johnston raising his hat to the Union officers, Breckinridge apparently unaware of their existence.

Just before swinging into the saddle, Johnston turned to the Kentuckian towering above him and asked his estimate of Sherman. Breckinridge replied with judicial deliberation, "Sherman is a bright man, and a man of great force."

Then anger exploded inside Breckinridge and he expostulated : "But, General Johnston, General Sherman is a hog. Yes, sir, a *hog*. Did you see him take that drink by himself?"

Johnston made some whimsical excuses for the Yankee general, but the Kentuckian would hear nothing in extenuation. "No Kentucky gentleman," he insisted, "would ever have taken away that bottle. He knew we needed it, and needed it badly."

Sherman proceeded to check the movements of his forces in other areas, relying entirely on Johnston's word of honor as to Confederate intentions. The Union general wrote Johnston, "I have almost exceeded the bounds of prudence . . . and only did so on my absolute faith in your personal character."

Davis reluctantly assented to the terms signed by Johnston. Then came word from Washington that the Federal government had rejected the peace terms offered by Sherman. Sherman informed Johnston of this veto and told him that he would resume hostilities at 11 A.M. on April 26 unless Johnston surrendered "on the same terms as were given General Lee . . . purely and simply."

While preparing for the resumption of war, Johnston sought another conference with Sherman. The two met again on the 26th. The tension this time was greater than before. Both Johnston and Sherman paced the floor while General Schofield wrote out terms essentially the same as those which Lee had signed at Appomattox. Both Johnston and Sherman signed. Few, even among those Confederates who would not read the meaning of Appomattox, could fail now to realize that the war was over.

The final disbandment of the Army of Tennessee came early in May. In the warm intimacy of the spring night, the voices of officers reading to their men Johnston's message of farewell had a nearness that rendered the words peculiarly poignant:

Comrades: In terminating our official relations I most earnestly exhort you to observe faithfully the terms of pacification agreed upon, and to discharge the obligations of good and peaceful citizens at your homes as well as you have performed the duties of thorough soldiers in the field. By such a course you will best secure the comfort of your families and kindred and restore tranquility to your country. . . . I now part with you with deep regret, and bid you farewell with feelings of cordial friendship and with earnest wishes that you may have hereafter all the prosperity and happiness to be found in the world.

The men could not hope to catch a parting glimpse of their old commander, but they knew that somewhere in that spring night in North Carolina a diminutive figure, erect and soldierly in defeat as in all the fortunes of war and life, was riding off into the deepening shadows.

In the years that followed, Johnston settled first in Richmond, where he served as president of an express company. Then he was made president of the Alabama and Tennessee River Rail Road Company and moved to Selma, Alabama, hoping that the climate would benefit Mrs. Johnston's declining health. Next he moved to Savannah, Georgia, where he headed an insurance firm serving as general agents for English and Northern companies operating in the South. In 1877, he returned to Richmond, where he continued to work as an insurance agent.

Meanwhile, he had published a book on his military operations during the war. He was also then and in later years embroiled with Davis partisans in arguments over the wisdom of his Fabian tactics. Johnston had his enthusiastic champions, but others accused him of folly and timidity. These accusations worried him, partly because he coveted the good opinion of his contemporaries and partly because he cared greatly about his place in history. He would have been consoled to know that in 1953 an *Encyclopedia of American History* edited by one distinguished Columbia University professor in consultation with a famous colleague of the same New York institution would list him with Lee, Jackson, Grant, Sherman, and George H. Thomas among the half-dozen leading generals of the War of 1861-1865.

Even in his own time, though, Johnston enjoyed considerable prestige in both North and South. The political disabilities imposed upon him as a former general of the Confederacy were removed by act of Congress in 1877. President-elect Rutherford B. Hayes considered appointment of Johnston to the cabinet as a means of promoting national harmony, but General Sherman, then General-in-Chief of the Army, advised against it on the grounds that the move would be offensive to veterans of the Union Army.

Some astute Richmond politicians maneuvered Johnston into running for Congress. Other Democratic aspirants signed a petition for Johnston in the belief that the little general, who had seldom gone out of his way to be politic, would never run for office. To their surprise, he did, and they then could not oppose him for the Democratic nomination.

In the general election that followed, some of his supporters were near apoplexy. He seemed not to trouble a whit whether his forthright opinions offended the voters. And he would not tolerate any campaign advertising that misrepresented his views. When he saw a banner suggesting that he might not be opposed to a protective tariff, he called a meeting of the campaign committee and told them : "Gentlemen, this is a matter about which I do not propose to ask your advice, because it involves my conscience and my personal honor. . . . that banner in Clay Ward comes down today or I retire from the canvass by published card tomorrow."

He won on his own terms. In the House, his most conspicuous service was in helping to right a wrong that the Federal government had done one of his Yankee opponents of the war days, Major General Fitz-John Porter. Partly through Johnston's efforts as a member of the Military Affairs Committee, a court-martial decision against the Union officer was reversed. Johnston was as zealous in helping Porter as if he had been a Confederate colleague. When the matter was still pending, the Virginian wrote the Yankee : "You may be sure that I will leave nothing undone. I had rather lose an arm than see your enemies succeed in preventing the righting of your grievous wrongs."

Johnston did not run for re-election, but lived on in Washington.

As he moved into his seventies, he remained true to the heroes of his youth. When he read Lyman Draper's *Kings Mountain and Its Heroes,* he wrote the author, "I find it the most interesting American historical work I have read." His youthful admiration for Robert E. Lee was once again undimmed by the slightest hint of envy, and he developed a real affection for the Yankee generals who had been participants in the great drama that was the high point of his own life. Once, praising McClellan and Grant to a fellow Southerner, he called Sherman "the genius of the Federal Army." Then he said with measured emphasis, "But, young man, never forget that Robert E. Lee was their superior in any capacity."

On February 22, 1887, Mrs. Johnston died. Johnston was not given to open expression of his emotions, but his friends read the magnitude of his grief in the fact that he never again mentioned her name and that he kept everything in the house exactly where she had last placed it.

In the spring of 1890, when Johnston was 83 years old, he accepted an invitation to Atlanta to attend the Confederate Memorial exercises. In a carriage covered with flowers and drawn by two black horses, he rode through the streets, escorted by the governor's horse guard. The little general seemed to have shriveled some, but the figure was still erect and soldierly.

"That's Johnston! That's Joe Johnston!" yelled an excited spectator. Instantly, Confederate veterans surrounded the carriage, lifting its wheels off the pavement, reaching through the sides of the vehicle to grasp Johnston's hand. Even the Atlanta police force could not hold back the surging crowd. But gnarled hands unhitched the horses and the old veterans, fighting for places in the traces, drew his carriage up Marietta Street to the custom house and back to the opera house that was his destination, yelling with a volume that drowned the best efforts of a welcoming band. The crowd parted as the old general stepped down from his carriage to enter the building. On the steps, an aged veteran stopped him to plead: "Marse Joe, let me touch your garment. I fought through the war and have traveled 200 miles to see you." Johnston grasped the man's hand, then vanished inside.

To be so received in the city for whose loss he had been blamed was solace indeed!

In February 1891, he was asked to serve as an honorary pallbearer for General Sherman. Sherman had often praised Johnston's military ability, and the Virginian was grateful to him. The 84-year-old Johnston could not be dissuaded from undertaking the winter trip to New York City to pay final tribute to the foe who had become a friend. The day of the funeral was cold and damp. Johnston stood bareheaded before the flag-draped coffin. There was a lesson for all Americans in this tableau. But a spectator, mindful of more immediately practical considerations, said, "General, please put on your hat; you might get sick." With the same finality with which he had said no to the President of the Confederacy and laid down the law to his Congressional campaign committee in Richmond, he replied, "If I were in his place and he were standing here in mine, he would not put on his hat."

He caught cold, and the illness placed extra strain on his already ailing heart. Realizing that the end was near, he received his last communion. Watchers at his bedside heard no memorable last words. As in other scenes which moved his companions to strong expressions of emotion, he maintained his reticence. On March 21, 1891, he died peacefully.

What of the two paradoxes of General Johnston's career?

"Old Joe" was loved by junior officers and the men in the ranks for his democratic simplicity. General Joseph E. Johnston was intensely jealous of the prerogatives of his rank in dealing with superiors. How could these two men inhabit the same skin?

Some would almost have us believe that the general's personality bordered on the schizophrenic. They overlook the fact that many proud and sensitive people are far more diplomatic with their subordinates than with their superiors. The supposed paradox dissolves when we reflect that this trait is particularly common among men whose physical height is not commensurate with their mental stature and professional elevation.

The other paradox is not so easily dismissed. How could a man so fearless in combat—one whose personal valor and even recklessness were attested by his many wounds—leave to posterity a name indissolubly linked to a policy of retreat? Apologists for the general justly argue that his strategy of saving armies rather than territories was one which the Confederacy would have been wise to adopt. It is also true that the retreat for which he was most severely censured, the withdrawal before Atlanta, is now seen to have been a masterly operation, dictated by common sense and executed with brilliance. But the fact remains that in other instances—notably on the Centerville line in 1862 and in the Peninsula campaign—Johnston retreated when a Lee or Jackson might have bluffed and dared and won.

Again pride seems to be the key. Johnston was a man of vast ambition. His thirst for reputation dominated vital areas of his life. Having won an enviable reputation, he guarded it fiercely. This fact is evident in his correspondence from shortly after Bull Run through the entire war, and in the postwar years of apologia. Johnston guarded his fame more carefully than his person. For such a man, to risk life is far easier than to risk reputation.

Lee in the War of Secession is often, and aptly, compared with Washington in the Revolution. Each disciplined himself in selfless devotion to the cause he served. Johnston might profitably be compared with an earlier Washington : the Washington of the French and Indian Wars. At that stage of his career, before revolutionary zeal burned away personal vanity, Washington was as jealous of his prerogatives as Johnston ever was. He was every bit as troubled by matters of rank. Like Johnston, he was the product of a proud plantation society that valued honor above life. Like Johnston, he was a man of unshakeable integrity. But, also like him, he thought of honor as an amalgam of character and reputation.

There was greatness in Johnston. It came to the fore when he described as fortunate the wound that took him from command on the Peninsula and made Lee his successor. It reappeared on numerous occasions, including the last days of Johnston's life, when he paid tribute to the man to whom he had surrendered in 1865. The essential nobility of his character makes his faults more obvious. His swollen ambition offends our sense of symmetry, just as any deformity seems greater in an otherwise flawless physique.

But the great defect does not deprive Johnston of heroic stature. In the Iliad of the Confederacy, he is like those larger-than-life characters of Greek tragedy whose monumental proportions are dramatically flawed by a single excess.

JOSEPH E. JOHNSTON
Bibliography

Govan, Gilbert E., and Livingood, James W. *A Different Valor.* Indianapolis, 1956. Carefully researched and the best available biography of Johnston, although it is a eulogy at Davis's expense.

Hughes, Robert M. *General Johnston.* New York, 1893. Written by one
of Johnston's kinsmen, this book contains invaluable material on
his family background, youth, and personality in the home.

J. E. Johnston Manuscript Collection in Library of College of William
and Mary, Williamsburg, Virginia. An invaluable collection of letters to, by, and about General Johnston. Heavily drawn on by R.
M. Hughes and Govan and Livingood, but other students of Johnston's life may draw quite different conclusions from a study of the
same material. Of particular interest is an eyewitness account of
First Manassas by Thomas C. Preston, written July 20, 1891 but
based on "written records made cotemporaneously with the
events." Preston was with Johnston much of the time and helped
him make his original report of the battle. Especially interesting
also is a diary kept by Colonel B. S. Ewell, which sheds light on
circumstances preceding and succeeding Johnston's removal from
command before Atlanta.

Johnson, Bradley T. *A Memoir of the Life and Public Service of Joseph E.
Johnston.* Baltimore, 1891. A little-read work, but one of the most
valuable on Johnston. The author, a former Quartermaster General of the United States, had been a Confederate brigadier under
Johnston. An admirer of both Johnston and Davis, he perceptively

appraised their conflict in Chapter XVIII, pp. 251–269. Includes good anecdotes and picture of Johnston's home life, and account of last illness and death, pp. 270–271. Book also contains reminiscences of Dabney Maury, rich in anecdote and dating back to Mexican War, pp. 291–306; and reminiscences of Col. Archer Anderson, revealing influence on Johnston of ancestral pride and early reading of Sir Walter Scott, pp. 307–317.

Johnson, R. U., and Buell, C. C. (eds.). *Battles and Leaders of the Civil War,* Vols. I–IV. New York, 1887–1888. Especially rewarding is Volume II, pp. 160–277, containing Johnston's own account of operations from the time of his withdrawal from Manassas through the Battle of Seven Pines, written in reply to Davis's statement in *Rise and Fall of the Confederate Government;* General G. W. Smith's account of the Battle of Seven Pines; General George B. McClellan's description of the Peninsula Campaign; and firsthand anecdotes about General Johnston. Vol. III contains Johnson's own version of the Mississippi Campaign.

Freeman, Douglas S. *R. E. Lee,* Vols. I–IV. New York, 1934–1935. Valuable chiefly for information on Johnston's association with Lee (especially Vol. I, pp. 51, 55, 74, 83, 119, 123–124, 219, 221, 226, 235, 260, 266, 272; Vol. II, pp. 41–80; Vol. III, pp. 461–462, 494–495; Vol. IV, pp. 4–6).

Freeman, Douglas S. *Lee's Lieutenants,* Vols. I–III. New York, 1942–1944. Numerous and enlightening references to Johnston throughout this splendid work.

Henry, Robert S. *Story of the Confederacy.* Indianapolis, 1931. Johnston's activities in the context of the war.

Chestnut, Mary B. *A Diary from Dixie.* Boston, 1949. Sheds light on feud between Johnston and Davis.

De Leon, T. C. *Four Years in Rebel Capitals.* Mobile, 1890. Has much the same value as *A Diary from Dixie.*

McElroy, Robert. *Jefferson Davis, the Unreal and the Real.* New York, 1937, Vols. I and II. Valuable interpretations of relations between Davis and Johnston, especially Vol. I, pp. 325–326, 340–342, 346; Vol. II, pp. 373–374, 382, 416–417, 450–451, 479–483, 643–644, 660–663.

Dodd, William E. *Jefferson Davis*. Philadelphia, 1907. Light on Johnston's relations with Davis, especially pp. 251–254, 294–299, 330–333, 340–341, 350.

Davis, Varina Howell. *Jefferson Davis, Ex-President of the Confederate States of America, A Memoir*. New York, 1890. Information on Johnston from a hostile source. Volume I contains little or nothing of interest to the student of Johnston's life. Volume II, however, contains many interesting references, especially pp. 86–158, 185–197, 262–265, 270–293, 620–626, 848–881.

Johnston, Joseph E. *Narrative of Military Operations*. New York, 1874. Johnston's own account of his operations. Valuable for its presentation of the general's side of controversies with Davis and others such as those over Harpers Ferry, pp. 14–31; failure to follow up effectively the victory of First Manassas, pp. 52–65; Johnston's rank, pp. 70–73; removal of Johnston from command before Atlanta, pp. 430–465. Important, too, for revelation of Johnston's sense of values.

Meade, Robert Douthat. *Judah P. Benjamin*. New York, 1943. Narrates difficulties between Benjamin and Johnston.

Williams, T. Harry. *P. G. T. Beauregard, Napoleon in Gray*. Baton Rouge, 1954. Much information on Johnston's role at First Manassas and in opposing Sherman in the Carolinas.

Vandiver, Frank E. *Mighty Stonewall*. New York, 1957. Especially pp. 143–167.

Commager, Henry S. (ed.). *The Blue and the Gray*. Indianapolis, 1950. Firsthand accounts by many men, including Johnston himself and Sherman, pp. 102–115, 741–742, 923–968, 1,112–1,118.

Douglas, Henry Kyd. *I Rode with Stonewall*. Chapel Hill, 1951. See especially pp. 5, 14, 65–66, 70, 95, 234.

Taylor, Richard. *Destruction and Reconstruction*. New York, 1955. Especially pp. 14–16, 22–25, 42–45. Taylor, who was a devoted friend to both Johnston and Davis, makes particularly valuable observations on the controversy between the two and on Johnston's personality.

Thomas J. Jackson Papers, Virginia Historical Society, Richmond, Va. Includes some of Johnston's military correspondence and two letters—January 13, 1863 and July 30, 1863—from Wade Hampton to Johnston, illustrating the affection in which Johnston was held by those who had served under him.

(Confederate Museum, Richmond)

VI

JEB STUART : The Knight of the Golden Spurs

VI

JEB STUART : The Knight of the Golden Spurs

Legend on Horseback

GAUNTLETED AND SPURRED, his tossing gray cloak revealing its crimson lining, a white-toothed grin parting the chestnut forest of his mustache and beard, a young cavalier rode off to battle with a banjo-strumming troubadour at his side. Jeb Stuart, who went to war in the most romantic traditions of chivalry, himself became a chivalric legend. He is like a hero of European minstrelsy, and yet he is as Virginian as the accents in which he and banjoist Sam Sweeney sang "Jine the Cavalry." Stuart was like those young lords and knights of old English ballads who reappear in different garb in the songs of the Virginia hills.

James Ewell Brown Stuart was native to those mountains. He was born February 6, 1833 at "Laurel Hill," his father's farm home in Patrick County, Virginia. When he rode to war, he thought of himself in the knightly role. His family's record was such that he might be pardoned for aspiring to be one of "the knightliest of a knightly race." His father, Archibald Stuart, a veteran of the War of 1812, had been elected to Congress after serving in the General Assembly of Virginia. Jeb's grandfather, Alexander Stuart, had been a member of the exclusive Virginia Executive Council, before trying his fortunes

in Missouri, where he became speaker of the State House of Representatives and a federal judge. Alexander was the son of Major
Alexander Stuart, Revolutionary War hero, wealthy patron of the
arts and a founder of Washington College, now Washington and Lee
University. Archibald Stuart, first of the line in America, ended his
days as a rich landholder in the Shenandoah Valley, but earlier years
had been spent in some role that forced him to flee a turbulent Ireland
in 1726.

Stuart must have remembered his aristocratic and romantic past,
as well as been mindful of his own adventures, when, during the War
Between the States, he signed some personal letters as "The Knight
of the Golden Spurs." Of course, his keen blue eyes must have glinted
with humor when he inscribed the title, but he must not have thought
the matter was entirely laughable.

Jeb Stuart's first years, in most respects, were like those of many
another country boy delighting in the sights and sounds of farm and
forest. But in several ways the boy foreshadowed the man to an
unusual degree. His esthetic sense was strong and he was a devoted
collector of flower specimens. However, none of the little savages
among his playmates would have dared to call him a sissy. Few things
were more characteristic of young Jeb than his actions at the age of
nine when he was attacked by some hornets. Persisting despite
repeated, vicious stings, he climbed a tree to the very nest of his
enemy and destroyed it. Influenced deeply by the intensely religious
atmosphere of his home, Jeb swore that he would never touch liquor.
Many years later, in an army that had too many hard drinkers for
its own good, Stuart declined whisky even when the refusal made him
unique among the assembled officers.

After brief schooling at Emory and Henry, he secured an appointment to West Point. Then seventeen, with his long arms and legs and
short body, he must have looked something like an awkward spider
when he walked. His blue eyes were brilliant and his high forehead
was expansive, but his fellow cadets were more aware of such
features as his receding chin. Only on horseback did he appear grace-

ful. His schoolmates, in the derisive friendliness of teenage boys, nick-named him "Beauty."

At the end of the first term, he stood eighth in his class in general merit and in his second year became seventh. His conduct was as commendable as his academic record. Fitzhugh Lee, who was at the Point with Stuart, remembered Jeb's role there as orderly sergeant of his company. "There was so much music in his voice . . . ," he recalled, "sounding like the trumpet of the archangel."

In his last two years, Stuart, who had grown to feel quite at home at the Academy, became as distinguished for fisticuffs around the barracks as for finesse on the parade ground. Demerits mounted.

But this same rough-and-tumble young man, with all the fighting predilections of a barbarian prince, wrote letters of the most delicate sensibility to young ladies. The same hand that blacked the eye of a fellow cadet could write to a pretty cousin, "Myriads of flowers leaned forth, laughing with joy. . . ."

Despite his delight in feminine beauty and romantic turn of mind, Stuart, when he was in the presence of attractive young women, appears to have been acutely and uncomfortably aware of his homeli-ness. He was more at ease with older women. Among two whom he charmed were Mrs. Robert E. Lee, wife of the Academy's superin-tendent, and Mrs. Winfield Scott, wife of the General-in-Chief of the Army. By his own testimony, both women were like mothers to him.

But, despite the diversions and delights of West Point, Jeb's heart was elsewhere. In one letter, he said : "I am very well pleased with West Point for the limited stay which I expect to make . . . but so long as there is such a bright spot as Virginia, I can never be content to take up my abode here permanently. If it could be grafted on Virginia soil, I would consider it a paradise."

In Stuart's time it was not a foregone conclusion that a young man studying at West Point would enter upon an army career. Not long before graduation in July 1854, he wrote his father :

"Two courses will be left for my adoption, the profession of arms and that of the law. . . . Each has its labors and rewards. In making the selection I will rely upon the guidance of Him whose judgment cannot err, for 'It is not with man that walketh to direct his steps.' "

To his cousin Bettie Hairston, he wrote more revealingly :

Were I to consult my own inclination at present, I would continue in the army. It has attractions which are . . . overpowering. There is something in "the pride and pomp and circumstance of glorious war" which makes "Othello's occupation" the most desirable of all. Now tell me candidly, would you not rather see your cousin a bold dragoon than a petty-fogger lawyer?

By mid-October, he was assigned to duty in Texas as second lieutenant in the Mounted Rifles, "a corps which my taste, fondness for riding, and desire to serve my country in some acceptable manner led me to select above all the rest."

There he found plenty of quail and deer to hunt but no Comanches. And, having little use for his sword, he busily employed his pen. His letters were full of allusions to Shakespeare, who had been a passion with him ever since the night when, as a West Point plebe, Jeb had secretly and with the excitement of discovery read the dramatist's works for hours after "lights out." There were also allusions to Byron, Scott, and Irving. Stuart himself was an interesting writer, as he fully appreciated, sending some of his missives to a newspaper back home as well as to relatives and friends. For all their weakness of high-flown rhetoric, the letters are remarkable revelations of the author's keen eye for significant detail. They also reflect the duality of the young soldier's own nature. He bemoaned the lack of opportunity for mortal combat, and at the same time was deeply moved by the sight of "a beautiful flower on the roadside." "Fond as I am of flowers . . . ," he wrote, "I did not pull it, but left it as an ornament to the solitude."

During his Texas service, Stuart grew the beard which, glinting red in the brassy Southwestern sun, became his oriflamme of battle. With this newly acquired personal trademark, he cut a dashing figure. He was delighted that his receding chin was now hidden by so handsome a covering. His confidence in social relations with young

women soared, and he found that he could charm them as effectively as he used to charm their mothers.

Soon he was concentrating his attentions on one, Flora, daughter of
Col. Philip St. George Cooke of the Second Dragoons. The facts that
her family was Virginian and that she was an expert horsewoman
may have counted for as much as her bright blue eyes. Rides down
the bridle path led to the bridal march.

After a simple ceremony at Ft. Riley on November 14, Jeb and
Flora left for a new home in the barracks of Leavenworth. Stuart's
sincere devotion to his bride did not crowd out all sentiment for other
girls. To one gentle friend he sent a piece of the wedding cake and
wrote : "Our correspondence shall never stop with my consent. What
say you ?"

Though a romantic fellow, Stuart was also a strictly moral man. His
new father-in-law, writing of Jeb to another member of the family,
said : "He is a remarkably fine, promising, pure young man. . . ."
Col. Cooke also noted that Stuart had received "an extraordinary
promotion" to 1st lieutenant, 1st Cavalry.

Kansas has always been noted for its storms, and in those days
there were tempests of human passions to match the fury of the
elements. Border Ruffians and Free Soilers lynched and massacred
until a mighty tornado of hatred threatened to sweep the entire population of the Territory into its frightful vortex. In the course of his
duties, Stuart saw a colonel of the United States Army forced to
negotiate with the bearded, gnarled, fanatical old leader of a lawless
band. The man's name was a common one, but Stuart remembered
it. The old man was called John Brown. Some people said that the
actions of men like this fellow Brown might lead to civil war.

But there was little time to meditate upon such things when there
were Indians to fight. In the summer of 1857 Stuart at last had an
opportunity to face the Cheyennes in open combat. He was so eager
that he spurred his horse on and outdistanced his company in pursuit
of the fleeing enemy. Plunging among the tribesmen, firing his gun
and slashing with his saber, he fought like a madman until he received

a pistol wound in the chest. After convalescence, he led his men on a hard march back to the fort. In the course of this adventure, he swam a swollen stream to prove to fellow officers that it could be forded on horseback. He relished the romantic elements of the expedition, but did not seem to consider his safe return remarkable. "From the first," he told his wife, "I prayed to God to be my guide."

The next month, September, Stuart became the father of a little girl. Stuart had his wish that she be named Flora for her mother. For his safe return and for this new life, Stuart was grateful to God. He wrote his mother that he wished to contribute $100.00 to start a building fund for a new church near his old home at Laurel Hill. In 1859 he was confirmed in the Episcopal church.

To Stuart there was never any conflict between the spiritual and the practical. Soon after his confirmation, he returned to Virginia to attend a church convention in Richmond, gratify his nostalgia for his native State, and visit the War Department in Washington in hopes of selling his new inventions, a saber belt fastener and "Stuart's lightning horse hitcher."

Stuart was in the War Department trying to sell one of these devices when an officer suddenly asked him to deliver a message at once to Col. Robert E. Lee, then across the Potomac at Arlington. Lee had orders to report to Washington. There was an insurrection at Harper's Ferry. Stuart accompanied Lee to a White House conference with President Buchanan and Secretary of War John B. Floyd. The President declared martial law. Lee was named commander of all forces at Harper's Ferry and Stuart, by his own request, was the colonel's aide. That night, after a wild ride, the two officers dismounted from a locomotive that wheezed and sighed to a stop in Harper's Ferry. Like a man conscious of his role, Stuart, rakish in a broad-brimmed brown hat, jauntily strode forth to embrace destiny.

A little before 6 : 30 the next morning, Stuart went with a party of marines to the engine house which had been seized by a man called Smith. Inside were Smith's followers and civilian prisoners whom he had seized. To avoid killing the innocent, the marines would use bayonets to storm the house. The signal for attack would be a wave of Stuart's rolled-brimmed hat.

Standing outside the door, Stuart read Lee's demand for surrender of the insurrectionists.

The door opened about four inches. Through that narrow crack, Jeb caught sight of a cocked carbine, then something even more startling : the instantly recognizable bearded face of a wild-eyed old man. Stuart knew at once that the Smith of Harper's Ferry was the John Brown of Kansas.

The two talked. In vain, Brown sought an amendment of the terms. At last, finding Stuart adamant, Brown concluded : "I would as lief die by a bullet as on the gallows."

"Is that your final answer, captain?" Stuart asked.

Brown's affirmative reply brought a wave of Stuart's hat. Using a ladder as a battering ram, marines splintered the door. There were three minutes of firing, slashing, and stabbing in the smoke-filled, reverberating engine house. Then Brown's followers were dead, dying, or prisoners and Brown himself was a blood-smeared captive. Stuart held Brown's Bowie knife, which he had seized as a souvenir.

A short while later, Senator James M. Mason of Virginia was questioning Brown regarding his military forces. "What wages did you offer?" Mason asked.

"None," was Brown's reply. But Stuart, looking more the bearded prophet than the cavalier, intoned " 'The wages of sin is death.' "

All over so soon ! But all was not over. North and South, many would agree that "The wages of sin is death," and many would be ready to exact payment. But there were great differences of opinion as to where the sin lay. Many in the South remembered the murders committed by Brown and his followers. Many in the North could not forget the courage of the carpet-slippered old man who walked so calmly to death on the gallows. They saw him as the martyred leader of a holy war and would not let his body lie "a-mouldering in the grave."

Stuart knew that his meeting with destiny had not been a hit-and-run encounter. In the fall he wrote Governor Henry A. Wise: "I . . . respectfully and earnestly urge you in view of the exposed situation of Virginia to attack from the North . . . to take into serious consideration the issue by the State to every organized military company in the State the same number of uniform suits as arms."

As sectional passions mounted, Stuart suffered no qualms of indecision. From his Western post of service, he wrote his brother: "The moment . . . [Virginia] passes the ordinance of secession, I will set out immediately for Richmond. . . . I had rather be a private in Virginia's army than a general in any army to coerce her."

In May of 1861, when Stuart received an appointment as captain, First United States Cavalry, he was already packing to return to his native State, which had seceded. Promptly resigning from the federal service, he was soon in Richmond with a commission as colonel of infantry.

Richmonders were speculating on the role to be played by Stuart's father-in-law. Jeb wrote his wife, "The greatest anxiety is manifested for your Pa to arrive." Again he sent an urgent message: "How I hope your Pa will resign! If he could only see things in their true and right light—which is difficult to do from so far—he would resign instanter."

Stuart was very fond of his father-in-law, and his own infant son bore the imposing name of Philip St. George Cooke Stuart. But family tragedy was portended by the message which Colonel Cooke had written on learning that both his son and Stuart had resigned their commissions in the United States Army. "Those mad boys!" he exclaimed. "If only I had been there."

Once again the impending struggle between North and South carried Stuart to Harper's Ferry, this time as second in command to Colonel Thomas J. Jackson. The Calvinist and the cavalier were soon good friends. Stuart acknowledged a greater eagerness for combat than Jackson would admit even to himself. "I strive," Jeb said, "to inculcate in my men the spirit of the chase."

FROCK COATS AND EPAULETS

Soon Jackson was relieved of command by General Joseph E. Johnston, Stuart's friend of earlier days. Stuart was quickly commissioned lieutenant colonel of cavalry, much to his delight. Johnston evacuated Harper's Ferry, but early in June Jeb saw action along the Potomac. In savage delight, he wrote : "The ball is open up here. . . ."

He took a boyish pleasure in writing his wife about the strawberries, bouquets, and other gifts which the ladies of Winchester were sending him.

But ceaseless patrols punctuated by occasional brushes with federal cavalry did not provide enough excitement for Stuart. To gratify his sense of humor, he would unnecessarily lead his men into areas surrounded by the enemy and then extricate them with dash and daring. Once he exchanged horses with a young trooper and the two rode across the Federal lines, inviting pursuit by Union cavalrymen. Jeb's companion excitedly pointed out that there was a Federal post ahead besides the troops in their rear. But Stuart would not hear of turning aside. "They won't expect us from this direction," he said. "We can ride over them before they make up their minds who we are." The two horsemen galloped through the astonished post with bullets flying all around them. Zest in his voice and sparks of enthusiasm in his eyes, Stuart called to his friend : "Did you ever time this horse for a half mile?"

Perhaps some of the Union soldiers had been temporarily thrown off guard by the fact that Stuart was still wearing his United States army uniform. Many a veteran of "the old army" wore one in the early days of the Confederacy. For this reason, Stuart was not surprised when, on one of his morning rides with a single companion, he encountered Duane Perkins, an old West Point classmate, in similar attire. All cordiality, Stuart shouted "Howdy, Perk! Glad to see you have come over. What is your command?"

Perkins laughingly shouted : "Hello, Beauty! How are you?" He pointed behind him where a Union battery loomed into view. "That's my command, right there!"

"Oh, the devil!" Stuart exclaimed. "I didn't know you had stayed with the Yankees." He wheeled his horse about and was off with a speed that left his would-be captor frustrated.

Soon he practiced a little deception of his own by means of the Federal uniform. With Confederate forces retreating before Federal troops in Northern Virginia, Stuart became separated from his men in wooded country. Suddenly he was alone, facing an enemy company in position behind a rail fence. He boldly rode toward them and, in the trumpetlike voice that dated from his West Point days, commanded : "Take down those bars!" Immediately they obeyed the orders of this blue-coated officer. Not until the barrier was down did skepticism enter their minds. But Stuart was prepared. "Throw down your arms," he shouted, "or you are all dead men !"

The Yankees could not imagine such boldness in one who did not have them surrounded. They dropped their arms and fell on their faces in meek surrender. Stuart was a merry man as he rode back to his own lines with his 49 prisoners. Single-handedly, he had captured an entire company of Pennsylvania volunteers.

Such exploits quickly made Stuart a legendary figure. Jackson and Johnston heaped praise on him. His own men regarded him as an extraordinary phenomenon. He converted many to his belief that "a good man on a horse can never be caught." When forced to retreat, he did so at so slow a pace as to seem nonchalant. "A gallop," he told his men, "is a gait unbecoming a soldier unless he is going toward the enemy."

With seemingly inexhaustible energy, he saw personally to innumerable details of his command and was out scouting so much that he was rarely in camp. When he was there, he would have enough surplus energy to challenge strapping young men to wrestling matches and laughingly pin their shoulders to the ground.

Soon this man of action proved that he was also a master of subtlety.

On the night of July 18, Johnston learned by telegram that Beauregard was under attack at Manassas. The Army of the Shenandoah must go at once to Beauregard's aid. Johnston knew that Federal

General Robert Patterson would attempt to interpose his force as soon as he learned that the Confederates were on the way to Manassas. He therefore ordered Stuart to conceal the movement.

Stuart must have exceeded Johnston's fondest hopes. He kept his handful of cavalry so busy and employed so many ingenious devices that Patterson not only concluded that the entire army still faced him in the Winchester area, but that it had been reinforced.

Stuart and his men bivouacked near Manassas the night of July 20 and were ready for action on the bloody Sabbath of Bull Run.

From the time the battle opened, Stuart was miserable. Repeatedly he informed the Confederate command that he was ready for action, but no orders arrived for him and he rode back and forth in the restlessness of frustration. The sounds of battle, rising and falling on the wind, told him that the Confederates were losing ground. It was some time before Stuart knew that Jackson had stood like a stone wall. By 2 P.M., in an agony of impatience, the cavalryman had dismounted and was pacing back and forth when a courier arrived in breathless haste. The message was all that Stuart could have wished: "Col. Stuart, Gen. Beauregard directs that you bring your command into action at once and that you attack where the firing is hottest."

Springing into the saddle, Stuart led his men over a field of the wounded and dying toward the wavering Confederate lines. Spying a regiment of scarlet Zouaves through the blue fog of battle, and assuming them to be from Louisiana, he called out, "Don't run, boys. We are here." In a moment, he realized his mistake. They were Federal troops.

Into their midst, Stuart's cavalry charged, clubbing and slashing, splashing the bright uniforms with the darker red of blood. Soon the Zouaves were on the run, spreading their panic like a contagion among other Federal troops. Stuart borrowed two guns from the infantry and accelerated their rout.

He sent a quick report to General Jubal Early and that officer brought up his forces in time to prevent re-forming of the Federal lines.

One of history's great battles had been fought, and in it Stuart had proved the possession of solid qualities behind the façade of glamor. By his judicious use of artillery as well as by dash and daring, he may have tipped the teetering balance of battle. General Early gratefully testified: "But for his presence there . . . the enemy would probably have ended the battle before my brigade reached that point. Stuart did as much toward saving the Battle of First Manassas as any subordinate who participated in it."

Disappointed at receiving no orders for carrying the war across the Potomac, Stuart set up headquarters at Munson's Hill, within tantalising sight of the capitol in Washington. Soon afterward John Esten Cooke, Flora's cousin, a distinguished author, joined Stuart's staff. Thanks to this fact, we have an intimate portrait of life at headquarters.

Stuart had just been made a full colonel, but the newly acquired distinction nowise diminished his boyish informality. Yet there was something princely about him too. Stretched on a blanket by the road, he would hold court among his civilian admirers. Even in that posture, he conveyed an impression of latent energy rather than indolence. Cooke said that, whether the colonel was writing at his desk or discoursing with one leg thrown over the arm of his chair, anyone in his presence "could discern enormous physical strength."

One day a pretty 17-year-old girl and an elderly female companion, captured while attempting to slip past Confederate pickets, were brought to Stuart's tent. At first they disdained to eat in the company of the vile rebels, but Stuart's good humor was unaffected. Like the young lord of a castle, he brought forth his entertainers. They were three Negroes: a guitarist, a ventriloquist, and a dancer with limbs amazingly obedient to the wildest of imaginations. Soon the elderly lady was smiling and the laughter of the younger one was mingling with Stuart's own.

After the fun, Stuart pointed out the bullet holes and blood spots on a Confederate coat, much as Mark Antony had pointed out

similar places on Caesar's toga. He told his guests of the brave boy
who had worn that coat on picket duty.

The next day Stuart gallantly helped the two women into their
carriage and they left under guard for Richmond. He kissed the
younger one's hand. The two were captives of the Confederate States
of America. Stuart personally had captured their hearts.

The entertainers were part of a troupe to which Stuart added as
the war progressed by asking that a great many men be attached to
his staff as couriers. By a curious coincidence, each of these couriers
was a soldier or orderly celebrated in his regiment as a singer, dancer,
ventriloquist, fiddler, banjoist, master of the bones, or clown. One of
these performers, Sam Sweeney, banjo player extraordinary, became
Stuart's personal troubadour.

No court in the romantic tradition is complete without pretty
women. Stuart always won their attention and often gained their
affection. He found time for gentle gallantries and the penning of
innocent missives that quickened feminine hearts. In his relations with
women as in so many other things, Stuart was superficially a cavalier
with a devilish gleam in his eye, but beneath the glittering surface
was a character of stouter weave and soberer hue. His adjutant,
William Blackford, who shared his quarters and often slept next to
him in the field, wrote : "Though he dearly loved to kiss a pretty girl,
and the pretty girls loved to kiss him, he was as pure as they. . . .
I know this to be true, for it would have been impossible for it to have
been otherwise and I not to have known it."

The usually good-natured Stuart became angry once, even with
so devoted a companion as John Esten Cooke, when the young
writer jestingly charged him with a hint of infidelity.

When Stuart captured a Federal officer's trunk and found in it
loving letters from a wife and risqué ones from a mistress gloating
over successful deception of the wife, he bundled them all together
and dispatched them to the officer's spouse.

A vein of seriousness always underran Stuart's light-hearted
behavior. Once when he appeared wholly absorbed in the sheer

physical delight of wrestling with a member of his staff, he paused to speak a word of grim warning to some soldiers whose conversation indicated that they were not taking McClellan's army seriously enough. "The war is going to be a long and terrible one," he said. "We've only just begun it, and very few of us will see the end. All I ask of fate is that I may be killed leading a cavalry charge."

The serious side of Stuart's nature was impressed upon his men in other ways. Seemingly utterly tireless, he appeared to have no appreciation of physical weakness in others. Once when a spokesman for a company on patrol reminded Stuart that they had been on duty ten days, and without food for 26 hours, he retorted: "Nonsense! You don't look starved. There's a corn field over there. Jump the fence and get a good breakfast. You don't want to go back to camp, I know. It's stupid there, and all the fun's out here."

Some of Stuart's troopers thought he was heartless and hated him. But others had a love little short of idolatry for the colonel who chose to sleep on the ground because his men could not enjoy the comfort of beds.

There was no question of how Stuart's superior, General Johnston, felt about him. In an official report, he stated:

"He is a rare man, wonderfully endowed by nature with the qualities necessary for an officer of light cavalry. Calm, firm, acute, active and enterprising, I know no one more competent than he to estimate the occurrences before him at their true value. If you add a real brigade of cavalry to this army, you can find no better brigadier general to command it." On September 24, Stuart—only 28 years old—was commissioned a brigadier general.

The tender letters that Stuart wrote Flora from his winter camp near Manassas, sometimes inditing them in sentimental verse, were in sharp contrast to the growing bitterness which he felt for her father, especially after the older man became a brigadier general in the Union forces.

A captured Yankee captain ushered into Stuart's presence warned him that the Federal cavalry would be no easy mark in the future.

When Stuart asked, "How's that?" the captive replied : "New commander. General Philip St. George Cooke. He'll make you smart."

Stuart's bearded mouth was a grim line as he said : "Yes, I know he has command, and I propose to take him prisoner. I married his daughter, and I want to present her with her father. So let him come on."

Stuart did arrange for the unhappy Flora to communicate with her mother through enemy lines, but he insisted that his son, Philip St. George Cooke Stuart, be renamed James Ewell Brown Stuart, Jr.

Further references to the little boy in Stuart's letters were those of a doting father. Nor was little Flora forgotten. He asked that her portrait be painted.

In December, Stuart's men fought an engagement at the village of Dranesville with a Federal foraging force greatly outnumbering them. The results were inconclusive and the Confederates suffered many more casualties than their enemy. Nevertheless, Stuart construed the affair as a victory for the cavalry. He could endure many things, but he could not bear to acknowledge defeat, even to himself.

The event would have had no great significance, except for the fact that it convinced Stuart of the need for a better organized and more mobile artillery. He built up a horse artillery with the aid of John Pelham, "the gallant Pelham" of future fame.

He also acquired the services of scouts as talented and colorful as the entertainers with whom he had earlier surrounded himself. Three were particularly outstanding. Two were still in their twenties : William Downs Farley, a polished young South Carolinian who shared Stuart's enthusiasm for Shakespeare when he was not chasing foxes or Yankees, and Frank Stringfellow, intensely brave but eminently practical, a man who once literally took refuge under the generous hoopskirts of a sympathetic Virginia lady when pursuing Federals were close on his heels. The third, Redmond Burke, was old enough to be the father of Farley or Stringfellow, and indeed was the parent of three of Stuart's troopers. Around the campfire, he could tell thrilling stories of hairbreadth escapes. To these men and others,

John Esten Cooke said, Stuart was "more like the chief of a hunting party than a general."

But, for the aggressive Stuart, there was not enough hunting. He found delight in pelting his troopers with snowballs, but he longed to shoot cannonballs at the enemy with his newly organized artillery.

When orders came from General Johnston in the spring of 1862 to burn the stores at Manassas and withdraw from Northern Virginia, Stuart complied immediately. But Jeb was both a man of action and a gourmet, and there rose in his bosom fires of resentment to match the blue and yellow flames that licked at the vast mounds of bacon. Even when 20 miles distant from these pyres, he could smell the cooking hogmeat, and that fact did not improve his disposition.

He was in much better humor by the time he reached Richmond and his spirits soared as he rode with his men up Franklin Street to Capitol Square. There were adoring women here. Handkerchiefs fluttered from the sidewalks and the windows of nearby buildings, and flowers were tossed in the path of the "Knight of the Golden Spurs."

Soon he was absorbed in the Peninsula Campaign as McClellan's army moved nearer and nearer to Richmond.

He distinguished himself at the Battle of Williamsburg and made sure that his wife learned of it. In a letter revelatory of the dichotomy of his character, he wrote : "Blessed be God that giveth us the victory. The Battle of Williamsburg was fought and won. . . ." Then, having given God the credit, he added : "For myself, I have only to say that if you had seen your husband, you would have been proud of him. I was not out of fire the whole day." Not very thoughtfully, he also said, "I came within an ace of capturing my father-in-law."

Then came the Battle of Seven Pines. Among its many wounded was Gen. Joseph E. Johnston. Robert E. Lee succeeded him in command of what he called the Army of Northern Virginia, a name soon to find its place in official records and world history.

Stuart was quick to urge the new commander to launch a major offensive against the enemy. "We have an army far better adapted to attack than defense," Stuart said. "Let's fight at an advantage before we are forced to fight at a disadvantage." Jeb scarcely tempered his brashness by adding, "It may seem presumption in me to give these views, but I have not thus far mistaken the policy and practice of the enemy." Stuart even went so far as to submit a plan of attack.

Ride to Glory

The time was one when few responsible persons, gravely viewing the threat to Richmond by McClellan's powerful army, were thinking in terms of bold offensive strategy. But bearded and benign Robert E. Lee, calmly reading Stuart's recommendations, had already decided upon a scheme of attack sounder than the one proposed by the young cavalryman, but not a whit less audacious. He thought that Stuart's boldness could be put to good use.

On June 10, Lee ordered Stuart to scout the rear of the enemy, gaining what information he could about Federal lines of supply and communications, seizing cattle and grain and destroying wagon trains. The bulk of the cavalry must be left with the main army. On this expedition would go only men who, whether officers or privates, were selected with the care of Gideon preparing to do battle with the Midianites.

Stuart set out on June 12 with about 1200 horsemen. With him were Colonels William F. H. (Rooney) Lee and Fitzhugh Lee, the son and the nephew of Robert E. Lee, and Colonel Will T. Martin of Mississippi. Fortunately for historians and interested posterity, there was also with him John Esten Cooke, historian and novelist, to leave a graphic description of what became one of the most famous raids in history. In this adventure, more than any other, Stuart seemed to leap full-bodied from the pages of Alexandre Dumas.

Cooke never forgot how Stuart looked when, at two o'clock in the morning, the young general, drenched in moonlight, sat astride his horse, "the gray coat buttoned to the chin; the light French sabre balanced by the pistol in its black holster; the cavalry boots above the knee and the . . . hat with its black plume floating above the bearded features, the brilliant eyes and the huge mustache." Five years later, Cooke wrote with a poetic hyperbole truer than literal truth, "The glance out of the blue eyes of Stuart at that moment was as brilliant as the lightning itself."

Stuart's cavalry saw no Yankees until the next day when, riding past fields of grain golden in the summer sun, they entered the village of Hanover Courthouse. United States Cavalry horses, saddled for action, were massed in the little, tree-shaded street near the old brick courthouse. Keeping his column hidden behind a wooded knoll, Stuart sent Colonel Fitzhugh Lee and his troopers to the right with the intention of flanking the enemy and cutting him off. Before Lee could execute this move, shots rang out. The Union soldiers had spotted the Southern scouts and were springing to their saddles.

Stuart shouted, "Charge!" With him in the lead, a yelling, thundering torrent of gray rushed downhill toward the Bluecoats. The Yankees, about 150 in number, galloped away in a cloud of dust punctured now and then by the blaze of a carbine like lightning in a storm cloud.

Stuart and his men galloped on, eating the enemy's dust, until suddenly, in a spot where thick woods pressed against the narrow road, the Yankee cavalry charged the Confederates. Just as suddenly, their leader fired his pistol, wheeled about and led his detachment back down the road at a gallop.

"Form fours! Draw saber! Charge!" shouted Stuart. A chorus of rebel yells followed as the Graycoats bore down on their quarry, firing as they came. Like fox hunters, the shouting troop galloped after the Federal soldiers until the gray horsemen reached the Totopotomi, "a sluggish stream, dragging its muddy waters slowly between rush-clad banks, beneath drooping trees."

By this time, Stuart had acquired many prisoners. They belonged to the company of which Fitzhugh Lee had been a lieutenant in "the old Army," and soon he and they were having a delightful reunion and exchanging information about mutual friends.

No such pleasant meeting awaited Fitzhugh Lee's cousin, Colonel W. H. F. Lee, who led his men across a rustic bridge to high ground where the enemy waited in battle formation. The gray and the blue forces met in a clash of bodies and swords amid a deafening cacophany of clanging metal, neighing steeds, shouting and screaming, and exploding powder.

Then the Union line gave way and once again the Bluecoats were in headlong flight with the Confederates chasing.

Soon the pursuing force was in the deserted camp of the enemy, near Old Church, and busily appropriating supplies. One of Stuart's men, the valiant Captain Latané, had received a mortal wound. Many of the enemy lay dead. With a single loss, Stuart had accomplished the mission on which he had been sent. He had the information which General Lee wanted. Prudence would dictate his quiet return to Richmond along the route by which he had come.

Stuart himself must have realized this. Certainly the bearded cavalryman seemed to be absorbed in inward cogitation before he turned quickly to Captain Cooke and said : "Tell Fitz Lee to come along. I'm going to move on with my column."

In a flash, Cooke knew that Stuart contemplated riding completely around McClellan's army. Gamely, he laughed and said, "I think the quicker we move now the better."

"Right," said Stuart. "Tell the column to move on at a trot."

Cooke was probably not the only one of Stuart's men who, at that moment, expected that within twenty-four hours he would "be laughing with . . . friends within the Southern lines, or dead, or captured."

Death might stare them in the face at any turn of the road, but the men in the ranks had so much confidence in Stuart and in themselves that they gave occasional false alarms of the enemy's approach to gratify their boyish humor.

Soon there were incidents enough without manufacturing them. As Stuart skirted the Pamunkey, he detached a force to set fire to several Federal transports anchored in the river. Hurrying on, the

Confederates left far behind the dark cloud of billowing smoke that rose from the river as they neared the railroad. Blue-coated infantrymen guarding the rails were swept up by Stuart's cavalry. The Confederates laid down their sabers and took up axes, felling telegraph poles right and left. The whistle of an approaching troop train shrilled an interruption, and Stuart quickly lined up his men on one side of the tracks. Round the bend the train came. At the command to halt, the engineer pulled out the throttle. As the flat cars of Union soldiers came abreast Stuart's line, the Confederates opened fire. The engineer slumped over at the controls and the masterless engine roared down the track and out of sight with all its passengers, the quick and the dead and the dying.

Stuart rode on as twilight deepened into night. A few miles farther, he found thirty acres of Union supply wagons and left thirty acres of roaring flames.

Yankee sutlers' stores furnished a late banquet. The hungry men earlier had passed Federal hospitals without touching so much as a loaf of bread.

As Stuart rode on in the bright moonlight, he was fully conscious of the drama as well as the danger of his position. He was menaced, as he had been every foot of the way, by cavalry commanded by his father-in-law, General Cooke. He was attempting to lead twelve hundred men completely around an army of 100,000. Like many reckless adventurers, Stuart not only loved life but was also half in love with death. The Great Adventure lured him and his most exciting flirtation was with Death. "There was," he later recalled, "something of the sublime in the implicit confidence and unquestioning trust of the rank and file in a leader guiding them straight, apparently, into the very jaws of the enemy, every step appearing to them to diminish the faintest hope of extrication."

But Stuart was intent on keeping his romance with the grinning skull strictly a light flirtation. He placed on mules, two to a steed, the 165 prisoners he had acquired so that his progress would not be slowed by men forced to march. By pressing ahead with no pause for rest, he should reach the bridge across the Chickahominy before daylight. Once the marshbanked river was between him and his pursuers, he would be able to breathe easily.

A lieutenant native to the Chickahominy country said that he knew of a short cut, a plantation ford nearer than the bridge. Stuart decided to take it. He needed every minute he could gain, for his activities by now had alarmed McClellan's army and fresh Yankee cavalrymen would soon be on the Confederates' heels.

Riding from Talleysville to the Chickahominy, Stuart's forces became divided and there were some anxious moments before they were reunited. Then Stuart, that problem solved and his route decided upon, put one knee over the pommel of his saddle and nodded into slumber. Down the white ribbon of moonlit road he clopped, the plumed head drooping on the barrel chest, the swaying body held in the saddle by Captain Cooke who rode beside him with a firm grip on his arm. Behind him rode a strange, and most unmilitary, caravan of drooping riders on staggering horses.

The gray light of dawn had chased the silver of the moon when the cavalry column came to the Chickahominy. The usually shallow ford was far beneath rushing flood waters that had inundated the river banks. Colonel W. H. F. Lee, first officer of rank to see the swollen stream rushing past half submerged tree trunks, plunged with his horse into the river to test the danger. Despite his strong arms and legs and the best efforts of his horse, he was almost drowned. "What do you think of the situation, Colonel?" Cooke asked the gasping man. "Well, captain," was the reply, "I think we are caught." The men in the ranks sank to the ground in weariness and resignation.

At that moment, Stuart rode up. There was no trace of sleepiness in the flashing eyes which he turned on the scene. Silently he sat his horse and twisted his beard. Cooke noted that Stuart was the only man there who did not surrender to despondency. Instead, "he was cool and looked dangerous."

Sending one remarkably good swimmer across the stream with a dispatch to General Lee requesting a diversion to occupy the Federals on the Richmond side of the river, Stuart addressed himself to the immediate problem. A bridge must be built at once. In an instant, Stuart had the men ripping timbers from a nearby barn and laying them on the abutments of an earlier bridge. As the sun climbed higher, the Federal cavalry drew nearer: just how near, nobody knew. Planking was hastily laid down, the general himself working with his men from a boat bobbing in the stream, singing gaily as he lifted the boards into place.

The structure was shaky, but it held as the artillery rolled across, followed by the clattering horsemen. The rear guard crossed. Torches were hastily applied to the bridge. As the flames leaped up from the old lumber, Bluecoats galloped into view on the shore just left. Their bullets sprayed futilely about the hard-riding Confederates and Stuart could indulge in a hearty laugh.

He paused for only two hours of sleep in friendly Charles City County. At nightfall, the column stopped, but Stuart did not. With a display of energy that appalled his weary staff, he spurred his horse on to Richmond. Before daylight he had gone thirty miles, and his horse's hoofs were clattering through the streets of the sleeping city. An hour later, President Davis and General Lee had the story of the raid straight from Stuart's own lips.

General Lee summed up Stuart's achievement in an official order:

The general commanding announces with great satisfaction to the army the brilliant exploit of Brig. Gen. J. E. B. Stuart—in passing around the area of the whole Federal Army, taking a number of prisoners and destroying and capturing stores to a large amount. . . . The expedition re-crossed the Chickahominy in the presence of the enemy with the same coolness and address that marked every step of its progress. . . . The general commanding takes great pleasure in expressing his admiration of the courage and skill so conspicuously exhibited throughout by the General and the officers and men under his command.

Debate over the long-term value of Stuart's raid still rages. Some say that it alerted the enemy. Others, pointing convincingly to the

fact that McClellan's troop dispositions remained substantially unaltered after Stuart's raid, say that the seemingly madcap enterprise
gave Lee the knowledge necessary for an attack on the enemy. Certainly Lee's own estimate of the service rendered by Stuart should
weigh heavily in the young man's favor.

But the famous "Chickahominy canter" did have indisputable results. It captured the imaginations of men in its own day and in succeeding generations. This most characteristic of Stuart's exploits lifted
the morale of the South and limned a bright new chapter in the
annals of military adventure.

The results were not happy for General Cooke. Stuart, enjoying a
well-earned rest in a story-book setting almost too good to be true,
romped with his children and listened delightedly as his wife filled
with romantic song the warm air heavy with the scent of roses,
honeysuckle, and magnolias. But, meanwhile, his father-in-law fretted
under a cloud of suspicion. He became the scapegoat for the cruelly
embarrassed Federal Army, and many believed that he had relaxed
his vigilance because his daughter's husband was his quarry. Whatever his potentialities for high command, he never got a chance to
prove them.

Stuart played an effective but unspectacular role in the Seven Days'
Battles in which McClellan's Army was beaten back from Richmond.
He made no effort to disguise his disappointment at his inability to
make "an overwhelming charge."

During the period of general inactivity that fall, Stuart left camp
in impoverished Hanover County for a trip to Richmond with one
of the most colorful members of his staff, Heros von Borcke, a former
Lieutenant of the Guard in Berlin—a blond giant with, as one
Richmond belle delightedly noted, "great curling golden mustaches."

One morning as he rode down a Richmond street, Stuart was
ambushed by a group of girls who placed a wreath of flowers around
his horse's neck and presented a bunch of roses to Jeb himself. The
bearded cavalier willingly surrendered and recited poetry to his fair
captors until a column of infantry marched onto the scene and startled

him out of romantic reverie with rude calls in falsetto voices. Their taunts accomplished something that enemy bullets seldom had. Stuart spurred his horse and made a hasty retreat.

On July 30, Stuart returned from Richmond with a major general's commission.

Not long after the street incident, the jeering infantrymen would not have recognized the dandified cavalry officer. One day in August, he and von Borcke and a few other members of his staff boarded a train at Hanover for Orange County where he was ordered to confer with General Lee. Accommodations for the officers' horses were easily found in a stock car, but room for Jeb and his companions could be made in the passenger cars only by disturbing the rest of sprawling troopers. Rather than wake the men, Stuart and his staff seated themselves on the fuel logs in the tender behind the locomotive. Thick, black clouds of smoke obscured most of the scenery, but they did not choke Jeb badly enough to prevent his singing at the top of his voice. On arrival in Gordonsville, he exploded into hearty laughter with his companions. All were covered with soot and Stuart's own face and beard were as black as his sable plume.

The infantry soon had another laugh at Stuart's expense. Lee planned to cross the Rapidan below Pope's forces and entrap the Union general. Stuart was to cut off the enemy rear and burn the bridge over the Rappahannock. Riding into the village of Verdiersville after midnight with his escort, Stuart chose to rest there and await the arrival of Fitzhugh Lee with the cavalry corps. Stuart stretched out on a farmhouse porch, his scarlet-lined cloak under him and his plumed hat by his side, and was soon deep in slumber. Aroused by the sudden arrival of Federal cavalry, Stuart had to flee. While Yankee soldiers delightedly tossed his hat about on their sabers, Stuart made good his escape.

Jeb wrote Flora that he was "greeted on all sides" by infantrymen asking "Where is your hat?" For him the war was now a personal contest between himself and Pope. He told Flora, "I intend to make the Yankees pay for that hat."

Stuart collected a first installment on August 20 when he put Bayard's New Yorkers to flight. Two days later he began in earnest to collect payment. With a raiding party of 1500 men, he set out for the railroad bridge at Catlett's station, a great distance behind the supposedly secure Federal lines. At Lee's headquarters, the expedition was classified as an effort to disrupt Pope's communications. But, as Jeb swung into the saddle, he flashed his famous white-toothed grin, laughed like a cavalier riding forth in a tournament, and gaily called, "I am going after my hat."

Before sunset, dark clouds suddenly rolled across the sky, lightning flashed and the rain poured. Stuart thought the night the darkest he had ever seen. While he was wishing for a guide, a loud rendition of "Carry Me Back to Old Virginny" broke through the drumming of the rain and rolling reverberation of thunder. The singer was a Negro serving one of the Federal officers and he consented to guide the Confederates to Pope's camp.

Soon Stuart learned that Pope's own tent was pitched on the Rapidan among those of the other officers and that only a few pickets were on guard. One of Stuart's men so successfully infiltrated the camp that he was seated at the enemy's supper table when the main body of cavalry swept down on the scene. Stuart charged directly among the tents. Tables were overturned and lanterns knocked down as tents toppled when fleeing Federals found exits where none had been before. Some, not so fortunate, wound up in the canvas "like fish in a net." Flaming kerosene consumed the tents with a hunger not dampened by the pouring rain.

Jeb had destroyed some wagons and captured some prisoners. But that was not all. General Pope's own tent had been ransacked, and Stuart could send him a saucy message : "General : You have my hat and plume. I have your best coat. I have the honor to propose a cartel for a fair exchange of prisoners."

Among the flesh-and-blood prisoners was a young man whose name Stuart had taken down in advance of the raid after promising a pretty Warrenton girl that he would take him for her. Another pretty young woman was a prisoner herself. She wore a Federal uniform but begged for release on grounds of her sex. Maybe Jeb's chivalry did not extend to women who wore trousers. He told her, "If you are man enough to enlist, you ought to be man enough to go to prison."

In the ensuing campaign, Stuart did his part in driving General Pope from Virginia. New legends clustered around his name. General Longstreet was amazed at this young Virginian who, with a stone for a pillow, could go to sleep on an active field of battle until his services were needed, and when called on, would spring into his saddle and gallop off singing, "Jine the Cavalry." On nights between battles, he could visit with friends until the light of day began to steal through the windows, and then ride back to camp, to all outward appearances as fresh as if he had had a good night's sleep.

On September 6, when a magnificent sunset flecked the Potomac with red-gold and gilded the shining arms and accouterments of his troopers, Stuart and his men crossed from Virginia soil to the northern bank of the river in time with the brassy strains of "Maryland, My Maryland." Lee was leading the Army of Northern Virginia on an invasion of the United States.

By noon of the next day, Stuart was in the village of Urbana, where he established headquarters.

The day after that, he was the toast of the community, especially the feminine part of the population. After a dinner party in their honor, Stuart and his staff strolled in the moonlight with some of the attractive young ladies. Looking out from the gallery of an academy building at a landscape bathed in silver, Stuart suddenly exclaimed to von Borcke: "Major, what a capital place for us to give a ball in honor of our arrival in Maryland!"

The next night, hundreds of candles lit a transformed interior. Von Borcke had decorated the empty hall with roses and battle flags. A regimental band played "Dixie" as young ladies and their escorts arrived in carriages and buggies. Soon the walls began to glitter as candle gleams danced on the hanging sabers which trembled to the vibrations of a spirited quadrille.

Few dancers even noticed the orderly who had jostled his way through their midst to Stuart's side until they heard him exclaim : "The enemy, sir! They've driven the pickets and are coming on. They are in camp, lots of them." The crack of a pistol outside added its own exclamation point. The music stopped. Stuart and his troopers grabbed their sabers and dashed from the hall.

The huddled women inside heard the sound of hoofbeats, loud at first but quickly diminishing. Then came the crackle of small arms, followed by the thunder of artillery.

At 1 A.M. Stuart, grinning with satisfaction, returned to the hall to report that the enemy attack had been broken and some of the Bluecoats had been captured. The candles were still burning. The musicians began again where they had left off and Stuart and his officers returned to the dance. Soon the welter of girlish laughter was pierced by a scream. Stretcher bearers were bringing bleeding men into the hall. Gay dancers instantly became sympathetic nurses. One of Jeb's wounded troopers spoke in the spirit of his commander : "I'd get hit any day to have such surgeons dress my wounds."

On the 11th, in the cold, gray drizzle of a dismal September day, the Army of Northern Virginia was forced to quit the vicinity of Urbana. Stuart was not at the head of his column. He lingered in Urbana even after a mounting crescendo of gunfire was clearly audible. He left the house where he was staying only when artillery shells began to explode around him. Von Borcke afterwards complained : "I was kept riding to and fro directing the retreat in the name of the General who, with the other members of the staff, to my intense disgust, still lingered on the verandah with the ladies."

The general spent the night near Frederick in the humble farmhouse of an old Irishman. He appeared to enjoy dancing with the lively daughters of his host as much as he had with the polished belles of Urbana. But he did not forget to write to Flora—albeit, he wrote more like an eager adolescent than a responsible commander in retreat. "The ladies of Maryland," he said, "make a great fuss over your husband—loading me with bouquets—begging for autographs, buttons, etc. What shall I do?" She knew very well what he would do, and so did he.

But a few days later, gloom sat heavily on Stuart as, after the bloody battle of Sharpsburg, he rode through misting rain over muddy roads to the Potomac. Through two harrowing days of skirmishing and bluffing, Stuart and his cavalry held off the enemy while the infantry escaped to Virginia across the river. Then the cavalry crossed, their faces ruddy in the light of the burning houses of Williamsport. "High over the heads of the crossing column and the dark waters of the river," wrote von Borcke, "the blazing bombs passed each other in parabolas of flame through the air, and the spectral trees showed their every limb and leaf against the red sky."

By the end of the month, Stuart had moved into quarters at The Bower, the hospitable plantation of the Dandridges, near Martinsburg. The place was much like the "bower of loveliness" in Spenser's *Faerie Queene*. Days were spent in boating and in woodland walks. Instead of attacking the enemy, Stuart and his staff daily attacked great platters of delicious food served by beautiful girls and admiring women of the neighbourhood. The charming Dandridge girls and their equally fascinating cousins added to the gayety of nightly dancing in the mansion. Concerts featuring Stuart's band drew people from miles around. Negroes were encouraged to participate in the entertainment, and their lively jigs were popular features of nearly every program. Whenever Stuart appeared, pretty girls dashed up to shower kisses on him—and there were no jeering infantrymen.

Even more demonstrative females lay in wait for Stuart when he and his staff visited a home near Shepherdstown. There a mob of young girls surrounded the cavalry hero, almost smothering him with kisses. When he could draw a free breath, his uniform had been shorn of its buttons and he was hard put to retain his locks of hair. Stuart's chief pleasure that day, though, seemed not to be in this excessive attention, but in quiet conversation with Lily Parran Lee, the young widow of an old friend.

In the course of the day's visit, Stuart was inspired to write an ode more notable for fervor than grace. The verses were a frank parody and the refrain was "Maryland, My Maryland."

Maryland was, indeed, on the General's mind. At 1 A.M. on September 9, Stuart staged by torchlight a "Farewell Serenade to the Ladies of The Bower." When the strains of music brought sleepy girls to the bedroom windows, Stuart himself sang four solos. Stuart had been ordered by General Lee to lead a detachment of cavalry across the Potomac into Maryland with the object of destroying enemy communications, discovering enemy intentions, and invading Pennsylvania to take city and state officials as hostages.

He instantly put behind him all fun except the fierce joy of conflict. Stonewall Jackson would have approved the tone of the cavalryman's address to his troopers : "Soldiers : You are about to engage in an enterprise which, to insure success, imperatively demands at your hands coolness, decision, and bravery, implicit obedience to orders without question or cavil, and the strictest order and sobriety on the march and in bivouac."

Stuart and 1800 men at 4 A.M. forded the Potomac. Their stomachs were empty, for breakfast fires would have been a giveaway to the enemy. In the dense, gray-white fog, they might have been riding to the end of the world.

Enemy fire greeted them on the opposite shore, but the opposing force was a small one and the Yankee commander finally watched helplessly as the long, inexorable line of gray dissolved into the grayness of the morning.

Telegraph keys clattered out the alarm in Maryland and Pennsylvania. Stuart would have to cross enemy lines as well as rivers, canals, and railroads. As the Confederates rode on, they encountered communities of complacent civilians who, despite the evidence of their eyes, insisted on believing that Stuart's men were Federal troopers. Forty miles of riding, practically without incident, brought the Confederate cavalry after nightfall to Chambersburg, Pennsylvania.

The frightened townspeople quickly surrendered. They were soon amazed by the manner and demeanor of the invading forces. Only one store was broken into by the Rebels, and Stuart's provost guard arrested several men for stealing private property. Colonel A. K. McClure, a local bigwig who had participated in the surrender of the town, was astonished at the behavior of the shivering Confederates who sought the hospitality of his blazing hearth. He lost count, but believed that more than 100 entered his home. He reported: "All, however, politely asked permission to enter and behaved with entire propriety. They did not make a single rude or profane remark."

The townspeople were so reassured that many of them chatted in friendly fashion with their conquerors. Stuart was much more uncomfortable that night than many of the citizens in his power. With his staff, he lay on the floor of a little toll house. The hard drumming of rain, hour after hour, drove away sleep. Three times when the sound became unbearable, he rose and waked his guide, always to ask the same question: "Won't all this rain make the rivers rise before we can get back? Can we ford the Potomac in this weather?" The guide assured him that the cavalry could race the flood waters back to the Potomac. Stuart, knowing that the whole countryside and Washington besides were aware of his activities, could find little comfort in the suggestion.

Morning was cold and damp. There was a chill in Stuart's heart as well as his marrow. With town officials as hostages, Stuart and his men rode out on the road to Gettysburg. Behind them, they left flaming machine shops and warehouses. A series of explosions told the fate of Federal stores of ammunition. No gleam of triumph lightened the tense earnestness of Stuart's face as he leaned from his saddle to speak to Blackford, who rode beside him. "Blackford," he said, "I want to explain to you why I took this route for the return. And if I don't survive, I want you to vindicate my memory."

His finger moved on the map that he held. "You see," he said, "the enemy will think I will try to recross the river above, out west somewhere, because it is nearer home and farther for them. They will have strong guards at every ford and scouting parties will be looking for us, so that they can concentrate at any point. They will never expect me to move three times that distance and cross at a ford below them but so close to their main army, and so they won't be prepared for us down there to the east.

Stuart's red eyebrows were like accent marks over his troubled eyes. "Now, do you understand what I mean?"

"Perfectly," Blackford replied.

"Don't you think I'm right?"

"You are," Blackford answered. "They won't think of it. And if anything should happen to you and I get through, I'll see that the army understands."

Tears welled in Stuart's eyes. He spurred his horse on and was gone.

As Stuart led his men to Cashtown, just seven miles from Gettysburg, and then by a circuitous route toward Emmitsburg, Maryland, the Federals were preparing a trap for him. "Not a man should be permitted to return to Virginia," General Henry Halleck warned McClellan. And McClellan replied, "I have given every order necessary to insure the capture or destruction of these forces, and I hope we may be able to teach them a lesson they will not soon forget."

The enemy's couriers were repeatedly captured by the Confederates. Stuart's men could not afford to attract attention by gunfire. They were using the silent saber. Twisting and turning over Maryland roads, the Confederates rode through the night without pausing to rest, even though the snores of the riders were sometimes louder than the hoofbeats of their mounts. During that fearful night, Stuart and some of his officers galloped six miles off the route to call on girls whose company they had enjoyed in Urbana, and then had to ride at breakneck speed to rejoin the cavalry column by daylight.

A Federal force spread across Stuart's southward path retreated in haste before one of his magnificent charges. A second Federal force was bluffed into retreat.

Before McClellan knew what was happening, Stuart and his men had forded the Monocacy River into Virginia while a hapless Federal force on the hills to the north indulged in futile threats. By a civilian courier, Stuart had sent his compliments to acquaintances among the sorely vexed Yankee officers.

A broad grin parted Stuart's luxuriant beard. A little later, another bearded man was looking grim. "When I was a boy," Abraham Lincoln said, "We used to play a game—three times around and out. Stuart has been around McClellan twice. If he goes around him once more, McClellan will be out."

Again there were idyllic days at The Bower, cut short by a fresh Union invasion over the Potomac. Stuart's cavalry won new glory in hard fighting in the mountains and around Fredericksburg.

There were ever closer brushes with death in the succeeding months. In the fighting around Fredericksburg as the year died, Stuart ordered charges so rash that they were countermanded by both Jackson and Lee. One bullet made a hole in his haversack. Another pierced his collar.

Worse to Stuart than any blow of the enemy was news from home that his little daughter had died. He wrote his wife, "I feel perfect resignation to go at His bidding to join my little Flora." He poured out his grief in a letter to Lily Parran Lee : "I can think over her sweet little face, sweet temper and nature and extraordinary sensibilities and weep like a child to think that their embodiment who loved her Pa like idolatry is now lifeless clay. May you never feel such a blow."

Flora joined Jeb at camp and he was the tender husband.

Death was much on Stuart's mind now. His beloved scout, Redmond Burke, was killed, and once again Stuart was moved to write to Lily Parran Lee of his grief. By now, he corresponded with her frequently, sometimes on happy subjects. He told her of the receipt from a Baltimore admirer of a gift of golden spurs, which were his special pride. Once he wrote, "If a truce . . . should take place, I shall be sure to visit you to get that kiss I have strived in vain for heretofore."

Early in the new year, Pelham, a great favorite of Stuart's, was killed and the general bowed his head and sobbed. Later, bearing his black plumed hat like a sable symbol of mourning, he knelt at the bier and wept.

John Esten Cooke could write in his diary :

"The General has got his banjo and has gone out frolicking. He is a jolly cove." And the General's wit still crackled like lightning, but an invisible comrade rode with him always now. The name of that companion was Death. Writing Flora about Pelham's death, he said : "He was noble in every sense of the word. I want Jimmy to be just like him. . . . I wish an assurance on your part in the event of your surviving me—that you will make the land for which I have given my life your home and keep my offspring on Southern soil."

In April, massive Federal forces moved across the Potomac into Virginia at almost every available ford. Lee was trying to concentrate his numerically inferior forces in the tangle of The Wilderness. Stuart's men, tired, wet and hungry, arrived on the scene on a night made miserable by sleet. On May 1, Lee, having pressed on toward Chancellorsville, sent Stuart and his men to the flanks of his line to search out a route of attack on "Fighting Joe" Hooker. The next day Jackson, at Lee's direction, swept around the left with his entire corps. General Stuart covered his movement.

Stuart, who worked with Jackson as well as Jackson did with Lee, was a useful subordinate on a day that saw panic-stricken Union soldiers fleeing before Rebels in full cry. Night came, but Jackson was not ready to count the day as over. He must attack again. Stuart was preparing to assault a fire-lit camp in the woods when a courier dashed up and called out, "You will have to come, General. Quick! General Jackson's shot."

In one sentence he completed his orders to the men around him and then galloped off. In an instant, the cavalry officer had become the commander of a whole corps of infantry.

Jackson's plan of battle, as usual, was locked tight within his own skull. Stuart sent to Jackson for instructions, but the dying general only sent back word that Stuart should use his own judgment, that he had complete confidence in him.

When the next day dawned, the woods seemed to be lit with the ruddy gold of sunset rather than the paler beams of sunrise. It was soon discovered that large areas of The Wilderness were on fire. Like Prince Rupert reincarnated, Stuart, waving his plumed hat and urging the men on, stormed the ridge that was the kingpin of Hooker's position. Then he led charges and countercharges through a hail of bullets. Above their whine and the clash of battle, his powerful voice rang out in an improvised song, "Old Joe Hooker, come out of The Wilderness." Before noon, "dense and huddled masses" of bluecoats were "flying in utter rout."

After that day, few of the infantrymen who had seen action at Chancellorsville were disposed to laugh, except indulgently, at Stuart's foibles and vanity. Col. W. L. Goldsmith described Jeb's personal leading of the charge on the ridge as "the bravest act I ever saw." And all marveled at the skill, daring, and quickness with which Stuart had led a force of less than 1,000 out of a wilderness trap held by 80,000—and all of this when he had been abruptly elevated to the leadership of a corps whose dispositions he did not know. E. P. Alexander, Jackson's faithful artilleryman, voiced the opinion of many when he said : "I don't think there was a more brilliant thing done in the war than Stuart's extricating that command from an extremely critical position . . . as promptly and boldly as he did."

Army gossip had it that Stuart would succeed to the permanent command of Jackson's corps. But, when the appointment went to Gen. Richard Stoddart Ewell instead, Stuart showed no disappointment. When Jeb was told that Jackson on his deathbed had expressed the wish that Stuart succeed him, the cavalryman replied, "I would rather know that Jackson said that than to have the appointment."

In the midst of somber thoughts, Jeb still retained his sense of humor. An erroneous report that von Borcke had been killed in fighting Stoneman's troops at the battle of Chancellorsville brought a request from Governor Letcher that the body be sent to Richmond to lie in state. Back went a reply generally attributed to Stuart : "Can't spare body of von Borcke. It is in pursuit of Stoneman."

On June 19, 1864, there was no joking about von Borcke's death. On that day, the enemy, mistaking him for Stuart because of his fancy uniform, shot him from his horse. The doctor told Stuart that the German could not live overnight. Stuart bent over his fallen comrade, the General's tears flowing on the Major's face, and said, "Poor Von, you took this wound for me."

Von Borcke lived, though he was never again fit for military service. But there were others—some of them almost as close to Stuart—who did not live. And some men were saying that the Confederacy itself was dying. Indeed, much of its vitality seemed to have departed when breath left Jackson's body.

Lee was preparing for a great gamble that, for good or ill, would hasten the end. Once again, he invaded the North.

Knight Errantry Errs

On the afternoon of June 22, 1863, Stuart received orders from General Lee outlining the role intended for the cavalry. First of all, Lee wanted reports on the enemy's whereabouts and activities. "I fear he will steal a march on us and cut across the Potomac before we are aware," the commander wrote. "If you find that he is moving northward and that two brigades can guard the Blue Ridge and take care of your rear, you can move with the other three into Maryland and take position on General Ewell's right, place yourself in communication with him, guard his flank, keep him informed of the enemy's movements and collect all the supplies you can."

The next night, Stuart, sleeping out of doors in a rainstorm because he insisted on sharing the privations of his men, was waked by further orders from Lee. Substantially they were the same as those of the day before, except for an additional command : "You will, however, be able to judge whether you can pass around their army without hindrance, doing them all the damage you can, and cross the river east of the mountains." Such latitude in dealing with Stuart was an invitation to daring.

Two days later, Stuart's cavalry, after an heroic crossing of the swift Potomac, rode into Rockville, Maryland, less than 17 miles from Washington. Students from a girls' seminary there formed a wildly enthusiastic chorus after this new adventure. By this time, Stuart had 400 prisoners, whom he spent about half a day in paroling according to the accepted codes of arms and chivalry, and had seized 125 wagons from the Federal supply train.

On June 30, slowed by the captured wagons, he arrived in Hanover, Pennsylvania. A regiment of the Confederates charged Federal troops in the town. But the Yankees were part of an entire brigade under command of General Hugh Judson Kilpatrick and they countercharged the small force of Confederates, driving them back along the main street of the little town while Unionist civilians took pot shots from the windows. Stuart and Blackford, unaware of the plight of the advance troopers, were riding into town when met by Graycoats galloping in retreat. Stuart laughed, flashed his saber, and jumped a roadside hedge with all the enthusiasm of a winner in a steeplechase. Blackford followed. The two galloped on. Ringing in their ears were demands for surrender, and then pistol shots. Suddenly, a 15-foot ditch yawned before them. Stuart did not halt a minute. Blackford afterwards wrote : "I shall never forget the glimpse I then saw of this beautiful animal way up in mid-air over the chasm and Stuart's fine figure sitting erect and firm in the saddle."

Stuart roared with laughter as fellow officers, one after another, landed in the ditch and clambered out with visible annoyance and a goodly share of mud.

While Blackford was admiring "Stuart's fine figure sitting erect and firm in the saddle," another fine figure of a man, also in Confederate gray, was pacing back and forth with considerably less poise. General Robert E. Lee, in Pennsylvania on his most daring venture of the war, was fumbling in hostile country without benefit of his "eyes and ears." He not only did not know where the enemy was. He had heard not a word from his own cavalry.

After daring exploits reminiscent of his famous "Chickahominy canter" around McClellan, Stuart, on the hot afternoon of July 2, reported at last to General Lee. With boyish eagerness he awaited commendation, but at sight of the cavalryman, Lee's face flushed with anger and he demanded, "General Stuart, where have you been?" Stuart's face fell in anguish and surprise and even his plume seemed to droop. He began a halting explanation.

"I have not heard a word from you for days," Lee said, "and you the eyes and ears of my army."

"I have brought you 125 wagons and their teams, General," Stuart replied lamely.

"Yes, General, but they are an impediment to me now," said Lee. Then the fire died in Lee's eyes and a note of sorrow replaced the rasp of anger in his voice. "Let me ask your help now," he said. "We will not discuss this matter longer. Help me fight these people."

Stuart did help all that he could, but by then one day of the Battle of Gettysburg had already been fought and the succeeding days were proof that Stuart's help had come too late.

Stuart redeemed himself in the eyes of his beloved commander, but the people of the Southland that he loved would always hold him partly responsible for the Confederate defeat at Gettysburg.

In the months that followed, Stuart was even more reckless than before in exposing himself to enemy fire. But he went to great pains to spare his officers from undue risks without wounding their pride. And there was a new gentleness about him, or rather the application to all of that gentleness which he had formerly reserved for the wounded and for women. One morning, beset with trying problems of command, Stuart heard a driver grumbling about missing his breakfast. He dipped into his own haversack, handed two biscuits to the astonished man, and then rode off without waiting for thanks.

Stuart's temper was growing gentler in a time when his task was becoming more exhausting and more irritating. He could not find replacements for lost men and lost horses, and the enemy cavalry was increasingly stronger and better mounted from month to month.

Virginia's rolling green fields were peaceful in the May sunshine as

Stuart, intent on blocking the advance of Sheridan's cavalry, rode into Yellow Tavern. No longer yellow with paint, but silvered with age, the tenantless old inn brooded over the landscape. One of the officers said: "We will never catch Sheridan. He is too fast and too big for us."

"No," Stuart protested. "I would rather die. . . ."

Stuart's men and horses, by his own report, were "tired, hungry and jaded," but the next day they distinguished themselves in bitter hand-to-hand fighting and eventually hurled back the Federal cavalry. The next day, Stuart saw Col. Henry Clay Pate, a brave Confederate officer but his enemy for years, inspire his outnumbered men to stand off a horde of Yankees. He rode up beside Pate and held out his hand with an expression that brought a smile from the colonel. "You have done all any man could do. . . . You are a brave man." As Stuart rode back in a hail of fire, his chief bugler accused him of loving bullets. And Jeb replied: "No, Fred. I don't love 'em any more than you do. I go where they are because it's my duty. I don't expect to survive this war."

Late in the afternoon, the Confederate position was critical. Wherever the danger was greatest, Stuart seemed to be. The men of Company K were surprised to see their general come riding through the woods, whistling as though on a solitary canter. In a moment, charging Yankees were within fifteen feet of the spot. Stuart called out, "Bully for old K! Give it to 'em, boys." Then, "Steady, men, steady!"

Suddenly Stuart clutched his side. His head rolled forward and the plumed hat fell in the dirt. "Are you hit? Wounded bad?" came the anxious cries.

"I'm afraid I am," the General said, "but don't worry, boys, Fitz (Lee) will do as well for you as I have."

By now, the gold-sashed waist was drenched with blood. But Stuart begged the officer at his side to leave him to return to the fray. And he did not permit a single groan to escape him as he was lifted from his horse to the ground.

Behind the lines Dr. John Fontaine begged Stuart to take whisky as a stimulant. But he stoutly refused. "I have never tasted it in my life," he said. "I promised my mother that when I was a baby." Finally persuaded that a drink might save his life, he consented.

That night he was carried by ambulance to a house in Richmond. A thunderstorm rolled over the city while the wounded man slept fitfully. The light of dawn disclosed a weeping throng of women standing in the wet street outside.

Stuart wanted to see Flora and she hurried to him aboard a locomotive commandeered for the purpose.

His speech interrupted by paroxysms of suffering, Stuart talked of Flora and then, after a pause, he added : "My spurs. I want them sent to Lily Lee in Shepherdstown. The gold ones, I mean."

Gaunt and nervous, President Davis entered the room. "General," he asked, "How do you feel?" The answer was firm. "Easy, but willing to die if God and my country think I have fulfilled my destiny and done my duty."

Then the minister came. Did the General have a request? "Let's sing 'Rock of Ages,' " Stuart said. And, as Stuart had when going forth on many another adventure, he sang, sang as lustily as he could as the life flowed from him. A little later, he told the doctor : "I am going fast now. God's will be done. . . ."

The guns of the enemy boomed around Richmond when Stuart was laid to rest in the city's Hollywood Cemetery on May 13. Despite the desperate plight of the city, flowers were brought to Stuart's grave every day by loving feminine hands like those whose gifts he had prized in life.

But Stuart had been more than the beau ideal of an admiring feminine populace. He had earned the full confidence of that great Puritan warrior, Stonewall Jackson. And Lee, learning that Jeb was mortally wounded, had said, "He never brought me a piece of false information." Still later, he expressed the feeling of many of Stuart's own men when he said, "I can scarcely think of him without weeping."

Almost exactly a year after Stuart's death, Lee, depressed by the fearful slaughter of the Bloody Angle in The Wilderness, peered fecklessly through the falling rain. Somewhere in the gray mists Grant's great army was maneuvering or ominously biding its time. "If my poor friend Stuart were here," said Lee, "I should know all about what those people are doing."

J. E. B. STUART

Bibliography

Thomas, Emory M. *Bold Dragoon: The Life of J. E. B. Stuart.* New York, 1986. The best of the Stuart biographies, enriched by much research in primary sources.

Davis, Burke. *Jeb Stuart, the Last Cavalier.* New York, 1957.

McClellan, H. B. *The Life and Campaigns of Major-General J. E. B. Stuart.* Boston and New York, 1885. Valuable not only for Major McClellan's personal reminiscences of Stuart, but even more for selections from Stuart's correspondence ranging from West Point days through service in the West, duty at Harpers Ferry, and Confederate service.

Blackford, W. W. *War Years with Jeb Stuart.* New York, 1946. A lively account of Stuart, his daring exploits and his fun-making by one of his closest companions in camp. This volume is a source of many anecdotes in the foregoing chapter.

Cooke, John Esten. *Wearing of the Gray.* New York, 1867. Cooke's account of Stuart's famous "Chickahominy canter" around McClellan's army, pp. 174–191, is the principal source of our narrative of that event. A novelist and historian, Cooke was one of Stuart's partners on the ride and his story makes exciting reading. Also reported are incidents of charming the two unwilling feminine guests, pp. 197–203, and other firsthand descriptions and fascinating anecdotes, especially pp. 2–43, 204–219, 223–227.

Von Borcke, Heros. *Memoirs of the Confederate War.* New York, 1938, Vols. I and II. Though not the most accurate of reporters, Von

Borcke captured effectively the flavor of many incidents to which he was a party or a witness. His *Memoirs* are filled with delightful anecdotes, such as Vol. I, Verdiersville surprise, pp. 105–109; the "black face" train ride, pp. 102–103; fording the Potomac at sunset, pp. 184–185; grand ball at Urbana, pp. 191–198; Vol. II, snowball fight, pp. 82–85.

Freeman, Douglas S. *R. E. Lee,* Vols. I, II. New York, 1934; Vol. III, 1935.

Freeman, Douglas S. *Lee's Lieutenants,* Vols. I and II. New York, 1942 and 1943.

Dowdey, Clifford. *Death of a Nation.* New York, 1958. Stuart in the Gettysburg campaign.

Vandiver, Frank E. *Mighty Stonewall.* New York, 1957. Stuart's record of cooperation with Jackson.

Douglas, Henry Kyd. *I Rode with Stonewall.* Chapel Hill, 1940. These reminiscences of a member of Jackson's staff contain more valuable observations concerning Stuart than most sketches written specifically about the cavalryman.

Thomason, John W., Jr. *Jeb Stuart.* New York and London, 1929.

Henry, Robert Self. *The Story of the Confederacy.* New York, 1936. Places Stuart's operations in the context of Confederate grand strategy.

Johnson, R. U. and Buell, C. C. *Battles and Leaders of the Civil War.* Vol. II, New York, 1887. Firsthand account by Col. W. T. Robins, C. S. A., of "Chickahominy canter." Confirms data in John Esten Cooke's account.

Southern Historical Society Papers, Vol. XXVI, ed. R. A. Brock. Richmond, 1898. Account of Chickahominy Canter by Capt. R. E. Frayser of Stuart's staff, pp. 90–92; account of the same exploit and defense of its value by Col. John S. Mosby, pp. 246–254.

Johnston, Joseph E. *Narrative of Military Operations.* New York, 1874. Events at Harpers Ferry when Stuart served with Johnston, pp. 14–31.

Mapp, Alf J., Jr. "Virginia's Fighting Yankees; General Philip St. George Cooke: Troubled by In-Laws." *Virginia Cavalcade.* Vol. 8,

No. 3 (1958), pp. 25–28. Information on Stuart's relations with his father-in-law.

Riggs, David F. *East of Gettysburg: Custer vs. Stuart.* Ft. Collins, Co., 1970.

NOTE: For some impressions of Stuart's personality, I am also indebted to the recollections of a keen observer of retentive memory, my great-grandfather, the late Rev. A. B. Dunaway, D.D., who participated in the historic "Chickahominy Canter."

EPILOGUE

As was forecast in " My Purpose," the six chief protagonists in *Frock Coats and Epaulets* have not submitted to confinement within the separate book sections assigned to them. Each has had his hour at center stage, but each has appeared also as a supporting player or foil or spear carrier, or perhaps only a disembodied voice offstage, in the life dramas of several of his fellow actors.

And this is as it should be, for each man's life is an inseparable part of the larger drama that involves his colleagues and his enemies. When we view an era as a drama with one figure in the forefront, we achieve design at the price of monocular vision. The human drama is played in theaters-in-the-round, so that the idea that one particular figure stands in the forefront is an illusion varying with the vantage point. Arnold Toynbee has wisely observed that the idea that one is the center of the universe is an intellectual error as well as a moral one.

Not only have the same actors appeared again and again in the foregoing pages, but some of the scenes and actions have been reproduced several times—reproduced, but not repeated. For, while the elements of each scene and action have remained consistent, aspect and emphasis have altered with a change of vantage point. Twice we see the end of John Brown's raid, but the drama is not the same through Jeb Stuart's eyes as through Lee's. Twice also we see the battle of First Manassas, or Bull Run, but our perspective is very different when we view the whole scene through the binoculars of the cautious Johnston as over-all commander from what it is when we stand in the

481

thick of battle with the eager Stonewall Jackson. We look over Jackson's shoulder as he writes his resignation because of the Loring incident and, though the words remain the same, they are read differently in the light of the oil lamp in Johnston's headquarters, the gaslight in Benjamin's office, and the hazy sunlight stealing through the windows of the White House of the Confederacy.

Nearly every major event in this volume is seen variously in the light of each man's vision, and therefore in the color of his experience. These individual colors have collectively a prismatic range. Yet, as only a fusion of the separate colors in prismatic refraction produces the clear light of day, so the separate colors of the lights of individual experience may be needed in combination to approximate the light of reason in which things are seen in what we like to consider their "true" colors.

The prism, though it separates rather than unites the elements of light, is an appropriate symbol for the process by which we have attempted in this volume to obtain a clearer view of one segment of a climactic drama in the life of a nation. Orthoptic exercises using the prism are frequently employed to gain the normal perspective of binocular vision.

Another phase of our approach may also be explained in terms of a scientific principle, although we are not so fatuous as to believe that history can be reduced to the abstractions of physical science. Lawrence Durrell has suggested that the relativity proposition may furnish a literary form that will become "classical" for our time. In this morphology, some of the separate books in a work, as in his own *Alexandria Quartet,* would be "siblings" rather than "sequels," interweaving in a purely spatial relation. The same action may be depicted in separate books of the work, but the subject viewing it (or believing that he initiates it) in one book will be seen as the object in another. In his observation, Durrell was primarily concerned with the structure of the novel. But there is no reason why the same form, freed of the rigidity of a continuum composed inevitably of three parts of space to one of time, cannot serve the historian.

To be more specific, how is relativity seen at work in *Frock Coats and Epaulets?* Or, to sound less pompous, what are the relationships among the lives depicted in these pages?

It would be extremely boring for the reader if we attempted to point out all the relations that appear to us. And even then perceptive readers would discover relationships of which the author was unaware. But—as a starting point, if not a stimulus, for the sort of conversation between writer and reader which every reading experience should be—let's consider some of the more obvious ones.

Most of the characteristics that affected the protagonists' relationships with their contemporaries, and thus influenced history, were apparent early in their lives.

The series of clashes between two proud, sensitive, and inflexible personalities, Davis and Johnston, imperiled Confederate operations at many points and sealed the doom of Atlanta.

Johnston's fear of losing reputation, as evident in a game of billiards or a quail hunt as in the deadly business of war, made a reckless soldier a cautious commander. Many military critics think that his caution was costly to the Confederacy at times when its only hope lay in boldness, even rashness.

Davis had important intellectual and moral qualifications for leadership. But his self-conscious adherence to code (rooted in his status as a member of the just-landed gentry) and his seclusion-bred dogmatism antagonized supporters of the Confederacy, took a heavy toll of his own nervous system, and caused him to take refuge in paper work at a time when dramatic measures were required to win support at home and abroad. Personality problems kept him from using as President of the Confederacy the imagination that helped to make him a great United States Secretary of War.

Judah P. Benjamin's early life taught him that he must be unusually agreeable to get ahead and must assume the protective coloration of the society in which he found himself. As presidential confidant, his habit of telling Davis agreeable things confirmed the President in unwise courses. His facility with protective coloration enabled him to be with equal ease a pillar of that elusive entity, "the Southern way of life," and a mainstay of her Majesty's justice among roastbeef Englishmen.

The repressed aggressiveness that tortured Stonewall Jackson's mind and body, when squared at last with his Calvinist faith through participation in what he believed to be a holy war, was released with a force that wrote a new chapter in the military annals of the world. But the belief that he was God's instrument led him to think that those who disagreed with him impeded the work of the Almighty. This conviction complicated his relations with the Davis government and created many problems to plague his command.

The "splendid folly" of Stuart's anachronistic knight errantry, nurtured by early influences, and the love of glamor related to West Point days when he was nicknamed "Beauty" in irony, brought the Confederacy some of its most glorious moments but helped to frustrate Lee at Gettysburg.

Lee's hard-learned lessons in self-control, coupled with his audacity, helped the Army of Northern Virginia to become one of history's great fighting forces. His excessive politeness toward subordinates, derived from his code of *noblesse oblige,* was misconstrued as weakness by the blunt Longstreet and helped bring ruin at Gettysburg. More important, Lee's levelheadedness from youth upward, together with his conviction that a Christian should learn to deny himself and should eschew hatred, reinforced by a strong national patriotism rooted in his personal heritage, made him the most effective agent in the reconciliation of North and South. Had he acted differently in the postwar years, the United States might not have attained real unity by the time of the Spanish-American War. Lee is the most tragic of the six protagonists because, from the time that he cast his lot with his native state, he was acutely aware of the probable consequences and yet felt that no other course was possible for him. But, in another sense, Lee is the least tragic of the six, for he outlived the war without outliving his faith. Urging fellow Southerners to work for a greater

South and a greater America, he told them, "History teaches us to hope."

Admission of the obvious fact that these men were the products of heredity and environment, and that their individualism was therefore the result of differences in these two factors, is in no way a denial of the existence of that individualism or its influence. The gray uniform of the Confederacy had none of the molding qualities of Madison Avenue's gray flannel suit. Confederate gray was not the gray of anonymity. Most Confederate leaders had not been taught the virtues of conformity; as a result they sometimes amused the group, sometimes shocked it, sometimes were in conflict with it, and often led it.

Despite all that the economic and social determinists may say, individuals influence events. That fact is amply illustrated by the lives of Confederate leaders, some in frock coats, some in epaulets. It is apparent in the lives of the six men with whom we are here primarily concerned. It is apparent, too, in the lives of others barely mentioned in these pages, but who are in some cases equally deserving of treatment in a volume of this sort : Longstreet, who may not have been as unsophisticated as he seemed; Beauregard, who believed he was a Napoleon and convinced others, too; Nathan Bedford Forrest, the blacksmith who may have been a natural genius; Raphael Semmes, who with one ship nearly suspended the carrying trade of the United States; Stephen Mallory, the superlatively inventive Secretary of the Navy who was reared in a boardinghouse for sailors; red-shirted A. P. Hill, the man for whom both Lee and Jackson called in deathbed delirium. And there are many others.

But, if there is no demand for a sequel, or a sibling, to *Frock Coats and Epaulets,* the reader who desires to view the Civil War from the coign of each of these colorful individualists need not despair. The spate of books on the Civil War now pouring and yet to pour from the nation's presses will include lives of all these men. Not only are some of these productions more exciting than our effort, but they can afford the discerning reader the delight of devising his own orthoptic exercises.

Yes, though individuals are the products of heredity and environment, each product is unique and is influential in its uniqueness. Even in our far more regimented twentieth century, the premise holds. Who will deny that the history of our times might have been radically different if Sir Winston Churchill had not surprised the physicians who feared he would die before attaining manhood?

Not only the famous, but obscure individuals, too, influence the course of events. Would history have been the same if Samuel Davis had not left his log cabin in the Lincoln country of Kentucky, carrying his sons Joseph and Jefferson to the rich delta lands of Mississippi? Would the record of the Confederacy be quite the same if Philip and Rebecca Benjamin had not elected to leave the Virgin Islands to settle in the Carolinas, or if the couple had separated some years before Judah's birth instead of some years afterward? How many generals of the Union Army did as much to insure Federal triumph as the obscure North Carolina soldier who, either through a habit of unquestioning obedience to orders or an uncurbed impetuosity, put the fatal bullet in Stonewall Jackson?

The determinists may be right in asserting that individuals do not change the ultimate destination of a nation or of mankind. But individuals can alter the course and the character of the journey, and they can change its timetable. To those embarked on a voyage fraught with perils and enlivened with adventures, the manner of traveling can be almost as important as the destination.

INDEX